JUDAISM AFTER MODERNITY

Papers from a Decade of Fruition

EUGENE B. BOROWITZ

University Press of America, Inc.
Lanham · New York · Oxford

Copyright © 1999 by
University Press of America,® Inc.
4720 Boston Way
Lanham, Maryland 20706

12 Hid's Copse Rd.
Cumnor Hill, Oxford OX2 9JJ

Library of Congress Cataloging-in-Publication Data

Borowitz, Eugene B.
Judaism after modernity : papers from a decade of fruition / Eugene
B. Borowitz.
p.   cm.
1. Judaism. 2. Judaism—20th Century. 3. Reform Judaism. 4.
Borowitz, Eugene B. 5. Spiritual life—Judaism. I. Title.
BM45.B66 1999 296.3—dc21 98-52554 CIP

ISBN 0-7618-1329-2 (cloth: alk. ppr.)
ISBN 0-7618-1330-6 (pbk: alk. ppr.)

⊖™ The paper used in this publication meets the minimum
requirements of American National Standard for Information
Sciences—Permanence of Paper for Printed Library Materials,
ANSI Z39.48—1984

This book is dedicated to
the good people of Port Washington, NY
among whom my family and I have happily lived for
nearly half a century now
and in particular
to my wonderful neighbors of
the "greater" lower-Reid Avenue community
and to my fellow worshipers and study companions at
The Community Synagogue, Temple Beth Am.

The publication of this book was made
possible by the Ilona Samek Institute at the
Hebrew Union College-Jewish Institute of Religion
to whose founders thanks are hereby gratefully expressed.

Contents

Part Three. What Does Judaism Say About...?

Part Four. My Teacher, My Friend, My Dialogue Partners

Acknowledgments

"Continuity and Creativity in the History of the Jewish Religion" was originally published as "Judaism: An Overview" and is reprinted in this volume with permission of Macmillan Reference USA, a Division of Simon & Schuster, from THE ENCYCLOPEDIA OF RELIGION, Mircea Eliade, Editor in Chief. Vol. 8, pp. 127-149. Copyright c 1987 by Macmillan Publishing Company.

Alicia Seeger, my neighbor and oft-time publishing collaborator, was reading the page proofs of this book when, after a long bout with rheumatoid arthritis, she died. May God grant her the rich reward she deserves even as those of us who knew her remember her with great warmth and appreciation.

Dorothy Albritton designed and set this book in type with high competence and a fine eye for what graces a page. My thanks to her reach out to include the staff of the University Press of America for their pleasant and efficient handling of the publishing of this volume.

E. B. B.

Introducing the Collection

Some thinkers have a brilliant insight early in their lives and spend the rest of their lives working out its implications. More frequently thought tends to ripen with experience, study and reflection. Clearly I am one of the latter stripe. Though I had a systematic bent as a young man and knew I wished to apply it to Judaism my several efforts to do so were fruitless, though they did indicate to me intellectual paths I would not find useful. For reasons unclear to me and for which the term maturation will have to stand in, only toward 1980 did I begin to gain a glimmer of how I might make a systematic theological statement about Jewish faith and duty. Though I began to have a new confidence in the direction my thinking was going I did not realize at the time how much work remained to be done.

The best example of this process is, not surprisingly, what happened to my thinking when, at the end of the 1980's I wrote *Renewing the Covenant, a Theology for the Postmodern Jew* (Philadelphia: Jewish Publication Society, 1991). I was able to draw on various of my prior theological papers, most from the 1970's and 1980's but, in one case, from a paper that appeared in 1957. In retrospect the process seems to have moved steadily, though slowly, forward but it certainly did not seem that way to me during the periods when I was floundering. When I was finally ready to write up my comprehensive statement not only did the older materials require substantial revision but, a number of new topics demanded attention if my presentation was to have decent systematic form. When the manuscript was finished I realized that though the years leading up to the book had taken me very far forward, what I had then learned writing the book seemed a theological quantum leap ahead of where I had been when I began to write.

That exciting experience did not prepare me for what followed. For, as it turned out, integrating a non-Derridean postmodern stance with the relational notion of Covenant generated a depth of understanding which went on beyond the book. As various intellectual tasks came my way or suggested themselves to me, I began to realize how much I could now see that simply had not occurred to me while writing *Renewing the Covenant*. Once the book's theology had taken residence in my psyche, I could approach matters with what seemed to me a growing depth of insight and understanding. The book was not merely a climax but an empowerment.

So my work in the past decade plus has largely passed through three phases. Some of my papers of that time point toward a riper Covenant theology, others exemplify it and still others extend that vision or give it fruitful application. In presenting this collection of my recent theological papers, I hope not only to illustrate these not uncommon stages in intellectual development but also to illuminate substantively the meaning of Jewish faith and practice today.

The essays gathered here have an unusual range of diction. While formal, published papers make up the bulk of this offering, others diverge from this standard in contrary directions. Three unusually extensive papers carry formality far forward. These days most journals strictly limit the length of the papers they will consider and they have good reasons for asking authors to eliminate what is not essential to their purpose. But that makes it difficult to undertake a comprehensive theme in anything less than a book. Two of the lengthy papers reproduced here, no. 5 on the history of the Jewish religion and no. 10 on the 20th century movement from modern to postmodern Jewish thinking, could not have tracked the sweep and flow of the developments that occurred had they been limited to the normal journal size. And the other long paper, item 2) of no. 4, which biographically tracks an aspect of my piety, would have had to leave out some critical events were it shorter. Of course, all authors protest at what their editors think desirable brevity in their writing but I will leave it to the reader to judge if my defense of these extended essays makes its point. In any case, in such materials, one can often come to know a thinker in ways that brief papers do not allow.

On the informal side, there is a quite diverse, numerous group of writings. Some are statements which I created for this book from tape recordings of occasions when I spoke from notes. I have tried to do this in such a way that even after substantial reworking and supplementation they retain something of their oral quality and spontaneity, the freshness which can arise when no prepared text restricts the speaker's living response to the listeners' ongoing reactions. I have even included some letters I wrote to thoughtful readers though when I did so, I did not have their publication in mind (the open letter in no. 12 is an exception). Here even less guardedness makes itself felt and the reader is exposed to the thinker communicating privately one on one. These "informal" papers offer a glimpse of the thinker away from the podium and remind us of the simple humanity of the thinker, who in a postmodern time should no longer claim to be an oracle of universal truths for all rational minds. That interest is, in fact, the focus of the first of this book's four parts, so let me turn to it and begin my introduction of the articles awaiting the reader.

Part One. Fragments of a Spiritual Autobiography

The word "spiritual" has been so over-used in our time that one can be tempted to join those who think a moratorium on its use for a year or two would improve our intellectual atmosphere. The difficulty with that is that the term, better than any other, speaks to the special change in our human self-understanding in the past decade or so. To some extent, it has achieved that status as much by what it obscures as by what it reveals. Where moderns were self-confident about the powers of the human mind, even arrogant, postmoderns, without becoming know-nothings, recognize there are certain limits to what we can know and, very likely, do well. So where mind once ruled and cool detachment was the hallmark of intellect, room now must be made for the whole person and feeling or, if you prefer, intuition. And where science once was god, now a sensitivity to the universe and other people makes valid claims on us. In this climate, varieties of religiosity become more than curiosities and meditative or other practices begin to find a place in our lives. The term "spiritual" sums up that mood, hence its ubiquity. And it has the special merit of doing what I have done above, not refer to God, a term with which many Jews remain uncomfortable even though the pieces of the old modernist idols lie all around them. So one may add to the virtues of "spirituality" that it allows one to begin a personal approach to God without ever having to admit it directly.

As I indicate at the beginning of "My Inner Life," a paper of the mid-eighties, I hadn't much thought about my spiritual life before the invitation arrived to join the first symposium on that topic at the annual conference of Reform rabbis. I'm certain that unconcern was true of most of my colleagues though we had spent our lives praying, studying, caring for people and working to improve our society, all in conscious discipline to our way of being "religious." What was new about "spirituality" in those days was that it now needed to be talked about communally, as long as sanctimony and self-serving were taboo. And it has helped us — as we went on to help those we served — to learn that many of our secret religious anxieties are well known to others while certain of their ways of staying open can often freshen up our inner lives as well.

Today, rabbinic and cantorial students come to us not only to learn Judaica in depth and the skills that will help them make their learning live in the lives of their communities, but how to acquire or deepen a spirituality they generally did not grow up with. The paper, "My Father's Spirituality and Mine," was my response to their request to their teachers for statements about their ongoing piety. As I read the original documents it seemed to me that some people construed the spirituality they were looking for quite narrowly while others could not stand the way sentimentality, emotionality and body language had come to be the hallmarks of the new pietists. So when I was able to turn to my own statement I mused about the difference between my sensibilities and those of both my father and my rabbinic school teachers. They were, in their generation, quite different from each other and distant from what I can be, yet I knew that in their different ways they reflected a genuine spirituality I should emulate.

One area in which my religiosity differs from that of many of my students is that I often find closeness to God in the hard work of cognition and intellectual analysis. Of course, I am a Litvak on my father's side (and a Chasid on my mother's) but his was not the way of intellectuality. So when recently I was honored for my life's scholarly attainment, I could not help but ruminate in "My Way Beyond the Modern" about the intellectual/spiritual highlights of my development. Something like that was on my mind when Larry Hoffman proposed that he and Arnold Wolf do a festschrift for my 70th birthday. Insisting the old scholarly varieties of such celebrative volumes were obsolete, I proposed instead that we invite a number of my students instead to tell the stories of their *Jewish Spiritual Journeys*. I was formally presented with the initial version of the manuscript shortly after my birthday and in my "Response to the Gift of 'Not a Festschrift'" I tried to say something about the spirit which has structured my life as a teacher. And not wanting to ask others to do what I would not do, my own contribution to "not a festschrift" was — to my great surprise — the rather lengthy account I made reference to above, "My Pursuit of Prayerfulness." Prayer remains a continual challenge and joy to me because in the honest effort to "stand before" God one cannot utilize all the evasions which usurp the place of a felt, personal relationship with God. I have tried to give an account there of how one person has spent a life working at becoming God's intimate. When after some unavoidable delays, the book finally appeared, six of its contributors came and spoke about what they had written and I, brimming with joy, added some remarks in "A Reflection on My Sense of Certainty" about what I had learned about my soul as a result of their perceptions of me.

Part Two. The Emergence of a Postmodern Judaism

The first two papers of the eight in this section are somewhat unusual in my writing. I have rarely written about the history of ideas in Judaism and while neither of these papers would qualify as an academic offering in that discipline, the first paper, at least, is my theological take on Jewish history. While I try to keep somewhat abreast of what the historians of ideas are doing, I see so large a gap usually between what "they believed then" and "what we ought to believe today" that I have given my efforts to the latter question. "Continuity and Creativity in the History of the Jewish Religion" allowed me to see if my contemporary understanding of Judaism would help or hinder me in trying to intelligently weave together the multiple strands of our faith and practice over the centuries. Some academic students of religion protested that an encyclopedia article of such breadth should have been written from the perspective of the academy, though in a way sympathetic to that of the synagogue. But it seemed to me that without practitioners of a given faith seeking to explain it from the inside — albeit in a way sympathetic to the concerns of the academy — it would not be clear how students of religion would ever get inside the tradition they were studying. In any case, a broad spectrum of Jewish readers found my construal of our spiritual journey based on the notion of Covenant reflective of their views and that gave me particular satisfaction indeed.

Two examples of my interactions with classic Jewish texts then follow. In the first, I wrote a brief commentary to the first of the Ten Commandments. I cannot say that I consciously set out to do so in a postmodern theological mode. I simply read the text anew and reflected on its many layers of meaning to me, scholar, believing Jew and writer. The result rather surprised me but has pleased those who solicited it from me. In "What does the Halakhah Say About . . .? Joseph Karo's Preface to the *Bet Yosef*" I assayed the role of translator, something I had never attempted before and am unlikely ever to venture again. I still do not know what tempted me to this undertaking. However, members of the rabbinate and the laity alike have for years been troubled by my, our, inability to give concise answers about what Jewish law says on even moderately complex issues. And if one wishes to consult the guidance of our tradition then it is precisely the law one needs to inquire about. Yet "the" law is not a ruling but a dynamic, ongoing series of opinions rendered by individual sages about what, in given specific situations the law requires. When I chanced on the explanation of the last great codifier of Jewish law as to how he could know what decision needed to be codified, it was clear to me that he provided a more authoritative answer to the queries about the difficulties of legal determination than I ever could. So I made his words available in English.

The remaining six papers here deal with how a new ethos came into our community. "American Jewish Modernity Comes to Self-Consciousness" discusses the kind of books about Jewish thought which began to appear after World War II ended and what this signaled about

American Judaism. From there we move forward nearly half a century to an early effort I made to apply my nascent postmodern Judaism to a particular problem, in this case the possibilities of creating a common religious language among Jews of several groups. "B'rit, Mitzvah and Halakhah: In Search of a Common Vocabulary," never saw publication and I never saw any other papers from the conference at which it was tape-recorded, which perhaps was a sign of the problems this effort at unity was to run into in the following years.

Once *Renewing the Covenant* was behind me, I could read the history of twentieth century Jewish thought somewhat differently than I had before. For two decades, at least, I had been teaching modern Jewish thought in terms of the systems which still spoke to our ongoing discussions. I tried to show how the various successor points of view had arisen out of discontent with the prior views yet with an appreciation for some of their contributions to our thinking. Now, in "The Way to a Postmodern Jewish Theology," I could weave that pattern so as to indicate how my thought grew out of what had gone before. In writing "Postmodernity and the Quintessential Modern Jewish Religious Movement," I could identify the growing discontent in Reform Judaism as arising from our commitment to a modern spirit which many among us had begun to find outmoded. This essay was particularly rewarding to me because writing it brought home to me that the clarity I had gradually attained about the differences between the two points of view was much richer than I had when writing *Renewing the Covenant*. I remember wishing that I could go back now and put this more mature clarity about postmodernity into the book.

My new self-understanding was in no little way occasioned by the various thoughtful readers who, though appreciative of what I had done, nonetheless raised critical questions about my stance. The first of my "Five Letters to Readers of *Renewing the Covenant*" explains to a historian friend the limited sense in which I believe the terms "modern" and "postmodern" are distinct periods. Another friend, proud of his Reform heritage and religiosity, chided me for my adulation of contemporary Orthodoxy, thus educing my explanation of what I believe we can learn from the Orthodox but where we also necessarily differ with them. That brings me to my greatest practical problem as a Jewish thinker: speaking with philosophers about issues of religious belief. While I begin my philosophizing with confidence in my religious experience and tradition, they object both to the violation of the postmodern principle that foundations for thinking can no longer be validly asserted, and to my unwillingness to argue for my positions in the common logical manner. Thus one correspondent felt I could bring more substance to my thought if I grounded it in the philosophy of Gadamer. In my response I try to explain to him why I believe that philosophic as against theological language is generally unsuitable to convey any full-bodied sense of what constitutes religious life these days. And a final letter was occasioned by a conversation with someone troubled by my idiosyncratic use of terms like "autonomy" and "experience."

The final response in this group of letters is more formal, being written to answer Elliot Dorff's published critique of my thought based on my being widely identified as the chief religious ideologue of Reform Judaism. Dorff, though a careful reader of *Renewing the Covenant*, insists on deconstructing the views stated in my book since they differ from what he takes to be the central commitments of the Reform movement. My response could have stopped with my simple assertion of my right to be myself, regardless of the movement in which I happily if critically take my stand. It should occasion no surprise that thinkers think for themselves and not as agents of a group. But returning Dorff's compliment, I then go on to try to indicate why I believe my Covenant theology explains the Conservative movement better than does its own ideology.

This section of the book concludes with a glimpse at an intriguing effort to "push the envelope" of postmodern Jewish thought, the attempt to bring textual scholars and philosophers together to see if textual reasoning may be a new path for those who think seriously about Judaism. I was one of the summary speakers at a two day conference on this topic and I share here my responses to it and to the promise and problems of developing a new intellectual syntax.

Part Three. What Does Judaism Say About . . . ?

There is something prototypically Jewish in the fact that the greatest number of papers in this book are directed to issues of practice rather than to theory. Of the twelve essays in this part only the first, the fourth and the last — "Covenant," "Postmodern Jewish Ethics" and "Life After Death" — may be said to deal with theoretical issues. (However, it should immediately be noted that the Covenant question was generated by the course of study for Reform Jewish *mohalim*, M. D. circumcizers. Similarly, clarifying postmodern Jewish ethical decision-making would have immediate impact upon specific issues of Jewish duty.) Deeds as the classic means of expressing Jewish piety here make their claims upon the contemporary Jewish thinker as they did upon those of the past.

While the "Zionism" paper arose from an invitation by a Reform Jewish group and my response was put in terms immediately relevant to them, I believe its message applies to any religious Jew who believes Jews should be granted a certain measure of self-determination in matters of belief and practice. A similarly broad sector of our community is unlikely to share so common a point of view with regard to "Apostasy." On this and similar issues American Jews have three different perspectives: those who identify themselves as persons who happen to be Jewish, often happily so; those who consider themselves to be fundamentally Jews, which term they understand to include a good deal of common humanity; and those — the largest group — who are made quite uncomfortable by this issue of boundaries and prefer to evade it. My postmodernity puts me in the second group and guides what I take to be my irenic response to the issue.

Though we often boast that the notion of "Human Rights" rests upon Hebrew Scripture and the Decalogue, a close scrutiny of the data indicates this is only partially the case. Modernity, no villain in this book, is really the source of our contemporary sense of human rights and their importance to our existence. This issue clarifies the way in which, in a significant sense, postmodernity is a continuator of certain modern values.

The papers on "Money" and "Finding a Jewish View of a Just Economy" deal with parallel issues. Note how the postmodern emphasis on community rather than simple individualism has a major bearing on each issue and serves as a critique of certain contemporary views. While on two such complicated matters no simple, single position can be stated, the wisdom of our faith applied to both problems leaves us with a significant, action-shaping point of view.

The "Psychoanalysis" paper describes the new ways it and religion have begun to work as allies. Even the suggestion of such a partnership would have been unthinkable in the days when analysts considered themselves the vanguard of modernity and their practice a science in the making. In that heady time, unmasking the emotional overlays of religion was good enough reason for jettisoning it. But when one comes across such certainty in mind and method these days it seems quite unrealistic. Instead, the greater humility which has come to both groups with postmodernity makes it possible for them to work together in mutually beneficial ways.

In a quite similar vein the sense of superiority which many religious groups once manifested has been increasingly difficult to defend except for certain fundamentalist and anti-modern groups. Surely this has been due more to the reality of inter-human encounter and the experience of democracy than to any intellectual developments. Nonetheless, the sense that all of us think out of a particular situation has made it difficult for thinking people to be as self-assertive as they once were. Hence relationships with people of other faiths now becomes an important living issue to us, the theme developed in "Religious Pluralism."

The suggestion that religion had a substantial role to play in "Healing" was also laughable not too long ago. Today, prayers for the sick and religious self-help practices for them have become a commonplace in many Jewish communities. In few areas of human life has the postmodern perspective on science and on being human had a more significant direct effect. The same cannot be said of the topic of "Aging" which has become an increasingly important issue to us as scientific medicine has made it possible for many people to live longer and often better at the same time. How, on the one hand, we are to avoid the demon of depression as our debility increases, and, on the other hand, shake off the futility which arises from the effort to spur the aging on to ever new adventures, requires an exquisite balance of realism and idealism.

The material on "Life After Death" is unique in this book in that, in the absence of any direct writing on this topic by me, two rabbinic colleagues kindly and thoughtfully gathered together a number of my writings which bear upon this issue. Though increasing age has brought me to think about life after death more frequently than I did years ago, I do not find myself ready yet to go much beyond what this anthologized statement says.

Part Four. My Teacher, My Friend, My Dialogue Partners

It is more than fifty years now that I sat in the classes of Abraham Heschel or — to remember him in the role in which he had even more influence upon me — strolled with him along the Cincinnati campus of the Hebrew Union College. Yet he remains a significant influence on my life, more for who he was than for any of the theological notions for which he became famous. The three articles here about him are indicative of those occasions when I have tried to come to terms with some aspect of his thought and person. Their variety of approach indicates how he remains a continual spur to me to combine thinking about Judaism and exemplifying it nobly.

The name of Arnold Jacob Wolf comes up in a number of the articles in this book. We were roommates at rabbinical school and became brothers in ways that neither the years nor the miles that have often separated us have ever been able to lessen. Arnold was one of the two editors of my "Not a festschrift" and here in "Arnold Jacob Wolf at Seventy" I introduce a collection of his writings published in honor of the fiftieth anniversary of his ordination as a rabbi. I seek in these pages to convey something of Arnold's incomparable human quality and know that, for all I have managed to communicate, very much more remains to be said about this unusually wonderful human being.

As my thought has gained a certain measure of acceptance I have had the opportunity to become involved with a number of the keenest religious thinkers of our time. The final three sections of this book are the results of my encounters with representatives of three different faiths (if I may be permitted to stretch a point about John Hick). In thinking about the exchanges with them that are presented here I realized with something of a start that each had, in a way, made an effort to convert me to his faith. There is no touch of the vulgar missionary in any of these teachers whose concern for the dignity of others is utterly admirable. They addressed me and others with reasons for their position and were fully prepared to listen to what I would have to say in return. But being convinced that the truth they had come to was the fullest available to anyone, they sought to share it in as persuasively logical a way as they could. To have done anything less at this level of intellect would be to patronize others as not being worthy of discussing what best explained reality. John Hick, the eminent academic philosopher of religion, found his truth in the image of the religiosity which his study of the world religions indicated to him lay beyond any one of them but integrated the best insights of them all. For Frans Jozef van Beeck, S. J., the esteemed systematic theologian of Roman Catholicism, it is the truth God has graced him with through Jesus of Nazareth. And for Masao Abe, the great Zen Buddhist challenger of the adequacy of Western philosophy and religion, it is Sunyata, the dynamic Nothingness underlying everything. Each, in his own way, has indicated to me as to others, why I should radically modify if not give up my Jewish theology for their more adequate truth. And I, who have learned much about the meaning and validity of Judaism from these exchanges, have steadfastly pointed to the questions I have had with their teachings and, in contrast, to the truth of Jewish faith. I hope the papers of my exchanges with these thinkers indicate how these demanding discussions have created a special measure of respect and even friendship between us. And if I see a touch of redemption in such relationships, you may ascribe it to my Jewish hopefulness or to human reality or, as I see it, to both at once.

The Sources of these Papers

1. Originally published as part of the symposium on "The Inner World of the Rabbi — My Spirituality," *Central Conference of American Rabbis Yearbook*, Vol. 94 (New York: CCAR Press, 1985).

2. Originally published in *Paths of Faithfulness*, Carol Ochs, Kerry M. Olitzky, and Joshua Saltzman, eds., (Hoboken: KTAV Publishing House, 1997).

3. Originally published in the *CCAR Journal*, Spring 1997 as "How a Discipline Became Established."

4. The first two papers in this section are in *Jewish Spiritual Journeys*, Lawrence A. Hoffman and Arnold J. Wolf, eds., (West Orange, NJ: Behrman House, 1997). The third paper was occasioned by the public launching of the book May 1, 1997.

5. "Judaism: An Overview." Reprinted with permission of Macmillan Reference USA, a Division of Simon & Schuster, from THE ENCYCLOPEDIA OF RELIGION, Mircea Eliade, Editor in Chief, Vol. 8, pp. 127-149. Copyright c 1987 by Macmillan Publishing Company.

6. My contribution to a volume on the Ten Commandments being published in honor of Arnold J. Wolf's fiftieth anniversary of ordination and his retirement as rabbi of KAM Isaiah Israel Congregation.

7. Originally published in the *CCAR Journal*, Spring/Summer 1996.

8. Originally published in the Jubilee Volume of *Jewish Book Annual*, Vol. 50 (New York: Jewish Book Council, 1992-1993, 5753) as "Jewish Thought — on the Emergence of a Genre."

9. Adapted from a tape made at a 1989 conference sponsored by CLAL to discuss the possibilities and limits of inter-denominational Jewish cooperation.

10. A substantially revised version of three lectures given at the University of San Francisco in 1992. One involved the presentation of a paper; the other two were tape-recorded and then transcribed. Upon revision, they were privately published by the University Department of Jewish Studies but the three divisions, and thus the content, of the extended paper prepared for this volume only partially correspond to the original presentations.

11. From *The Human Condition*, The Alexander Schindler Festschrift, ed. Aaron Hirt- Mannheimer (New York: UAHC Press, 1995), where it appears as "Reform: Modern Movement in a Postmodern Era?"

12. Over the years a number of readers of *Renewing the Covenant* have written me, raising such cogent questions about my thought, that I have responded to them at length. Four of these responses are presented in this section. Elliot Dorff's critique of the book was published in *Conservative Judaism*, Vol. XLVIII, No. 2, Winter 1996 as "Autonomy vs. Community" and the

open letter reproduced, with a cordial response from him, is in that same journal Vol. L, No. 1, Fall 1997 (which actually appeared Spring 1998).

13. My statement introducing the summarizing panel at the Drew University conference on Textual Reasoning and Jewish Philosophy, June 1996.

14. Originally published in *Berit Milah in the Reform Context*, ed. Lewis M. Barth (no city: Berit Milah Board of Reform Judaism, 1990) where it appears as "The Concept of Covenant in Reform Judaism."

15. Originally published in *The Journal of Reform Zionism*, Vol. II, March 1995 where it appears as "What is Reform Religious Zionism?"

16. The first paper in this section was originally published in *Modern Theology* Vol. 11, No. 2, April 1995 as one in a series of responses to an open letter by Michael Wyschogrod to a Jewish convert to Christianity. Writing that response motivated me to do another article on the same topic with a broader horizon of apostasy and readership in mind. It appeared in *Reform Judaism*, Summer 1996.

17. The two papers in this section are from my introductory statement and concluding reflection in *Reform Jewish Ethics and the Halakhah*, ed. Eugene B. Borowitz (W. Orange, NJ: Behrman House, 1994).

18. Originally published in *Concilium*, April 1990/2 in a special issue devoted to Religion and Human Rights edited by Hans Kung. It appeared there as "The Torah, Written and Oral, and Human Rights: Foundations and Deficiencies."

19. Originally published in *European Judaism*, Vol. 27, No. 1, Spring 1994 where it appears as "Human Aspiration, The Lessons of a Century."

20. Originally published in *Signposts on the Way of Torah*, ed. Jacob Neusner (Belmont, CA: Wadsworth, 1998) where it appears as "Contemporary Reform Judaism Speaks: Finding a Jewish View of the 'Just Society'."

21. Adapted from a tape recording of a presentation to the March 1996 conference on Psychoanalysis and Religion: The New Alliance, sponsored by the Long Island Center for Modern Psychoanalytic Studies.

22. Written together with Dr. Sherry Blumberg, Assoc. Professor of Education, HUC-JIR, New York, this article appeared in *Religious Pluralism and Religious Education*, ed. Norma H. Thompson (Birmingham: Religious Education Press, 1988) under the title "Religious Pluralism, A Jewish Perspective."

23. The first of these two papers was one of two keynote addresses to the conference *Ma-ayin Yavo Ezri*: Whence Shall My Help Come? An Academic Exploration of Sources of Healing Within Judaism, November 1995 sponsored by the National Center for Jewish Healing, Hebrew Union-College-Jewish Institute of Religion, the Jewish Theological Society of America and the Reconstructionist Rabbinical College. Published by them

as Monograph Series, No. 1. The second paper is a brief commentary to Psalm 90 published in *Healing of Soul, Healing of Body*, ed. Simkha Y. Weintraub (Woodstock, VT: Jewish Lights Publishing, 1994.)

24. Written with Dr. Kerry Olitzky, then National Dean of Jewish Living and Learning, HUC-JIR, and published in *Aging, Spirituality, and Religion*, ed. Melvin A. Kimble, Susan H. McFadden, James W. Ellor and James J. Seeber (Minneapolis: Fortress Press, 1995) in the section on "Theological Perspectives," and entitled, "A Jewish Perspective."

25. I have not written a direct treatment of my views of life after death but Daniel Syme and Rifat Sonsino were good enough to accept my suggestion that they anthologize the several places where I have touched upon the topic. This selection from their book, *What Happens After I Die?* (New York: UAHC Press, 1990) appears under the heading, "Covenant Theology" and is here briefly introduced by them.

26. The first paper in this section appeared in *What Kind of God? Essays in Honor of Richard L. Rubenstein*, Betty Rogers Rubenstein and Michael Berenbaum, eds. (Lanham: University Press, 1995). The second is the manuscript of a Nostra Aetate lecture delivered at Fordham University, Lincoln Center, in November 1997 in commemoration of the twenty fifth anniversary of the death of Abraham Heschel. The third is adapted from the tape recording of my presentation to the Jewish Theological Seminary conference The Legacy of Abraham J. Heschel, March 1998.

27. Originally published in *Unfinished Rabbi, Selected Writings of Arnold Jacob Wolf*, ed. Jonathan S. Wolf (Chicago: Ivan R. Dee, 1998) where it appears as "Foreword."

28. Adapted from a tape recording of my response to Prof. John Hick's second lecture on the occasion of Auburn Theological Seminary's Conference on "Christian Faith and People of Different Faiths," held at Union Theological Seminary, New York, April 1994.

29. These two brief items illustrate aspects of my ongoing exchanges with the Catholic theologian Frans Jozef van Beeck, S. J.. The first is a "Foreword" I wrote to his original study of the reception of the famous Holocaust document "Yossel Rakover's Appeal to God," a topic on which further research has now permitted him another publication on the topic. My "Foreword" appeared in *Loving the Torah More than God*, Frans Jozef van Beeck, S. J. (Chicago: Loyola University Press, 1989). The second item is the exchange of letters which his sermon on the Holocaust occasioned between us and which he later suggested we submit for publication to *Cross Currents*. They published the text of his sermon in their Summer 1992 issue and our correspondence in that of Fall 1992.

30. As one of the thinkers who had been in discussion with Prof. Masao Abe concerning his lengthy statement about Zen Buddhism and Western religion in *The Emptying God*, John Cobb and Christopher Ives, eds. (Maryknoll, NY: Orbis Books, 1990), I was invited to prepare a rejoinder to his original response to me. The first paper here is that rejoinder, published in the annual, *Buddhist-Christian Studies*, 1992 (University of Hawaii Press). The second paper was my submission to the farewell volume occasioned by Prof. Abe's return to Japan after many years of teaching in the West: *Masao Abe: A Zen Life of Dialogue*, ed. Donald Mitchell (Rutland, VT: Tuttle, 1998).

Part One

Fragments of a Spiritual Biography

Chapter 1

ℰↄℭℛ

My Inner Life

I had not thought much about my spiritual quest over the years until Jack Stern graciously asked me to help start this discussion.

As I see it now, much of my Jewish religious life derives from an ambivalent impression of my Ohio childhood. I liked being Jewish. I even enjoyed religious school and going to services. But it exasperated me that my teachers and my rabbi could never explain Judaism in any way that made sense to me. When I discovered that philosophy and the social sciences were not any smarter, I decided to become a rabbi.

Then my ambivalence intensified. I loved the Hebrew Union College in theory but only occasionally in practice. Once again, my teachers left me badly disappointed. Along with my two close friends, Arnie Wolf and Steve Schwarzschild, I figured I had better build my own sort of Jewish faith and find my own way of explaining it. And that is what I am still doing.

A consequent student experiment was critical. I was not worried about my intellectual life. That came easily to me. But making personal contact with God was strange to my American upbringing. So I decided to try to learn to pray, not just at the daily College service but by myself. That way there would be no dodging God. Besides, I and some others of

my classmates wanted to be more Jewish. We knew we were modern.
What bothered us was how to be Jews. Another lifelong quest. So I tried
to learn to pray alone from a prayer book. I started with the Union
Prayer Book and worked with it for some years. Later, I pushed my
religious growth further by extending my davvening through gerrymandered *siddur* services. Daily prayer has been the bedrock of my
Jewish life — and a continual judgment. Let me explain.

Early on, I decided to pray in my office, to link my work and my
faith. Nothing I regularly do is more difficult for me. I find it a terrible
trial to pay attention to God when all around me are reminders of things
I need to work on. Frequently, I discover my *kavanah* has broken, and I
am thinking about one of my projects instead of talking to God. I hate
that. But it is the fundamental spiritual problem of my life. How do I
keep God ahead of all my schemes? How do I subordinate everything I
do, especially all the good, Jewish things, to God and what, as best I can
figure it out, God wants of me and the Jewish people? In sum, how, in
my life, do I make and keep God one?

I do many other Jewish things, but I now want to say a word about
my other search, the intellectual one. Here I have been fortunate. I have
been spared the religious pain of having to surrender early religious
beliefs I have later found inadequate. Instead, much of what I always
thought was a poor explanation of Judaism has fallen by the way. At the
same time, the path I started on as a student — radically theological yet
deeply practice-, text-, and community-oriented; personalist, not
rationalist; richly particularistic without being ghettoizing or a-ethical —
now holds a substantial number of our community. Of course, it also
helped that I started out more with questions than with certainties. And I
have been content to accumulate partial insights and be patient until I
gained a more rounded vision.

Sometimes I am troubled that I have not been overwhelmed by the
problem of evil. Surely, there is enough of it around, and we Jews have
seen it at its worst. Intellectually, I think my turmoil has been relatively
moderate because I never believed God was, in Dick Rubenstein's words,
"the ultimate, omnipotent actor in history." It also helped that I did not
believe I had to have, or was entitled to, rational explanations of
everything. For an intellectual, I seem to be able to live with a good deal
of mystery.

Humanly, I simply find I cannot rail at God for long. Here an
experience was instructive. In 1953, I went to do a funeral for a colleague

who was off at the CCAR meeting. On the way, my automobile was hit by a semi-drifter who had borrowed an uninsured car without brakes. Two days later I was in my naval base hospital with a ruptured kidney. Waiting for it to heal, it occurred to me the rabbis were right to have a blessing for excretion, so I taught myself the text. Ever since, when my kidneys work or I defecate, I have said it. It does not always mean much to me — but it, more than any of the other blessings I daily say, continually reminds me of what God regularly gives me.

I have also been spared great personal tragedy and physical pain. There has been suffering, to be sure. My family has known cancer of the brain and of the pancreas, two cases of Alzheimer's disease, several instances of coronary artery disease, and disturbing if not incapacitating neuroses. I obviously cannot take *rofe kol basar* at face value, but I remain fundamentally moved by *umafli laasot*.

I struggle with many of the things that bother other rabbis. People do not seem to care very much about Judaism. Regardless of my best efforts, they do not take it very seriously or find my understanding of it very compelling. Despite the occasional life I have touched and the faithful remnant who care, I often feel that, on the human level, my work does not really mean very much. It helps when I can remember that God will one day win out even without my success. I found it hard to acknowledge that I was not the Messiah, not even the bringer of the Messianic Age. It is harder still remembering that I am not God.

My greatest spiritual shock has come from the intense loneliness I feel as a Jew. My ethical and cultural friends think religion odd. My Jewish companions, the few who are learned and serious, think Reform Judaism intolerably undemanding. I do have the rare good fortune to have Reform colleagues with whom I can discuss Jewish intellectual, issues. But we go rather independent ways when it comes to understanding our Judaism, particularly should we ever talk of Jewish faith.

My sense of isolation is intensified by my strong commitment to the notion of Judaism as a community religion. Even desiring a rich Jewish ethnicity makes one an alien to much of American Jewish life. But if one wants to be a self and fulfill oneself in a Jewish community of selves, in Buber's sense, then alienation becomes the common stuff of one's Jewish existence. In this respect, my experience differs from that of many colleagues. I have spent almost all my rabbinic years working on someone else's staff. I have not been able, therefore, like congregational rabbis, to take the leading role in shaping the community in which I function. I am rather more like a congregant who can only be an active but highly subordinate participant. That can easily intensify the loneliness.

I have some partially effective strategies to alleviate my solitariness. I am blessed with a good marriage and children who still talk to me, and I work hard at keeping it that way. I have a few friends and enjoy a few pleasures. And I try to create community wherever I can. My greatest challenge is to transform my classroom from the rigid, hierarchical one of my school years to one of inter-personal exchange, while not sacrificing the demands of Jewish learning. That effort has also given me my greatest rewards. Furthermore, I have the joy of working with colleagues who agree that we must make a serious effort to have our school less an institution than a community. And from time to time, we and our students actually bring it into being.

Mostly, I have learned a new aspect of Jewish messianism. Of course, I hope for justice and look forward to peace. I still aspire to the ultimate vindication of the Jewish people and, through it, of all humanity. But now, too, I long for redemption from the *galut* of loneliness, for that day when we shall all be one as persons and one in community — for only on that day will God be in our lives as God, to God, is God.

Chapter 2

ℰℴℭℛ

My Father's Spirituality and Mine

M y father was as good a Jew and human being as I have ever met. Yet I wonder if people in this generation would have considered him "spiritual." (I think they would respond more immediately to my mother's "spirituality" but, because it was so primally entwined with her fineness of soul, it would take more poetic skills than I have to describe it.) He and my mother attended Friday night services with great regularity and late Saturday afternoons my dad would often take me, as a young teen-ager, to the temple's *shaleh-shudas* (= *shalosh seudah*) where he was often one of the youngest people present (a smallish number to begin with). I vaguely recall that his davenning on these occasions seemed more perfunctory than intense. Though he enjoyed having certain rituals performed, he always managed to find ways to have more "learned" people conduct them, e. g. our Seders. Thus, I never recall his having made *kiddush*. His "study" consisted of a thoughtful perusal of the daily *Forverts* (which, in Columbus, Ohio, the mailman delivered.) He esteemed learning and the educated, so my sister was long the only female college-graduate in our extended family and the academic expectations of me were lovingly high.

His outstanding Jewish virtue, after devotion to our family, was his love of Jews, an attitude he then also applied to everyone else in the world. When as a young man he read in the Communist daily, *Freiheit*, that the Jewish settlers in Palestine were exploitative colonialists who had provoked the Arab riots of the late 1920's, he threw the paper in the garbage and became a reader of the Socialist *Forverts*. He represented the Jewish Labor Committee to the Columbus Jewish Community Council (though he managed production in a large trouser factory) and I remember sitting outside the room of one hot Council session waiting for him when the issues of refugees and Zionism were boiling. He was aroused and told the Council that he could not say what he needed to say in his English (ordinarily quite workable) so he asked for the right to address the Council in Yiddish, the only time that ever happened in that German-American dominated august body. (I could only hear muffled sounds coming from the room but I could tell that he had been most passionate.) During World War II he was instrumental in racially integrating the production lines in his factory, the first time that happened to an industrial plant in Columbus. (And only the Jewish admonitions of clean speech keep me from repeating the line by which he spurned those workers who wanted segregated bathrooms.)

In the 1960's with their death-of-God agitation, I once asked him if he believed in God. He looked at me as if that was a peculiar question to ask and said, "Of course," as if no sensible person would do otherwise. That was that. When some years later he was dying of pancreatic cancer, fortunately without intractable pain, and I was walking with him in Sloan-Kettering Memorial Hospital, he quietly said to me at one point, "*Ich hob mein's getun*," "I did mine." That was as much a summing up as he needed, as much a statement of purpose and duty as I ever heard from him. The rest was all good-hearted deed.

By today's preferred understanding of "spirituality" I doubt that my father would qualify as a model. He certainly wasn't very self-conscious about God or his relationship to God, nor did he judge his acts by whether they made God more present in his life or that of society. People now use "spirituality" to refer to a religiosity which is more interior, more subjective, more explicitly God-oriented than my father's. I never heard him use that term or anything like it to speak of others and certainly not about himself. He probably would have shaken his head in incomprehension at it, considering it another of those American things others found valuable but he didn't understand or value.

The gap between my father's living Jewishness and our concern about Jewish spirituality set me to thinking. If, by the American Jewish standards of his time, my father was a good Jew without our kind of spirituality, what might I learn about our sense of Jewish piety by thinking of him and some other fine Jews I have known.

Over the years I have often been reminded of my father's dedication when talking to one or another rabbinic colleague, generally not people on the national scene or of great reputation. When they talked about their work, I was moved by their simple devotion to it, the unending round of services, hospitals, *simchas*, committee meetings, community affairs and more. They also complained a good deal, particularly about the heavy work load. I was, after all, a rare safe, sympathetic ear, one unlike their spouses whom they felt might already be suffering from an overload of their *kvetching*. Yet once the ventilation was over, what remained was their quiet determination to carry on with their rabbinic tasks as best they could. They knew that this was what they most wanted, most needed to do. God bless them, they sent me away from such encounters renewed in shouldering my own kind of rabbi-burdens, convinced that there were more good Jews in the rabbinate than our critical community — myself included — ever appreciated.

I now think of these colleagues and my father as exemplars of a classic type of Jewish spirituality. In their different ways they followed the rabbinic ideal of the *tzaddik*, the Jew whose good deeds win God's approval. Most contemporary Jews, I guess, will more readily identify this type of activist Jewishness with people who have devoted their lives to great ethical issues. That was surely my sense of some of the (apparently secularistic) colleagues who put themselves on the line in the early days of the civil rights struggle and who tried to carry on the good fight in less dramatic ways ever since. But where *tzaddik*-hood of ethical devotion has often been celebrated in our movement, its more ordinary, everyday elaboration, deserves greater attention.

In some ways my father's activist Judaism accords poorly with his childhood for it was tied up with another ideal Jewish type. My father grew up in the home of his maternal grandfather, awaiting for over a decade his American immigrant father's call to his wife and children in Poland to join him. Of Hershel, his grandfather, of whom my father always spoke with reverence, he particularly remembered how he stopped being the *rav* of Sokoly and instead, since he had the special *smichah* allowing him to grant others *smichah*, turned his house into a modest *yeshivah* over which he then presided. He was, apparently, a Jew in the classic Litvak mode, one whose spirituality took the form of study and the intellectual exercise that accompanied it. I no longer remember whether he was a *musmach* of Volozhin or Slobodka (as I once wrote) but it was clear he was a *misnaged* who observed the ban on Hasidim. So he was undoubtedly influenced by the classic text of Litvak spirituality, the *Nefesh Hachayyim* of Hayyim Volozhiner (the Vilna Gaon's disciple and the Volozhin *Rosh Yeshivah*). That work identifies Torah with the *En Sof*, making study the Litvak equivalent of the *unio mystica* some Jews today take to be the goal of spirituality. Being a *masmid*, an unceasing student of Torah, was for such Jews a literal way of being in God's presence. Despite his love of Hershel, my father did not have the *sitzfleisch* to become a *chacham* and, though he urged education upon me, he made it clear that he thought intellect without deeds a betrayal of Jewish responsibility.

Perhaps the purest Litvak-style intellect I ever came across was my teacher Samuel Atlas. He was an acknowledged master in both philosophy and Talmud, the two disciplines he taught at HUC. It remains one of the great regrets of my life that his understanding was so advanced and mine so rudimentary that I could not benefit from his utterly uncommon inter-disciplinary mastery. Some of my other teachers, themselves dauntingly learned, also exemplified the Jewish piety of determined intellectuality. Julian Morgenstern, a leading Semitic linguist and Biblical scholar of his day; Samuel Cohon, who taught theology from what seemed like an encyclopedic knowledge of Judaism; and Sheldon Blank, who meticulously attended to the words of the prophets and gently made them the standard of his life — they were all people who realized themselves most fully in the exercise of the mind. These scholars considered their subjective lives a private matter yet their piety in and through their intellectuality was evident to anyone sensitive. *Mutatis mutandis*, they were not what the rabbis meant by *chachamim* nor my great grandfather's kind of Litvak, yet a single kind of Jewish religiosity linked them — and, if I may say so, is what animates the instruction at our New York School. That I followed Hershel's way was no rebellion against my father. He not only encouraged me in it but kept me a lifetime doer as well as thinker.

The more personalistic, felt piety that we today largely identify with Jewish spirituality was not without its exemplars years ago, though it was no one's spoken goal. To stay with rabbis — though some marvelous lay examples could easily be adduced — let me say a few words about a colleague somewhat older than me, Byron T. Rubenstein. "B. T.," as everyone called him, always seemed an unusual spirit. It's hard to know why people universally felt that way about him but perhaps it indicates that we all have a certain openness to genuine piety even if we insist it is not our own way to live. B. T.'s aura of spirituality didn't have anything to do with what he said about himself or directly urged on others. On the surface he seemed like most other good rabbis. And it didn't keep him from the life of deeds — he was the oldest rabbi (forty-something, I would guess) among the sixteen of us (and Al Vorspan) who answered Martin Luther King's telegram to a CCAR convention to come get arrested in his campaign in St. Augustine, Florida. Yet you knew he was a person of great inner depth, an unusually elegant spirit, someone whose simple wholeheartedness you would like to emulate if you ever could.

Our present discussion of spirituality has, I think, gone somewhat further on B. T.'s road by making interiority a value to be sought consciously, by struggling with how to give it adequate verbal expression and by identifying it unambiguously with personal experience of God. Those are not small gains for in our time the subjective side of religion has not been given its due so we are engaged in an effort to add the Judaism of the heart to that of the deed and the mind. We are learning to value not only the *Tzaddik* and the *Chacham* but the Psalmist as well.

Some have gone even further and seek the path of the Kabbalist. Zalman Schachter-Shalomi, Art Green and Larry Kushner each in their own ways set before us models of contemporary Jewish mystic spirituality. Within limits, I can appreciate their form of Jewish spirituality. I say that because though I admire how mystic experience has affected them and their teaching, I have not shared their experience of merger with the Divine. Like Buber, I find the apparent fulfillment of the self becoming one with the Ultimate less significant than standing on my own side of the I-thou hyphen, marvelously involved, yet respectful of the Other's individuality — and my own.

So I have known four kinds of Jewish spirituality in my lifetime, ones amply attested in Jewish tradition. What gives me pause in my otherwise wholehearted appreciation of the new personalistic emphasis among us is what often troubled me about one or another forms of Jewish piety in the past, that emphasizing one aspect of Jewishness, they will not give proper scope to its other ones. At the moment, I do not see much danger that the new interiority will decrease a concern with ethics and rite. The Psalmist is no stranger to the needed deed. But there is a certain American anti-intellectualism which easily co-opts subjectivity to deny or constrict the role that learning and thinking play in the service of

God. Not everyone is gifted to be a *Chacham*. Most of us would be happy to qualify as their disciples, *Talmidei Chachamim*. What concerns me only is properly holistic spirituality, one in which, depending on temperament and opportunity, we do not turn our backs on either the doer, the student or the believer in us but find our way to give them a dynamic unity in our lives.

Chapter 3

ဆၣ

My Way Beyond Modernity

I f I now followed the American Jewish *minhag,* I would say the *shehecheyanu* — but our sages limit that blessing to personal benefits. Since the Foundation assures me that my work has been of value to many, I should express my thanks to God by saying the blessing for joys that are shared, *hatov vehametiv,* "God the good and the doer of good." However, *Magen Avraham* and *Ba'er Heteiv,* commentaries to the *Shulchan Arukh,* specify two conditions for doing so. If you hear about your good, you should be sure the reporter is trustworthy, which, the medal hanging from my neck, is surely more than mere news. The other condition is that if one is ambivalent about the good that has come to one, one should add a second blessing. The commentators base this on paragraph 382 of *Sefer Hasidim,* the 12th or 13th century masterwork of the *Haside Ashkenaz,* those extraordinary Franco-German Pietists whose life, among other things, has been studied by Bob Chazan, the retiring Chair of the Academic Advisory Committee of the Foundation. The text there tells of a certain poor man who on marrying a wealthy woman he did not like recited not only *hatov vehametiv* but also the blessing for evil news or events, *dayyan haemet,* "the truthful judge." Chided by his colleagues for applying an unusual halakhic usage to his situation he said he was only being honest: he loved the money but hated her. So ambivalent beneficiaries are warned to add an offsetting blessing.

I have no ambivalence about this unexpected, overwhelming honor. A 1930's product of a Columbus, Ohio synagogue afternoon Hebrew school, my language skills were so problematic that I was admitted to the Hebrew Union College in 1942 only as a special student. After ordination in 1948 I found myself one of that dozen or dozen and a half rabbis from the College and the Jewish Theological Seminary who, to the surprise of teachers and friends, were seriously interested in Jewish theology. But unlike my dear friends Herschel Matt, Seymour Siegel, Jakob Petuchowski and Steven Schwarzschild, I have been granted years. We pioneer American Jewish theologians fantasized about creating a new systematic statement of Jewish thought and of all that gifted group I alone have managed to fulfill that dream. I have not accomplished this unaided. Looking about, I see the two Deans, Paul M. Steinberg and Norman J. Cohen, who over my 34 years of teaching have also been my loving colleagues; I see some of my increasingly fine students, those teachers of their teachers; I see dear friends of many years' standing; and I see the representative of my utterly admirable children and grandchildren. Best of all I have known the abounding joy of having the love of my youth grow into extraordinary personal fulfillment yet still find me a worthy companion for her life. Unambivalently, then, I say *Barukh atah adonai, elohenu melekh haolam hatov ve hametiv.* "I call you 'blessed,' *Adonai*, ruler of the universe, who is good and does good."

My kind of Jewish scholarship remains so uncommon that I want to devote these remarks to explaining how this field of study emerged and what I see as my present place in it. Our standard for modern Jewish scholarship was set by that extraordinary 19th century figure, Leopold Zunz of whom Mike Meyer has written so insightfully. Zunz commandingly demonstrated that if Judaism and its literature were studied by the university's critical historical method, a newly intelligible, culturally credible picture of our tradition would emerge. Since his day, our modernized community has most admired the masters of philological and textual history, virtuosos of footnoting, like my two accomplished colleagues of this evening, Judah Goldin and Michael Meyer. And in recent years we have expanded our appreciation to Jewish achievement in other humanistic disciplines.

We neophyte Jewish theologians, however, were most concerned about an issue the traditional disciplines could not help us with. We wanted to know what a modern Jew ought to believe and why. Rejecting Moses Mendelssohn's original response to this issue, that we compartmentalize our minds and separate what was Jewish from what was modern, we sought to integrate the two. If we studied history, that would only tell us what Jews had once believed but not why they ought to believe it today, a particularly pressing problem since our lives are so substantially based on putting our ghetto/shtetl history behind us. Academic Jewish philosophy was of equally little help. Insofar as it was Jewish, it studied medieval thinkers exercised about reconciling Judaism to neo-Platonic or Aristotelian worldviews, clearly not our problem. And insofar as it was contemporary philosophy, it was radically anti-religious. Besides, philosophers could not agree on how they knew anything for certain, a shaky foundation indeed for rebuilding the structure of modern Jewish belief. Some of us, then, took the path of eclecticism, demonstrating Jewish continuity by the copious citation of appealing Jewish texts. I among others rejected the eclectic approach since its practitioners could never explain why they chose and highlighted certain Jewish texts and by-passed opposing ones. Today, when the issue of hermeneutics dominates our intellectual life, what constitutes a text worth reading and how one should interact with the text, are questions demanding a response. Moreover, footnotes have only an ambiguous role in the realm of thought. They can testify to learning and adduce outside authority. Neither establishes the cogency of your argument and cogency is what thinking is all about.

The discipline euphemistically called Jewish thought — thereby avoiding the term "theology" and its Christian overtones of dogma and required Jewish belief — was born out of the desire to think by university standards about the questions of belief posed by classic Jewish texts and modern Jewish experience. I rejoice that as the notions of academic objectivity and value-free inquiry have changed from dogmas to dubious assertions, the university has become hospitable to open intellectual inquiry into belief-oriented thinking, including courses in modern Jewish thought.

I have tried over the years to enhance the development of this field by writing about its emerging contours and by describing the thinkers, the methods and the issues which constitute it. To begin with methodology, I identified six separate, incommensurate ways of arguing for a special understanding of modern Jewish identity that were systematically elaborated in the first two thirds of the twentieth century, four of them rationalistic, two of them non-rationalistic. One of the rationalisms, classic Zionism, insisted on a secular basis to Jewishness, namely, nationalism, but the others, though variously resistive or influenced by the Zionist claim, all believed Judaism to be ineluctably religious, inevitably involving beliefs about God, Torah and the people of Israel as well as their interaction. Hermann Cohen elaborated a philosophically tight interpretation of Judaism based on neo-Kantianism and explained Judaism as ethical monotheism *par excellence.* Leo Baeck accepted Cohen's ethical rationalism but violated his philosophical integrity by yoking reason to Rudolf Otto's concept of religious consciousness. Mordecai Kaplan, considering these theories too individualistic, read Judaism out of the new science of sociology, thereby making the Jewish folk the generative element in Judaism.

The non-rationalists thought these thinkers were too optimistic about the mind's capacity and insisted that some kind of non-rational experience must precede reasoning and be the standard for the rational explication of its meaning. In the Buber-Rosenzweig view — the latter unfortunately leaving only the beginnings of a system — a real, independent God enters into relationship with people, non-verbally to be sure. In the Jewish case, the folk as a whole accepted this involvement with God as basic to their corporate existence and called its consequences Torah. Abraham Heschel considered the Buber-Rosenzweig model still too human centered and thoughtfully rhapsodized a return to the biblical-rabbinic teaching that God is in search of us and our response.

All that was in place before the theological discussion of the Holocaust and the "death of God" began. Hindsight suggests that the emerging field of Jewish thought largely provided the language and context of the debates about post-Holocaust theology during the decade-plus period that they remained significant. I have argued that the Holocaust discussions produced no ideas of God not previously known to the thinkers and their students. Thus, every significant modern Jewish thinker of the 20th century — or the 19th, for that matter — had abandoned the Biblical idea that God actively runs history, punishing evildoers and rewarding the righteous. Almost all the thinkers had taught or intimated that God has limited power. Some few argued for the traditional belief that people have only a limited capacity to understand what God does.

One thing emerged clearly over time: the death of God radicals were wrong. God has not only not died among us but today Orthodoxy continues a vibrant resurgence while Jewish mysticism and its more genteel surrogate, the search for spirituality, speak to a sizable minority among us. The truth seems to be that our civilization no longer believes that secular reason can supply us with a commanding ground of value. Thus today what we can believe and therefore must do has become a burning issue of our personal and communal existence.

If this last third of the 20th century has seen theological issues, not system, seizing the Jewish theological agenda, its greatest contemporary promise is seen in Jewish feminist theology. Its powerful, persuasive polemic against the patriarchal character of classic and contemporary Judaism demands, among other things, that we males cease the pretense of claiming to think universalistically, that is, for all truly thoughtful people. Human beings, embodied and engendered as they are, are thoroughly particular so women must be allowed to think out of their own feminist particularity. I am confident that as Jewish feminist thinkers elaborate the positive understandings of Judaism that feminine religious experience mandates, our community will be newly enriched in ideas and practice.

I have had my say on many of the specific issues of recent years but to my delight, I have also finally been able to work out a new systematic Jewish theology. How much of this was due to the maturation of my thought over the years, I cannot judge. But surely my work was facilitated by my encounter with that family of new intellectual languages we call postmodernism. Here, too, I have had to take an uncommon stance. I reject postmodernism's customary academic form which agrees with Jacques Derrida that everything is ultimately undecidable and therefore rules out the reality of God, the importance of the Jewish people and the imperative to live by Torah. Thus too, though I celebrate my young colleagues' renaissance of academic Jewish philosophy based on Emanuel Levinas's passionate reaffirmation of ethics, I do not see how his thought avoids the problems Herman Cohen's universalistic rationalism made so clear or how one can Jewishly validate Levinas's key notion of infinite ethical responsibility. Alternatively, I find the more particularistic colleagues who seek to educe postmodern Jewish thought from the study of classic Jewish texts encountering the opposite problem. While their communitarian situatedness is clear, how will they ever be able to move on from comments on a specific text to the kind of generalization we expect today when we ask for meaning or explanation?

My thought begins by rejecting the assumption of the earlier systematic thinkers, Heschel excepted. They believed that meaning must stem from individual experience, philosophical or religious. I do not see how any individualistic beginning can ever lead on to the robust Jewish particularity much of our community has been seeking. Judaism is primarily located in the Jewish people's corporate relationship with God. Therefore we need to begin with the corporate religious experience of the Jewish people in our time. In my view, our community unconsciously learned two theological lessons from the Holocaust and they have increasingly surfaced in recent years. First, we discovered that we are more deeply Jewish than we thought and that, as feminism and Marx and Freud and anthropology have been trying to teach us, the particular precedes the universal. Second, that what died for us in the Holocaust was not the biblical God most moderns never believed in but the one deity they truly trusted, themselves and their capacities. It turns out that we and western civilization generally are not as messianically competent as we once confidently proclaimed. So in Orthodoxy or mysticism or spiritual searching or the like, we have grudgingly begun to admit our need for God or God's surrogate.

These two new stands invert two cardinal modernistic assumptions about the self and Judaism. I therefore see them as the basis of a postmodern understanding of Judaism. Yet one truth that modernity taught remains utterly precious to us: that human dignity demands people be allowed to exercise a significant measure of self-determination in belief and action. Moderns called this notion autonomy, a concept I have sought to transform by recontextualizing it in terms of the Jewish self's situatednesss amid the people of Israel and its ongoing, historic relationship with God. Our tradition called its version of this association Covenant and we call its continuing consequences Torah. Explaining all this in detail is the stuff of my postmodern theology.

Chapter 4

ℰ❀ℭℛ

My "Not a Festschrift:"
Jewish Spiritual Journeys

1) Response to the Gift of "Not a Festschrift"

S ince I want to share with you something of my experience as a teacher and also to thank a few people, I thought it best to contain my cascading thoughts by putting them on paper.

With deep apologies to many others, let me offer five statements of gratitude.

First, thanks to you all for your gracious reception. I think of myself as a rabbi and therefore care very much what my rabbinic colleagues think. It has always pained me that I seem to arouse more than the negative transference all rabbis receive and I have tried to overcome the failings which induce it. Still, it remains a reality and that makes this occasion all the more precious to me.

I owe this event and half the *festschrift* project to the devotion of Larry Hoffman. You know him as one of that handful of academics who really have something to say. I know him also as a faculty leader and dear younger friend. He loves our students, loves teaching and loves our College despite its shifting mismatch of ideals and reality. And he includes me in that love, which honors me greatly.

Larry's partner in *Jewish Spiritual Journeys*, my name for the *festschrift* is my fraternal twin, Arnold Jacob Wolf. At seventy he remains as annoyingly intelligent, as excitingly verbal and as provocatively action-oriented as ever. When this luncheon is over he will, as always, do a critique of this talk. Not to worry. I, at a semi-private occasion during his recent congregational 70th birthday weekend, unhesitatingly upbraided him for speaking about an author personally in a way I deemed out of line. So it has gone for fifty two years, demanding much of each other, trying like Akiba being reproved, to remember that anything less is not real love.

To the extent that I am the person, Jew, rabbi I ought to be it is largely because of the love, the human sensitivity, the far-reaching intelligence, the greatness of soul and the idealistic patience of that beautiful, radiant, ever flowering woman who for nearly forty seven years now has graced my life. Most graduates of the New York School know her as the gracious mistress of our home and they can testify, if I can persuade her to stand for a moment, that I am guilty only of understatement. Estelle —

And a special *modim* to God who has brought me to this day. I hope I have not been unnecessarily resistive to the One who has sought to guide my life and direct my stubborn will, nor to the Love which has kept me close, showering on me the blessings of life, of love, of a remarkable family, of worthwhile work and some accomplishment. May God remain so good and gracious to me and mine for yet many years to come.

I would now like briefly to share with you some thoughts about my way of being a teacher. My pretext for doing this is that it shaped the *festschrift*. Most such collections show what smart academic or important friends the honoree has. As books they are rarely readable. I suggested we might get something more useful by plugging a gap in contemporary Jewish religious literature. We would do so by inviting some colleagues whose lives have intersected with mine to overcome their reticence and say something about their spiritual life's journey.

Focusing on them, not on me, was, of course, another act of what, twenty years ago, I called leadership by *tzimtzum*, leadership by strategic withdrawal rather than self-extension. That notion characterized my way of being a husband, parent and rabbi long before I knew what to call it, and it still drives my ongoing effort to teach more effectively. To my great pleasure it still seems significant and recently my article about it was the only reprint included in Torah Aura's fine collection of papers called *What We Know About Jewish Education.*

The biographical essays for *Jewish Spiritual Journeys* were sent as seventieth birthday tributes and as I read them I was deeply moved by their religious diversity and human depth. This is one of the greatest virtues of leadership by *tzimtzum*, that it draws forth the extraordinary things most of us, in our own way, have to offer each other. No group determinedly agenda- or leader-dominated will do that. So I am thrilled by the content of the *festschrift* as I hope you will be.

Let me, in turn, respond with a reciprocal *tzimtzum* gift. Next winter, thanks to the heroic exertions of Paula Dubrow, a lay student at the College who professionally does design by computer, and thanks to Behrman House we will publish a 460 page book, *Reform Jewish Ethics and the Halakhah*, the work of 26 of our youngest colleagues, a number of whom I see here. These are its bound page proofs, not yet trimmed to size. The book contains fourteen studies on topics that range from Hazardous Waste Disposal through Counseling Germ Cell Gene Therapy to Synagogues Accepting Tainted Gifts and the like. It resulted from a course in which student-teams became Reform *poskim*, rendering a decision on an issue of their choosing — but only after a reasonably exhaustive survey of the diverse ethical and halakhic positions toward it. The volume is introduced and assessed by an outside reader, Prof. Louis Newman of Carleton College, probably our leading contemporary critic of applied Jewish ethical method. It concludes with my essay on the possibility of a postmodern Jewish ethics. If you can stop by the Behrman House display some time this afternoon, you can see the page proofs up close.

But life by *tzimtzum* has its problems and I want to touch on three I live with. It is one thing for the teacher to make room for true student participation but quite another when you need to take seriously what they then say. Over the years that has sometimes been easy and sometimes not. Thus, once my consciousness was raised, I had little problem shifting to inclusive language as it seemed so just a demand. Wearing a *kipah* for prayer was harder. I certainly did want to identify with the Jewish people rather than the Protestant west when I prayed but making a public religious change caused me an embarrassment I had to struggle to overcome. And this year, for the first time in 37 years teaching at the College, I find there are some students whose personal religiosity I not only admire but seems to have moved somewhat ahead of my own. I am not speaking here of ritual observance; on the whole traditional practice, always a minority phenomenon at our school, has decreased over the past decade. Rather I find these students in their personal relationship with God and their effort to see what that requires of them suggesting possibilities I hadn't thought of. And I admit that I find that scary. I've also sometimes had the experience that what students see as new Torah I see as fad, the reinvention of the wheel, or simply wrong.

That leads me to a second, presently perplexing issue. For some years now, students have been calling on us to provide a more nurturing environment. Those words sound strange to someone whose rabbinic education proceeded under a pedagogy of harassment and shaming, yet they also carry a strong religious appeal. Many aspects of our human relations are pretty bad compared to the loving helpfulness that is our ideal. This winter our student publication adverted to the need for nurture in new terminology, students not feeling "safe" or "secure" at services because someone — and not just faculty — might criticize them. On the one hand, they do want to be educated but they want it done in a way which respects them as they are and affirms it. Now I am glad to reach out to them as "thous" but that doesn't mean to me that I should overlook faulty spelling — with spell-check, yet! — or not knowing what they are talking about. So the *tzimtzum* challenge changes from student generation to generation with this one certainly striking me as particularly awesome.

One last issue. To be a rabbi one must practice a certain emotional asceticism. We come to Jewish acts with total dedication and try to bring our whole selves appropriately to a given situation. Our congregants want no less. But they come with a lesser Jewish involvement, sometimes momentarily intensified. Their transient Jewish need satisfied, they go on to more important things, grateful, perhaps for what they received, sometimes touchingly so.

All rabbis live with this emotional imbalance of giving and receiving. However, if our lives long intertwine with theirs some special event may allow the otherwise unexpressed love momentarily but honestly to surface, something I saw so notably at Arnold's seventieth birthday celebration. By contrast, teachers spend only a few intense and formative years with their students. Some they never see again and most of the others only sporadically. The rabbi who becomes a professor must therefore sacrifice the ongoing increment of enduring association with some families and individuals, and then often passes into retirement with little or no ceremony. In melancholic moments, I feel even more asceticism is demanded of the teacher who practices *tzimtzum*, the one who seeks to be as unintrusive as the student's growth allows. Stepping aside so as to give the student room, it sometimes seems they did little. There may be some truth in that — but not at this moment, for as it were, *atem nitzavim hayom kulchem...* we are standing here, all of us, to renew the special covenant which binds one rabbi to every other one. And it is this faith which brings me always to conclude my private davvening: *al yisrael, v'al rabbanan, v'al talmidayhon . . .*

2) *My Pursuit of Prayerfulness*

When Larry and Arnold told me about the *festschrift* they proposed to do for my 70th birthday I was pleased indeed. To gather in reunion with a few friends and some of the students with whom I have spent the past three decades seemed a lovely way to celebrate. Now, reading the resulting essays, I am freshly conscious of my blessings. I never was able to find a teacher to guide me, so these keen souls, most notably Arnold, have worthily served me in that role. Gratefully, I acknowledge their patience with my pedagogic failings, ones exacerbated by my lofty goals and risky expectations. Here, once again I have pushed us all quite far, asking them to break out of our common reticence about such matters and speak of our inner religious lives. I take it as a special sign of their affection that they have done so with such openness. God has been very good to me.

In one respect, their accounts surprised me. They contravene our mythic picture of the inner lives of caring Jews in the second half of the twentieth century. These spiritual journeys reflect little *sturm und drang* over the Holocaust or its theological implications. The lives they describe were not greatly moved by either the founding, the traumas, the culture or the spiritual impact of the State of Israel. And mostly they display a remarkably positive tone.

Like so much else, that set me to thinking. Do these accounts indicate it is time for a revision of the accepted picture of the Jewish psyche overwhelmed by momentous events? Was this stereotypical perspective the experience of *amcha*, the Jewish people as a whole? Or was it merely what a small-ish group of culture-shapers thought ought to have happened to our broad masses? Perhaps I am reading too much into the accounts of this quite exceptional group of contributors. Would any group of respondents, influenced by this celebrative context, have produced equally positive reflections? Or are these writers merely mirroring my preoccupation with Diaspora Jewish existence?

Whatever the case, their generous context prompts me to tell something of my own story.

I was blessed with a simple soul, albeit needled by a complicated, busy mind. Issues that bedeviled others have often seemed quite clear to me even when — a common case — my overactive analytical faculty did not find my explanations of my stand very satisfactory. I owe the gift and nurturence of that core simplicity to my caregivers, first my marvelous parents and then, these near fifty years, to my wife, she of the exquisite soul. I cannot even hope to begin unwinding here the skein of their ongoing spiritual tutelage (or that of my daughters — their mother's soul sisters — their admirable husbands and remarkably diverse children, my mentors all). Instead, I will try to recount something of my lifelong struggle to pray wholeheartedly.

By my simplicity of soul I surely mean that even as a youngster in the 1930's, I knew that Judaism was deeply good and true — and thought it abominable that none of my teachers or my rabbi could explain it sensibly. Our Columbus, Ohio Sunday and Hebrew schools taught mush and the services I often attended were mindless. At Columbus East High School I finally got some indication of what it meant to think as moderns did, but, naturally, not in a class. I tried out for the debate team with a speech overflowing with statistics. The debate coach, Martin E. Horn, then gently inquired how all these numbers proved the proposition under discussion. For several years, then, he taught me speech by speech what it meant to give a good reason and how one best combined reasons so as to be persuasive. In my Synagogue High School Department I met Manuel Brandt, a research chemist, who taught us his thoughtful, university structured understanding of Judaism. The one started me thinking rigorously, the other gave me hope that my life project aborning — to explain modern Judaism in an academically sound fashion — might be possible. I mention both their names with continuing appreciation.

For a congenital thinker, I was also determinedly practical — another uncomplicated commitment of my life — yet, having sampled and ruled out all the sensible choices of a bright Jewish boy, I wound up in the Ohio State University philosophy department. I suppose I thought I could always teach and I really wanted to see what reason could do for me and the world.

In the Spring of 1942 I had a critical intellectual experience, one so decisive I can recall no other like it. At 18 I was about to enter the university's senior class. My good academic record got me admitted to a graduate seminar on epistemology being taught by a professor visiting from Johns Hopkins. One afternoon, walking to where my jalopy was parked, I kept going over the day's discussion. If one was an epistemological dualist, how did the independent realities outside one's mind ever get into it? But if one was an epistemological monist, all that ever was in the mind was one's own mental devisings and one could never really know their relation to the world outside one if, indeed, there was such a thing (for how would one ever know it?). The seminar group had not resolved the issue; they never did (nor has contemporary philosophy). It suddenly occurred to me: if I didn't know philosophically how I knew anything then I could never know anything for certain. So as a philosopher I would spend the rest of my life surer of my doubts than of anything else — and that included being surer of our doubts about the difference between right and wrong than about its reality and the consequent need to do something about it. That struck my practical soul as ridiculous and I ceased believing reason could validate anything deeply significant. (Later I learned how true that also was of even what we think reason is.)

That was the beginning of my abandonment of the primacy of rationality, of philosophizing which hoped to start from doubt and arrive, if one was still religious, at faith. I came to realize that everything serious begins with a measure of faith and then, if one is reasonable, one tries to think as sensibly as one can about what it means to see reality that way. That, concisely, is what I mean by that problematic term, "theology."

I came to the Hebrew Union College in Sept. 1942 hoping to learn about Jewish theology and thus gain the reasonable explanation of Judaism I desired. Despite a summer's study with a tutor at the College my Hebrew skills were still so weak that I was admitted only as "a special student." In the College dorm I soon found some classmates who felt as I did that American Judaism was barren, not only in its thinking but in its practice. We wanted to be able to pray with *kavanah*, "direction, intention." For some that probably only meant praying with fervor but I now feel that our quest also had overtones of more personal engagement with God. The upper classmen found all this ludicrous and brandishing the cynicism that passed for sophistication in those days, they began deriding us as "the *kavanah* boys." Our independent service did not last long. We were few and the heavy course load as well as the dormitory taunting had their effect. Perhaps we would have been consoled had we known that we were among the forerunners of what has since become the search for "spirituality."

Whatever remained with me from that experience helped me bring my own *kavanah* to our services in "the Chapel." I still recall being exalted by some sunny Shabbat morning services as our student soloists and choir provided the music. Remaining determinedly analytic, I knew this might only be an effect of community and rite for I had little direct sense of the presence of God. But if there were no God, no real God, no God not myself, as the basis of Jewish and ethical existence, then the whole enterprise made no sense. So I decided to find out whether I truly believed in God.

Knowing that reasoning, mine or others', could not resolve the issue, I decided to take the experiential route. I would pray privately to God and see if "anybody was there" and I would do so using the *Union Prayer Book*, which I had come to love. That was how my pursuit of prayerfulness began and with it my life of prayer which, despite my shortcomings, soon became a mainstay of my relationship with God.

I shall shortly tell my story but I first want to make some additional comments about the spirituality these narratives depict. They exhibit three different foci in Jewish piety and, if some license is granted, one can see something of a chronological sequence to them. In the two which dominated the post World War II decades there is little explicit mention of spirituality, a theme much too pious for a time when our modernization-secularization project was at full throttle. In those years I knew many admirable people who expressed their Jewish dedication in their intellectual intensity. Perhaps that now leads me to see that devotion to the cognitive (in several varieties) as a common form of the "spirituality" of some of the earliest ordainees writing here. I suggest it is our academicized version of the "Litvak" devotion to mind and surfaces here as thinking, research, or, more recently, literary study. Somewhat concurrent with this but only topping our religious agenda in the activist mid-sixties, was the concern for religion as action, particularly a moralized politics. In these biographies it is manifest in the energetic determination to be a worthy rabbi, teacher, and/or ethical leader, our modernistic, if somewhat restricted, version of the Rabbis' spirituality of duty. Only as we move to more recent years does personalism establish itself and spirituality emerge in language and self-consciousness. The uncommon theme of this *Festschrift*, spiritual journeys, is an outcome of that new sensibility and unthinkable a decade ago. Despite some bows in the direction of Kabbalah and Hasidism, I find little classic mysticism — access to higher religious realms via exceptional experiences or leaders — in this community of sharers. That would be a fourth way in Jewish spirituality, one with significant minority manifestation in the contemporary Jewish community but not represented in these writers.

Permit me a bold comparison, one prompted by some people's insistence that true spirituality is found only in Asian faiths. Since devotees of the spiritual say that their piety is the essence of all religions, I suggest, despite my inexpertise in Asian religions, that considerable similarities exist between "Litvak" intellectuality and Hindu metaphysical Yoga, between Rabbinic duty and Hindu Bhakti Yoga, and between Psalm-like personalism and the Yoga of self-discovery.

My schema, Litvaks, Rabbis, Psalmists, reverses Jewish history but roughly characterizes non-Orthodox American Jewish life as I experienced it and now read about here. Shortly after World War II the *Wissenschaft* in which Jewish intellectuality then gloried found itself joined rather charily by an unanticipated theological interest. It did not take long for Jewish intellectuality to link up with Jewish duty, particularly social action, and emerge as modern Jewish style. But with time, academia and activism lost their salvific auras, religiosity became identified with inner experience, and felt piety became the living edge of Jewish spirituality.

All this is typological abstraction. I make no claim to have seen these types as one-dimensional in reality as I described them above. The personalists are often ethical activists and the most abstract thinkers have felt great passion for their ideas. People are far more deliciously, maddeningly complex than our theories about them. I suppose I made this historical detour so I could say, with considerable trepidation, that it seems to me that Arnold's and my religious lives, from our first acquaintance in 1942, were unusually three dimensional. Though I have written more, he has read more. Where he has been more socially active and politically involved than me, I have my own record of community activity. But where his family's German-American Jewishness has tended to formalize his life of faith, I suggest that the expressiveness of my East European home encouraged me to a more subjective and personal religiosity.

That is something of my context as I see it. That being set, let me
focus on one aspect of my Jewish interiority, my effort over the years to
build a rich prayer life.

The Doer Who Would Be God's Intimate

I am not by nature a prayerful person. My religiosity, such as it is,
has more easily been exercised as thought or action. Others find analysis,
argument and system-building, in which I have delighted, cold and
detached, and often find it odd that I find them apt vehicles for my piety.
But I consider my urge to conceptualize a gift from God and try to
exercise it in faithfulness to its Source. I have also loved doing good
Jewish deeds, from soliciting in our Columbus teen-age "Federation"
campaign, to loading sandbags to stave off a Cincinnati flood, or going
to jail in St. Augustine in a Martin Luther King campaign. I didn't think
much about the presence of God as I did these and other things; they
simply seemed (then and today) the most natural thing for a Jew to do.

Thus, when as a young rabbinic student I set out to pray to God on
my own, I had to fight my inclination to ease into some comfortable
abstraction or busy-ness. I just had to stand there (it seemed too casual
to pray sitting down) and talk as naturally as I could to God all the while
not taking (skeptical) note of what was going on. Memory suggests that
I stood facing the East wall of my dormitory room, feeling embarrassed
and silly, fearful that someone would come barging in and find me praying,
of all things. It was far more unsettling than learning to dance as an
adolescent. But I persisted, "reading" one or another of the *Union Prayer
Book* daily services until the strangeness gave way to familiarity and I
could reach for *kavanah*. It was not easy. I regularly shifted my attention
from God to thinking about the meaning of a phrase in the text or some
task I really had-to, ought-to, do. So began a lifetime's spiritual struggle.

It took some weeks, I recall, before I felt satisfied that I learned what
I needed from my inquiry. Happily, I now knew I could turn to God
directly and often experience God being there, before me, with me. It
was — I still cannot find decent terminology for it — a "knowledge," a
"sense," an "intuition," that with varying intensity and clarity has since
accompanied me and grounded my existence. I am saddened when that
experience fades, sometimes for long periods, and joyful when it reappears,
sometimes quite unexpectedly. Not only as a believing Jew but as a
theologian much concerned to understand and write about our relationship
to God, I have been much exercised with how to be true to this reality in

my theologizing and mitzvah-ing, particularly my praying. (How my thought-work influences my piety, as it surely does, turns out to be a mystery I have not, despite some effort, been able to clarify significantly.)

This new consciousness allowed me to bring a new interiority to the College's corporate prayer-life and regular attendance at services helped sustain me during my six years in rabbinical school. The five years after ordination in 1948 were filled with momentous happenings — marriage (in 1947); our first pulpit (an assistantship for two years in St. Louis); a return to the College to do doctoral work; the Korean War (which limited my resident study to one year); two years' service as a Navy chaplain at the huge East Coast boot camp in rural Maryland; and the birth of our first daughter. In these years, prayerfulness retreated from the fore of my consciousness yet I vaguely recall the special challenges of trying to conduct services with *kavanah* in a large congregation and later in a military chapel. Little else stands out liturgically.

Then, in June 1953, two months before I was to be discharged from the Navy, an event occurred which had a substantial impact on my life of prayer. Being stationed not too far from Wilmington, Del., I had agreed to cover for Rabbi Herbert Drooz — an older friend from student days — while he was at that year's CCAR meeting. One day I received a call from the congregation asking me to conduct a funeral. On my way there my car was broadsided by an uninsured ne'er-do-well, the brakes of whose borrowed car had failed at a stop sign. The next day, after slipping in the wading pool where our baby was frolicking, I discovered that my urine was the color of *kiddush* wine. I felt fine otherwise but the Navy doctors insisted on hospitalization, various unpleasant tests and, though the color of my urine cleared, they refused for complicated medical reasons to release me. They treated my immediate problem, an apparent tear in the kidney wall, with an injunction to drink as much water as I could. Of the odd ramifications of that case all that is relevant here is what it taught me about my body and prayer.

One day in the hospital after the umpteenth trip to "the head," it occurred to me that the Rabbis had a blessing after a visit to the toilet. Of course, as a properly modern sophisticate I had learned to pooh-pooh such backward, uncouth elements of traditional Jewish practice. (How barbaric it seemed to me a few years earlier, at Steve Schwarzschild's mother's funeral, that the mourners and others actually threw a shovelful of dirt on her coffin — a practice I have since often tenderly participated in.) Now I needed to do something about my primal sense of thankfulness every time my kidneys and bladder worked well. So overcoming my smugness, I first studied and then began to recite the *asher yatzar* prayer. "We call you 'Blessed,' *Adonai* our God, ruler of the universe, who fashioned human beings wisely and created in them many orifices and hollows, all the while knowing most clearly that if one of them should gape or seal, it would be impossible to stand before You. You are 'Blessed,' *Adonai*, curer of people, worker of wonders." That articulated just what I wanted to say; no, it said more than I would have thought to say and said it better.

I gained three things from that experience. First, I began to appreciate the aura of a life punctuated with *berakhot*. That started me learning how to respond to various situations with blessings, traditional ones or ones I make up to fit an occasion. To this day I have not been able to fully implement that insight, though I still work at it fitfully. Second, I learned to appreciate the Rabbis as spiritual guides. Though I had already completed my first doctorate, I, like many a Reform Jew, felt quite superior to the rabbinic tradition and many of its quaint ideas about how to serve God. But while I had thought I could transcend my body, the Rabbis, despite their smelly privies, knew the excretory system was too important a part of being human to be barred from our relationship with God. From then on, I began to trust them and their "way" more and to approach their behests as spiritual disciplines which might enrich my impoverished inner life.

The third consequence deserves special attention because it was so unexpected that it remains something of a continuing surprise to me. I have come to recite many prayers during the day but I do so quietly, to myself. I do not find my old friends and neighbors, though respectful of my practice, comfortable when I do so on anything but formal occasions. Of all the prayers I say, none surfaces more constantly in my consciousness than the *asher yatzar*. It is, I suppose, my closest equivalent to a *mantra*. Perhaps that may be attributed to the innumerable times I have said it (a sum increased as the years have passed with their predictable prostate problems and the diuretic I take for mild hypertension). It took on fresh urgency a decade or so ago when one of my coronary arteries closed down. Whatever the external impetus, I see that comparatively lengthy blessing as a demanding, ongoing spiritual exercise in accepting my contingency — my mortality, to be blunt. It speaks to me of life's fragility, of its utter dependence on countless teeny apertures not closing up or gaping wide. To a physically vigorous, intellectually adventurous, act-oriented, busybody like me, that is a daunting message. More, the prayer says that this dependency is perfectly clear to God. And I, thankful that this arrangement still works for me now call God "Blessed" or "Praiseworthy" or whatever one makes of that overloaded symbolic package, "*barukh.*" I do not bridle that the closing words praise God as "healing all flesh" for I do not see that as a nonsensical denial that some illnesses are chronic, others destructive and many fatal, but a celebration of the curative role of excretion. There is something quite "wondrous" about this work, as the final words of the *berakhah* put it and so I, leaving the toilet, sanctify this otherwise profane moment through words the Rabbis taught me. Surely it took a rare combination of realism suffused with spiritual genius to direct us to love God afresh each time our organs have produced our urine or feces and I am its grateful beneficiary.

The lessons of this *berakhah* have had a de-Copernican effect on my soul and my theologizing. Modernity put humans at the center of the universe so we are shocked, even outraged, when it does not conform to our desires. But each *berakhah* teaches that the world is ordered more as God would have it than as I would. Whatever else the classic metaphors for God, "Creator" and "Ruler," imply, they convey the primal Jewish intuition that God (whether limited or infinite) is the most basic reality in the universe. I may be very significant but the world is God's, not mine. It is humbling that, having devoted myself to reestablishing God's reality in non-Orthodox Judaism, I only came to understand this in "my flesh," as the Psalmist says, by praying the blessing for going to the toilet.

Knowing the world is more God's than mine, I have come to realize that "Anything can happen to anybody at any time" and I have made that scary sense of contingency a part of my piety. Though I still regularly get nauseous when confronting another tragedy, I try to face it determined to do what I can to overcome it and, when that is unlikely, with something like the classic Jewish mood of acceptance. Paradoxically, not evading what may transpire has intensified my appreciation of the present and all the goodness God continually showers on me.

Let me extend this theme a bit. Understanding the universe as God-centered and not me-centered has helped me also appreciate God's greatness. There is something awesome about this world and every revelation of the sub-atomic or the astrophysical realm only heightens my appreciation of the mystery. We need to remember that the Awesome One behind this cosmos is the One before Whom we stand in prayer. So the first act of prayer is to put aside our private agendas and "set God before us." That, I take it, is the reason for the lavish praise of God at the start of our services. The Rabbis, knowing most people then, as now, come to services preoccupied with themselves, have tried to help us transcend it. Knowing we could never praise God's greatness sufficiently (so the *nishmat kol chai*), rabbinic realism limits what we say and modern Judaisms have tended to be even more concise.

A paradox accompanies this awareness of transcendence for it is just I, excretory animal that I am, who know this. More, the Present One, the Fundament of all being, is involved with me personally. How incredible it is that nothings such as me may often easily be intimate with God, no less. That special closeness gives humans unalienable honor, dignity, challenge — and in this extraordinary "far-near" experience, Jewish prayer came to be and flourished.

I have introduced these not uncommon themes of Jewish piety to explain two additional aspects of my prayer life. I have not been able seriously to argue with God. That has often been suggested in our day as a way of responding to intractable evil. It has some basis in Jewish tradition (though I think it a lot less prominent than do many of its protagonists). In this respect I share something of Abraham Heschel's piety, one which, because it begins with an acknowledgement of God's incomparable greatness, transforms what one finds one can say to God. This seems so miserably passive that I have tried to do what others suggested and indict God for some evil I should think God would find intolerable. I have not been able to carry it through for my strong sense of God's greatness arises to preempt that. I have also come before God and sought merely to ask some penetrating questions about a given outrage, yet I have been met only by implacable silence. None of this has ever made me feel rejected or spurned by God simply for coming to God and honestly trying to pour out my heart. I know God is great enough to pay attention to me in any momentary distress I bring to my prayer. Sometimes, coming to pray, I realize that what has been riling me is really too silly to pray about. (Is that one meaning of God answering before we ask?) But I also am confident that if a matter, even a small one, is important enough to me to bring to God — who else will fully listen and understand me? — then God, the incomparable Transcendent, "cares for" me enough to "want" me to do just that.

What part of these reflections was directly the outcome of my saying the *asher yatzar* blessing and how much I have come to connect with it over the years, I do not know. I only wish to make one more observation here. I have found that the nodes around which my spirituality have turned, like this *berakhah*, arise on their own and can decline in power in an equally incomprehensible way. Thus I would never have imagined that the *asher yatzar* blessing would have such resonance for me over all these years. Yet the *birkhot hashachar*, which for long powerfully suffused my getting up and dressed each morning, now has mostly lost its special magic. Therefore, despite all the benefit one gains from the discipline one's spiritual guide teaches, one must finally also discover and go on one's own soul-enlarging way.

I have made prayer a habitual but uncompulsive life discipline that has its own urgency. This involved me in one aspect of the famous clash between the contrasting Jewish prayer ideals *keva* — fixity — and *kavanah*. People generally think of it as a fight between spontaneity and rule. Identifying prayer with an uninhibited upsurge of the soul, they bridle at praying fixed prayers at fixed times, as Jewish tradition prescribes. But should the value of prayer be measured by human experience alone? If God is real, indeed the Ultimate Reality, then we ought to pay attention to God, regularly. And if our relationship to God is not merely a private creation but one that derives from and contributes to the Jewish people's ongoing Covenant with God, then our prayer life should largely be structured by the wisdom of corporate Jewish spirituality. Giving new weight to *keva* does not resolve the *keva-kavanah* problem but only restores *kavanah* to its place as the strived-for, difficult prayer-ideal. Let me quickly add that I have rarely been at ease with the balance I have achieved.

But I have been theologizing when I mean to tell my story. As prayer became a regular part of my life I learned to do it better. The words and phrases began to flow more easily from page to eye to heart to mouth to God. I came to love the services and the wisdom behind them, at least as they refracted in shifting ways through my soul. I came to trust their language more and resist the difficult phrases less, though some passages have never opened up to me and I now doubt that they ever will. I also discovered a new talent. Though I was never a good memorizer, I gradually, almost naturally, became able to recite long passages of the liturgy by heart. That too made it easier for me to find the service an incomparable means of learning-expressing-renewing old Jewish pieties.

I had made my way into prayer via the Union Prayer Book (the "Newly Revised" edition of 1940) and am still deeply moved by its prayers. (I occasionally make a pilgrimage to Temple Emanu-El so I can once again be stirred by its elegant English.) But with my knowledge enlarging alongside my soul, I now wanted to benefit from more of the numberless overtones of the classic Hebrew text. This soon became so much a part of me that it once led me into a somewhat embarrassing situation. In 1964, the CCAR meeting in Atlantic City received a telegram from Martin Luther King asking its members to come to St. Augustine, Florida and participate in his crusade against segregation there. Two days later, seventeen of us were in jail there, held, at our request, in one large cell. The colleagues asked me to lead an evening service for us. We had no books, of course, so I began by memory. The group had no trouble with *maariv aravim* but as I continued with *ahavat olam* there was grumbling. They primarily knew the English text and, ignoring the congregation, I had simply continued on my, by then, familiar way. As I remember it, at that point our jailers intervened, complaining at our insensitivity for making so much noise when the warden's wife was suffering with cancer in the room beneath us. When they retreated we adjusted our service and continued.

When I felt I had fully mastered the considerable portions of our tradition in the *Union Prayer Book* I moved on to a gerrymandered version of the traditional *siddur*. The length of what I could meaningfully pray grew considerably over the years but eventually reached a stopping point. Still holding on to *kavanah* as my prayer-ideal, I found there were limits to what my activist, reflective soul could stretch to. Or to be clearer about my sense of duty, I expanded my service agenda to something just beyond what I regularly could make come alive, hoping this would stimulate me to continue growing in prayerfulness — but apparently I can assimilate no more. I did become reasonably proficient in the spiritual art of praying in the traditional *presto* rhythm, one quite different from the *adagio* of Reform services. The latter seeks the revelations of doing less but doing it intensively (when worshippers are not simply following this generation's variety of decorousness) while classic davvening revels in the flood of brief, half-assimilated flashes of insight we associate with multi-screened, multi-media shows (when worshippers are not just racing to get it over with). These two spiritual styles take different liturgical skills for granted. The breakneck traditional pace demands that congregants have great familiarity with lengthy texts and can recite them fluently. In the Orthodox Great Neck Synagogue where I often go for *shacharit* on Shabbat morning — there being few other places I can hear the whole *sedra* read and also not be overwhelmed by Bar Mitzvah tourists — there are some davveners who astound me with their fluency, not the least because they understand what they so nimbly say. Whatever the service, I love being in a congregation where the *kahal* really knows its spiritual style and makes it, in its own way, work. A fine rabbi or cantor can give invaluable leadership to worship but where they displace the congregants in carrying on the service, the result is rarely what I seek in Jewish prayer.

By these many positive remarks I do not mean to imply that I have not suffered the problems of regularity in prayer. While I am fairly good about *shacharit*, I have never been able to fulfill my desire to also recite the *maariv* service daily. Glorying in the Hebraic lushness of the traditional Shabbat *shacharit* service as I do, I must also put up with a maddeningly impossible traditional rhythm for reciting the morning Psalms, one which grossly violates these gorgeous texts. I have now reconciled myself to saying thoughtfully only about the first half of the poems. And as the pews fill, my struggle for *kavanah* must often battle with nearby conversations on real estate, politics (often Jewish) or a moderately excusable argument about a *sedra* text.

At home, too, much of my daily davenning is more dutiful than exalting. Not infrequently, the length of the service I seek to pray weighs heavily on me. And in some periods of my life, as recently, the moments of connection are fewer than the schizoid experience of a mind gone elsewhere while the lips declaim the familiar words. I have come to see this as a central spiritual struggle of my life: transforming my desirably strong ego into the I who exists hyphenated with God as Thou. As I now think about it, turning back to God with a full heart after finding my consciousness elsewhere has become a major spiritual challenge for me. I am so prone to distraction, my will to pray is so flimsy a defense against the subtle wiles of the *yetzer hara*, that my inability to do something supremely important to me is often quite depressing. Thus, this act of wholeheartedly turning back to God, while a poor substitute for having properly fulfilled my prayer hopes, is as much as I can often do.

My continual failure to pray as I would like makes it difficult to believe that another act of turning will result in anything but a new sin of inattentiveness. If prayer depended only on what went on in me, some days I would quit in disgust. But my Thou has not given up on me and I know that what God most wants of me is to keep honestly trying. I am not given to anthropo- or other morphs of God but I have occasionally had the sense that when I am stewing around about my wayward soul, God is smiling indulgently at me. *Kivyakhol*, it is as if God were saying to me, "Knock it off, Gene. Don't take yourself so seriously. Leave the judgment to Me and just keep trying." As quaint as my semi-detached theological soul finds that I know that there is a reality in that reverie (read, *chizayon*) that far transcends whatever the psycho- or other analysts would make of it.

Thus far I have touched only peripherally on the fuller expression of my (Covenantal) spirituality, praying among a Jewish community. I was able to live this ideal most fully in the years I created and participated in the worship style of the new congregation in Port Washington, NY to which we went after the chaplaincy. I had, of course, gained much from my prior corporate prayer experience. My ideals took shape praying with the HUC congregation, were strengthened by Arnold's and my experiments with youth-created liturgy at the first NFTY Leadership Institutes, given realism by leading the semi-classical service at my St. Louis assistantship and expanded by the diversely "traditional" Eastern Seaboard Jewish boots-in-training at our Naval Base. The Port Washington congregation was at first more desire than institution. Most of its young, newly suburbanite families had never thought of themselves as synagogue members, but some vague stirring of responsibility for their children's Jewishness brought them to the only place they could now find Jewish contacts. In short, they were, at best, Kaplanians and I was one of the few people who cared instead about what Buber had said about community.

Aside from the sociology, I had some marvelous help, most notably, the congregation's true soul-guide, Marjory Hess, whose memory is indeed for blessing. The daughter of a learned Reform rabbi, Felix Levy, herself extraordinarily well informed and intellectually alive, and a former concert singer, Marjory cared passionately about congregational participation in services, most particularly in its music. Her willing ally in this (and my uncommonly able colleague) was a reasonably well known voice teacher who had become a certified cantor at the College, a *basso profundo* named Maurice Jampol. They had already taught these neophyte worshippers to be active in the service, so all [!] I had to do was add a sense of transcendence to their we-feeling. With the Buber stories of Hasidic rebbes as prayer leaders in my head, I set about being, without benefit of mystic powers, a praying role-model (though I don't recall that term being current then).

I would occasionally explain the sense behind a prayer or liturgical practice. I also tried to explain why the God they treated with agnostic aversion was largely a literalistic image taken from the Bible and *siddur* but a far cry from contemporary Jewish belief. At one point I started to write a little book about the structure of the service and its goals but I never finished it. Apparently I managed to communicate to them that I took prayer quite seriously even though my outsize cerebral cortex had not atrophied and neither had my agile sense of humor. I imagine that the majority of the congregation didn't know what to make of me but they were not sufficiently disturbed as to increase their customary limited involvement with the congregation. One way or another, I found my caring minority and they slowly began to be the core of much that happened in the congregation.

What joy it was when occasionally I was able to give living spiritual shape to an entire service and not merely one or another of its prayers. I have long felt that services have an intrinsic form, a structural dynamism, and I have sought to bring that out in "conducting" services. So when I could use the totality of place, music, word, chant, movement, silence, teaching and community to fill a given moment with the Rabbinic sense of God's present/past relationship with us and our people, I believed I had fulfilled an important part of being a good rabbi.

The opposite has also been true; I have received as much as I have given. On many an occasion I have come to a service, whether to lead or to participate, and found myself flat, empty, unable to do more than fulfill my role responsibly. Not infrequently on such occasions, either the words-rites themselves or the congregation's momentum — it need not be its fervor — has brought me into the davenning in ways I could not do myself. I think it an important part of being a prayer leader to learn not only to do what you can for others but to realize how often you must lean on them and let them do for you. (In all of this there is an aspect of God's own activity but I cannot as easily speak of that subtle reality as I can of group and *siddur*.)

When I left the congregational pulpit in 1957 after four intense, wonderful years, I did not know that I would never again regularly shape a community's prayer. In the nearly forty years since in which I have served as bureaucrat and professor, I have had no doubt about which rabbinic function I most missed: regularly leading a congregation in prayer.

When I arrived at the Union of American Hebrew Congregations in 1957, soon to succeed Dr. Emanuel Gamoran as Director of Education, I continued my practice of saying the morning service in my office. (Office prayers remind me, not always successfully, of what is supposed to be Number One in my life.) I recall how startled someone was who came through my door early one morning and found me davvening (the *UPB*). Whether it was the irony of that event or just the simple logic of it, I found it peculiar that a religious organization had a "chapel" but no daily service within it.

I had not then heard the account which Gene Lipman, z"l — a great story teller but an uncommonly reliable one — later related to me. When the sizable parcel of land opposite Temple Emanu-El at Manhattan's Fifth Ave and Sixty Fifth St. became available just as the Union was seeking to move from Cincinnati to New York, it seemed too good to be true. However, the zoning laws prohibited office buildings that far North on Fifth Ave. and that was what the Union sought. But some fine legal (dare I hope, "Talmudic"?) mind pointed out that the code does permit Houses of Worship there and would not dare rule how much office space a faith finds appropriate in a house of worship. So it was as a synagogue that the Union got a building permit — though no one ever remembered the chapel being used, except to show visitors to the building.

I floated the idea of a daily service in the chapel and got permission to go ahead. We held it at noon so that people could take the first fifteen minutes or so of their lunch time to stop by. By getting various members of the staff to lead the service for a week, we got it going. Only when we had a meeting in the building or a noontime group of visitors were we likely not to have our customary sparse attendance. I and some others were rather regular and in a unique way, that little struggling service often had a special effect on me. (I've often felt something like that at lay-led daily services in various Reform synagogues.) At one point we got some unexpected help from an odd source, New York City. It began requiring a moment's test of all the air-raid sirens at noon each work day and the sound became a signal that services were about to start. But it was largely my determination that kept the service alive and some months after I left the Union in 1962 to teach full time at the College in New York, the daily service came to an end.

I had better luck at the College but I don't remember whether it all started before or after I joined the Rabbinical School faculty. (Shortly after coming to Port Washington, in 1954 or '55, I began teaching part time in the then quite active School of Education, becoming an adjunct instructor in the Rabbinical School in 1957.) At the College I was appalled to discover that, since the days of Stephen S. Wise, the New York School (a) did not have a daily service and (b) had a weekly compulsory "service" each Friday morning where the students could practice reading the Sabbath liturgy, sing various Sabbath tunes and listen to another student preach a sermon. At first Dr. Wise — and later Dr. Tepfer — would demonstrate proper rhetorical skills by tearing apart the sermon — and sometimes the student. ("Nurture" was then not a major student concern or, for that matter, desire.) This play-acting "service" suited the students well for cynicism was their standard psychic defense against having to face up to what they weren't sure they believed despite their determination to become rabbis.

Fortunately our Dean, Paul Steinberg, agreed that a new arrangement was needed, and the next fall, to the derision of the students and the incredulity (*sic*) of most of the faculty, a daily weekday service began at the New York School. Attendance was not compulsory (it still isn't) so attendance varied from sparse to non-existent. But each student had to lead services for a week (they still do) and were free to design or shape a service for our congregation (they still are). In those first years, some of the conscripts tested the limits of their "authority" by finding creative ways to mock the new practice. I attended whenever I was in the building and I still recall the special hardness of the pews and the equally austere atmosphere of the 68th Street building chapel. It was designed after Mrs. Wise, a sculptor of some note, had seen the Rashi Chapel in France and decided (ca. 1922) to model much of our building after it. Neither our chapel, which could perhaps seat 75, or the first floor auditorium, which probably sat 300 or so people, originally had an ark. Ever the great preacher, Dr. Wise believed the sermon was the center of the service and he held his Carnegie Hall service on Sunday morning. Some time later Mrs. Wise had a lovely, neo-Gothic vertical chest built to serve as the chapel ark and it provided a plain but attractive home for our small *sefer Torah*. (The ark in the auditorium was a hideous plywood contraption, apparently built when the Free Synagogue transferred its services from Carnegie Hall Sundays to Friday nights on 68th Street.)

One of the ongoing joys of my life has been the transformation of the daily congregation at the College from student circus to, dare I say it, a *kehillah kedoshah*, an ofttimes pious community. To be sure, neither the faculty nor the students, rabbinic and cantorial (plus a smattering of others), have turned saintly or walk around being unctuous, may God preserve us. But the American Jewish psyche began esteeming Judaism with unprecedented appreciation as a result of the confluence of the Six Day War in Israel, the American race riots and the disillusion brought on by the Vietnam War. The quality of our student bodies then radically improved as did their general attitude toward their studies with us. The synagogue service was the last aspect of our school life to be transformed, the late 1960's being the time of Death of God theology. But whether it was the slow recognition of the collapse of messianic modernism, as I have termed it in *Renewing the Covenant*, the cultural shift to the intimacy of *chavurot* and the personal intensity of mysticism (first Asian and then Jewish), or the marvelous leadership of our then young instructor in Liturgy, Larry Hoffman, a new religiosity began to make itself felt. It not only gave a new tone to our services but to the feel of our community in general.

That etiology does an injustice to another major energizing force which I have reserved for special mention here: the growing piety and participation of School of Sacred Music students in our services. Obviously a congregation of Rabbinical School students has solid liturgical skills and above average motivation. But imagine what happens when a congregation abounds with worshippers who are also musically expert and talented. I have known no other congregation where the service is so robust, so rich in knowledgeable davenning, said and sung. Since student-cantors co-lead (and co-plan) our daily services, regular davveners are exposed both to the vast treasury of Jewish music past and present (some of it by our students). The unfamiliarity of the new music usually does not dampen the participation of our *kahal*, for student-cantor worshippers often know or quickly learn the unfamiliar setting.

This is, of course, the experience of recent years, the ones in which students have become more personally concerned with realizing their Jewish spirituality. However, its germ was always there and was significant enough to help keep me content to be in a seminary rather than a university. Nonetheless, I never imagined years ago that our services would reach the spiritual level they sometimes do these days. Everything I said above about what one can gain from the congregation when one's own personal prayer resources are temporarily depleted holds doubly true of praying in the College congregation. Life in this particular, often prayerful community is a very special blessing, one of the many spiritual gifts students have given me over the years. I do not mean to disparage what our administration or faculty have sought to do to bring this about when I say that its primary cause has been the spiritual activism that the students themselves have brought to our school in recent years.

Thinking about the many things they have given me personally prompts me to say something about my oft-mentioned practice of starting class with the *berakhah* for study. That began at home years ago as an effort to add a touch of *kavanah* to the *torah lishmah* with which I had learned to begin my home morning prayer routine. Back then, when Jewish Studies programs were new, I often served as a visiting professor at various universities teaching something like my College courses. The similarities made me think about what made teaching academically at a rabbinical school special. I certainly expected my HUC students to work to high academic standards, yet in our study we were also fulfilling a religious duty. Because professional moralizing was abominated then (and is only somewhat more patiently endured today), I decided to do in class what I had been doing at home — after all, this was what the study meant to me. Nonetheless, I was quite squeamish about starting it for it radically broke with academic convention and could easily be derided. Perhaps people did make fun of it — me — behind my back. But in the strange ways that God sometimes works, I doubt that there is anything I have said or written — as significant as I think they are — that has affected my students more than this simple act. It once led to what I quickly accepted as a "chastisement of love." I came charging into class one day, near-frantic about the dozens of things I needed to remember and get done, and plunged directly into the day's material. A gentle voice quietly inquired about the *berakhah*. I have not forgotten my responsibilities since and I am no longer surprised when students now join me in saying the blessing.

That practice was an indirect gift from my students. Were they not there, I could not be a teacher, a fact I rarely forget and one occasionally forced on me when no one signs up for an elective I am offering. At home, in fact, I have made the distinctive paragraph of the *kaddish derabbanan*, the last words of my daily order of prayer so as to link my life with the special community of rabbis and students with whom I particularly identify. Every once in a while as I pray for "the Rabbis, their disciples and their disciples' disciples," an image of this or that old student, now my colleague, flits through my consciousness.

There are also specific things our students have taught me. When a minority among them began wearing *kipot* ages ago, it struck my old Reform sensibilities as peculiar. But to my inquiry about this they said that they did it to identify with the people of Israel. So I now had to ask myself, who was my reference group when I prayed, the Christian community? Should I then continue praying in churchy bareheadedness, a *minhag* rarely found elsewhere in the World Union for Progressive

Judaism, or should I identify with the people of Israel? Mastering my trepidations once again, I began wearing a *kipah* when I prayed. The use of a *talit* as a participant at College services came more easily to me for I had always worn one as a rabbi leading my congregation — but it took the practice of a minority of our students to embolden me to do so when sitting in the daily congregation at school. Later, when I carried this over to formal College service occasions, it caused a bit of a murmur but I did not see why grand versions of *shacharit* should require me to give up a normal Jewish aspect of my daily worship.

Tefilin are another matter. We have also had a few students who wear *tefilin* at our daily services, though I, as someone who customarily wears a jacket and a long-sleeved shirt, have not found it congenial. Once, however, I came close to adopting it. We were visited by a high administrative official who became apoplectic at seeing *tefilin* worn in our synagogue. He was then reported as threatening to demand that students give up the practice. Had he persisted in that folly I surely would have become a steady wearer of *tefilin* at daily services and who knows what good it might have done me.

I have had some discomfort learning some other things from my students. One is the great variety of spiritual styles which, over the years, they have found meaningful. Some of these, say their manner of leading a service, their kind of creativity, or the kind of music which now speaks to them, seem essentially another manifestation of their student experimentation with life. Being of another generation and having a deeply ingrained personality, I try to be benignly indifferent to these. Other innovations have spoken to the needs of many students and lasted among us for years. I have tried to benefit from exposure to these cultural currents which, in my tower, I simply had not come to know and which now expand my spiritual repertoire. These days, I do not judge too quickly what will or will not work for me but consider that each new fashion may possibly freshen up my prayer life.

Early on, with our students taking it for granted that we should vocalize Hebrew as the Israelis did, I realized I needed to exchange the familiar Ashkenazi pronunciation of my youth for the Sefardi. Years before, at the Union, I had tried unsuccessfully to get the Commission on Jewish Education to change the transliteration in our new books to the Sefardi mode. And I had made good progress in converting my private study vocalization to the Sefardi but my Hebrew prayer fluency, which had not come easily, was borne along in the emotional ties of my Ashkenazi pronunciation. After deciding to make the shift, I stumbled around for weeks over old familiar texts, watching my pronunciation instead of talking to God and even when some fluency returned the sounds simply didn't carry the memories of my childhood. I don't know how long that annoying process went on but now, despite an occasional lapse into Ashkenazi when speaking, I rarely revert when praying.

More recently inclusive prayer has given me a similar problem. Believing in the justice of the cause, I have tried to follow the lead of our feminists in adjusting our liturgical language. That hasn't been much of a problem for me in the English and I can now almost automatically convert third person masculine pronouns referring to God to the inclusive second person — "You" — or say "God" (a term the consensus apparently allows to have a certain trans-sexual status). I slip occasionally in converting "King" to "Ruler" or "Sovereign" but console myself that in a few years new inclusive services will be widely available.

Hebrew, however, my preferred home medium, has been more troublesome. Early on, in the *Avot*, the names of the Matriarchs were linked to each of the Patriarchs; *chasdei avot* was expanded to *avot veimahot* and *ezrat Sarah* was joined to *magen avraham*. My old habits made the introduction of these changes something of an anti-*kavanah* nuisance but I persisted. Just as I had made the new version reasonably habitual the *minhag* changed and now we bunch the *imahot* together and mention them by name after the *avot*. For an old dog this has been annoying. But how could I stand easily in God's presence if I felt I had not done justice to the feminist search for our greater integrity?

In one respect I have not been able, despite some effort, to follow the feminist lead with regard to God-language. To avoid the gender issue and perhaps also to bring God closer, Marcia Falk has created impersonal images, e.g., "Source of Life," to substitute for the classic masculine terms for God. Many students, male and female, have found this meaningful but I have not. I do not see how I can establish an intimate personal relationship with something impersonal and therefore not reciprocally involved with me. (And if mind may make a claim on prayer, it seems quite odd that I, so conscious of being a person, should at my most significant level be created in the image of something impersonal.) I know my espousal of personalistic language leaves us with all the troublesome gender problems and I do not know how to meet them. But I cannot simply accept a creative proposal which contravenes the basic reality of my prayer experience, one with deep Jewish roots.

Let me conclude this lengthy account by speaking of a most precious thing students have in the past few years given me and others. For some time, there had been student efforts to hold a regular *minchah* service at our school. The problems were daunting: most students rush out of our building at three each day to get to their Hebrew school or other teaching jobs. The service had no required leaders, rabbinic or cantorial; it was to be done purely in the "pick up" style. And the students who cared about it wanted an informal, traditional mode — reasonably speedy davvening of the required Hebrew prayers, in a classroom and not "the Chapel," a mode of worship not congenial to many other students. So the initial attempts failed. But then one year there was a sufficient core of regulars to make the service go, with or without *minyan*, and it now continues its somewhat precarious existence with an official place on the day's schedule. Each afternoon we have the problem of reminding people still on the classroom floor that we are getting ready for services. Then we must cajole someone into leading the service. Then lickety-split, off we go, we nutty few, insisting on facing God in the middle of another crazy Manhattan day and without the accoutrements that we count on at our earlier, better attended and carefully led service.

I love that odd-ball service not the least because it has enabled me to do — at least whenever I teach — what I have never been able to get myself to do alone, to pray a second service. I generally stand facing the front, East, wall but near the windows fronting on Fourth Street (my reminiscence of Daniel praying at a window). Again and again, this 18 minute romp through *minchah* touches me quite differently than other services. When the students are on vacation and I pass the empty Room 509 I think wistfully of that service but do not have the courage yet, there or elsewhere, to say it on my own. It is a spiritual gift which has touched me more deeply than I could ever have imagined.

Afterword

Writing these pages — among some of the most difficult I have ever tried to set down — has affected me quite paradoxically. It has made my thinking more prayerful, as if I were doing that work as a conscious form of devotion. I did not realize that until I came to write these words but it has surely been true. Yet the decision to write intimately about my prayer journey has disturbed my praying. I have always had a problem of shifting from address to reflection, of thinking about something the praying suggested rather than making it my own and saying it to God.

But it has been much worse in the weeks I have been writing this essay. I regularly found myself collecting data for these pages or correcting what I had said or was getting ready to say. So now that I approach the final paragraphs I hope I can return to the greater measure of concentration that I used to have. I know my old urge to do or think rather than to pray will not end with the conclusion of this effort but I hope it will lessen its grip on me.

One final thought and then a story. In all this talk about prayer I miss the actual praying itself. It's a little like the people who write about humor and do so very seriously. Why can't I pray with you and by the doing convey the reality I am discussing? I once had such an experience. Many years ago I was visiting the College in Cincinnati and went to the daily service with an old friend I had run into there. I noted afterward that he seemed quite overcome by the davenning and discreetly inquired about it. In a voice filled with feeling he said, "My God, you were actually praying the service." I know there was nothing special in what I did that day but he apparently was affected by something he had not previously encountered or been ready for. But nothing so explicit has ever happened to me since. Still, would that I could convey the reality of my praying to you by doing it rather than talking about it.

I tried beginning this paper with a prayer I wrote expressing to God what I felt as I approached this task. The first several times I came back to the computer to work on this essay I looked at what I had written, thought it awful, deleted it and wrote a new prayer. And then I realized that I could not find a properly prayerful way of praying my readers into my theme. So I began as you have seen.

But I want to begin my leave-taking by citing a piece of a prayer to which I resonate greatly. Ber. 28b reports that: Our Rabbis taught, on entering [the Bet Hamidrash] what should one say? "May it be Your will, O Lord my God, that no offense should occur because of me, that I not make a mistake in a matter of *halakhah*, that my colleagues rejoice in me, and that I not call the unclean clean or the clean unclean. And may my colleagues not make a mistake in a matter of *halakhah* and may I rejoice in them." When one leaves [the *Bet Hamidrash*] what should one say? "I thank You, O Lord my God, that You have made it my lot to sit with those in the *Bet Hamidrash* and not with those who sit on street corners. I rise early and they rise early, but I rise early for the words of Torah and they rise early for frivolous talk..." That old prayer speaks with an invidiousness that I do not like but its positive message and declaration of love for the student's way of life speak to my heart.

I conclude by recalling an incident through which a colleague taught me a great deal. I was teaching at the Jewish Theological Seminary as part of an inter-denominational course. My colleagues were Seymour Siegel, z"l, Professor of Theology at the Seminary, and Norman Frimer, z"l, the dynamic, learned Orthodox Director of the Brooklyn College Hillel Foundation. One day when Norman was making the major presentation, he kept citing Hebrew passages from the book he held in his hand. At one point in his fervent lecture he inadvertently dropped it. Not lessening his cogent stream of language, he bent, picked up the book, kissed it, and continued. I had not seen anyone kiss a *sefer* since I was a youngster. But surely, I mused, that was as sensible a custom as could be for one who loves the Torah and the books derived from it. So I have since kissed my book when I am done studying it — and even have done so with photocopies. But I have not yet been bold enough to do so at the College or otherwise in public. This is my first foray in that direction. By telling you this tale I mean to kiss this book in gratitude for all those who have participated in it. And were they here in person, I would kiss them on the cheek for all they have done for me.

3) *A Reflection on My Sense of Certainty*

In these remarks I propose to make two oracular statements and, by explaining the first one biographically, lead up to the second. Here is the first one: The book, *Jewish Spiritual Journeys,* marks a decisive moment in the modern Jewish community's turn from agnostic human centeredness to its dawning postmodern acknowledgment that a living relationship with God is the heart of Judaism. I plan, while defending that thesis, to comment on two intriguing passages in the book.

I began teaching for the College in the winter of 1954 as the entire faculty of the Rockville Centre branch of the HUC School of Education. In Sept '57 I became an adjunct of the Rabbinical School Faculty and in '62 a full-time professor. Like all professors, I hoped to save my students from the faults I had found in my education but trying to find a way to speak to their needs rather than just my own put me in a vexatious quandary.

Until relatively recent years most of them wanted to think about Judaism, consciously or unconsciously, in resolutely secular terms. Having done well at good schools they were eager to save Judaism by reinterpreting it in terms of the high humanism they had mastered at the university.   Most of my Faculty colleagues found that attitude quite congenial since they were trying to show how their disciplines could be pursued in the best academic fashion, one which regularly ruled out issues of belief and commitment as irrelevant to the learning at hand. But after my first few years in the rabbinical school, I increasingly specialized in what I called Jewish theology and that created my pedagogic predicament.   My students, except for their dedication to Judaism, were typical products of the American Jewish community and so sought an elevated humanism that could pass as the Jewish religion if it were adorned with a garnish of Hebraic rite and text.   I was convinced that their path and that of our community led to an intellectual and religious dead end. Moreover, as far as I can tell, I wasn't fazed by the fact that American culture as a whole promoted the idea that, if you will excuse the expression, belief in man was now the only sensible kind of religiosity, a people-centered optimism that reached its high point in the "Death of God" movement of the seventies.

To explain my obduracy I must now turn to the first phrase in the book on which I wish to comment. It taught me something about myself that rounded out an important part of my religious self-understanding. When I first read it, I was a little shaken by Larry Hoffman's observation in his forward to *Jewish Spiritual Journeys* that a "tone of knowing finality...often accompanies his [my] insightful pronouncements." I was shocked, even a little hurt, by the truth that people often take me as a dogmatist when I know of no one who spends more hours trying to write clearly and persuasively to explain his or her belief, and fewer still who dare to publish anything because publication invites criticism. But on reflection, I realized Larry was right and I had simply never understood how oddball my modicum of belief can sound in a society where, following Descartes, doubt is king, and parading one's anxieties proves one's sophistication. At least now I have some insight into why I regularly put some people off.

But that revelation led me back to a phrase of self-description I had written in my own autobiographical essay for the book since I would not ask others to do what I would not do myself. Larry thought it utterly incongruous of me to say that, "I was blessed with a simple soul" - - but the more I have thought about it the more I think it accurate. Besides, it also explains a lot of things about me. Some things about life and reality just seem obvious to me and I am regularly surprised that most people don't see them my way. Which, of course, is the reason I sometimes speak, as Larry said, with a tone of knowing finality. That's my religious simplicity asserting itself.

Let me expand on that a bit. I make no claim to be a person of great and overwhelming faith, one whose every step and act is accompanied by an unshakeable sense of the presence of God. And I am not the sort of person who has known such irresistible moments of God's enveloping reality that nothing after could negate their gift of meaning. I am — here, I go again — too simple a soul for that, though I sometimes wish I could have the more grandiose kind of religious experience others know. If you read my essay in *Jewish Spiritual Journeys* you will be able to judge for yourself how quiet and ordinary, yet real and significant, my inner religious life has been. Perhaps I can convey my meaning and advance my argument by a brief reference to an experience I tell about in my essay. It was decisive for my life. I was eighteen, a new senior at the university. Walking across the campus after an advanced seminar in epistemology, I realized that contemporary philosophy was at a dead end, that rationalism couldn't any longer supply the foundation for a commanding ethics or for the robust modern Judaism I vaguely knew we needed. It just made no sense to me not to realize that there are some things people must not do and others that they must do, as difficult as it is to put those imperatives into words. I knew I didn't believe much but I certainly didn't believe as little as most people around me. From then on my mind no longer dominated my soul and I started learning to give faith a certain priority to reason. Moreover, I now insisted that religion have equal time to criticize culture instead of supinely accepting as unchallengeable what the secular intellectuals said about the spirit.

None of that came to me in a flash of insight, or with a tremendous flow of emotion, or an experience of great relief, or, if I recall correctly, anything special at all. It is only in retrospect that I realized that a certain growth or unfolding, perhaps a certain ripening had taken place in me that day. With some nice highs and few significant lows, that is about the quiet way my religious life has gone on ever since, though nothing as momentous as what occurred in that walk across the campus has ever again resulted.

To my surprise and delight, that intuition of mine in 1942, has increasingly been shared by our culture as a whole and by a growing minority in the Jewish community. It powers the current Jewish search for spirituality and has found dramatic expression in the spontaneous, widespread rise of Jewish rites for the healing of the sick. Jewish books on theology are now staples of our publishing and feminist Judaism promises to add a new religious understanding to our community. Even rabbinical students in recent years, tend to pursue their questions about God in a general context of belief rather than in the old fervent agnosticism.

However, it seemed to me that one thing more was needed to bring this religious turn to its full potential: personal examples of how contemporary Jewish spirituality grows and expresses itself. In an age so concerned with the self, so interested in the person behind the facade, religious language without religious autobiography is likely to have limited impact. We need people to break the wall of silence in the Jewish community which quarantines us from hearing about personal belief and we need models of the many ways people can go about building their personal relationship with God despite doubt and trial. A particular burden therefore rests upon the rabbinate. If rabbis are to exercise effective spiritual leadership today they need from time to time to speak of their Jewish spiritual journey. So when Larry spoke to me about the possibility of doing a Festschrift, I countered with a project that would round out one of my life's major themes, restoring God's place in liberal Judaism. I suggested the publication of a series of Jewish spiritual autobiographies. I hope that reading my twenty colleagues' fascinating statements will move you along on your own Jewish spiritual journey.

But that leads me to my second statement that comes with a "tone of knowing finality." God was a prior generation's major theological problem. If *Jewish Spiritual Journeys* among other things succeeds, it will empower us to turn to the critical challenge facing us: knowing God only situates us in the covenant of Noah, all people's relationship with God; but is the Covenant of Sinai, God's particular relationship with the Jews, still binding for us? Do we take it seriously enough to acknowledge that the Jewish tradition and the Jewish community properly make significant claims on us despite our espousal of some measure of autonomy? And are we ready to assert that the intimate relationship between God and the Jews means that the Torah's way lays unimpeachable claims on us and our descendants despite our appreciation of the truth in other religions? *Jewish Spiritual Journeys*, I hope, will not only round out one era in American Jewish religious life but start us into the next one.

Part Two

The Emergence of a Postmodern Judaism

Chapter 5

ℰↄ◯ℛ

Continuity and Creativity in the History of Jewish Religion

An Overview

Neither of the sacred Jewish classics, the Bible or the Talmud, speaks of "Judaism." Hellenistic Jews created this Greek word to describe their uncommon way of serving God (2 Mc. 2:21, 8:1, 14:38; Gal. 1:13-14). All such mediating terms, because they utilize alien categories as the means of self-representation, necessarily distort as much as they explain. Thus, while the Jews of the first century C. E. integrated their ethnicity and their religion, Paul, writing Galatians for gentile readers, must sunder faith from folk in order to communicate.

Contemporary Jewish thinkers radically disagree as to the nature of Judaism and even the advisability of employing the term. Interpretations of Judaism today range from steadfast traditionalism to radical universalism. The traditionalists themselves differ strongly on accommodation to modernity. The right-wing Orthodox resist accommodation, while the Modern Orthodox accept any cultural good not forbidden by God's revelation. Debates over the role of mysticism add further diversity. Other contemporary Jews, have rejected Orthodoxy because they deem it incompatible with the practice of democracy and the findings of the natural and social sciences, especially critical history.

Among nonreligious Jews, some are humanists who assimilate their Jewishness to contemporary culture, especially ethics. Others identify Judaism with Jewish folk culture. Zionism and the state of Israel represent the secularization of Judaism at its fullest.

Among liberal-that is, non-Orthodox-religious Jews, four differing emphases occur. (1) Jews who have an ethnic attachment to Judaism often find that it acquires a core of universal spirituality that, in turn, revitalizes their attachment. (2) Jews seeking a more disciplined Jewish religiosity direct their ethnic life through Jewish law, dynamically interpreted, as a historicaliy evolving structure. (3) Jews concerned with the demands of rationality assert that Judaism uniquely comprehends the idea of ethical monotheism, a universal truth that is reinforced by their sense of ethnicity. (4) Jews who adopt a personalist approach conceptualize Judaism as a relationship, a covenant mutually created by God and the Jewish people and re-created in every generation. This article describes postbiblical Judaism in terms of the evolving expression of the Jewish people's covenant with God, understood in liberal religious terms.

From the Bible to Rabbinic Judaism

We have little hard data by which to trace the progress from biblical to rabbinic Judaism, despite some help from the biblical Book of Daniel. From Ezra and Nehemiah (Hebrew leaders of the mid-fifth century B.C.E.) to the earliest rabbis (the authorities mentioned in the Talmud) in the first half of the first century CE, the sources in Jewish tradition that are considered authoritative provide little reliable historical information. Learned conjectures can fill this gap, but as their validity rests on hermeneutic foundations that often shift, all such speculations are best left to historians.

The rabbis themselves affirmed an unbroken transmission of authoritative tradition, of Torah in the broad sense, from Moses to Joshua to the elders, the prophets, and thence to the immediate predecessors of the rabbis (Avot 1.1). By this they meant that along with the written Torah (the first five books of the Bible, also known as the Pentateuch or Law) Moses also delivered the oral Torah, or oral law, which contained substantive teaching (legal and nonlegal) as well as the proper methods for the further development of the Torah tradition. As inheritors and students of the oral (and written) law, the rabbis knew themselves to be the authoritative developers of Judaism.

Modern critical scholarship universally rejects this view. For one thing, the Bible makes no mention of oral law. Then, too, it is reasonable to think of Torah as undergoing historical development. When, over the centuries, Judaism grew and changed, later generations validated this unconscious process by introducing, retroactively, the doctrine of the oral law.

We may see rabbinic Judaism's mix of continuity and creativity more clearly if we briefly note these same features in their late biblical predecessors. Ezra and Nehemiah believe that God and the Jewish people have an ancient pact, and they seek to be faithful to it by their lives. Though they acknowledge that God rules the whole world, they and their fellow Babylonian Jews manifest a deep loyalty to a geographic center returning from an apparently more prosperous land to resettle Jerusalem and restore God's Temple there. They are ethnic separatists, rejecting offers of help from the Samaritans and requiring Jewish males to give up their gentile wives. They carefully restore the Temple cult and insist on observance of the Sabbath. But their Judaism involves sensibility as well as statute. When Nehemiah discovers people collecting debts in a time of hardship, he denounces such hard-heartedness as incompatible with covenant loyalty, and they desist.

Ezra and Nehemiah also evidence a new religious concern: acting in accordance with "the book of God's Torah" (Neh. 9:3). In a great public ceremony, the book is read to all the people, men, women, and children, and explained to them in detail. By the mid-fifth century B.C.E., then, a written tradition has taken the place formerly occupied by divination, prophecy, and priestly teaching.

Nearly three centuries later, Daniel gives us another glimpse of late biblical Judaism. Daniel, the paradigmatic Jew, lives outside the Land of Israel, among idolaters. He perseveres in the prescribed Jewish patterns of eating, drinking, and praying, despite the threat of severe punishment. A heavy eschatological focus distinguishes this book, as do its bizarre visions and their cryptic interpretations. After calamitous persecutions of the holy people, including wars against them by foreign powers, God intervenes, sending one who defeats their foes and establishes their kingdom forever. A time of cosmic judgment follows that dooms the wicked to eternal reprobation while the righteous live on forever. The biblical prophets' expectations of an ideal king, descended from King David, who would one day establish worldwide justice, compassion, and recognition of God have here been radically extended.

The Judaism of the Rabbis

Rabbinic Judaism appears as a mature development in its earliest datable document, the Mishnah, a compilation of Jewish traditions redacted about 200 C.E. We can flesh out its bare-bone texts by consulting the more extensive classic works of the movement. These are the Talmuds (essentially, discussions related to the Mishnah; that of the Land of Israel, the *Yerushalmi*, redacted about 400 C.E., and that of "Babylon," the *Bavli*, "the Talmud" proper, redacted about 500 C.E.) and the various early books of *midrash*, "the Midrash" (homiletic and other exegeses of the Bible, the earliest compiled from the third into the sixth century C.E.). They proceed on a startling presumption: the Temple, destroyed by the Romans in 70 C.E., will be rebuilt only in "the days of the Messiah." The rabbis refer to the cult mainly as memory, hope and study material, Their Judaism centers about the Torah, particularly the Oral Torah. To the critical eye, the distinctive features of rabbinic Judaism reflect creative development more than reverent continuity.

A structural innovation of the rabbis provides a convenient entry into their Judaism. They operate with parallel, mutually reinforcing modes of instruction, what later generations neatly split into the realms of *halakhah* and *aggadah*, respectively "the way," that is the required pattern of living, and all else, including lore, preachment, speculation and, thus, "theology." Both are Torah, literally (God's own) "instruction." In rabbinic texts, they are thus often found organically intertwined but they carry diverse authority. When dealing with *halakhah*, the rabbis, for all their disagreement and debate, seek coherence and many times decide what alone constitutes authoritative practice. (The rabbis' courts can inflict severe penalties on transgressors.) By contrast, the realm of the *aggadah* seems astonishingly unregulated. The rabbis appear to delight in finding ingenious ways to amaze their colleagues with their imaginative exegeses and dicta. In all their contradiction and contrariety, these teachings too are part of Oral Torah.

The Way of the Rabbis

For the rabbis, the Covenant entailed a way of life faithful to God more than it required holding a specific faith to ground it. All later varieties of Judaism, including, despite radical differences, the modern ones have echoed these spiritual priorities. A description of Judaism, therefore, should begin with some highlights of the rabbinic way. What follows represents the norms found in authoritative rabbinic texts much more than it does the realities of community practice about which we have no direct independent data.

Responsibility of the Individual

The bulk of rabbinic literature concentrates on how the ordinary Jew ought to conduct himself *(sic)* so as to sanctify his life. Feminists have correctly pointed out that the rabbis take men to be the primary focus of God's instruction with women essentially considered as adjuncts to male Jews. Thus, men make all the halakhic decisions about women's duties and though any man might qualify to render such decisions, traditionally no woman can. The rabbis did assign women a comparatively high personal and communal status. Nonetheless, by egalitarian standards, differentiating women's duties from those of men — the standard — imposes on them a loss of dignity and worth as well.

The troubling issue of sexism aside, rabbinic Judaism is remarkably democratic. It calls all Jews to the same attainable virtues: righteousness in deed, piety of soul and education of the mind. It may derogate the wicked and the ignorant but it never denies they might change and attain the highest sanctity. This elite, the rabbinate, remains open to anyone and recognizes no substantial barriers between itself and other Jews.

With the Temple destroyed, rabbinic Judaism made the ordinary Jew a "priest." That is, they transformed many rituals once connected with the cult so that they became a way of sanctifying one's everyday life at home or in the market place. Before eating or after excreting, one was to wash ritually and recite an appropriate blessing. Each morning and the afternoon — the times of the Temple sacrifices — one worshiped in a prescribed liturgical structure. Later, an evening service was added. In the morning, one said one's prayers wearing head and arm phylacteries with their compartments for biblical citations. (The pious wore them all day.) The doorpost of a Jewish home had its own small container with Torah texts written in it. So too a special fringe on the corner of one's garment served as a reminder of one's responsibility to God.

The Jew's table became an altar. What came to it had to be ritually acceptably, *kosher*. The list of foods proscribed by the Torah book was amplified by rabbinic interpretation. Animals had to be slaughtered in a religiously acceptable, humane manner, including an examination of their carcasses for diseases. Rabbinic law extended the biblical prohibition of boiling a kid in its mother's milk and prohibited mixing any meat with any milk products. It also mandated various blessings prior to eating different foods such as bread, fruits, grains, vegetables, and the like. After a meal, a longer, preferably communal grace was to be said.

More blessings accompanied one through the day. Hearing good news or even bad news, the sight of the Mediterranean, or a flowering tree, or an odd looking person, or a meteor, the smell of spices, acquiring something new or passing a place where a miracle had been done, all required brief words of prayer.

The conduct of business also exhibited this intermingling of the commonplace with the transcendent. The Covenant embraced the treatment of one's workers and their responsibilities to their employer, what constituted reasonable inducements to customers and what illegitimate restriction of trade, the extent of a fair profit and one's responsibility in the face of changing prices, one's duty to testify in the rabbinic court and how contracts were to be written. The rabbis spell out in detail their religious equivalent of what others call civil law. And disputes between Jews on any of these matters, were to be taken to the rabbinic court, with its detailed standards for administering justice.

The rabbis made daily study — for its own sake and as a means to observance — a religious responsibility of the highest significance. The minimum requirement might only be some biblical verses and rabbinic passages but the liturgy reinforced this with its numerous texts and regular Torah readings. Besides, knowledge gained one community esteem, a typical example of ethnicity strengthening rabbinic ideals. The rabbis endowed Jewish religiosity with its bookish cast and their argumentative, analytic form of study made Jewish life uncommonly verbal and cerebral as well.

Much that the rabbis valued could not usefully be made law so they surrounded their precepts with highly individualistic teachings about the good person and community. Like the Bible authors, they abominate lying, stealing, sexual immorality, violence and bloodshed. They decry gossip, slander, faithlessness, injustice, hard-heartedness, arrogance and pride. They glorify the industrious, honest, compassionate, charitable, trustworthy, humble, forgiving, pious, God-fearing soul. Believing in the Jewish community's good sense, they urged individuals to acquire a "good name."

They do not underestimate the difficulties involved in striving to be a good Jew — yet they never doubt that, with God's help, one can be more righteous than wicked. They picture human beings perpetually conflicted between their Urge-to-do-evil and their Urge-to-do-good. The former they describe as a relentless, wily, indefatigable foe who can be defeated only momentarily. It seeks to dominate human consciousness and easily infects human sexuality. Realists that they were, they acknowledge that it often leads to good. Its driving energy brings people to marry, build homes, engage in useful commerce and the like. Though one ought never to underestimate its destructiveness or one's own vulnerability, human beings can harness some of its strength for their good and God's work.

One can best fight off or sublimate the Urge-to-do-evil by study, piety, good companions and, above all, observing the Torah. However, nothing guarantees its defeat and self-righteousness practically invites its victory. Death alone terminates the struggle and only at the "end of days" will the Urge-to-do-evil itself be destroyed. Until then, the Jew continually beseeches God's help, confident that, as the Bible teaches and the rabbis continually reiterate, God will aid him in his striving for purity.

With Moses as their model, the rabbis do not expect anyone to remain sinless. Having sinned, one should then do *teshuvah*, "turning" or "repentance." Elaborating a biblical theme, the rabbis specify the stages by which sinners right their relationship with God. One begins by becoming conscious of having sinned and therefore feels remorse. That appropriately should lead to a confession of one's sin before God and thus confrontation with one's guilt. But morbidity leaves no energy for sanctification. Instead, guilt should motivate one to recompense those one has wronged and ask their forgiveness. Having firmly resolved never to repeat the iniquity, one may then beseech God's mercy with confidence. For God so loves this returning of the human will that God's atoning grace responds immediately to every sincere initiative.

One need not be Jewish to do *teshuvah* and the rabbis directed that the Book of Jonah be read on the Day of Atonement to remind Jews that even the wicked Ninevites had once done so. Even for Jews it involves no special rites or sanctified personnel. Rather, each day's dynamic of striving but often failing to fulfill the Torah, involves the individual in practicing *teshuvah*. (On the Day of Atonement, the people of Israel, in a unique sequence of four services, carries through an annual corporate *teshuvah*.)

Family in Rabbinic Judaism

The rabbis do not usually think of individuals as isolates but organically connect them to their families and their people. For them, the Jewish way primarily involves an ethnic group's unique Covenant with God and, consequently, the lives of the individuals who comprise it. The Jew's family replicates in miniature that greater Covenant community.

The rabbis consider marriage a cardinal religious obligation, though they tolerate some exceptions. Through it one carries out the biblical command to have children. Marriages being arranged in this period, the rabbis provide much counsel for this important process. They strongly urge early marriage, to a wife from a good family who has a pleasant personality. They practice monogamy but do not require it (which sages of the middle ages finally did). They subordinate good looks, love, sexual pleasure and even fecundity — in all of which they delight — to their goal of Jewish family well-being, *shalom.* And that comes from a couple's mutual dedication to the Torah.

The rabbis hope a deep love will arise between the spouses but do not say much about how they should develop their relationship over the years. They enjoin sexual fidelity, initially more rigorously for wives, though later becoming more strict with husbands. They expect male dominance in the household but counsel the temperate use of the husband/father's power. They also display a canny sense of the critical, even decisive role the wife/mother plays in family affairs.

Despite this exaltation of marriage, the rabbis included divorce in their sacred way of living. Though they decried the break-up of a family, they did not make divorce administratively impractical and divorced women often remarried.

From Bible times on, Jews experienced infertility as grievous suffering. Without offspring, the Covenant expires. Through them, all prior Jewish devotion hopes to reach completion. Children, particularly sons, therefore come as a great blessing and if they grow up to be good children, Jews respected in the community, their parents have inestimable fulfillment. Should they be wicked, their parents will consider it a major judgment on their own worth. Some rabbis identify suffering because of one's children as the worst of visitations.

Only occasionally do the rabbis discuss the parents' obligation to a child, perhaps because they believed that natural sentiment guided by Jewish folkways would adequately direct them. By contrast, they say much about children's duties to honor their parents. Their amplification of the Fifth Commandment not only reflects their regard for wisdom and experience but testifies to the covenant between the generations which revivifies the Covenant between God and Israel. Jewish personal names add to this intimacy for one is called the child of so-and-so and thus carries one's parent in one's personhood all one's life.

These relationships functioned within the Jewish home, the primary scene of ongoing Jewish observance. Particularly since it might also be one's business place, the Jewish home brought the diverse aspects of Jewish life together in mutually strengthening integrity.

Jewish Community and Jewish People

In rabbinic times most Jews lived away from the Land of Israel — in the Diaspora — and, in time, Babylonian Jewry exercised preeminent religious authority. To carry on their odd faith, Jews scattered across the Parthian and Roman empires would live alongside other Jews. Anti-semitism also brought them together. As always, the social and the sacred interpenetrated.

Each Jewish community's Covenant responsibility surfaced most visibly in liturgy (from which obligatory individual prayer derives). Ten males, the smallest group to stand for all Israel, constitute a prayer quorum. At Monday, Thursday, Sabbath and festival morning worship (and Sabbath afternoons), they read a portion of the Torah scroll, often followed by a selection from the prophetic books. If there were someone learned enough, there might be a sermon.

Anyone with the requisite knowledge may lead the service or read from the scroll. Various religious functionaries would enhance the community's life but a rabbi is a luxury not a requirement. Both a ritual slaughterer (so there can be *kosher* meat) and a teacher for the children would likely have higher priority. Devoted volunteers attend and bury the dead — and the same is true of other such duties.

When the community had a rabbi, he functioned as scholar and judge. He modeled the Jewish duty to study and he answered questions about Jewish law, when necessary convening a rabbinic court. (As part of the Oral Torah, these decisions carry God's authority. Yet they can be appealed by writing to a greater scholar elsewhere who may, by the authority of his knowledge and piety, indicate that the ruling was faulty.) Rabbis in the talmudic period were not employed by the Jewish community but, like other Jews, worked at some ordinary occupation.

Corporate life moved about several institutions. One, the synagogue, may have pre-existed the rabbis but they established it as a surrogate for the Temple. They substituted prayer for sacrifice and laymen for priests. They also made it possible for a synagogue to function anywhere a quorum meets, so a populous settlement might have many of them and a prosperous community would erect an appropriate building to house its activities.

Another institution was the study-house. Those devoted to learning would find a place to study and to meet with other students of Torah. Often this will only be a room in the synagogue. But we have few facts to go on.

The court, the *bet-din*, comprised of three learned people, did more than hear significant cases. It bore responsibility for the community's spiritual well-being and had appropriately great authority. In special situations, its executive power had few limits. In a way, it also had legislative power for it could institute enactments binding on the community. But, again, the data is not unambiguous.

The learned shared power in unspecified, shifting ways, with the community lay-leadership. These Jewish communities often lived in some legal independence and their rulers expected Jewish community leaders to collect taxes, regulate the markets, and generally supervise Jewish internal affairs. All these matters were handled by applying the Torah's teaching to the immediate social and political realities.

Community leaders, carrying out a prime Jewish obligation, collected and disbursed *tzedakah*, literally "justice," effectively, "charity." Every Jew had obligations to every other Jew, particularly those who needed help; many communities so esteemed *tzedakah*, even its recipient gave to others. And gathering and distributing the funds were among the most honored community tasks.

Geography and cultural division produced variation in Jewish practice between the leading centers, that of the Land of Israel (under Roman rule) and that of Babylonian Jewry (under Parthian and later Sasanid rule). No central agency existed to bring uniformity into practice or theory. Instead, a relatively loose pattern of authority emerged. From time to time, certain institutions or individuals arose whose scholarship and piety commanded the respect of many Jews. In time their teachings established precedents for later Jewry.

Despite the open texture to this orthodoxy, the rabbis exhibit a clear-cut sense of the unity and identity of the Jewish people. They know that it alone has God's Torah and thus bears unique witness to God. They detest the idolatry and immorality they see all about them. Hence they consciously seek to distinguish and separate Jews from the sinful nations. But most rabbis happily accepted sincere converts. Jewish isolation made hospitality to strangers a critical value. Wherever he might travel, the Jew could expect to find a welcome in the Jewish community which, despite some different practices, clearly followed the same Torah he did.

Three Rhythms of Jewish Time

A Jew lives in three inter-related dimensions of time, the personal, the annual-historic and the eschatological-anticipatory. The critical passages of each individual life are marked by sacred rite. On a male's eighth day, his birth is heralded by his circumcision. At thirteen he assumes personal responsibility for performing the commandments. Should he complete the study of a classic text, a small celebration follows. A formal betrothal signals a coming marriage. The wedding itself will be as elaborate as one's means and community allow. Some suffer the pain of divorce. Many have the great joy of children and all experience bereavement. Inevitably, one's own death comes and with it one's own funeral and mourners. Prayer and act sanctify many of these moments; all involve community participation.

Jews similarly mark the great moments of each year. Six workdays climax in Sabbath rest, worship, study and feasting. On Friday eve (Jewish days begin at sundown) one's wife lights the Sabbath candles and says a blessing over them. Before one eats one sanctifies the day by a prayer over a cup of wine. So, too, the rabbis directed that the Sabbath end with blessings over wine, spices, a multi-wicked flame and the separation of secular and holy time.

Each year begins with solemn synagogal rites celebrating God's sovereignty, justice and mercy, climaxed ten days later by the Day of Atonement's fast and all-day liturgy, beseeching God's promised forgiveness. The ancient pilgrimage festivals, *Pesah*-Passover, *Shavuot*-Weeks/Pentecost and *Sukot*-Booths marking the agricultural seasons, became rabbinically historicized. Passover celebrates the Exodus, *Shavuot* the giving of the Torah, and *Sukot* God's providential care in the wilderness. Thus, the undeviating natural year became a reminder and renewal of the Jewish people's unique historical experience.

Rabbinic creativity likewise embellished the forms for lesser occasions. Special psalms, prayers and a reading from the Torah scroll greeted each new lunar-solar month. On the fast of the Ninth of Av, commemorating the destruction of the Temple, the rabbis enjoined a dolorous reading of the Book of Lamentations. They memorialized other tragic events with lesser fasts. So too, the salvation of Persian Jewry recounted in the Book of Esther, became the feast of Purim. And even without biblical warrant, the Maccabee's rededication of the Temple (167 C.E.) after its desecration by the Syrian ruler Antiochus IV, was celebrated as *Hannukah* mainly by kindling lights at home cumulatively for eight nights — fittingly, at about the winter solstice.

The number of each Jewish year indicates the time since creation even as its rhythm directs one toward history's promised climax, God's rule on earth. A messianic hopefulness infuses all Jewish observance for the End might begin now; yet the heartbreaking Jewish experience with premature messianism — particularly that of Bar Kochba (in the rebellion against Rome of 133 C.E.) — indicated that the Messiah would come only at "the end of days."

We can surmise something of the lived tone and human quality of the rabbis' Judaism from what their traditions tell us about the way they lived. They can be wildly playful though they are usually highly serious, exuberant in celebration yet careful of minutiae, free in opinion yet obedient to discipline, grief-stricken at sinning yet confident of forgiveness, desirous of pure intention yet content with the done deed, esoterically mystic yet rigorously rationalistic, emotionally demonstrative yet devoted to structure, picayunely practical yet eschatologically oriented, individualistically themselves yet absorbed in community, foolish sinners yet pious martyrs, ordinary people who might be one's neighbors yet saintly in an uncommon intellectual, activist and spiritual sense. And the communities their teaching guided seem much like them, bustling, human and holy at once.

Above all they have a passion for life, this life, despite the finer one to come. They delight in its opportunities to serve God through the routines specified by Torah. Yet should a life be at stake, any Jewish law that impedes saving it *must* be broken — except three: those against idolatry, murder and sexual sin. So too, when the survival of the Jewish people seems at risk, the rabbis accommodate to reality — but not by compromising principle. For they know, above all, that the world was created for the sanctification of life and through holy Jewish living alone can it hope to endure and reach completion.

Beliefs of the Rabbis

It is characteristic of the rabbis that their faith is inseparable from their way of life. Their test for heresy was behavioral, not creedal. Their explicit statements of belief are generally more poetic than precise, more fragmentary than general, and they exhibit little interest in systemic coherence.

While acknowledging the notorious elusiveness of what they call rabbinic theology, some modern scholars have yet found it possible to explicate some of its major themes. The rabbis' theological creativity operates mainly in their reshaping of the multitudinous ideas and images of biblical belief. In this process they continue the millennial Jewish experience of reinterpreting the covenant as times change and as their own intellectuality and religious sensitivity demand.

The primacy of continuity in rabbinic belief helps explain what modern readers often consider the rabbis' surprisingly modest response to the Temple's destruction. Though they were deeply traumatized, the rabbis did not see the loss of the Temple as a disaster requiring major theological reconstruction; rather, they found it a confirmation of the Bible's teaching. God had done what God had promised to do and had done once before (in 587/6 BCE). Sin eventually begets punishment, even to the destruction of God's Temple and the exile of God's people. But the punishment has a covenant purpose, to bring the people back to God's service. In due course, the rabbis believed, God would again restore the holy people and their Temple. Continuing the faith of the Bible as they understood it, the rabbis indomitably transcended profane history.

God

Monotheism anchors the rabbis' faith, just as it anchors the later biblical writings. The rabbis abominate idolatry and passionately oppose the notion that there are "two powers" in heaven. That does not prevent their speaking of God's heavenly retinue, the subordinates by whom God's governance of the universe usually proceeds. Similarly, they exhibit no inhibition about using metaphors to describe God. These may be abstract names, such as "the Place," "the Power," "the Holy," or images drawn from human life, such as references to God's phylacteries, or daily schedule, or emotions.

Another typical rabbinic dialectic moves between the utter greatness and the immediate availability of God. The ineffably glorious Sovereign of all universes attends and responds to a human whisper or fleeting meditation.

Rabbinic theology often pivots about God's justice and mercy. The declaration "There is no Judge and no justice" seems to be the rabbinic equivalent of atheism, but the rabbis give elaborate validations of the reliability of God's justice. They believe that the world could not survive if God were absolutely just: human fallibility and willfulness make such stringency impractical. For people freely to come to righteousness, God must also be merciful and compassionate. But if there were mercy without justice, this same rebellious humankind would never become responsible for its own actions. Undaunted by the paradoxes, the rabbis affirm that the one and only God is both just and merciful, demanding and forgiving, the ultimate idealist and realist in one.

Much of what other people might take to be evil the rabbis steadfastly consider the subtle working-out of God's justice. They do not deny that unmerited suffering occurs. Sometimes they explain this as "chastisements of love," torment given to the pious in this world so that rewards will await them in the afterlife. Some times they merely ascribe it to God's inexplicable will, God's "harsh decree." (Parallel reasons are offered by the rabbis for the gift of God's unmerited blessing-that is, it comes because of the "merit of the patriarchs," or simply because God loves or chooses to bless the recipient.) Less frequently, the rabbis will picture God, as it were, as somehow unable to prevent a tragedy or as lamenting its occurrence. With reason or without, they hold God to be the ultimate source of evil as well as good and so call for the recitation of a blessing upon hearing evil tidings. They devoutly trust God, whom they know they cannot hope to understand despite all their study and piety.

Perhaps they evince such confidence because they have a strong, full belief in life after death. Several stages of the afterlife may be identified in rabbinic traditions. At death, the soul is taken from the body for preliminary judgment and purification and stays with God until the general bodily resurrection that will take place at the "end of days." Then the soul, rejoined to its purified body, receives judgment. The wicked are utterly destroyed, and the less culpable receive a limited term of expiatory punishment. Finally, the individual enters the "future to come," the blissful but indescribable reward God has promised the righteous.

Humankind and Human Destiny

The rabbis' conception of humankind stands behind their Jewish self-understanding. Human beings literally constitute a family since God created them from one pair of progenitors. And God made and maintains a covenant with all the descendants of Noah. Under it, God promised that there would be no more annihilatory floods and commanded all people to obey seven laws: six negative-not to blaspheme God, or worship idols, or steal, or murder, or commit sexual offenses, or eat the limb of a living animal-and one positive-to set up courts of justice.

Human nature being so torn between its evil and good urges, people regularly transgress these simple laws. So God brought a special nation into being, the Jews, to serve God devotedly by accepting a covenant of 613 commandments. In the rabbinic sociology of religion, people are either Jews, faithful servants of the only God, or part of "the nations," idolaters and therefore sinners. The Jews' experience of anti-Semitism reinforced this view and strengthened the Jewish commitment to separatism for God's sake.

The customary strife between the nations and the people of Israel will greatly intensify as the "end of days" nears. But God will send the Messiah, a human, Davidic king descended from King David, to lead God's people to victory. Once again, the rabbinic accounts grow hazy and irreconcilable. Some see the nations converting to Judaism; others see them accepting Jewish leadership. There is little elaboration of the biblical poems that prophesy a time of universal justice, peace, contentment, and lack of fear. However, the rabbis anticipate that at the final judgment the nations will be found guilty of wickedness and denied entry to the "future to come." Some rabbis mitigate this attitude by teaching that individuals who are "pious among the nations of the world have a share in the world to come."

Of course, any sinner might become righteous by repenting. The rabbis tell-occasionally with considerable envy — of a number of gentiles and Jews who by a heartfelt act of *teshuvah* immediately gained the life of the world to come.

Most of these matters became part of rabbinic law concerning non-Jews. Hence this doctrine, in general, may be said to be authoritative rabbinic teaching.

Rabbinic Theory of Torah

Radical theological creativity appears starkly in the rabbis' doctrine of the oral law. Unlike some of their other distinctive ideas, such as repentance, the Messiah, and resurrection, the notion of the oral law has no explicit biblical foundation. Since it undergirds all of rabbinic Judaism, it may be said to be the rabbis' most characteristic doctrine. To reiterate what has been said above, the rabbis taught that God gave Moses not only the first five books of the Bible (and, by implication, the rest of it) but also unrecorded verbal instructions, including specific duties and the methods for educing further oral law.

The rabbis also delimit the content of the written law in its broader sense of holy scripture, that is, the Hebrew scriptures. They apparently inherited fixed versions of the five books of the Torah and of the Prophets (including Joshua, Judges, Samuel, and Kings) and they determined what would be included in the Writings, admitting Ecclesiastes, for example, but rejecting Ben Sira. With these three divisions (Torah, Prophets, Writings; abbreviated in Hebrew as *Tanakh*) they closed the canon, for they believed that revelation ended with Haggai, Zechariah, and Malachi and that the books of the Writings had preceded these prophetical books. Though the rabbis occasionally hear a "heavenly echo" concerning matters under discussion, they may disregard it. Effectively, therefore, postbiblical Judaism derives from the rabbis' delimitation of the written law and their continuing explication of the oral law.

God excepted, no aspect of Jewish belief arouses the rabbis' awe as does Torah. They describe it as existing before creation, as God's guide to creation, and as God's most treasured possession, one so precious the angels tried to keep it from being taken to earth. The people of Israel, by virtue of having been given and having accepted the Torah, have become infinitely precious to God and central to human history. The rabbis acknowledge that wisdom may be found among the nations, but for them Torah contains God's fullest truth for humankind, making it the arbiter of all wisdom.

The rabbis do not detail the correct means or institutional structure for amplifying the oral law. Rather, the living practice of the master (rabbi means "my master") sets the model for his disciples. From time to time various institutions have emerged that temporarily exercised some general authority, but none lasted or created a form that later generations utilized. We have no way of gauging the extent to which Jews accepted the rabbis' leadership even in their own time. It seems paradoxical to seek control and integrity with such lack of structure and tolerance of diversity, but the arrangement has persisted to the present day.

With God's teaching available in verbal form, learning became a major Jewish religious activity. On a simple level, study motivated Jewish duty and specified its content. On a more advanced level, pondering God's instructions-even those of only theoretical relevance, like the rules for the Temple service-enabled one to have intellectual communion, as it were, with God. Gifted men sought to become rabbis, perhaps even to have their teachings cited by others, but always to set a living example for other Jews. Often reports of a master's deeds themselves became part of the oral law.

This heavy intellectual emphasis should not be divorced from its religious context. The intellectually keenest rabbis are also depicted as deeply pious, passionate in prayer, caring and virtuous in their dealings with people, intimately involved in the ordinary activities of life. Many also were mystics, though we have only hints about their esoteric spirituality.

The rabbinic doctrine of Torah brought fresh dynamism to Judaism. By authorizing new and open forms of authority and practice it enabled the Jewish people to keep the covenant vital, no matter what changes were brought by time and dispersion. With Judaism now centered on the individual and communal practice of Torah rather than on the Temple cult in Jerusalem, one could live as a faithful Jew anywhere. And as life created new problems, one only needed to find or become a learned Jew to determine what God wanted now, God's continuing command, and hence feel God's continuing care and concern. This oversimplifies a highly sophisticated process, but also conveys its providential gist.

The Jews as God's Treasured People

The people of Israel uniquely serve the one God of the universe by living by God's teachings. Whatever superiority the people of Israel might claim over the gentiles derives from their faithfulness in living according to the covenant. Having the Torah does not exempt the Jews from God's demand for righteousness; if anything, because they have more commandments to fulfill they bear more responsibility before God. At the same time, God has a special love for the people of the covenant. When the people of Israel sin, God patiently waits for them to repent and helps them do so, sometimes by punishing them to remind them of their responsibilities.

The rabbis directly applied these beliefs to their situation, with the Temple destroyed and Jewish life in the Land of Israel degenerating. They lamented the calamities of their time: their inability to fulfill the commandments regarding God's cult and the material and spiritual distress brought on by dispersion and Roman rule. But their faith did not waver. They held that this people had been justly punished for its sins, though they often pictured God as pained at having had to execute so dire a sentence. To the rabbis, this new exile came because of the covenant and not as its negation; God had fulfilled what the covenant called for in response to egregious iniquity.

The Jews' political and social insignificance in the Roman empire did not negate their faith in their continuing spiritual uniqueness. Rather, the idolatry and immorality of the Romans proved them unworthy of Jewish admiration and God's esteem. To keep their service of God uncontaminated, the Jews set a distance between themselves and the nations. They also lived in the hope that their stubborn loyalty to God would one day be vindicated before all humankind. The eschatological savior described in the Book of Daniel had become an important figure in rabbinic Judaism, the King Messiah. One day — perhaps today — God would send him to restore the holy people to its land, defeat its enemies, reestablish its throne, rebuild its Temple and reconstitute its cult, institute a world order of justice and compassion, and usher in a time when all the promise of creation and the covenant would be fulfilled.

This was a human and historical expectation. As a consequence, some Jews would, from time to time, declare one or another figure of their day to be the anticipated Son of David, in the hope that the Jewish people had so lived up to its covenant responsibilities that God had sent the Messiah. Even if the folk did not merit him, it was understood that God would, in God's own time, send redemption. In either case, the rabbis could only fantasize as to what God would then do to transform and perfect creation. They imagined nature pacified and responsive, the nations admiring of the Torah or even converted to Judaism. Diverse as these conceptions were, all the rabbis agreed that this glorious time will be succeeded by the resurrection of the dead, the final judgment, and the climactic but indescribable "future to come."

The rabbis taught the people of Israel to remain confident of God's rule and favor and to await in history and beyond it God's sure deliverance and blessing — a faith that carried them through history until modern times.

From Talmudic to Modern Times

After the editing of the Talmud, countless variations of the rabbis' way appeared as Jews lived in diverse countries, cultures, social orders and historical circumstances. Mostly they added observances, some of which became universal practice. Among the most famous of these are the ninth day of the festival of Booths, *Simhat Torah*, the Joy of Torah holiday, or the much later practice of memorializing a close relative's day of death, the *yohrtsayt*. A selective factor also operated, as in the abandonment of the triennial cycle of liturgically reading the Torah scroll in favor of an annual lectionary. Jewish ethnicity greatly extended the range of this cultural creativity.

Two major, continuing cultural streams emerged. The Sefardic tradition roughly embraced the Jews of the Mediterranean Sea basin and those in Arab countries. The Ashkenazic tradition encompassed the rest of European Jewry and became dominant in the Americas. Sefardic rabbis gave particularly significant leadership to world Jewry from the eleventh through the sixteenth centuries. During this period, the Ashkenazim created a halakhic scholarship which would later bring them to the effective leadership of Jewish life.

Each cultural style itself encompasses diverse national and local ways of living Judaism which changed over the centuries. Sefardic spokesmen have, however, often taken pride in their community's urbanity, its respect for form and decorum, its devotion to liturgy and esteem of clear intellectuality. Similarly, Ashkenazic leaders have proudly noted their group's passionate energy, its fierce individuality, its dedication to study and love of talmudic erudition.

Developing the Rabbinic Way

We have little data about the actual practice of Jews for much of this period and the many rabbinic statements testifying to its multi-faceted development do not admit of summary. But the quasi-institutional means which evolved to control this process so evidences the spirit of Judaism that it deserves description. In their far-flung Diaspora, Jews recognized no institution or group as universally authoritative. Yet despite the slowness or lack of communication and their immense local variegation, the Jews remained and recognized each other as one Covenant people.

Persecution intensified this inner sense of identity. With the rise of Islam early in the seventh century, Jews became a tolerated but socially degraded people. Among Christians, the early centuries of occasional anti-semitic outbreaks gave way after the First Crusade (1096 C.E.) to nearly seven centuries of harassment, including economic limitation, forced conversions, pogroms and riots, communal expulsions, culminating about 1500 C.E. in the creation of the ghetto, the walled-in Jewish quarter. This pariah status strongly affected Jewish practice and attitudes, including an elemental spiritual resistance founded on the certainty of possessing God's revelation and favor. The immediate contrast between their way of life and that of their oppressors empowered Jews to live and die steadfast in their faith.

Jewish communities vested authority in those whose learning and piety evoked it. Early on, the leaders, the Gaonim, of the Babylonian institutions, the *yeshivot*, which produced the Talmud, began responding to questions addressed to them by distant Jews. This pattern of questions and answers, *she'elot uteshuvot*, established itself as a way to get and give authoritative guidance. To this day, responsa remain the preeminent device for Jewish legal development. The power of a *teshuvah* derives entirely from the prestige and scholarship of the issuer. Many merely became additions to the body of Jewish "case law." Others became widely authoritative, like one of Rav Amram (Gaon of Sura 856-74 C.E.). His lengthy answer, from Babylonia, to a Spanish question about liturgical practice became the prototype for the many other later Jewish prayer books.

The Gaonim and other sages sometimes wrote commentaries to portions of the Talmud or composed treatises on an aspect of the law. Eventually, the growing accretion of law led some teachers to compile codes. None lacked critical commentaries, some of which now appear published alongside the code text. One, the *Shulhan 'Arukh* of Joseph Karo (1488-1575 C.E.), a Sefardic master, published in 1565 C. E., became generally accepted among Ashkenazi Jews as well after Moses Isserles (ca. 1525-1572) wrote glosses to it reflecting Ashkenazi practice. Though scholars continue to rework various of its sections, it has not found a successor.

Only one serious challenge to rabbinic Judaism emerged in this period. The Karaite, that is, biblicist, movement rejected the authority of the Oral Torah and created a pattern of practice based on the Bible. Beginning in the eighth century (C.E.) in the Middle East, it reached the peak of its appeal and literary productivity in the eleventh and twelfth centuries. Not long after its inception, rabbinic authorities declared Karaism heretical and, for example, prohibited intermarriage with Karaites. Some few thousand Karaites still exist, largely in the State of Israel.

In many other fields as well as law, the range of Jewish study continually expanded. Biblical exegesis, homilies, poetry, mystical accounts, chronicles, polemics, explorations of piety, handbooks for good conduct, philosophy — every period produced its books and the students to ponder them. The invention of printing added further impetus to Jewish learning.

Accounting for Judaism's continuing integrity during these difficult centuries has proved problematic. Some have attributed it to an indomitable Jewish will to live, while others emphasize God's corresponding Covenant faithfulness.

New Ideas and their Effect on Practice

Four particularly significant, if not always distinguishable, intellectual currents moved through much of the Jewish middle ages: pietism, mysticism, philosophy and polemic. It will help to consider pietism, the most popular, first, though mysticism, an elitist enterprise, predates it.

Medieval Pietism

The Talmud and *midrash* books devote much attention to the virtues a Jew should manifest but always do so in passing. About the eleventh century, a highly appealing, specifically pietistic literature, *musar*, began to appear. Well into modern times, large numbers of Jews read and sought to live by the high spiritual standards its authors advocated.

The title of the early, exemplary *musar* book, *Duties of the Heart*, written by Bahya ibn Pakuda in the late eleventh century, epitomizes the movement's aims. While the Talmud focused on the good Jew's acts, Bahya stressed the inner life which ought to be its basis. He and other pietists call attention to the intimacy between individuals and God, stressing the humility of the one and the greatness of the other. This consciousness should strongly motivate one to cultivate personal holiness, particularly by loving behavior to others — an emphasis so pronounced that these are often called "ethical" books.

Two concerns of *musar* teachers gradually became common to most medieval Judaism. First, they strongly contrast the purity of the soul with the grossness of the body. This duality, attested in the Bible and manifest in the Talmud, became central and intense in *musar* piety. With corporeality the soul's antagonist, the pietists commend a measure of asceticism and social withdrawal. Yet they do not go so far as to become full-fledged dualists for they know that the good God created the body and ordained social life.

Second, the pietists commend high anxiety about sinning and advise being fearful of incurring guilt. How can anyone intensely aware of God's greatness not find defying God utterly reprehensible? One of the most common *musar* strategies for avoiding or surmounting temptation is to remember the punishment awaiting the wicked in the next world. The musarists therefore urge heartfelt remorse and repentance for every sin, even suggesting compensatory atonements one might undertake. No small measure of the conflict between the values of modern life and that of pre-modern Judaism arose from their conflict over these matters.

The Maturation of Jewish Mysticism

Whereas pietism reached out to ordinary Jews; mysticism, *kabbalah*, limited itself to select individuals initiated into an esoteric doctrine by masters who often concealed as much as they revealed.

The Jewish mystic writings exhibit phenomena known worldwide: stringent disciplines, bizarre language and exalted spiritual expression, techniques for gaining mystic experience, visions of the heavenly realm, physical images of God coupled with assertions of God's utter ineffability, cosmogony, theosophy, longing for religious consummation and ways of hastening it — all this and more appears refracted in perplexing and fascinating fashion through sensitive temperaments affected by highly diverse situations.

The main tradition of Jewish mysticism is known as Kabbalah. Developed in response to God's revelation of a holy way of life, it has a highly cognitive content that is concerned with cosmogony and theosophy. Its most significant document, the *Zohar,* the Book of Splendor (a late thirteenth century Spanish creation), claims to be a commentary on the Torah. In it, too, a growing theosophy matured into a mysterious doctrine of God's dual-single nature. Ultimately, God is *En Sof,* without limit, hence the one about whom nothing at all can be said. Yet God is also intimately known, contemplated and related to as ten interacting loci of divine energy, the *Sefirot,* literally, spheres or numbers. The mystics speak of the *sefirot* with an almost limitless freedom of metaphor, including sexual anthropomorphism. Feminine metaphors for God, rare in the Bible and occasional in the Talmud, now become fully present in explications of God's nature.

The Jewish mystics, for all the immediacy of their relationship with God, know that Torah remains primary to Judaism. They therefore eschew antinomianism for meticulous observance. By ascribing supernal significance to commandments and customs reason cannot explain, they easily provide absolute justification for them.

Two late mystic developments have had continuing repercussions. The cosmogonic explanation of evil by the Sefardic adept Isaac Luria (1534-1572) explains that creation began with an act of God's self-contraction. When God projected generative light into prepared vessels of materiality they proved too fragile and shattered. Creation thus consists of unsanctified shards or husks, in which only sparks of God's creative, transformative light dwell, thus explaining the prevalence of evil. The Torah comes to teach us that by observing God's commandments we can gather the heavenly sparks and mend the broken vessels, our world. God appears passive in this process and human piety brings the Messiah, a striking anticipation of modern liberalism.

A century or so later, in southern Poland and the Ukraine, the Hasidic movement transformed kabbalistic tradition through a radical appropriation of God's accessibility (prompting charges the Hasidim were "pantheists"). The good God's nearness now implied living in joy and enthusiasm. For such cleaving, one need not be a spiritual virtuoso but only give God one's heart. Though this encouraged new, often strange practices — laxity said its enemies — it also led to fervent observance.

Hasidism became a mass movement which carried a dialectical tension. The humblest person could live the mystical life. The Hasidic leaders encouraged this egalitarianism by making much of their teaching exoteric in the form of tale, story and popular preaching, as well as promoting a close community life around them. They also created the unique Jewish leader, the *Tsaddik* or "*rebbe*" (a Yiddish form of "*rabbi*"). He represents Hasidism's esoteric principle, privately practicing an exalted mysticism and serving as the intermediary between his followers and Heaven. Their followers report the *Tsaddikim* to have worked wonders and thus beseech their intercession on every personal problem. Since each community thought no *Tsaddik* could be as great as their own, some Hasidic communities withdrew even from other Hasidim.

Later Hasidism became institutionalized around dynasties and antagonistic to modernity. The groups which managed to survive the Holocaust have had a resurgence in the State of Israel and the United States as Jews who have become disillusioned with secular culture and have sought out their own esoteric communities.

The Encounter with Philosophy

The Talmud knows nothing of Philo of Alexandria or any other Hellenistic Jewish philosopher. Possessing God's revelation, associating philosophy with idolatry, the rabbis spurned it. That hardly seemed possible when, in the ninth century (C.E.), Jews encountered Moslem philosophy claiming to adumbrate the purest possible monotheism. For the next seven centuries, that is, as long as cultural involvement persisted, a tiny intellectual aristocracy created Jewish philosophy. They had little impact on Jewish life though some of their ideas, e. g., Maimonides' excoriation of anthropomorphism, became widely influential.

The early thinkers, from Saadiah Gaon (882-942) on, demonstrated the creation of the world and from it deduced God's unity and sovereign power. They then sought to clarify such questions as miracles, providence, evil and why their faith had the true revelation. Rationality made the logically inexplicable commands of the Torah a problem, evoking considerable philosophic ingenuity.

Most of this thought operated with what were thought to be Aristotelian categories. The occasional neo-Platonic voice found little philosophic resonance though the mystics found emanation a concept congenial to their notion of levels of being. Sometimes, as in the case of Judah Halevy (c.1075-1141), a thinker became self-critical of philosophy and subordinated reason to revelation rather than making it an equal or senior partner.

Modern thought rejects the medieval concept of causality and so the philosophy based on it remains of living interest only to academic specialists. However, the contemporary clash between reason and faith seems pre-figured in the writings of Moses Maimonides (1135-1204), the preeminent Jewish philosopher. As author of the first great code of Jewish law, the *Mishneh Torah,* literally "the Second Torah," (1180), he had incomparable Jewish stature. He faced an intellectual crisis: newly discovered writings of Aristotle showed he repudiated creation and affirmed the eternity of matter. Maimonides would not deny the demands reason now made upon him and his masterful effort to harmonize Judaism with a new view of reality became the model for all later Jewish thinkers.

Post-Maimonidean Jewish philosophy displayed both more radical submission to the demands of reason and staunch validations of religious faith. But when the Jews were expelled from Spain and Portugal and left their cultural context behind them, this fruitful intellectual enterprise came to an end.

A more popular form of intellectuality occurs in the polemics against Christianity which circulated from the twelfth century on. The Talmud has remnants of earlier ones but not until major Jewish centers suffered under Christian religious oppression did books attacking Christianity appear. (Islam evoked few comparable works. Hierarchy rather than harassment, one often pragmatically enforced, characterized the relatively quiescent relations between Moslems and Jews after the early centuries of Moslem conquest.)

Jewish teachers had little internal need for polemics. The Covenant of Sinai denies only idolatry. Besides, the claim that Jesus of Nazareth was the Messiah seemed self-refuting: the world remained radically unredeemed. But as the church increasingly attacked Jewish belief, its claims demanded refutation and its doctrines invalidation.

Jewish polemics demonstrated the Christian misinterpretation of biblical texts by citing the Hebrew or the traditional Jewish understanding of them. When the church won some Jewish converts, the arguments also included talmudic and midrashic passages alleged to prove Jesus' messiahship. More sophisticatedly, the Jewish writers attacked the credibility of conflicting gospel accounts or their ignorance of talmudic law (which they assumed operative in Jesus's time). The authors also caustically exposed the irrationality of Christian doctrines like the virgin birth, the incarnation, and the eucharist. By contrast, they contended, Judaism was a religion a rational man could accept. It was a theme that Jews would continue to find persuasive in modern times.

Modernity: Opportunity and Peril

Emancipation, the fitful process by which the segregation and oppression of European Jewry ended, began in earnest with the French Revolution. Gradually, as nationality was severed from Christian faith, Jews and other "unbelievers" received equal political rights and social opportunity. As a result, most modernized Jews, despite their religious heritage, have avidly supported keeping government and social intercourse religion-free. With little separation of politics from religion, most Moslem nations were among the last states to grant their Jews complete equality.

After some 1500 years of degradation climaxed by centuries of grinding oppression, most European Jews enthusiastically welcomed equality. To those raised in the ghetto or *shtetl* (its unwalled East-European counterpart) every new freedom, no matter how hedged by qualification or anti-semitism (itself now secularized), came as a near-messianic fulfillment. Hope became the dominant tone of Jewish existence.

But the price of equality was conformity. The accepted conventions of European society did not allow for much cultural diversity — and for all that the expected forms were secular, they often reflected their Christian origins.

The consequences for rabbinic Judaism were devastating. As Emancipation proceeded, modernized Jews abandoned its disciplines and major doctrines, producing two radical responses to modernity: one Jewish group rejected modernization, the other, Judaism. Most Jews found these reactions too extreme, thereby indicating the middle way they proposed to take.

A small minority, rather than surrender anything of what they knew God had asked of them, spurned modernization. Thus, many pious East European Jews long refused to immigrate to America, a country where faithlessness was the Jewish norm. Consequently, staunchly Orthodox institutions arose in the United States only after those of the Reform and Conservative movements, an anomaly in Jewish history.

Most Jews rejected this strategy of separatism for pragmatic and intuitive reasons. Practically, Emancipation offered Jews a human dignity they had known only sporadically for two thousand years. Hence their embrace of modernity can be understood as an existentially transformed act of keeping Covenant. It arose from the intuition that western civilization, as evidenced by this act of liberation, contained a considerable measure of the universal truth of Judaism.

Some Jews carried this appreciation to the point of urging Jews to assimilate, allowing their parochial faith to die for the sake of participating in humankind's emerging universal culture. Again, most Jews demurred. Given their passion for modernity, their insistence on remaining Jewish has been difficult to explain, especially since no concretization or philosophy of modern Jewish living has ever become widely accepted. Anti-semitism has kept some Jews Jewish — yet its continuing virulence seems more a reason to defect than to stay. Moreover, even in the absence of overt Jew-hate, many Jews have refused to assimilate. Modernist believers see this as an act of Covenant persistence: Jews remain personally faithful to their ancient pact even if uncertain how now to live it, while God, in some inexplicable but accustomed way, does not let them go.

Post-Emancipation Jewry has chosen to be both modern and Jewish, thus fixing its continuing agenda: first, establishing a less separatistic, more adaptive yet authentically Jewish way of living and, second, validating its authenticity in Jewish and modern terms.

Sundering the Unity of the Way

Modernity made religion a private affair and defined religious groups in terms of Christianity, that is as communities united by common faith and ritual practice. Nationality was dissociated from religion and subordinated to the nation-state, an arrangement which can still disturb multi-national countries. On both counts, Judaism could not maintain itself as a religio-ethnic entity (the hybrid designation modernity has forced upon students of Judaism). As a result, an unprecedented dichotomy came into Jewish life: one group of Jewish life-styles became more "religious," one more secular than pre-Emancipation Jewish life had been.

The Religious Ways of Liberal Jews

Faced with the unacceptable options of staying Jewish but in a ghetto manner, or converting to Christianity to be modern, some early nineteenth century German Jewish laymen began experimenting with a Judaism adapted to European modes of religiosity. In that spirit, they reformed synagogue worship. Essentially, they adorned it with a new esthetic: eliminating liturgic repetitions and poetic embellishments, introducing solemn group decorum, vernacular prayers, sermons and contemporary musical styles (including the use of a pipe organ and female as well as male singers). They also abolished the separation of the sexes at services, allowing families to sit together in worship.

These Jews began Reform Judaism. Their social adaptation pioneered the several ways subsequent non-Orthodox Jewish movements would take. The early Reformers justified their Judaism with a culturally derived notion: eternal essences take transient forms. The essence of Judaism is an ethics based on one God. Its ritual and customs serve to transmit and strengthen this ethical monotheism. When times change and old forms no longer function well, they should be altered or abandoned and new forms created.

Most modernized Jews have accepted moral duty as the core of Jewish obligation. Many have believed that the Jewish people had a mission to teach humankind the religious primacy of universal ethics. In any case, modern Jews often reduce Torah to ethics and though allowing much else in rabbinic Judaism to atrophy, devote themselves to morally transforming society. This universalized sense of Covenant responsibility accounts for the astonishing record of modern Jewish contributions to the improvement of human welfare.

In the latter part of the nineteenth century, a new movement emerged, Conservative Judaism. East-European immigrants to America found that neither the adaptive tone nor the essentially ethical content of Reform Judaism satisfied their sense of Jewish modernity. While seeking to be modern, they also wanted to preserve a considerable measure of particular Jewish practice. Devotion to the Jewish people as the dynamic creator of Jewish law now became their counterpoise to ethics. Other, much smaller movements have arisen over the decades, positioning themselves essentially in relation to these central communal groups. The most significant of these is Reconstructionism, a movement which derives from the theory of Mordecai Kaplan (1881-1983) that the Jewish community, acting in democratic fashion, ought to be authoritative with regard to Jewish practice.

As the twentieth century concluded, the denominational lines had become blurred. At the same time, most Americanized Jews, regardless of affiliation, tended to follow one of several patterns of liberal Jewish living. These varied in their loyalty to classic observance and spirituality but showed considerable similarity in the cultural activities they integrated into their Judaism. The most obvious of these cultural/secular involvements are higher education, civic affairs and the arts, music and literature. But the interplay between Judaism and modernity can best be illustrated by the current Jewish devotion to inter-personal relationships. Jews today express the rabbinic commitment to family and community by their disproportionate involvement in the helping professions and their intense concern for family relationships and personal mental health. In these areas they demonstrate a dedication lacking in their observance of the dietary laws or the sexual relations between spouses. They seem to believe that sanctifying life, their Covenant goal, now requires giving these general human activities priority in Jewish duty.

Despite this heavy cultural borrowing, they manifest a significant measure of particular Jewish action. Even at the humanist end of the religious spectrum, ethics and other universal concerns are reinforced by an attachment to the Jewish folk. Such Jews invest energy and self in

Jewish charity, ethnic self-defense, support of the State of Israel and occasional ritual acts, most notably those associated with life-cycle events but also observances like High Holy Day services or a Passover home *seder*. In this group one sees clearly a problem that continues to bedevil all liberal Judaism: the freedom not to be Orthodox is often taken as a license to do and care little about Judaism altogether.

At the other end of the liberal religious spectrum stands a small minority whose lives are substantially guided by Jewish tradition, read now with a modern ethical and cultural sensibility. They exhibit the rabbinic devotion to self, family, people and God, seeking to live by rabbinic law wherever they can. This group constitutes the spiritual heart of non-orthodox Judaism and its Jewish fate depends upon their leadership in combining modernity and tradition.

The outstanding achievements of liberal Judaism derive from its pursuit of a mediating spirituality. It has radically enlarged the horizon of Jewish duty by its dedication to ethics and democracy. It has revolutionized the study of Judaism by its insistence upon the adoption of modern, academic methods. Above all, it has convinced most of the Jewish community that modernity and Judaism can successfully be integrated. What many in a prior generation passionately feared and fought, most Jews now consider of great benefit to Judaism.

Nothing so well illustrates the continuing promise and problem of liberalizing Judaism as its response to feminism. Early in the nineteenth century, the German Reformers recognized the ethical need to break with the Jewish laws and customs that discriminated against women. But it took more than a century for Reform congregations to have women officers and until 1972 for the first woman to be ordained a rabbi (women cantors then followed quickly). Since then the Reconstructionist and Conservative movements have accepted both innovations.

Much of the community has welcomed this development but that gives no good indication how far it will tolerate alteration of the old patterns, e.g. in removing the sexism of the prayer book or genuinely sharing power. If liberal Jewish daring in this matter eventually becomes part of the accepted Covenant way, then its experimentation will again have taught Jews a new way of sanctifying Jewish existence. But, as Orthodox critics point out, in breaking with the classic understanding of the Torah, the liberals may as likely be denaturing Judaism as winning its future.

The Ways of Orthodox Jews

As a self-conscious movement, Jewish Orthodoxy arose in response to liberal Judaism with the purpose of correctly delineating Jewish authenticity. Judaism knows only one standard of faithfulness to God, loyalty to God's Torah, especially the Oral Torah in its continuing development by contemporary sages. Hence the lives of believing Orthodox Jews — as against those only nominally Orthodox — display continuity more than they do religious change. Variations in observance among Orthodox Jews derive from local custom, from the differences between Ashkenazim and Sefardim, Hasidim and other Orthodox Jews, and from the variety of opinion passed down by various sages.

God's Torah having absolute primacy, modernity can come into Judaism only as the Torah allows. Determining the limits of that openness creates the major forms of Orthodoxy. It stands united, however, in defense of the Torah against the faithlessness of most other Jews. Even permissible innovations can be resisted lest they give credence to other Jews' radical departures from tradition.

Orthodox attitudes toward the acceptance of modernity range from antagonistic to embracing. The Hasidic sects visibly project their hostility to modernity and their distance from the gentile world (and other Jews) by their distinctive dress, hair, posture and language styles. Other Orthodox groups merely seek to recapitulate the relative cultural isolation of East European Jewry, a goal more easily accomplished in the State of Israel than elsewhere. The continued use of Yiddish, the Judeo-German vernacular of East European Jewry, as the Jewish language of choice, characterizes this entire wing of Orthodoxy. Its antagonism to modernity does not prevent the pious from utilizing technological advances that enhance observing the Torah or from having contacts with gentiles when necessary, as in commerce. A more significant effect of modernity on them appears in their sometimes large number of marginal affiliates, Jews who live in more modern fashion and maintain their group ties by keeping some of its special customs, by visits and by financial support.

Contrariwise, the "Modern" Orthodox contend that the law allows and many sages exemplify the virtue of embracing any cultural good which enhances human existence as the Torah delineates it. Thus, the only distinguishing visual sign that Modern Orthodox males present may be the wearing of a small, often knitted skull-cap. They have been most innovative in creating new instruments for Jewish education: the Jewish university and day school. These feature the sciences and sports, both once considered unJewish. So, too, they generally speak the vernacular, not Yiddish. But their disciplined loyalty to the Torah appears in such matters as prayer, food, Sabbath and festival observances and the like.

Orthodoxy enjoyed a significant resurgence as the twentieth century moved toward an end. Some Jews, like others, lost their prior confidence in western civilization and withdrew from it somewhat by adopting a more distinctive practice of Judaism. A minority joined the separatistic Jewish sects. Most Orthodox Jews, however, rejected self-ghettoization. They did want living a dedicated Jewish life as part of a community of the observant to differentiate them from an ofttimes pagan society. But they also wanted to live the life of Torah with a modern overlay their Orthodox great-grandparents would probably have opposed. Regardless, the movement to greater Jewish authenticity has debilitated Modern Orthodoxy's innovative zeal though the large number of nominally Orthodox testifies to the continuing inroads of modernity. They tend to be only sporadically observant and believing. Worse, they often commit the heresy of considering their private preferences in Jewish law a genuine Judaism.

Orthodoxy has notable accomplishments to its credit. Despite dire predictions of its death in modernity, it has created a cadre of Jews whose personal piety and communal life demonstrate the continuing religious power of rabbinic Judaism. It has kept alive and advanced East European Jewry's exalted standards of the study of Jewish law. Particularly in the field of bio-ethics but in other areas as well, it has shown the continuing vitality of the Oral Torah. Above all, Orthodoxy has fought for the primacy of the Jewish spirit while exploring acceptable way of learning from the surrounding culture. In showing how Jewish discipline and sensibility properly respond to modernity, it has added a notable chapter to the millennial record of Covenant existence.

Again, feminism best clarifies the continuing promise and problem of Orthodox Judaism. In refusing to grant women substantial legal equality, contemporary sages have defended the integrity of God's Torah as they received and understand it. Considering how modernity has shattered family life, they do not deem it to possess a wisdom superior to Torah. Rather, every genuine faith demands some sacrifice and Judaism, abandoned by so many and in such world-wide peril, deserves the obedient dedication of all who wish it to remain true to itself and God.

Many Orthodox authorities have long acknowledged that some laws regarding women create suffering, e. g. the woman procedurally barred from receiving her Jewish divorce. Liberal Jews perceive the sages' inability to move in this area a telling indication that the good will of the sages does not effectively remedy the law's inequities. Moreover, with most Orthodox Jews committed to women's general self-fulfillment, feminists cannot believe that Orthodox women will long be content with sex-segregated duties and roles. However, Orthodox Judaism has shown no significant loss from its defense of classic Judaism in this matter.

Culture, as "Torah" of Secular Jews

Living in large urban areas and educated at the university, many Jews believed that modernization meant the death of God and negated differentiating observance. They became thoroughly secularized but generally not to the point of assimilation. Large numbers retained a connection with the Jewish people if only by discovering that many of the humanitarians they enjoyed associating with were also secularized Jews. Two inter-related major patterns of secular Jewish living arose from this process, the one cultural, the other, political.

The early foes of Emancipation argued that the Jews could not modernize because they had no capacity for high culture. Liberal Jews sought to refute them by estheticizing Jewish worship. Secular Jews did the same with literature and the arts, engendering their later uncommon success in these areas. Existentially, secular Jews made high culture their "Torah," bringing to it the intense dedication they had once given their faith, for it now validated their existence.

To keep the Jewish people alive, some European Jewish secularists suggested that Jews participate in universal human culture through their languages, initially Hebrew, but later Yiddish as well. This movement toward Haskalah, Enlightenment, revivified the Hebrew language, long used only for scholarly and religious purposes. The long-range hopes of the Haskalah leaders did not survive the realities of anti-semitism and migration. Few Diaspora Jews maintain their Jewishness by utilizing Hebrew or Yiddish to pursue humanism. Yet modern Jews as good as consider cultural philistinism a denial of one's Jewishness.

Jewish secularity also directed itself to ethical politics, that is, redeeming the world through government. As political action had given Jews rights, correcting ancient wrongs, so other social injustices might be ended — and by a means more effective than prayer or piety. Being politically informed and involved therefore became the modern equivalent of a commandment.

This movement's effects have been felt in general society and the Jewish community. Jewish politicians and Jewish volunteers have been a significant influence in humanizing modern society. Simultaneously, the notion of pluralistic democracy has reshaped Jewish community life. Contemporary Jewish community life operates on a fully voluntary basis and features a broad inclusiveness, diverse busy organizations and a dynamism undaunted by emergency or changing times. Above all, it has raised more money for Jewish charity than any other voluntary philanthropic effort in human history. In the midst of such secularization, the lineaments of the Covenant appear.

Nationalism: Zionism and the State of Israel

The cultural and political drives in Jewish secularization climaxed in Zionism, the movement which reinterpreted Judaism as Jewish nationalism. Organized on a worldwide basis by Theodore Herzl (1860-1904) in 1897, the Zionists began a crusade to liberate Jews on both levels. First, they sought freedom from persecution by acquiring a land where the Jewish masses might find economic opportunity and political security. Second, they wanted to create a genuinely Jewish culture, one more expressive of the Jewish people's spirit than of European-Christian standards.

Liberal and Orthodox Jews both initially opposed Zionism for religious reasons. The former found its secularism Jewishly aberrant and its nationalism a threat to Jewish acceptance in democracies. The latter objected to its notion of a Jewish state independent of the Torah and found its nationalistic activism a usurpation of God's messianic role. Vestiges of these anti-Zionisms still exist but most religious Jews ardently support the State of Israel.

Before the founding of the State of Israel 1948, Zionism generated a new form of Diaspora Jewish living, one built on political activity, immigration and the preparation for it, and participation in Hebrew culture. The barbarity of Nazi Germany and the callousness of the rest of the world toward the Jews in the 1930s and 40s gave Zionism an additional concern: acquiring one place in the world where Jews controlled the immigration.

With the birth and growth of the State of Israel, Jews could return to a way of living they had not known for nearly two millennia, existence as a Jewish community living on the Jewish homeland in Jewish self-determination. The State of Israel is secular — though Orthodox Judaism retains special rights in it — and its ethos is democratic and welfare-oriented. Its extraordinary effort, amidst the most trying political circumstances, to hold itself to ethical standards higher than those pursued by most other nations, has won it the admiration and identification of world Jewry. Nothing in post-Emancipation Jewish life has remotely approached its ability to arouse Jewish devotion and action.

Israeli Jews, the great majority of whom consider themselves non-religious (that is, non-Orthodox), live by the rhythm of the Jewish calendar and draw their ideals from the Bible, the great national saga. Their everyday language is Hebrew and their culture increasingly reflects the concerns of individuals and a society facing the awesome dilemmas of modern existence. In every human dimension, Israeli lives are, even without thinking about it, Jewish. And for those who carry on Orthodox Judaism or the tiny minority who are Reform or Conservative Jews, the reconstituted Jewish society provides an incomparable context for religious Jewish existence.

Outside the State of Israel, Zionism as a way of life has as good as disappeared. Most Diaspora Jews do not carry on a Jewish cultural life in Hebrew or plan to immigrate to the State of Israel. They may be deeply emotionally attached to the State of Israel but it does not provide the essential content of their Jewish lives. Zionism has had an incomparable triumph in the high human and Jewish accomplishment of the State of Israel. Yet its thoroughgoing secularization of the Covenant has apparently rendered it incapable of guiding Diaspora Jewish life.

The Philosophic Grounds of Modern Jewish Life

Judaism makes its claims upon the Jew in the name of God and the Jewish people's corporate experience — but modernity radically individualizes authority. A modern philosophy of Judaism must mediate between autonomy and tradition as well as commend itself as doing justice to each of them. Thus far, theory has lagged far behind life.

Contemporary Orthodoxy does not wait for the mind to establish Jewish duty. It begins with faith and has felt no pressing need for academic expositions of its beliefs. It has therefore largely left to liberal Jews the task of constructing systematic Jewish theologies. Five major, distinctive intellectual statements have gained continuing attention — six, if Zionist ideology can be considered an equivalent system.

Two Rationalist Interpretations

Rationalism had irresistible appeal to nineteenth century Jewish modernizers. It compellingly distinguished between the lastingly valuable essence of Judaism, ethical monotheism, and its transient historical expression, ceremony and ritual. This early liberal criterion of continuity and change first attained sophisticated statement in the work of Hermann Cohen (1842-1918), the famed Marburg neo-Kantian philosopher.

In rigorous academic works, Cohen delineated the religion a rational person could accept. Cohen demonstrated that rationality required a philosophical idea of God to integrate its disparate scientific, ethical and esthetic modes of thinking. But ethics effectively dominated his system. In more popular essays and a posthumous book, he argued that this idea first appeared in human history in the prophets. As the earliest and purest representative of ethical monotheism, Judaism had a mission to humankind: to teach the universal truth of religion of reason. Messianism now no longer could be the miraculous advent of God's regent but became humankind's task of ethically perfecting itself. (This led him to oppose Zionism as a constriction of the Jewish ethical horizon.) All customs that strengthened Jewish ethical sensitivity or kept Jews faithful to their mission ought to be maintained; those which thwarted them ought to be abandoned. In greatly diluted fashion, Cohen's ethical reworking of Judaism became the accepted ideology of modernized Jews.

Leo Baeck (1873-1956), the German thinker who remained closest to Cohen's Judaism of reason, felt the need to supplement it with the experience of mystery, even though that meant sacrificing Cohen's logical rigor. Drawing on ideas like those of Rudolf Otto, Baeck pointed to religious consciousness as the deepest foundation of ethical monotheism. He evocatively described the human sense of being created yet also of being an ethical creator, of being utterly transient yet linked in spirit with that which is eternal.

However, Baeck's rationalism remained sovereign. Fearing the dangers of romanticism, he insisted that religious consciousness might lead to action only as ethics permitted. Thus, while empowering some non-rational observances, he ruled out anything that smacked of superstition and bigotry. He also conducted a vigorous polemic with Christianity and Buddhism, finding both of them deficient in their ethics and monotheism. Any rational, religious person, he concluded, would surely prefer Judaism. He so closely identified Judaism with this universal faith that, alone of all modern Jewish thinkers, he urged Jews to seek converts.

Baeck called for a broad horizon of Jewish obligation. He believed the Jewish people so historically identified with the idea of ethical monotheism that, should Judaism die, ethical monotheism would also die. The Jewish people, therefore, must survive. Its very ethnicity, in turn, mandates observances which perpetuate and strengthen it.

Rationally Validating the Primacy of Peoplehood

Zionist ideologists proclaimed the Jews a nation, not a religion and, looked forward to Judaism as the social life of the Jewish folk resettled on its ancient soil. Thus, they demythologized the biblical interpretation of Exile — which Jewish mystics had applied even to God — and made it purely political. Redemption would not come by a Messiah but with geographic relocation, cultural self-expression and political reconstitution.

One early Zionist debate still roils the community: is Jewish nationalism rigorously secular and thus value-free or does it contain a distinctive Jewish standard of quality? No one raised this issue more penetratingly than did the essayist Ahad Haam ("one of the people," pseudonym of Asher Ginzberg, 1856-1927).

Ahad Haam's Zionism drew on the concept of folk-psychology to assert that the Jews, like other peoples, had a folk "character" to which it needed to be true. The Jewish national soul exhibited a talent for ethics and high culture, as the Bible indicates. Jewish nationalism, therefore, had to work for the recreation of an ethically and esthetically elevated Jewish culture. A renascent Jewish state could serve as its worldwide "spiritual" center and Diaspora Jewish communities could survive by participating in its cultural life.

Most Zionist ideologists simply assumed that Zionism mandated humanistic values and rarely sought to explicate them. Besides, crises in Jewish life followed so hard upon each other that arguing such abstractions seemed frivolous. But various events in the life of the State of Israel have kept the issue alive. Its very persistence has testified to the odd secularity of the State of Israel. So too have the legal cases where Israeli courts have refused to sever fully the connection between Jewish nationalism and Jewish religion. Some thinkers therefore insist that, for all its putative secularity, the State of Israel can best be understood as an eccentric sectarian development of classic Jewish ethnic religiosity.

An American thinker, Mordecai M. Kaplan (1881-1981), created another distinctive Jewish rationalism in terms of philosophic naturalism. Kaplan based his thinking on the newly arisen science of sociology, which indicated that for Jewish life today to be meaningful, it must reflect the scientific worldview and democratic commitment of modernity. Kaplan therefore carried on a vigorous polemic against Jewish supernaturalism. He self-consciously inverted the central idea of traditional Judaism, that God gave the Torah to the Jewish people (thus giving it its distinctive character). Kaplan now argued sociologically that the Jewish people had created Judaism. It needed to be seen as an ethnic civilization, based on a land, a language, a history, a calendar, heroes, institutions, arts, values and much else, of which religion is the core and through whose concept of God the people expressed its highest values.

Kaplan did not see how anyone could deny that the Jews are fundamentally an ethnic group rather than another "church." The Jewish people's health could only be restored by fully reconstructing its folk life — so Kaplan called his movement Reconstructionism. The continuing American Jewish involvement in Jewish art, music and other cultural forms owes much to this Kaplanian emphasis. Kaplan also called for the Jewish community to reorganize itself institutionally as an ethnic group with many natural interests. Though pluralistic, it could then democratically seek to legislate for its members. But no Jewish community has yet so reconstituted itself.

Kaplan daringly proposed a definition of God: the Power (or Process) that makes for "salvation," by which he meant "human fulfillment". By speaking of God in impersonal, naturalistic terms, one indicates the symbolic status of folk anthropomorphisms and the modern rejection of miracles, verbal revelation and chosenness. Equally important, defining God finitely — only that in nature which abets human self-development — solves the theological problem of evil. Kaplan's God does not bring evil, only good. We can now maturely see evil as caused by nature and take it as a challenge to our moral creativity.

Kaplan's bold recasting of Judaism won him a small but enthusiastic following. However, as his equation of modernity with scientific rationality lost its appeal in the Jewish community, the interest in non-rationalist Jewish thinkers heightened.

Non-rational Jewish Thinkers

After World War I Franz Rosenzweig (1886-1929), the youthful German author of a magisterial work on Hegel, pioneered Jewish existentialism with his effort to situate Judaism in selfhood rather than in acts or ideas. Rosenzweig connected Jewish being with Jewish doing, that is, observing the law, but only as one was existentially able to appropriate its commanding quality. He thus specified but never clarified a greatly appealing balance between duty and freedom, bequeathing to later liberal Jewish thought one of its central issues.

Martin Buber (1878-1965), an older contemporary and sometime collaborator of Rosenzweig's, created a more extensive system. He suggested that human existence is dynamically relational, either in an objectifying mode he called I-it, or a value-conferring one of personal openness and mutuality he called I-thou. For all its indescribable quality, he carefully differentiates the I-thou relation from romanticism and mysticism. The former involves an I-it of emotion or experience; the latter, a loss of self in the One. Buber had in mind something as subtle yet much more common.

Like all significant personal involvements, an I-thou relationship with God (the Eternal Thou) evokes responsive action, thus it "commands." Transgression of such duty will involve guilt and the need to atone. All this has a corporate dimension for whenever two persons truly meet, God is present as well. Consequently, the I-thou experience directs us to create true human community, a society of thou's.

Religions arise from relationships with God which take on social forms. In time, institutionalization, instead of expediting, prevents living contact with God. Equally bad, faiths may designate one sphere of life holy, leaving the rest to be profane. But the I-thou relationship knows no limits and all life should be lived in its terms. Hence Buber opposed all "religion."

He found the Bible recounting the I-thou experiences of the Jewish people with God which, over centuries, created an indissoluble relationship between them, the Covenant. No other ethnic group has ever so identified its corporate existence with loyalty to God. Because of its Covenant, the Jewish folk undertook the messianic task of creating community among its members and thus, eventually, among humankind. While Jews sometimes lost sight of this task, it could never be completely lost, as early Hasidism indicated and Zionism might now show. During his decades of residence in the State of Israel, Buber's public insistence that it live up to his high sense of the Covenant made him quite unpopular.

The last great system-builder, Abraham Heschel (1907-1973), personally integrated much of twentieth century Jewish experience. The scion of a Polish Hasidic dynasty, he took a doctorate in Berlin, was brought to the United States by the Reform rabbinical school and later left it to teach a near-Orthodox theology at the Conservative seminary in New York.

Heschel faulted the existentialists for keeping religion a movement from people toward God. Our very scepticism should make us awestruck at the power Someone has given us. Such "radical amazement" will open us to the reality of the Giver, God. Then we can see, as the Bible indicates, that God pursues humankind, forcing upon it God's self-revelation. We dare not call the prophets liars but must acknowledge that they accurately transmit God's message.

Their meaning cannot be misunderstood: God is a God of pathos, one who suffers when people transgress and who rejoices in their holiness. Surely God would not be greater by not having feelings, a Stoic, not a biblical, conception. Revelation proceeds by sym-pathos, by uncommonly gifted individuals co-feeling what God feels. They may verbalize this individualistically but they do not interpose themselves between God and humankind. The commandments Moses and the sages transmitted to us accurately reflect God's injunctions. They are the divinely sanctioned media for meeting God by doing God's will.

Two themes in Heschel's thought mitigated his absolute acceptance of Jewish tradition. First, he emphasized the paucity of revelation compared with the subsequent plethora of interpretation, thereby suggesting the virtue of continuing development. Second, he carefully documented the prophets' intense ethical devotion, implying, perhaps, that human considerations should predominate in interpreting the Torah. He nobly exemplified this in his participation in the 1960s' civil rights and Vietnam War struggles. But he never indicated whether he would advocate changes in Jewish law for these or other reasons.

Since the creation of these six systems, much theological writing and discussion has gone on but no distinctive new pattern has won substantial acceptance.

Confronting the Holocaust

For reasons still debated, not until the mid-1960s did Jewish thinkers confront the implications of the Nazi murder of 6,000,000 Jews. With other Americans discussing the death-of-God, some thinkers proclaimed that Auschwitz — the great death camp — now rightfully occupied the place once held by Sinai and demanded a radically new Jewish theology.

World Jewry, catalyzed by the Six Day War of 1967, emerged from this agitation intensely identified with the State of Israel. In it, the Jewish people knew, it had given its deepest response to Nazi destructiveness: that it proposed to live and to do so with high human dignity. The Arab-Israeli Six Day War of 1967 which threatened Israel's (and therefore Jewish) existence catalyzed Jewry worldwide to identify even more intensively with the State of Israel. The State of Israel, therefore, for all its secularity, took on a numinous quality for those who maintain the Covenant. The survival of the Jewish people now became a central preoccupation of Diaspora Jews and a major motive for assuming or extending their Jewish responsibilities. Associated with this was a reassessment of the values of the Emancipation. Because of the messianic hope it awakened, Jews had surrendered much of their traditional way of life. Now, even as western civilization began to doubt its ultimate confidence in science, technology, education and culture — in utter human capability — so Jews started approaching their tradition with new receptivity. For some, this partial withdrawal from universal concerns led back to Orthodoxy. Most Jews found that while their social activism no longer could take on redemptive guise they also could not spurn the ethical lessons of the Emancipation. Again, feminism made the issue inescapable. The critical life problem of such chastened liberal Jews has become the delineation of their duty and the creation of communities to live it, a concern giving rise to considerable experimentation.

The theoretical response to the Holocaust had an ironic outcome. Experience made substituting Auschwitz for Sinai unacceptable. For despite continuing mass depravity, the Holocaust does not constitute the norm of human or Jewish existence. Sanctifying the routine, though not forgetting the extraordinary, remains the Jew's fundamental responsibility, as Sinai taught. The primary response to the Holocaust, all Jews agree, must be intensified human responsibility.

Some Orthodox leaders, like the Rebbe of the Lubavitch Hasidic sect, say with the Book of Deuteronomy that God grievously punished a sinful generation. Most Jews find it impossible to connect justice with the Holocaust. Rationalistic teachers assert God only has finite power and humankind must actively help God bring the Messiah. Others have come to a Job-like stance. They know that a qualitative difference of cosmic significance separates Jews from Nazis. No contemporary humanism endows that intuition with commanding authority. But if it is undeniable, then a more than rational reality must here impinge upon us with this demand for quality. Jewish tradition called it God. These thinkers remain stunned that God can entrust humans with the freedom to become as heartless as the Nazis did. Nonetheless — a word they give strong Jewish overtones — they accept God's sovereignty and seek to build their lives on it.

All these views of evil circulated in the Jewish community well before the Holocaust, leading some to suggest that what truly died in the Holocaust was the Enlightenment's surrogate god, the infinitely competent human spirit. As a result of this awakening, Jewish mysticism has gained a hold on a small minority of modern Jews. For others, Orthodoxy has gained fresh appeal. For most Jews, the Emancipation has only been qualified, not negated. Mediating between Judaism and modernity continues to be the central spiritual concern of the people who stand in Covenant with God, working and waiting for the realization of God's rule on earth.

Chapter 6

ഇരു

The First Commandment,
A Postmodern Reading

"I, Adonai *your God,* [am the one] *who brought you out of the land of Egypt, from a slave- house. "*

"I"

S omeone is talking to me. I am not standing at Sinai and I hear no voice. All I have is a text but that turns out to be not as inert as one might think letters on a page or screen are. As long as I can remember the text has been read, chanted, for my (and others') benefit. Even when I am alone with the text, the voice of the reader/chanter dimly sounds in me bringing the words to me as a living address. Mostly, I see/hear it in context, embraced in the story of our people's memory of what happened — and understood by them and me to be most sacred. Even read in utter silence, as happened just a moment ago when I prepared to begin writing these words, it came to me as address. (And were Jewishness not central to my being and were I only another reasonably sensitive participant in western civilization, the words would still come to me as someone speaking to me.)

Who is talking? As yet, I don't know. Normally I would look to see where the sound is coming from or concentrate on its timber so that the first few syllables of this Hebrew "I," might identify the speaker. But while the very word "I" makes the act of address plain, there is no one to look at and no sound pattern to identify. And in all the times that I have read/heard this text there has been no vision or sound connected with this "I" that I might now bring to this hearing.

Yet the word, which in its unadorned articulation seems so devoid of content, is, after all, a symbol and thus necessarily a conveyer of meaning. It cannot literally say nothing for even our supposedly emptiest words — "nothing," "null," "negative" and their kin — say "something." I am spoken to by an unknown "something" that identifies itself — or, if you will, which Jewish spiritual geniuses described — as an "I." Something personal — or metaphorically verbalized as personal — is before me, calling itself to my attention. With a word, it announces its presence as a presentness which seeks me, which involves me with it by asking for a response, that, at least, I attend to it and not turn away. I, being an only somewhat considerate person, it risks my negative response. It does so by making no effort during this intrusion into my consciousness to defeat my freedom and determine my response. Thus I detect that it comes to me with a certain respect for what I am and care about being. In one word it has announced a certain linkage between us, indicating, as it were, that "I am an 'I' as you are an 'I' and I present myself to you in my 'I'-ness so that you will know that some measure of commonality exists between us."

In saying "I," it identifies itself as not-plural even as I know myself most truly to be a singularity, a one-ness, a unity to which I lay claim despite my frequently fragmented sense of self-hood. For me, I-ness is a process in pursuit of its ideal. Is that perhaps true of this I that now addresses me? Or is it far more integrated than I can ever hope to be and, knowing its I-ness to be the ideal which I so imperfectly emulate, I therefore acknowledge it as the standard for my efforts to achieve an ever more realized unity?

"I, *Adonai* . . ."

Oh, so it is You who speak, You, bringer-into-being, orderer-of-nature, sustainer-of-life, elusive-champion-of-the-right. For such an "I," no simple "you" will do and "You" barely hints at the mysterious distance/nearness I/we share with You.

You, not Moses, not one of the other prophets, You Yourself speak. You present Yourself to me/us momentarily making the Far-Off-One the Here-Near-One, approaching as close as our retinas or eardrums. To have been so visited, even if only in paltry recapitulation dignifies us unalienably.

You tell us Your name and by it we come close enough to glimpse who You are and are thereby debarred from ever presuming to call you by it. We mean to cherish Your name by our avoiding it, calling You other things instead, none of them unproblematic. Our oldest euphemism, "lord," now distorts our sense of nearness to You and is too gender-heavy to reflect the breadth of Jewish experience with You. Those today whose self-confidence disdains these old bounds and who assert their intimacy with ultimacy by readily calling You by name, are nonetheless guessing how to pronounce it as, tradition says, the High Priest did each year. Yet just when the climactic moment of utterance came on Yom Kippur day, the Levite choirs increased their volume so no distinct sound could be heard. Nonetheless, the very notion that the High Priest was calling You by name shook us enough that everyone in the Temple threw themselves to the ground before You.

Though we are confined to English, Your name still puzzles, dazzles us. No hint of the sacred four Hebrew consonants is found in the Indo-European root *gheu* — "to call, invoke" — from which our Germanic-English "God" derives and it surely is more an abstraction than a proper name. Nonetheless, some today reflect their Hebraic awe in their English usage. Reverence for "God" suggests not fully spelling out the word, so G-d or Gd become distinctive signs of North American Jewish piety. With disrespect for God rife, believers can well cherish these signs of honest concern. Yet as with so many symbols a shadow cannot be avoided. Deforming Your title/name seems a curious act of demonstrating regard for You. Does the *yetzer hara* of otherwise inadmissible doubt here subtly infiltrate piety and, in eery repetition do to "God" what the rabbis said to do to idols so that, once they are defaced, statues might no longer be offensive to the Jewish soul?

I, *Adonai*, your God . . ."

"My" God? Surely *Adonai* is God of everyone and everything. Why then this surprising singular, "thy God?" Why this personal address to me, or not to me or any other individual but to the Jewish people?

Your reach here is clearly corporate, communal, national but in all these Words You address me/us individually. In pre-Enlightenment days and certainly back in Bible times people did not suffer from today's fearsome gap between the self-legislating I and its society. Rather the self and its group so imperceptibly merged into one another that modern scholars must speculate whether the biblical poet's "I" refers to a person, the nation or, more likely, both at once in shifting emphasis. So meaning me, you mean all the Jews, each one preciously an individual to You.

Nonetheless, the singular "thy" comes as a twofold imperative. The nation, in responding to *Adonai*, must not forget the supreme value of the single self; and only as individual Jews, one by one, do what *Adonai* requires of Israel, can the nation fulfill its Covenantal responsibility. I must not forget that though the Jewish people has an existence independent of me, until I (and other individual Jews) carry out the commandments incumbent upon me (us) as one of all-Israel, it cannot be the Jewish people God is calling it to be. And that begins with knowing that *Adonai* is "my" God in a most personal and intimate way. Temperament, training, soul, experience, endowment — all mix to make me just who I am and the way I go about being/becoming me. You are asking me, *Adonai*, by Your addressing me personally, to fulfill the common duty of all-Israel as just the me I am, that is, in terms of my unique self. To be sure, I speak here, with some hesitation, knowing how much I have been affected by the special prominence modernity has given to the self. Yet our people has long cherished the many individualists and idiosyncratics who served You over its centuries and it has lovingly transmitted their stories to us. I/we respond to Your evocative address to the nation as a collection of single selves by carrying on our uncommon Jewish blend of individualism and corporate concern.

"I, *Adonai*, your God, [am the one] who . . ."

The English has now betrayed me badly enough that I must intrude upon its flow with bracketed words. Already in my problems rendering the sense of the previous Hebrew word, *elohecha*, the non-Hebraic soul of the English language made itself felt. Its "you" might well suggest a Hebraic ambiguity of singular or plural address. So I had recourse to the archaic "thy" to make the singularity of the Hebrew fully evident. Now, were it not for the Hebrew *"asher,"* here "who," the translation might have proceeded as the Hebrew does, without introducing here (or earlier, as most translations do), a verb speaking of existence, "am."

What shall we make of the fact that, compared to western languages, Hebrew seems to take existence for granted — or at least does not often see the need to introduce words to refer to being? Shall we say that existence does not seem so remarkable to the Hebrews that they find it worth mentioning — or is it the opposite, that non-being is so contrary to their way of facing reality that the wonder of existence becomes almost as ineffable as is God? Whatever the case, without *asher* I could have rendered the text without an interpolation this way: "I, *Adonai* your God, brought you out of the land of Egypt, from a slave-house." But the text says, *asher*, and thereby stresses the connection between "I, *Adonai* your God" and "brought you out . . ." requiring something like my "[am the one]" to render its sense in English. Shall I now simply pass over the fact that I have added some words to the Ten which the Torah declares God said directly to the people of Israel at Sinai? At least, I have called my act to your attention inviting you to join me in wondering about how much else I, in my English-ing of the Hebrew — or in my English-shaped thinking about Judaism — have reconfigured its message while transmitting it. Or should we be consoled that, like Heraclitus's river into which one cannot step even once, there has never been a moment when the Hebrew language stood still long enough to equip its words with some kind of prime, pure, essential meaning. Does not the Bible record show and our linguistic experience affirm, that words and their combinations never fix into one perfect meaning which all else adulterates. Meaning abides in these shifting connotations in as obvious and mysterious a way as I remain me while going through the passages of my life. In translation as in life one can only strive for ever greater integrity.

I, *Adonai* your God, [am the one] who brought you out . . ."

Of course You did. But I mean no disrespect by quietly remembering that if I hadn't walked I might still be in the land of Goshen. And, while the text doesn't make much of the minutiae of the journeying — relying, I assume, on our great Jewish talent for complaining — it isn't difficult to imagine what daily activity was like when Your cloud lifted, signaling that we were to fold up the tents, repack the goods, get the family together, find our place in the march and start another trudge. The daily mood, I would guess, was less the high that accompanied Your constant presence than the tedium of one foot after another and the hope against hope that today the ever-lurking problems wouldn't surface and further complicate our lives.

That recital in no way mitigates the wonder You did. Whenever we could lift our spirits so weighed down by each day's demands, we knew we could never have gotten out of Egypt solely on our own. It was as mighty an empire as the world had ever known. Why should they lose all our slave power so necessary for their awe-inspiring, slave-killing projects? Moses's charisma and group cohesion wouldn't have kept us going for very long. No wonder historians, pointing to the absence of confirming external evidence have argued that, though the exodus story is a marvelous national saga, it never happened; "history" doesn't work that way . That is, if you abide by the secular conventions of the academy which rule God out of their kind of "history." Our people, impressed by the continual improbabilities of what has happened to us over the centuries — not the least being that, against all odds, we are still around — knows that again and again God has showed up and, one way or another, brought us out. Not without our putting one foot in front of another, to be sure. Partnership, not unilateral action, has been our sense of God as taker-outer but with no confusion over who was the Senior Partner in the process.

Not all the great faiths which call You "one" proclaim you, as do we, Bringer-out. They apparently believe that to involve You in history this way is to compromise Your purity or the fullness of Your being. We, who identify You not only as creator but as the one who called creation "good" — though flawed since the primal parents were chased out of Eden — know You only as the participating One. To us, one sign of Your greatness is that You are involved with us (and others) and by such interaction do not compromise Your superlative status. As the daily prayer epitomizes You, "*Melekh-ozer-umoshia-umagen*," "King-helper-and saver-and shielder." The very one who is Most High is also the one who bends down low, not one without the other. And because You are our continuing Bringer-outer, we are a hoping people.

Not unproblematically so. If Your greatness rendered You neutral toward us, we would not have the problem of evil. Why should a universe indifferent to us not occasionally (or more often) erupt into evil? Why expect anything else? Our spirituality begins with wonder at how beneficent one finds creation, that is when one stops taking it for granted (I. e., as if there were no Grantor). And that is particularly true when after some depressing personal situation or historical calamity, Your help has brought us out once again. More than a hundred Jewish generations have wondered why You do not do that more often or more quickly, why You can let the people of Israel suffer long years of Egyptian slavery before bringing them out. And the last couple of generations have brought us an anguish over your inscrutable time schedule that we did not previously know. Yet we have also seen incomparable evidences of Your saving hand, though they cannot be said — vile thought — to compensate for the suffering that preceded them. A generation back some said You were dead, a curiously dated notion now that says more about human conceit than Your reality. We, a generation seeking Your nearness, are more apt to pray that You heal our sick than that You explain clearly to us just who You are and why You act as You do.

"I, *Adonai* your God, [am the one] who brought you out of the land of Egypt, from a slave- house."

If You had only brought us out of the land of Egypt, *dayenu*. Despite its plentiful leeks and cucumbers, its advanced culture and international status, it was also the country where rulers were gods and idols were as much animal as human. At least the statues did not have the fallibility which made the Pharaohs' claims to divinity unbelievable, at least to the children of the children of Jacob, Leah, Rachel, Bilhah and Zilpah. In such a country, to be created in the image or to seek to imitate the gods, could not lead to the society the Torah would envision and the Hebrews seek to establish. *Dayenu*.

Worse, Egypt was a slave-house, literally the place where we were not free, figuratively a land where the Jewish spirit could not find itself. Literal slavery is not to be underestimated just because we no longer have enough of it in our world that we have personal experience of slaves and slavery. The Torah, written for a world which took slavery as a human necessity insisted that Jewish slavery must be limited to six years and extended only if the slave wished to stay with the master. Nonetheless, the rabbis must have found even that institution sufficiently uncongenial that, while not abolishing Jewish slavery, they added severe restrictions on what the slave holder might do. It took a long time for economic reality to reflect religious idealism in this realm but the outrage we feel when evidence comes to light of people anywhere who have as good as enslaved others is a testimony to what God began by bringing us out from Egypt. *Dayenu.*

But release from a slave-house has its greatest effect on us today as a compelling metaphor for anything that releases us from any of the many bondages which impede our acting in proper freedom. The inescapable contemporary model of that exodus is what happened to our families as they went from the ghetto to emancipation. So when we or others now move from despotism to democracy, from ignorance to knowledge, from unemployment to a job, from discrimination to equality, from illness to health, from neurosis to maturity, from depression to hope, we know our lives have been touched by that same elemental force that so powerfully made its impact on our ex-slave forebears. And it is because God has not yet concluded all the taking out which humankind needs that we can believe that the long-ago promised days of sitting under vine and fig tree with none to make us afraid will one day come. And only when the great *shofar* sounds will we all be able to say the full, final, *Dayenu.*

"I, *Adonai* your God, [am the one] who brought you out of the land of Egypt, from a slave- house. You must not . . .

Ah. So that is why.

Chapter 7

ഇൗൻ

What does the Halakhah Say about . . .?
Joseph Karo's Preface to the Bet Yosef

(Casting about for a new pre-davvening torah lishmah *project, I chanced upon Karo's introduction to his magnum opus, the Bet Yosef commentary to the Tur. The more I read it, the more I found it a remarkably compressed introduction to that classic problem, determining what "the" halakhah says on a given topic. Hoping colleagues might find this text of some interest, I ignored my inexperience in linguistic matters and decided to prepare a fairly free translation. I am grateful to Henry Resnick of the HUC-JIR Library staff in New York for his invaluable guidance. I probably should have followed it more often than I did.)*

B lessed be Adonai, the God of Israel, who created His universe for the benefit of human beings and out of the whole human family chose as His treasured people "Jacob, His inherited portion." (Dt. 32.9) Because of His love for His intimate people He drew us near [Him] at Mt. Sinai and by means of the choicest of human beings, Moses, our Rav, peace be upon him, He endowed us with Torah and commandments, righteous rules and statutes [all] for our improvement, that we might walk in His ways and be seen as such in His eyes.

As the years have lengthened, we have been tossed from country to country, scattering as we went. Many successive, oppressive troubles, ones intertwined with each other, have come upon us so that, for our many sins, [the words of Scripture] have been fulfilled, "the wisdom of our Sages has disappeared, etc." [Is. 29:14] Then, too, the power of Torah and its students has been exhausted for the Torah is not expounded as if it were two *Torot* but *Torot* without number. The reason [for this] is the multitude of [printed] books available which seek to explain the statutes and laws. Moreover, even though they [the Sages], peace be upon them, intended to illumine our darkness [the opposite occurs], for out of that good light with which they, peace be upon them, benefited us, great doubt and confusion is drawn. The cause of this [calamity] is that everyone writes a book on his own, duplicating what has previously been written by those who preceded him; [or] he reverses a colleague's ruling without citing his language. For you can find that many decisors *[Poskim]* cite a certain law anonymously as if it were accepted with no one dissenting but when you research the matter you find that the Great Authorities differ over it. This situation is evident in innumerable places to anyone who has scrutinized the books of the decisors and studied the ground of their opinions in the Gemara and the early decisors.

[Then, too,] should anyone desire to investigate the source and origin of a law in the text of the *gemara* [as well as in] all the commentators and the decisors, it will be very difficult for him. This is particularly so because he will be exhausted trying to find an entry and discover where that law is [treated] in the Talmud unless the Holy One, *barukh hu*, graced him [so that he finds] the commentary of Harav Hamaggid, [Vidal Yom Tov of Tolosa, late 14th cen., author of the *Maggid Mishneh*, a commentary to Maimonides' *Mishneh Torah*], his memory is for blessing, or the work of Rabbenu Yeruham [Jeroham b. Meshullam, ca. 1290-1350, Spanish Talmudist, author of *Toledot Adam Vehavah*], who indicate to us the places where the laws [are discussed] in the Talmud. One who pores over them will surely understand what he is missing if he does not have a broad familiarity with the Talmud. It also happens that in many cases one will search [their text] and not find in their words an indication of the source for a given law. Should [for example,] the Maggid Mishneh state the law diverging from the text of Maimonides (his memory is for blessing) or from his [legal] system; or should Rabbenu Yeruham on occasion be brief rather than adduce all the opinions given concerning that law; or should the source-indicator only speak generally and have the source he may cite not review anything but a few aspects of the whole [topic] rather than [include] the rest [of them], then the one who is searching will weary himself seeking [the source of] all the aspects [of the law] in the place which [his guide] had indicated to him and still not find [them].

Even if he knows the Talmudic source of the law, he will need to understand its entire [original] Talmudic legal context together with the commentaries of Rashi and Tosafot. After that, he will also need to ponder the words of the Rif [Isaac Alfasi, 1013-1103, author of the classic codifying Talmudic abridgement], the Rosh [Asher b. Jehiel, 1250-1327, outstanding German-Spanish decisor], the Ran [Nissim Gerondi, ?-ca. 1380, premier Talmudic commentator] and the Mordecai [Mordecai b. Hillel, ?-1298, eminent German decisor]. Then he will need to study the Rambam and the other decisors as well as the responsa of the great authorities available to him. [He must do all this in order] to know whether there is general agreement on this law or whether there is a dispute or several disputes about it and according to whose ruling one should decide [specific cases].

It is self evident that this is a process which has no limit. If this is so with regard to a legal question which confronts someone, how much the more so is it true that one cannot attain [the goal] of wanting to know in depth the sources of all the laws and to comprehend the different opinions concerning them as well as the individual [reasoning] of all those holding dissenting views. For even if he investigates every individual law in the Gemara, the commentaries and all the decisors, which is a very great labor, forgetfulness is a common human [trait] and then too, many [legal] matters ramify [greatly], so that [in the end] one labors in vain, Heaven forfend. Should one then decide to choose [to study only] the abridged [legal] books, like the *Sefer Mitzvot Katan* [of Isaac b. Joseph of Corbeil, fl. 13th c.], [*Sefer*] Haagur [1487, by Jacob Landau] and the *Kol Bo* [the medieval legal, not the famous liturgical, work], in truth this turns into [both] a short and long path for he will never finally be able to understand any law in its authoritative formulation. (This is particularly true of the *Agur* for in many places it cites the *Tur* faithfully but that very language requires "a master craftsman and the son of a master craftsman" [A. Z. 50b] to unpack it for he [the author of the *Agur*], his memory is for blessing, cites it[s language] as he found it. In [other] places he also will cite without dissent a given decisor who rules permissively on a matter on which all the Great Authorities of Israel disagree [with him] and rule proscriptively. It also happens that this decisor who had ruled permissively on this matter indicated that there should be some hesitancy about this. Nonetheless, he [the Agur], his memory is for blessing, records the permissive ruling but has not mentioned the words of hesitancy recorded by that same [permissive] decisor. Study closely what he wrote in [the *Agur*] *siman* 434 about water wheels and about a wheel with permanently affixed small vessels with apertures so that they may draw liquids. Compare this with what the *Tur* says in *Yoreh Deah*, *siman* 201 and you will find that this is just as I have described it.

For these reasons, I, the least among the "thousands of Joseph," [a play on Gen. 33:17], one of the sons of *Kevod Morenu, Horenu, Rabbenu* Ephraim the son of *Kevod Morenu, Horenu, Rabbenu* Joseph Karo, his memory is for blessing in life everlasting, I have become "zealous for *Adonai* of Hosts" [so Elijah, 1K. 19:10] and bestirred myself to clear the road [of *halakhah*] of its obstacles. I have decided to write a book encompassing all the laws [currently] in effect with an explanation of their sources and origins in the Gemara together with all the diverse interpretations of the decisors (none will be lacking). However, I decided not to do this book as an independent work so that I would not have to once again cite the words of those who had preceded me. For this reason I decided to base it on one of the famous decisors and first thought I would base it on the book [*Mishneh Torah*] of the Rambam, his memory is for blessing, since he is the most famous decisor in the world. But I changed my mind since he does not present more than a single interpretation and I would then need to spend a lot of time citing the interpretations of the other decisors and their [substantiating] reasoning. As a result I decided to base it [my work] on the book *Arbaah Turim* which was written by *Harav, Rabbenu* Yaakov, the son of the Rosh [Rabbenu Asher], may his memory be for blessing, for he includes most of the opinions of the decisors.

This is the structure of the book: it aims to explain the law as stated by the author of the *Turim*, [clarifying] whether it is [based on] a *mishnah*, or a *baraita*, or a *tosefta*, or a statement in the Talmud Bavli or Yerushalmi, or the Sifra, or the Sifre, or the Mekhilta. [It also indicates] whether there is a consensus or a controversy [concerning the law] among the Tannaim or Amoraim, and whether the author [of the Tur] has ruled according to one of them, what reasoning led him to rule according to that source, and whether [he,] the author, cites the reasoning of the decisors who have a differing view on this law. It will [then] clarify the reasoning of each [dissenting] opinion and its Talmudic roots and origin. It will [then also indicate] whether the author has ignored the opinion of a given decisor since you find he often has, e. g., ignoring the view of the Rif or of the Rambam or the opinion of other decisors. [In that case, my book] will cite the opinions of the ignored sages and [give] their reasoning. Should the language of one of the decisors, whether one adduced by the author or not, be unclear, their words will be clarified. In particular [this applies to] the language of the Rambam, his memory is for blessing, for in many places his language is obscure and impenetrable and it will be explained in this book according to the commentary of the *Maggid Mishneh* and the Ran [no commentary by him to the *Mishneh Torah* is extant]. At times it [my book] will question an interpretation [of one of them] and will explain [the Rambam's language] in another fashion. One who ponders [the issue] may [then] be satisfied and hold fast to [whichever view] he chooses. In those few places where the Rambam's words require explanation but the above-mentioned commentators have not spoken about them, his language will be explained.

Moreover, should our author, the *Baal Haturim*, raise objections to [the rulings of] certain decisors, his difficulties or surprise [at what they said] will be resolved. Should there be a legal innovation in the words of a certain decisor or commentator which the author has not cited, this will be adduced and its reasoning explained.

The result will be that anyone who has this book before him will have an orderly presentation of the words of Talmud accompanied by the commentaries of Rashi, the *Tosafot*, the Ran, the rulings of the Rif, the Rosh, the Mordecai, the Rambam, the *Hagahot* [*Maimuniot*, a commentary on the *Mishneh Torah*, 13-14th cen. German], the *Maggid Mishneh, Rabbenu Yeruham, Sefer Haterumah* [13th cen. French-Palestinian], *Shibolei Haleket* [13th cen. Italian], the [*Sefer Ha*] *Rokeah* [12-13th cen. German], *Shaarei Dura* [13th cen. German], *Sefer Hatashbetz* [13th cen. German], *Sefer Haittur* [12th cen. French], *Nimukei Yosef* [15th cen. Spanish], the *Semag* [13th cen. French], the *Semak* [13th cen. French], the *Orhot Hayyim* [dubiously "The Will of R. Eliezer," 11th cen. ?], *Torat Habayit* [of the Rashba, 13-14th cen. Spanish], *Hagahot Asheri* [14th cen. Austrian], *Sefer Hamanhig* [*Olam*, 12-13th cen. various countries], the *Agur*, the *Baalei Hanefesh* of Rabad [12th cen. French], and the responsa of the Rosh, the Rashba, the Ri [Isaac] bar Sheshet [Perfet, 14th cen. Spanish], Rav Shimon bar Tzemah[.] [Duran, 14-15th cen. Algerian], the Mahari [Joseph] of Colon [15th cen. Italian] and

Terumat Hadeshen [15th cen. German]. All their statements will be thoroughly explained and, in some places, statements from the Zohar [as well]. Since it is well known that the Rosh, the *Mordecai*, the *Semag*, the *Semak*, *Sefer Haterumah*, and *Hagahot Maimon* generally follow the rulings of the *Tosafot*, therefore if one hears that I do not give their views in some places, let him not suspect me [of oversight] for when I indicate the views of the *Tosafot* I do not need to give the views of these holy [aforementioned sages] who generally say what they mean [and would therefore say so explicitly if they did not accept the opinion of the Tosafot].

Recently I acquired a copy of some of the responsa of the Rashba, written with "a pen of iron and lead," [Job 19:24, i. e.,] printed, which states at its beginning that they are responsa of the Ramban. When I cite something from these responsa, even though I know that they are the Rashba's responsa, I will write "So it is written in the responsa of the Ramban. [I will do this] because printed works now are found in everyone's possession and anyone who wishes to investigate the language of the responsum itself will thus be able to do so readily.

I [also] have acquired a lengthy commentary to the book *Orah Hayyim* [of the Tur; no longer extant] by our Rabbi, the *Gadol, Kevod Moreinu, Rav, Rabbenu* Yitzhak Abuhav [Isaac Aboab II, 1433-1493, of Castile], his memory is for blessing, and a commentary to the beginning of the book *Orah Hayyim* and [also] the beginning of the book *Yoreh Deah* by the *Rav, Kevod Moreinu, Horeinu, Rav, Rabbenu* Jacob ben Haviv [Jacob ben Solomon ibn Habib, ?1445-1515/16, Salonika], his memory is for blessing. I decided to cite their opinions in their names, and in places where I differ with them, I will indicate what troubles me in their positions and I will [then] indicate my opinion. An interested person can then choose [which view] he deems correct.

Since [the printings of] the book *Arba Turim* are full of transcription errors, I will in many places note the location of the errors and indicate the correct, authoritative language according to thoughtful and reliable books which I have pored over. It also occurred to me that after all the exposition I should rule as to what is *halakhah* [in this matter] and decide between the various opinions. For this is the goal: that we should have one Torah and one rule. But I well know that when we say we shall determine who among the decisors [offering] Talmudic arguments and proofs has [correctly determined] the law, behold the Tosafot, the Talmudic commentaries of the Ramban, the Rashba and the Ran, their memory is for blessing, are filled with arguments and proofs for each and every point of view. Who [then] wants to become involved [in these disputes] to add more arguments and proofs? Who is daring enough to put his head between these "mountains" [of legal authority], "mountains of God," [Ps. 36:6], to decide among them, on the basis of arguments and proofs, and contradict their clarification [and specification of a disputed law] or rule on something which they did not? [In truth,] because of our many sins our mental ability is too limited to understand their words let alone to outsmart them. Moreover, even if were it possible for us to follow this path it would not be sensible to persist in it for it is an exceedingly long one.

Because of all this, I decided that since there are three pillars of [legal] instruction upon whose decisions the house — the House of Israel — rests (surely they are the Rif, the Rambam and the Rosh, their memory is for blessing), it seemed to me that whenever two of them concur in a given ruling we should rule that their view is the *halakhah*; except, however, in those few cases where all Israel's sages or the majority of them disagree with that decision and as a result the contrary practice has spread. [Then, too,] in a case where one of the three aforementioned pillars has not indicated an opinion on this law and the remaining two pillars disagree on this matter, then behold, the Ramban, the Rashba, the Ran, the Mordecai and the Semag, their memory is for blessing, are before us [to guide us] to the place where the Spirit is, the Spirit of the Holy God, so that [we may] walk where we should walk [a play on *halakhah*?] — only according to the [ruling] of the majority and teach that as *halakhah*. When none of the three aforementioned pillars has ruled [on a certain law] we shall decide according to the famous authorities who have published their views on this law and [surely] this is a proper and reasonable "royal road" to clear the stumbling block.

If in some few countries the custom is to prohibit some few matters despite our ruling to the contrary, they should maintain their practice for they have already accepted upon themselves the opinion of the authority who prohibits [this action] and it is forbidden to them [now] to introduce a permissive standard as is clarified in the passage "[In] a place where the custom is . . ." [Pes. 50a and following — the printed text says 51 — the *locus classicus*].

[Moreover,] since the indices to the book *Turim* are so very brief, someone seeking [to find] a given law is occasionally unable to determine whether it is under one heading or another, or whether the author has referred to this law. Therefore I decided to create other indices which would indicate all the laws specifically treated under a given heading and after that I wrote brief indications of all the innovative legal determinations which I had made in my commentary called *Sefer Bet Yosef*. [All this has been done] so that anyone seeking a law can find it easily.

The usefulness of this book to sages is clear. Those who choose [to utilize] this abridgement [of the halakhic developments will find] it provides [both] a lengthy and a short path [of study]. Should one not have the vigor to endure [a thorough investigation] one can study it to understand most clearly what the author of the book *Arbaah Turim* intended [by his text]. Thus this book is nourishment for everything is in it. For this reason I have entitled it *Bet Yosef*, [Joseph's House], for just as [in Egypt] Joseph's house sustained everyone with bodily nurture, so this book will sustain them with spiritual nurture. The additional, second reason is that this is my [personal] portion of all my labors, my [Joseph Karo's] "house" in this world and in the world to come. I ask *Hashem*, the blessed of Self, to aid me in this matter [involving] the glory of His name, [so] that I compose a pure book, [one] stripped of all errors and mistakes. In Him, the blessed of Self, "my heart has trusted and I have been aided." [Ps. 28:17] He will have mercy on me and as a free gift He will be gracious unto us. For His gracious acts are gracious [indeed] and those who receive His mercy know [true] mercies, as it is written, "For I [truly] grace the one [to whom] I extend grace and I bestow [true] mercy to the one to whom I extend mercy." (Ex. 33:19).

Chapter 8

၈၁၈

American Jewish Modernity Comes to Self-consciousness

In the early *Jewish Book Annual*s the lists of new books published do
not contain much of what today would be called "Jewish thought."
The reasons for that are largely semantic and social. There have always
been thoughtful Jews and there is hardly an age in our long history when
they have not also been writers, seeking to share their ideas with others.
It was no different in the 1940s for all the special difficulties authors and
publishers encountered due to the war, the lingering economic tightness
and American Jewry's continuing cultural latency. As a result one can
find in these initial registers a steady sprinkle of books in the classic
genres of Jewish thinking: homiletics, commentary, Talmudic *hidushim*,
halakhic *psak* and, in a more recent style, ideology. Anyone who wants
to understand what intellectual Jews seriously cared about then and how
they carried forward a millennial style in an age dominated by a radically
secular culture must study this literature.

That the connotations of the term "Jewish thought" have changed
over the past five decades testifies to our contemporary conceptual
sophistication. It is only by the standards of our current riches that these
old lists seem quite impoverished. For today the term "Jewish thought"

carries with it the implications of academic competence, of books written for the university trained and culturally sophisticated reader — a reader, incidentally, who has benefited by the explosion of knowledge which has characterized this half-century. No longer can one expect commendation for one's writing as a simple matter of community pride, that the appearance of every Jewish book should be greeted with thanksgiving and its quality guaranteed by the Jewishness of its author and topic. Today's readers have been taught that a critical attitude is the beginning of wisdom and enough books make a claim on them that the need to be selective induces them to exercise it. Moreover, their horizons have enormously broadened. They bring to bear on their Jewish reading the same standards of judgment and taste that they apply to any book that seeks their assent. Our community did have some books fifty years ago which sought to meet these criteria for in that blessed intellectuality of ours there were some Jewish authors who, dissatisfied with what they saw around them, wrote far in advance of most of their readers, seeking to bring American Jewry from where it was to where it needed to be.

In this period what has changed spectacularly for the Jewish better — at least in this one respect — has been the symbiotic development of a public for sophisticated works of Jewish thought and of authors who address this group. In some ways this is only another by-path in the well known history of the post-World War II maturation of American Jewry, of its rise from penury to affluence, of its stunning academic and cultural ascendance, of its growth to self-conscious self-respect, and of its odd will to remain Jewish despite being bewitched by the pleasures of assimilation. But nothing in that record of the Judaization of our community prepared us for the emergence of a clear-cut interest in Jewish ideas per se. Our Jewishness, so it seemed, was a blend of American pragmatism — do first, you'll think later — and ethnicity. So it was not to be expected that abstractions about Jewish life rather than history or literature or how-to manuals would become a significant concern of our authors and readers. The result of this unexpected evolution has been a steady stream of cultured volumes of reflection, one so broad-ranging that even assiduous readers cannot any longer easily stay abreast of it.

Social historians have yet to probe the etiology of this phenomenon but even standing in its flowing midst a non-expert can discern three, perhaps four, factors as critical to its formation: the explosion of the number of Jews academically involved in Jewish studies, the crisis in ethics, particularly bio-ethics, and the recent intensive search for meaning with its attendant fresh appreciation of tradition. An extra energy has been given this flow by the emergence of Orthodox authors who write in English and in a genre that once seemed to belong to non-Orthodox thinkers seeking to demonstrate their Jewish validity.   Of particular significance in this regard has been the breadth of this development, one not limited to Orthodox "centrists" but one which embraces elements of the Orthodox right.   The centrists, believing in the Jewish authenticity of *halakhah* co-existing with general culture, might have been expected to make their case in the general culture's terms.   But the rightists are normally suspicious of modernity so their adopting the culture's forms to win Jews to their cause is a phenomenon worthy of investigation. Even more so is the historically unprecedented development that an impressive English literature has developed for adherents of the Orthodox right who seek Jewish authenticity via *laaz*, a foreign tongue.

The German forerunners of academically aspiring Jewish writing in the realm of ideas took the form of studies in medieval Jewish philosophy. In a culture where rationalism seemed the indispensable standard of modernity and philosophy its noblest exemplification, to show that Jews too had once been able rationalists, even influences on the development of the European canon of ideas, validated the emancipation of the Jews. In America, as philosophy departments began to overcome their addiction to continental rationalism or British analysis, Jewish students of philosophy found it possible to develop their interests beyond Saadia and Maimonides. Then as ethical questions increasingly moved to the foreground of philosophic concern and ethnicity and feminism cut the ground from under the old assumptions about universal rationality, the possibilities for philosophizing with a Jewish concern greatly expanded, as witness the current involvement with the thought of Emmanuel Levinas.

A more fruitful area of Jewish writing has come from the academic esteem of the history of ideas, a notion which has increasingly reached beyond rationalistic conceptualization to study non-rational forms of thought, mysticism being the outstanding Jewish beneficiary.   Gershom Scholem's contributions to our community cannot be limited to his having opened up a relatively unexplored because undervalued realm of Jewish cognition or even to his many publications, as valuable as these remain. Rather, in raising up many disciples and setting high standards for their future publications he made possible an ongoing, illuminating and horizon-widening production of literature.   No one but specialists can now reasonably hope to keep track of it, yet many of these volumes open up questions and concerns that promise many more fascinating books to come.

These works are the products of those who specialize in Jewish thought. But where shall we draw the boundaries of "Jewish thought" and thus include or exclude the writings of those many other academics who bring the expertise of their disciplines to bear on aspects of what Jews think or once thought? For example, shall we exclude from our evolving view of Jewish conceptions of reality the findings of students of government who extrapolate from Jewish practice and comment an understanding of Jewish political thought? or those of the anthropologists who uncover the worldviews buried in social practice or tale? Today, from every area of the social sciences the books of Jewish academics are awakening us to new dimensions of Jewish thought.

Perhaps the liveliest area for publication in recent years has been that of ethics. Oddly enough, though modernized Jews have for well over a century identified the essence of Judaism as ethics — in the Kantian sense of that term — there have been few books indeed on that topic and most of those merely illustrated how Jewish texts supported the precepts of liberal universalism. Ahad Haam's case is paradigmatic. Rejecting God and revelation and substituting high human culture for Torah, he was hard put to explain why one should care about the Jewish people and continue its culture. He tried to give special value to the Jewish folk by arguing that its unique national talent lay in the realm of high culture and ethics. Thus, he insisted that the fundamental distinction between Judaism and Christianity arose from their different understanding of ethics, a matter he hoped to make clear in a master work on Jewish ethics. He never wrote that volume and despite the fact that this has been a favorite ideological stance of Jews for decades, neither has anyone else. The alleged higher ethical concern of Jews has been more easily understood as a matter of action, particularly Jewish family life and liberal politics, than of a distinctive cast of Jewish thought, a not inappropriate set of priorities in Judaism.

As society changed and as history effected its transformations, those older understandings became strained. The role of government action in the moral improvement of society no longer could be taken for granted. Jews had long identified Jewish ethics with the espousal of such government leadership for they had benefited from it in the emancipation of the Jews. For decades this notion was reinforced by the Jewish belief that their people's security depended on their society affirming everyone's equality in law and practice. So enlightened self-interest reinforced Jewish liberalism. But as Jews changed from have-nots to haves, as their success depended on maintaining the current social order, as some Jews believed that "what was good for the Jews" was to be left alone in safety, the accepted liberal-political understandings of "Jewish ethics" demanded rethinking.

At the same time, the Kantian understanding of ethics which had dominated Jewish thought ever since the late 19th century no longer retained its philosophical dominance. Other ways of thinking about ethics have now vigorously reasserted themselves. Moreover, as Orthodox Jews increasingly found their place in our culture, a host of theoretical questions about the relationship between Jewish law and general ethics — particularly as it demeaned the particular and elevated the universal — prompted new writing. All this has led to a small but steady stream of Jewish books seeking to reconceptualize what had for so long been taken for granted as "Jewish ethics."

Most of the new publications in the realm of Jewish moral responsibility have dealt with the practical questions raised by contemporary ethical dilemmas and no area has received greater attention than bio-ethics. The writing about specific issues has not come from the source that one would have anticipated fifty years ago. Then ethics seemed to be the realm of secularists and Reform Jews. As it were, moral law was their substitute for Oral Law and they gloried in the universality of their ethical horizon, implicitly asserting its moral superiority to any which operated from an essentially particularistic Jewish basis.

Over the decades two developments occurred which as good as ended the ability of old-style secularists and Reform Jews to think seriously about Jewish ethics. First, their universalism, so liberating when Jews often had an ethnocentric, ghetto-mentality became increasingly irrelevant as Jews generally integrated into the society. Their "Jewish" ethics merely took what the reader of the journals of liberal opinion already knew and adorned it with quotations from the Bible or the rabbis. This might give the standard liberalism a certain Jewish flavor but added no fresh or specific Jewish insight in matters of increasing complexity. Writers from these groups remained most helpful to the community as they identified those general socio-political questions which had special Jewish implications.

Second, the universal, rationalist approach to ethical issues — Kantianism in one or another of its forms — lost its cogency. Partially this was a practical matter, the messianically touted socio-ethical programs of social reconstruction having caused very many serious new problems even as they partially resolved certain old ones. Partially it was an intellectual matter, for Kantianism lost its philosophic cache once thinkers began tightly associating rationality with logic and not with moral content while critics of philosophy exploded the Cartesian myth that anyone actually had access to universal rationality rather inevitably projecting a quite particular persona.

As a result, ethical thinking displayed a new hospitality to the particular sources of one's ethics, "communitarianism" as it has come to be called. Thus, what other ethicists thought Jews might contribute to any discussion of a societal issue was not their universalism but quite precisely the particular wisdom their tradition had worked out over the years, in a word, *halakhah*. And in our community as well, Jews now as much concerned to be Jewish as to be "American" wanted to know what Jewish law said about a given issue in the past and today. As against a morality which touted itself as fundamentally universal, this version of our ethics would have no difficulty qualifying as "Jewish."

The result has been a continuing stream of books in which writers explore themes as diverse as the limits of advertising (among other economic matters) or the range of attitudes toward suicide. Few themes which become major concerns of our society for any period of time will long be neglected by contemporary Jewish authors. A corollary aspect of this development has been the flourishing of a more popular literature in which Jewish religious guidance is given people facing one or another problem of contemporary life like overcoming addiction or being an effective parent.

This surge of publication has been most impressive in the area of bio-ethical issues, medicine in particular. As technology has opened staggeringly disturbing issues and easy answers, rational or paternalistic, have increasingly seemed unworthy of thoughtful and mature adults, the search for significant guidance has become a dominant theme of our intellectual lives — and no sooner have we come to terms with one set of problems than another is troublingly set before us. At this juncture, the millennium plus tradition of Jewish law comes to the aid of inquiring Jews. For Jewish tradition has long had an intimate concern with healing as an adjunct of the sanctification of life and human relationships. While technology and knowledge have changed the particulars of the problems we face, it is remarkable how many of them have direct analogies to living experiences of the Jewish past and thus lend themselves to contemporary halakhic adjudication. It should be no surprise then that Orthodox Jewish writers — physicians as well as scholars — have tended to dominate this burgeoning field of publication.

However, this has, in turn, stimulated others to enter the field, albeit not often with book-length publication. The motive for this development is the clash which often characterizes the fundamental interests of classic Jewish law and those that remain operative for most modern Jews. The *halakhah* speaks with authority and expects that those who inquire of a sage will abide by the decision rendered, God's authority being behind it. In contrast, moderns still have great respect for the individual conscience, connecting an ethical decision with one's personal conviction that a given position is ethically compelling. How to blend the objectivity of the tradition with modernity's esteem for autonomy has become a major theoretical problem in this field, one already generating a new area of ethical publication. To some extent one may see this in the books which begin to explore rather systematically what it might mean to speak of "Jewish ethics" in our time. Yet it is as likely to arrive in the context of given practical medical problem as the author considers how much weight to give to tradition, how much to individual self-determination. To a limited extent, this issue also surfaces indirectly in the differing approaches to a given decision by "stringent" and "liberal" decisors. It is but one step further to the possibility of presenting a comprehensive intellectual understanding of Judaism, a systematic Jewish philosophy or theology. During the fifty year period under consideration the thought of our two great American Jewish thinkers, Mordecai Kaplan and Abraham Heschel came to full maturity. In this era too translation and interpretation made available the ideas of the German Jewish thinkers, Hermann Cohen, Leo Baeck, Franz Rosenzweig and Martin Buber. Each gave voice to a distinctive interpretation of Judaism entire, one largely motivated by disagreement with the formulations of the other synoptic theoreticians. Most of the systematic writing, however, was devoted to specific issues, Zionism and Jewish identity being particularly prominent early on, the Holocaust dominating the middle period, while mysticism and feminism are evoking considerable attention now. These creative efforts need to be understood against the background of the academic concern with the history of ideas, already mentioned above. Thus we have many studies describing critical themes in the thought of one or another thinker, or in modern thought generally, or the outlines of the thinking of one or another writer. It must be noted, however, that often under the guise of an objective investigation of a given theme a writer is putting forward a personal Jewish agenda, hermeneutics and advocacy not being unrelated as postmoderns see it. All this publication has created and been made possible by a not inconsiderable reading public that has an interest in Jewish philosophy or theology. Its following among Jewish professionals, academics and clergy might be ascribed to their work, more cynically to a need for a "plausibility structure" to justify their continued activity. But there has been a growing interest in these once esoteric topics on the part of lay Jewry as well. Clearly it has to do with the loss of the self-confidence that characterized secularistic modernity at mid-century.

As the year 2000 approaches, western civilization as a whole seems quite unsure of itself, of its determining values and of its human direction. The search for a ground of value drives people into the most diverse faiths and saving therapies. For some people only the new and radically different can be valuable, for others it seems that only what has lasted for ages can be an adequate antidote to the permissiveness and nihilism around us. Jews, having been emancipated by western civilization, believed passionately in its spiritual significance. How could they not now be deeply affected by discovering it to be only another false Messiah? So many Jews today turn to their tradition to see what it might teach them about living in a world where evil and good too often come as a pair and transforming the one and exemplifying the other is the true task of maturation. In such a human situation we may expect that some Jewish thinkers will be moved to speak of Judaism as an integrated whole and by their books seek to teach this generation their Torah.

Chapter 9

ഇറ്റ

B'rit, Mitzvah and Halakha:
In Search of a Common Vocabulary

My theological work over the years has been largely involved with the Jewish domestication of personal freedom, that is, with the question of what autonomy might mean if taken into a serious, believing, and observing Jewish commitment. Autonomy is, obviously, a dangerous idea, one with fearful implications for Judaism. Why, then, should any caring Jew want to become involved with it?

Any historian looking at the Jewish people in modern times would see that after a wonderful career of almost two millennia, the overwhelming majority of Jews have now abandoned Jewish law. Why did that come about? Why is it that today only a rather small minority among us takes the notion of Jewish law seriously, which is to say, really disciplines its lives by the standards of the *halakha*? And, what have other Jews substituted for Jewish law? It is this latter question, raised to the level of truth, that has interested me and has occasioned a good deal of my theological reflection over the past several decades.

I propose here (as elsewhere) to try to speak out of the mind of the Jewish community that is not law-observing or law-believing. I try to articulate its best self-understanding. In comparing this community to any other, let us be scrupulous in comparing the best of the one to the best of the other or the worst of the one to the worst of the other.

As I understand it, the majority of modern Jews, uncompelled by anyone, has given up the notion of the law as discipline because they have come across a substitute notion which they believe to be true, that is, personally compelling in an axiological sense. It is the idea that people should be allowed to make up their own minds. They should not only think for themselves, but should do so most particularly when a decision on how they should act is at stake.

Let us, at this point, quickly dispose of one matter. No one is completely autonomous. All of us are part of families and communities, cultures and histories, and all of us come with specific genetic, emotional, and physical capabilities. Nonetheless, if you ask, "What is the ideal of the mature person in our time?", it is someone who is increasingly able to think for him or her self and to come to reasonable decisions based upon personal knowledge, experience, sentiment, feeling, and logic.

Paradoxically, individualism pervades the moral common sense of our culture. It is something our children learn from the time they are little and are allowed to ask us the question "Why?". "Why?" means, "Give me a reason." "Why?" means, "I will not really accede to what you want until you have given me a reason that convinces me." "Why?" means that you, the person who is asking "why?", have a certain personal dignity. You demonstrate this by your being allowed to reject command and dictation in order to ask for reasons whose cogency you will examine before making a decision. This notion of self-determination is enshrined in democracy and worked out as pluralism. It has captured the moral imagination of the best of the Jewish community, and it, rather than the received law as discipline, has become the primary principle notion by which modern Jews live.

I do not wish to be misunderstood. For a so-called "Orthodoxy," the Jewish tradition gives extraordinary room for individuals to think for themselves and make up their own minds. The difference between the classic and the modern Jewish sense of individuality and practice has to do with the extent to which we must act within the dictates of the Jewish tradition. In the clash between the individual "conscience" (as moderns sometimes call it) and the tradition, the individual conscience was expected by classic Judaism to give way to the law that God had made available to us. Autonomy operates only within *halakha*.

In the modern world the individual believes that he or she is entitled to be self-legislating. It is this self-determining aspect of autonomy that has made for its conflict with Judaism and raises the fearsome threats of anarchy and assimilation.

For all that, the more we have lived with the idea of autonomy, the more it has impressed us that it is the right principle by which to live. We think it is true that each of us has the capacity to know in a very deep and compelling way the truth to which we must address ourselves. At our best, each of us has a sense of what God wants of us and we know also that we must be faithful to that call of our soul. To be sure, knowing how limited, how prone to self-deception, how insensitive we can be, we will earnestly want to learn from others. We know we can benefit greatly from education, tradition, ritual, and discussion in developing our capacities. We need to develop the appropriate use of our precious, dangerous freedom. And law has an important role in any mature person's life. But, having had the dignity of being able to think for oneself, having seen what happens to one as one takes one's personal stand in testing and understanding and giving or withholding credence to others, we know this process of exercising autonomy to be the source of our sense of effective personal worth. It is the basis upon which most American Jews propose to live their lives, and I try to articulate the religious truth and Jewish significance/limits of those Jews who earnestly follow this nonlegal way.

This truth of our personal existence has been confirmed both by our social reality and its social results. The results are much easier to talk about. The emphasis on individual decision- making has led to the creation of a social order in which, because individual autonomy is taken for granted, we expect people of very different ideas and very different temperaments to live peacefully side by side. My commitment to your right to think for yourself is inherent in my assertion that I insist on thinking for myself. Americans therefore live with one another in remarkable peace. And as a further result of American pluralism, Jews in the United States have lived with their neighbors with a certain quiet and benefit and opportunity that their forebears did not have elsewhere. Moreover, applying this Americanization of pluralism to living out one's Jewishness with other Jews has been extraordinarily beneficial for our community. We live with one another with more tolerance of difference, with greater cooperation and unity than any variegated Jewish community in the past.

The social reality of our existence in the United States - indeed, anywhere in the modem world - also powerfully reinforces our intuition of the truth of autonomy. It is founded on the fundamental determination that each of us is entitled to vote. As a participant in the democratic process I share in deciding who legislates over me. American Jews may not be observant about very much else, but they are uncommonly involved in electoral activities. And, having learned from the process of democracy the importance of sharing in making their own law and being responsible for those who determine the laws, most Jews believe the notion of autonomy which grounds them is entitled to a special grip on the Jewish soul.

What, then, shall we Jews do about this truth? How are we to accommodate it to the greater truth we call Judaism? One thing is clear to me. We no longer exist in the good old days of modernization when whatever we learned from general society we simply brought over to Judaism, making our Judaism conform to it. To the contrary, having made a strong case for autonomy, I take the postmodern view that Judaism is also entitled to make its case against modernity. It is quite clear to me that we need to criticize the general secular, and specifically Kantian philosophic notion of autonomy from our Jewish perspective. Autonomy may be a truth, but the nature of that truth needs to be revised and reformulated from its secular understanding in order to find an appropriate place in our Jewish religious self-understanding. The core of my theological work for a quarter of a century or more has dealt with aspects of this issue.

I begin with a Jewish polemic. The secular notion of autonomy makes no sense whatsoever. The self does not explain its worth or validate its own high value. To know a self is not to have any particular reason to grant it special dignity, particularly the dignity of self- legislation. The more realistic we are about how people live and the more we know how conflicted and irresolute selves are, the more honest we can be about our own sins of omission and commission and the more we realize that the self is our problem, not our solution. Without a self-transcending ground for our selfhood I do not see how we can insist on the dignity of every self. By contrast, the worth of every self makes sense in terms of his/her relationship to God. Because there is a God and because that God is covenanted to all humankind, all selves have an unalienable dignity. This notion was the Judeo-Christian ground of the values that created Western democracy.

To be a self involved with God, however, is not yet to be a Jewish self. A Jewish self, as I understand it, is a self that shares a relationship with God as part of the Jewish people. My self is intimately tied up with the people of Israel and the people of Israel's ongoing historical relationship with God, the Covenant of Sinai and beyond. For me, this language of relationship is the least inadequate of all the contemporary theological languages to articulate the Judaism I know and affirm. It is the cultural intellectual form with which I am best able to express what it is that I fundamentally believe as a Jew.

If I want to come to a decision as a Jewish self, exercising "Jewish autonomy," I need to do so not only as a personal matter or only out of a living relationship with God, but also by trying to understand what God wants of me as a member of the Jewish people. As we share a historic relationship, one that has a history and cares about history, I am deeply concerned to know what Jews in the past have understood God wanted of them in this area. And as I live the Covenant in and with the Jewish community of today, I am deeply concerned to know what other Jews of every view understand God wants of them and us. And as this historic Jewish relationship with God is pointed toward the coming of the Messiah, whatever decision has to be made has to be faced in terms of its future thrust and its messianic, redemptive quality.

In an autonomous Jewish decision, all these factors come into play, but so does my self. It is I, me, the person, here, now, with my background, with all my determinants, and yet also with my freedom, standing personally before God as a member of the Jewish people who is making this decision. I understand this view of the autonomous Jewish self to give me very substantial basis for reaching out to other Jews as to our tradition and our Jewish future. I need to live my Jewish duty not as an isolate but as part of the Jewish people living up to its Covenant today. Nonetheless, I must most fundamentally live out my Jewish duty as me, as a single autonomous Jewish self whose life and dignity are ultimately quite individual.

I do not see how I can get Jewish law out of the notion of the concept of autonomy in covenant of relationship. But I can get pluralism and I am a committed Jewish pluralist. And the Jewish pluralism which was basic to my journal *Sh'ma* from its very beginning in 1970 came out of the theology I have been sketching here.

Today, therefore, all discipline must increasingly become self-discipline. To help individual Jews find better Jewish self-discipline, that is my aim and interest.

Chapter 10

ﺵﻭﻍ

The Way to a Postmodern Jewish Theology

I am a believing Jew who seeks to understand as best he can the nature of Jewish faith and the religious life its beliefs entail. Jewish tradition classically and many believing Jews today do not share my great interest in this reflective aspect of Jewish spirituality. Some consider it a foreign importation into Judaism and hence an activity no serious Jew should be associated with. Despite this, I carry on an activity I and some others loosely call "Jewish theology." I do so because I enjoy thinking and because I believe that trying to give words and intellectual structure to what I most significantly believe will make me a better Jew. I am encouraged in my uncommon Jewish religious activity by those people in our long history whom I perceive to be my predecessors, those authors whose writings indicate they lived in cultures that honored Hellenic ways of thought and who therefore also pursued abstraction.

One of my major theological concerns is generated by an issue unknown to my theoretical forebears, traditionalists all of them. While my Judaism is as primary to my existence as their faith was to their lives, I do not live the life of Torah within the parameters of its classic interpretation but in a modernized adaptation of them. Intellectually, it seems odd to me that my modernity has impacted on me sufficiently that I dissent from my tradition in significant measure. I say that because I know that no contemporary point of view is more basic to my life than is my Judaism. I would therefore like to understand this somewhat curious spiritual stance of mine — one, incidentally, I believe the overwhelming bulk of modernized, believing Jews share.

I am not the first modern Jew to devote a good portion of his professional life to thinking about this matter. Yet, to add to my puzzlement, I find serious fault with all the prior efforts to give an adequate intellectual description and cultural validation to this amalgamated Jewish faith which we thinkers have lived. So I have sought to create a new theoretical structure for my Judaism and that of many other present day Jewish believers. The resulting work of giving an orderly, abstract articulation of my life's truth I call "Jewish theology."

Having my most fundamental stance within Judaism drives me to understand myself theologically in relation to the classic Jewish tradition, a lifelong effort currently moving toward intellectual completion in a project currently under way. Nonetheless, since I also stand firmly within contemporary culture I have been involved in the related work of seeking to understand my Judaism in terms esteemed by one of its significant intellectual currents. It is this cultural task, what theologians call apologetics, that led me to my concern with the postmodern mind. The results of my mediating between Judaism and postmodernity as I understand it are now visible in my book *Renewing the Covenant,* a work whose theory and content provide the substance for this discussion.

I cannot directly continue the patterns of thought created by my teachers, the non-Orthodox Jewish thinkers of prior modern generations, because I do not share the unbounded confidence in culture that animated them. I have only a modest regard for the spiritual vitality of contemporary culture and the secular methods it commends as our most valuable ways of finding meaning. What troubles me about it is not so much its increasing fragmentation and contradictoriness but its low moral standards. And the university, which once seemed to offer the hope of providing a guiding humane vision for our civilization now seems, with many individual and some institutional exceptions, as much the cause and victim of our social malaise as its antidote.

To be more specific, my teachers and their teachers before them followed the accepted liberal Protestant method of doing theology. First they turned to the university and allowed it to prescribe a manner of speaking about religion that it considered acceptable. Then they sought to adapt their faith to it, glorying in those traditions which had long anticipated the new truths yet occasionally calling for certain modifications of the accepted secular wisdom in the name of their old faith. Thus in my lifetime various Jewish thinkers have demanded that we speak of Judaism in the terms of philosophies as varied as neo-Kantianism, naturalism, logical analysis, existentialism, process thought and neo-pragmatism. Others, abandoning the philosophic standard have found their formative truth in the social sciences, particularly sociology and its offshoot, anthropology while some seek cultural legitimation from one of the humanities like literary theory or the study of religion. In part because it has itself been fractured by this experience of rapidly shifting plausibility structures, in part because of its own honest critique of its own assumptions, neither the university as a whole nor any one of its disciplines can today easily command the spiritual authority it took as its due perhaps as recently as a generation ago. The root difficulty is that our academies and the modern ethos they advocate project far more expertise as relativizers of values rather than as the leaders whose secular vision can provide us with a freshly commanding ground for them. It is this value-vacuum, I contend, that has spawned the utterly unanticipated spiritual search and religious revival going on in western civilization, one seen most dramatically in the reborn vitality of classic fundamentalisms.

Sharing in religion's new self-respect if not in the certainty of those who know they possess God's own verbal revelation, I cannot, as my teachers did, allow the university to define how modern Jews should understand and live their faith. Nonetheless, respecting greatly what the university might still teach us, I, like many others, seek the fresh understanding that might come from articulating my faith in a university refined language. And the dialect that seems to me today most likely to allow me to speak least faithlessly of my Jewish truth I find among the babble that makes up the postmodern conversation. Let me now quickly but with some necessary detail, indicate the intellectual road which led me to my particular position.

The Winding Way of Twentieth Century Jewish Thought

For two centuries now the religions of the Western world have confronted a philosophical challenge, that sophisticated rationality says that what they assert to be true is, in reality, groundless. We need to understand, then, something of David Hume's intellectual challenge to religion and Immanuel Kant's initially impressive answer to it if we are to understand the core problem to which thinkers sought to respond.

In what we may call premodern times, culture was suffused with religiosity rather than secular. Medieval thought was built on the thesis that the human mind is capable of knowing the world as it really is and this notion was the basis of its remarkable efflorescence of religious philosophy. I can crudely picture this in the following way: even with my eyes closed, my mind — let us say a faculty associated with my brain — somehow goes out of my skull into the world, comprehends it in an idea and returns with it to my brain so that I now have a reliable understanding of how the world actually operates.

Modern philosophy, by contrast, begins by learning to doubt almost everything, the classic case being Descartes' insistence on skepticism toward ideas until he could grasp them as clear and distinct ideas. This inquisitiveness led the Scottish philosopher David Hume to ask how it was possible for the human mind to get, as it were, from inside a person, outside that person and into the world as it really is, and, acquiring knowledge about it, bring that knowledge back inside the person. That problem becomes particularly intense if one wants to still one's skepticism by adducing some reliable evidence that there is reliable evidence that what one has now come to know about the world is true. If, as Hume thought, the only reliable evidence is empirical, that one needs the testimony of one or more of our senses to verify what the mind now knows, how do we get from the raw sense data to abstract cognitive structures?

Consider, for example, the idea which was so indispensable to Hellenic and medieval thought, the notion of cause and effect. The mind finds it a most useful way to think about what transpires. But, Hume realized, no one has ever tasted, heard or felt a cause. We may think we have seen a cause as, in the classic example, when one sees a billiard ball hit another billiard ball and the second billiard ball immediately moves away. We quickly say that the first billiard ball caused the second billiard ball to move. But how can you prove that there really is something called a "cause" rather than something your mind has simply invented?

Once Hume unleashed that skeptical question and others like it the certainty of medieval philosophy collapsed and modern thought with its endless worry about how we know anything at all came into being. For a brief period it looked as if Immanuel Kant had once again brought stability to our intellectual life. Kant conceded Hume's point that there is no certain way that we can speak about what the world actually is. But he quickly added that we can, however, indicate with some precision how a rational mind functions in relation to the world. And as long as we are following rational patterns of thinking about the world, that is as reliable an understanding of reality as a rational person can hope for. Kant then proceeded to clarify how the good mind did that in relationship to science, to ethics and to aesthetics, the three diverse modes in which his analysis indicated the rational mind operated. Furthermore, he indicated how we managed to manifest one integrated rationality rather than devolving into a trizoid human personality.

The difficulty with this, however, was that anyone who accepted the Kantian solution to the Humean challenge had lost the world "outside." All that was left to the careful thinker now was how the rational mind properly functioned.

I have taken this detour into secular philosophy because its increasing skepticism left thoughtful religious believers in a fearful quandary. Religion is based upon the notion that God is real, that is, that God is not simply an idea of ours or an illusion but a reality independent of us. During the middle ages the thinkers of the three great religions of western civilization were convinced that the human mind could know — indeed, prove with conclusive evidence — that God was real. However, after the Kantian revolution one could not rationally gain access to anything metaphysical; all one could do was to work with how a fine mind operated. As a result of this revolution in certainty modern religious thinkers had to find a new way of asserting the truth of their faith. Mostly this took the form of beginning with some aspect of human experience and then arguing from its reality to the reasonable inference that there was a God to whom we should be devoted. For example, the Protestant theologian Friedrich Schleiermacher focused on our experience of dependency and most Jewish thinkers, following a theme of Kant's, built their religiosity on our rational ethical nature. In either case, they then indicated how religion grew out of our sense that there ought to be a God behind this experience, though this could now never be rationally established. In this kind of Kantian thinking — the language of most modern Jewish thought — God became an idea or a concept and to this day one encounters people in the Jewish community who cannot simply say "God" but must use a locution like "God idea" or "concept of God." There is, however, all the difference in the world between speaking of God as if God is an important or necessary aspect of one's thinking and knowing God as a real, independent other. Yet if one wanted to be rational it seemed necessary to live with God as desirable human idea.

Let me now turn to what Jewish thinkers have made of all this. In pursuing this strictly intellectual trail I do not mean to deprecate the importance of history and social experience. In many ways, I believe, they have more immediate effect upon a community than what philosophers are cogitating about. However, contemporary Jewish history and its effect on Jewish life and thought have been so thoroughly discussed that I am taking it for granted that you are reasonably familiar with the wars our country and the State of Israel have fought; with the State of Israel itself; with the Holocaust; and with the various major formative events of American Jewish life in our time. Since the intellectual figures who have accompanied this are less well-known, I wish to indicate how they have shaped the development of postmodern Jewish thought.

I begin with the early twentieth century German philosopher Hermann Cohen, the grandfather of modern Jewish thought. I have given this great neo-Kantian interpreter of Judaism this family honorific because he sets the pattern and standard for subsequent sophisticated thinking about Judaism. Of course, there were major Jewish thinkers in the 19th Century but none gave abstract, reflective thinking about Judaism such systematic coherence and intellectual cogency that it had long lasting consequences for later Jewish philosophy.

Cohen was an academic not a rabbi. He made his mark at the university with path-breaking secular work on Kant. That is critical to our discussion because he exemplified the modern approach to religious thought. Let me emphasize a point I have previously made: university intellectuality set the pattern of truth within which modern Jewish thinkers — like those of other religions — believed they needed to operate if they were to be persuasive. Cohen probably came to apply his philosophy to specifically Jewish questions due to the anti-Semitism which erupted in Germany in the 1870s — one which had a peculiarly academic slant because of its emphasis on race. Nonetheless, it should be noted that despite Cohen's extraordinary eminence as a German university philosophy *ordinarius* — our "full" professor — Cohen was always a loyal Jew. Even after years at the university he would return to his cantor father's *shul* and serve as one of the choir members on the *bimah*. So the sources of Cohen's Jewish philosophizing remain unclear. Nonetheless, at first in a series of essays and later (at the time of the First World War) in a full scale book, Cohen developed a systematic academic philosophy of Judaism.

It began from a consideration of human rationality and then reasoned its way to the divine. Cohen argued as the creator of one of the three great systems that revived Kant's thought late in the 19th Century. His philosophical premise was that every rational human being needs an integrated intellectual world view. That system had to encompass the three major ways in which the neo-Kantians taught that every rational mind operates, namely, in the scientific-mathematical realm; in the ethical realm; and in the aesthetic realm. For various philosophical reasons, Cohen gave ethics primacy in this process resulting in almost an identification of being rational with having ethical responsibility.

The climax of this analysis came in a quite secular question: how do you intellectually integrate these three disparate activities of the mind? He answered: in order to integrate your system you require another idea, one which will unite them without being involved in any of them except insofar as it grounds them all. And, he said, that uniquely significant, integrating, comprehensive idea is what religions call the idea of God. This purely philosophic argument for a universal concept of God, a God-idea primarily connected with human beings in terms of their universal ethics, Cohen later utilized to describe and validate Judaism. For he argued that, rationally understood, Judaism is the historical religion of ethical monotheism par excellence and thus, obviously, a fully modern yet true religion.

Even Jews who have never heard of Hermann Cohen know this view, one which became the basic ideology of most modern Jews in the western world. Until relatively recent years, when you asked Jews what Judaism was all about or the basic reason for any Jewish practice, their answer was, "It makes us ethical. And look how ethical we are." Cohen has had an extraordinary influence on modern Jewish thinking, not only substantively but as a model of philosophy being the means to explain Judaism. When later discussions indicated that a given philosophy would no longer work, thinkers would try another one, hoping eventually to

Judaism After Modernity

find one that everyone would accept as true and which would at the same time explain, validate and reinterpret Judaism. So for much of the 20th Century the goal for Jewish thinkers was to be a contemporary Maimonides who would take a philosophy given by the western world — a latter-day Aristotle — and expound Judaism in its terms.

But strangely enough, we do not find ourselves concerned with this version of our intellectual task at the end of the 20th century. Why is this the case? How is it that for much of this period intellectually minded Jews sought a rationalistic interpretation of their Judaism but today, while that quest is still being carried on, many thoughtful Jews are quite skeptical about philosophy's ability to yield a significant religious message and instead have far greater interest in Jewish mysticism. Nothing could have been further from Hermann Cohen and his colleagues' minds. They closely identified modernity with rationalism. Hence they denied the value of religious experience and considered mysticism, with its claims to a special realm of insight, the death of intelligent discourse.

Nonetheless, it became clear to many European thinkers after World War I, that they could no longer uphold the notion of human beings as fundamentally rational, as beings who would live by what reason indicated and whose character would be refined by the continual exertion of the mind. That optimism about humankind itself now seemed irrational and even as thinkers in the society sought new ways of thinking about religion some Jewish thinkers began to do the same.

In the United States, however, the optimism about humankind continued for far longer. Perhaps it was because war did not come to the U.S. with a similar immediacy until after World War II. Perhaps it was the exceptional opportunity that the flood of immigrants that came to this country until 1924 found here that gave them an inextinguishable optimism. Even during the days of the great depression of the 1930's, there was great hope. People who did not have the means or many of the protections that we today take for granted somehow had more confidence in themselves and their future — indeed, in the possibilities of America — than many in our affluent if often psychically depressed community now manifest. Whatever the reason, through World War II and the extraordinary economic expansion our country underwent for two decades, optimism ran high in this country.

One is therefore not surprised to find that the dominant philosophy among Jews in that period was another rational philosophy. This was no longer a philosophy founded on the basis of the neo-Kantian version of

German idealism, but an American way of thinking called naturalism. Instead of trusting to an analysis of how the mind at its best should work, these thinkers built their confidence on the scientific method. They hoped that if they could think about human problems in the manner that scientists went about their problem solving they would reach more useful and reliable conclusions than had the classic philosophers. The great Jewish proponent of this point of view was Mordecai Kaplan and he sought to provide a new rationalistic basis for Judaism, one based on naturalism. What made Kaplan particularly appealing was his pragmatic interest in going beyond abstract thought. He wanted to explain himself socially, why he and other Jews should be linked to the groups in which they found great meaning, not only America and humanity but the specific Jewish people as well.

To accomplish this goal he selected a scientific model for his thought which would make this possible. Note that working on the basis of a science would immediately indicate his rationalism and would also endow his thought with the high commendation that our culture gives to things scientific. So in the 1920s he set about modeling his philosophy of Judaism on the newly burgeoning science called sociology. Its study of human groups indicates that all human groups operate in a similar fashion: they create a culture, or, in the language of 1930's that Kaplan preferred, they create a civilization. Without any revelation or intervention by God every ethnic group naturally creates its own social self-consciousness and way of life. It connects this with its sense of its history, its response to its land and the special contours of its language; it develops its special calendar, designates its heroes, defines its celebrations, establishes its institutions, projects its values and celebrates all this in music, art and folklore. All this it transmits with great power through its folkways. To integrate all this and endow it with importance and immediacy, every group also creates a religion. And the apex of its religion is the idea of God it eventually sets forth.

This theory enabled Kaplan to make a most telling polemical point. The failings of Jewish life are intellectually due to our misunderstanding our true nature. We have been treating ourselves as if we were a religion; that is to say, another Western church. But the Jews are not a church. They are a people. And instead of creating a churchy religious style, which is what they thought was appropriate in the modern world, they need to establish a full-scale ethnic life, that is, live Jewish culture or civilization in its fully rounded form. When Jews see that their social reality is given full expression in a lively Jewish cultural life they will again embrace themselves as Jews and add their strength to the community.

Furthermore, Kaplan believed that this cultural emphasis would also go a long way to resolving the problem of making religion important. According to sociology, when ethnic life flourishes, there will naturally be a need for religion to tie its diverse aspects together. As the religion grows, sensitive people will create an idea of God as its capstone. But it needs to be an idea of God that is both culturally appropriate and fulfills its social function. Sociologically speaking the function of religion is to get people to try to improve themselves and Kaplan argued that this was the humanistic drive behind the classic religious term "salvation." He therefore proposed a definition of God that would meet these criteria. For Kaplan God is everything in nature that helps people to fulfill themselves. Note how it utterly fulfills the modern paradigm by beginning with the human and then moving to the divine. More significantly, Kaplan has not only defined God — a first in Jewish history — but done so in terms of human needs as science has helped us understand them. The trust in human rationality seems unbounded — even as in Cohenian neo-Kantianism — for once again our minds dictate what God can and cannot be.

It is this optimism about human powers which begins to fade as we move toward the latter part of the 20th Century. In Europe World War I forced people to face the dark and irrational aspects of human being; the way in which we regularly act so as to defeat ourselves; and how this is not simply remediable by further education, good government, full employment, or even psychotherapy. Increasingly all our strategies for trying to conquer our difficulties have their limits. Indeed they may create new evils. So it becomes necessary to account for our regularly showing ourselves to be unworthy of the trust we and others have had in ourselves.

I can trace the beginnings of postmodern Jewish thought — the proto-modern, if you will — to three figures who developed Jewish thought along new lines and recognized that they must begin to break with philosophic rationality. The lesser known one is Leo Baeck. He is particularly interesting because his book, *The Essence of Judaism*, in its greatly expanded second edition of 1923, is a conscious, rationalistic break with Hermann Cohen on the grounds that Cohen equates Judaism with philosophy and basically wants Jews to be philosophers. But if one looks at the reality of Jewish life — how people really practice it — it is not pure intellect that concerns believing Jews but intellect which acknowledges and celebrates a certain special experience. The religious person has a consciousness of the mystery which lies behind the ethics that rationality commands. More, it opens us to that which is beyond us, which brings us into being, which is permanent even though we are ephemeral. Out of this twin consciousness of rationality and mystery Judaism and its idea of God arise.

Baeck's understanding of God and religion marks a major break from the modern rationalistic understanding of human being. He still makes human experience fundamental but he is now willing to acknowledge that religion is founded on something beyond what the human mind can fully grasp. I see in this an opening toward the divine which, in more radical thinkers, will allow God to make an appearance as a fully independent reality.

We find that step beyond the human in both Franz Rosenzweig and Martin Buber. Again in books which appeared in the early 1920's two thinkers now say "Humanhood has its limits" and direct our attention beyond us to the reality to which religion points. In Rosenzweig's famous introduction to *The Star of Redemption*, he introduces us to the three elements which will be basic to his philosophy. They are "elements" of reality in the same way that we commonly have 92 elements as basic to our chemistry: that is, once you go beyond this substance, the material is no longer there. So for Rosenzweig reality has three givens, whether your rational mind likes it or not. One is, as he called it, "man." A second is the world and the third is God. Just that suddenly and bluntly God as a simply reality appears in a fundamental place in a non-Orthodox modern Jewish philosophy. Except insofar as Rosenzweig posits God as given, we do not have the common modern path leading from human experience to God. And this God, who is independent of human beings, can now be said to do something that had not previously been done in modern Jewish thought: God, and not just people, can be an active partner in the shaping of our religion. Despite this, Rosenzweig remained non-Orthodox and suggested that revelation is non-verbal with God "speaking" to human beings in the simple intimacy of love, where communication is real but beyond words.

Rosenzweig died before he could do very much about adumbrating this insight in Jewish life and institutions. But in the work of Martin Buber this same stance came to a somewhat different but more fecund working out. I think it so important to our time and our move beyond

Jewish modernity, that I want to give it some special attention in a moment. Suffice it now to say that Buber's God, whom we meet as a Thou, also has an independent role in our lives and that of our community as well. As we shall see, in his thought too, we move well beyond the modernist reliance upon the human but particularly since Buber's thinking ultimately exalted the experiential level it created problems of applicability as the decades passed. But it is an important milestone in the Jewish evolution to postmodernity which requires us to examine its successes and failures more closely.

We come back now to the United States and forward into the 1960s to talk about one further thinker, the only one besides Kaplan to develop his mature thought in this country, Abraham Heschel. He could not be satisfied with the thinking of Baeck, Rosenzweig and Buber — with whose thought he was quite familiar — for despite their departures from modernity he felt they remained too much a part of it. From his point of view they still made human experience too great a part of our understanding of who God is and what God wants of us. Heschel wanted to pursue God's reality more radically.

Where should we start our thinking about religion, you and I? Shall we begin, as Descartes urged us to, with doubt? But, Heschel will want to know why we trust our doubting so much Why should we be so devoted to our skepticism and take it utterly for granted? Should we not rather first recognize what a marvelous gift that we have, this ability to ask and to hope we can receive an answer? In Heschel's view we should begin our thinking with a sense of being blessed that we can think at all. We should never start our reflection with ourselves but with God, the grantor of these many beneficences. There is no way, Heschel insists, of making a beginning without God being there first to make it all possible. Not human experience on any level but the God who makes all human experience possible and gives us a basis for our thinking ought to be the starting point of our religiosity.

Again and again Heschel's thinking calls us to reverse the questions humanistic versions of religion have taught us were sophisticated. Note the very title of his major work, *God in Search of Man*. It is a quite conscious reversal of the modern notion that religion proceeds from the human to the divine. Heschel argues the Biblical case, that it is God who seeks us and he hopes that he can awaken us from our modern denial of such experience to recognize its ongoing truth. So Heschel's thought moves on to teach us a greater sensitivity to God and God's greatness. In his thought God's stature is raised to something approximating the Biblical vision of God with human beings now approaching God and religion with appropriate awe.

He completes this reversal by then arguing for God as the giver of revelation, specifically, of the prophets as accurate in their depiction of God and God's demands. Since in Jewish tradition Moses is the chief of the prophets this means that the Torah is now God's own revelation — both Oral and Written — so we are called upon to take it with a new seriousness. And that completes the reversal of modern Jewish thought. From rationalisms which began with setting human beings as the arbiters of God and religion we have arrived, two-thirds of a century later, to the point where we are being asked, in effect, to return to what is a sophisticated Jewish fundamentalism. In a way that I have sought to clarify elsewhere, I believe Heschel's stance corresponds closely to what has been happening in Western civilization generally. But I think we must turn to Buber's thought in some detail if we are to see how the case for most postmodern Judaism took shape.

The Teacher We Must Move Beyond

I cannot recall a thinker who has been more helpful to me and, I believe, should be more helpful to those in the Jewish community who seek to plumb the depth of their faith than Martin Buber. Moreover, his influence has extended far beyond our midst for the issues with which he dealt so creatively affected the entire Western religious world. He deserves proper intellectual honor, which means that we not only acknowledge how much we have learned from him but also that we transcend his teaching. I can best illustrate my meaning by retelling one of the many Hasidic stories that Buber recast in his special mode. After Noach had inherited his father Menachem's court as the Rebbe of Lekhovitz the elders of the community gathered and gently offered some criticism. "Rebbe," they said to him, "why is it that you do not carry on our community practices the way your father did?" The rebbe looked at them with great surprise, and said to them, "But I do exactly as my father did. He did not imitate, and I do not imitate."

It seems to me that we pay only a limited homage to great teachers if we simply take over their thought and carry it on without any modification. So I should like to explain to you why, despite Martin Buber's extraordinary helpfulness, his very intellectual success requires us to move beyond his ideas to that new way of understanding Judaism which I characterize as postmodern.

Martin Buber's solution to the problem of reconciling Judaism and modernity has clearly been of deep and lasting significance to many religious people. Note that I have shifted the discussion from rationality to "religious people." That is, I am speaking now not of professional philosophers or of their rationalistic followers at the academy or in the culture. Rather I speak now of the many people who have come to see that as rationality became ever more tightly defined it seemed ever more inadequate to the complexities of human existence. That was certainly true of those many Jewish and Christian believers — the people most influenced by Martin Buber's thought — who somehow knew that God is real, much more real than the philosophers could credit God with being. Knowing that God has a reality which extends beyond the mental and the intellectual, they sought a way to explain this to themselves and others in some intelligent fashion.

Buber approaches this problem not as a philosophical intellectual but as a religious person and this required him to express himself in a rather different and uncommon language. His stylistic oddity arises from his effort to give a description of the unusual way in which you and I go about knowing things in our complex world. He said we do this in a strange, two-fold manner. Most of the time our knowing takes place by examination and analysis. We stand back from the focus of our inquiry and try to be dispassionate about it so as to clarify our impressions, to seek definitive description and precise understanding. In this mode of knowing we often feel we have only come to true knowledge when we can take things apart and put them back together.

This has turned out to be marvelously useful to us. It has yielded the continuity on which we base our lives and the control of various aspects of nature which has astonishingly enlarged the opportunities before us. Buber is not an enemy of knowing in this fashion; he recognizes it as a mode of coming to terms with the universe which has great human value. But the marvelous successes resulting from knowing in this cool, analytical fashion have made us want to extend its competence to knowing everything and everybody. The malady of modernity, Buber felt, is that we no longer can easily reach out to the world in any other fashion than this quasi-scientific mode.

To take the simplest exceptions, that kind of knowing may be fine as long as we are speaking of objects but what happens when it gets applied, indeed applied with a certain privileged exclusivity, to persons?

Think back for a moment to your having a consultation in a medical clinic with a physician or technician who has learned more details about you from the file of your tests than you have ever known about yourself. This expert, to whom you have gone voluntarily and who specializes in cool-headed examination and analysis, now carefully correlates your data with that from many other people and seeks to talk to you about all of this. How do you feel when that person, perhaps harassed, perhaps trained in an older style, perhaps following an institutional manual for cases such as yours, addresses you as another instance of whatever it is you are diagnosed as but seems otherwise quite detached and unconcerned about you? Most of us in that situation will begin to feel, "That's not really me they are describing. I wish they would pay attention to me." Something similar happens when we are talking earnestly to an intimate and suddenly have the sense that they're not really listening to us. When that occurs we often simply stop talking — which will lead our friend to say, "Why did you stop?" If we respond, as we are likely to, "You weren't listening," they may indignantly retort, "What do you mean, I wasn't listening? I certainly was." And then, like an effective tape recorder they repeat every word you said. We are then likely to respond, perhaps sadly, "You may have heard me but you weren't really paying attention."

In this quite common human distinction between hearing people and really paying attention to them we encounter the subtle, other form of knowing of which Buber wanted to make us conscious. Consider another such ordinary interchange. Not uncommonly we have the experience of chatting with someone, perhaps someone we've known for some time yet, as we say, have never developed a relationship with. But on this occasion there is something about what transpires between you that leads you to think afterwards that there is a lot more to the person than you had realized, that, as we often put it, they are a "real person." Incidentally, nothing terribly important or notable may have occurred. You may just have simply bumped into one another at the laundry or at the supermarket and exchanged a few words. That was all, but, for a change, it was, as we say, "real."

Something similarly instructive may happen when you try to tell somebody something very important to you and find you simply can't say it properly, the words just wouldn't come out right. In that situation you can feel terribly embarrassed and foolish — that is, until you look over at the other person and realize that your inarticulateness is unimportant. They know what you wanted to say. More than that, you know that they know what you wanted to say. And were that not enough, they know that you know that they know what you wanted to say. Something has happened that was quite beyond words but utterly communicative. Persons have met and truly come to understand each other.

Buber wants us to have proper respect for this non-verbal, elusive experience. Though we often try to hide from such knowing or are encouraged by our culture to deprecate it, sometimes people get to know one another as the whole persons they really are. It is not just a matter of appreciating our looks, or our words, or the image we have learned to project, but us.

This is Buber's second way of human knowing and it has its own appropriate style. It cannot take place as long as we maintain our customary analytical and observational distance. We have to somehow "be there" for the other person, to be, as we say, "open" to them. And if it happens that the other person is somehow there available to you, this kind of exchange may take place. We cannot force it for all our good intentions. It happens or it does not in a rather mysterious kind of way, as any of us know who have hoped to have a memorable evening with someone we truly care about and for which we have made elaborate plans. Nonetheless, we can never know what finally will happen and thus we will be deeply grateful whenever a memorable occasion of true encounter takes place.

Buber also wants us to know that this is not a matter of our sensations, how much we felt moved. That simply makes us self-concerned. What gives genuine meeting with another its power is that it exposes us to an order of quality and human being which otherwise is often missing from our lives. Note its consequences. If such meetings take place with some frequency, we turn acquaintances into friends. If they keep recurring, we speak of loving someone. The love and understanding which builds between creates that precious thing we call a relationship. In a true relationship the intimacy that grows between us increasingly affects our individual lives. For if I am to maintain my relationship with you I know there are certain things I must do and others I must not. That is true even if you don't tell me explicitly what you expect of me. The astonishing rule is: "If you really love me, you should know." And regardless of its not being put into words it has commanding power for if this relationship is dear to me, I must do what it implies. Not to act that way is a transgression of what we mean to one another; it is a sin against the relationship and damages it. To restore it, I must make up for what I have done, most likely by confessing to you what I've done, trying to make up for it, resolving not to do it again and asking your forgiveness. That pattern of atonement may set our relationship right again. For perhaps you will accept me despite my failing; you will, in that touching metaphor, "bear" with me (yourself carry my fault). If you — we — can do this, our relationship will emerge from the trial even stronger than it was before, for now the human will to change is met by the freely given love of the one we have wronged.

Some further words need to be said about Buber's vision of the dynamic quality of living this way. Once we recognize that we humans have these two quite different ways of knowing we cannot expect our inner lives to be static. Most of our experience takes place as we make our way utilizing the first, the withdrawn kind of knowing. But in the midst of this, we can slip into the second, engaged one, rather quickly — so it seems — only as quickly to slip out of it again. So it goes, time spent in relationship to objects which is periodically punctuated by the knowing we most easily identify with persons. That's the way our lives go by and that is true even with people we dearly love. We cannot dwell on the level of intimate engagement for very long. Most of the time we slip into ordinariness and instead of being illuminating our life with them is dull. And then, the spark of true encounter will be there again explaining just why our entire lives are built upon this relationship. These moments are most precious indeed for they give our lives their lasting significance. And they allow us to return to the routine existence of the everyday knowing our lives are very much more than this, particularly as we seek to reshape the commonplace in terms of the true interpersonal.

This Buberian model thus gives us new insight into the problem of evil. You and I have a loving relationship; why then do you hurt me? Worse, you who are most intimate with me can now wound me in ways nobody else could. Often I don't understand why this terrible thing took place and neither do you. But if we are fortunate, if one of us is remarkably forgiving, perhaps because the other is seriously repentant, the relationship can survive even that grievous a blow. I can love you even though I don't understand you, and I am deeply, deeply grateful that you can do the same for me. That is love indeed.

After this long digression into human nature and relationship we are ready to move back to our Humean-Kantean problem: how can religious people claim to know that God is real? Once we accept Buber's understanding of our two ways of relating to reality we can ask, "Which of these is more applicable to religion? to God? Do we reasonably expect to know God by our ordinary way of knowing things, our way of knowing an object? Is reflection upon faith best carried out by examination and demonstration, by asking for proofs such as that given by taking something apart and putting it back together? Should its great confirmation be to yield a description or a definition? In Buber's terms, do we know God, so to speak, in the way that we customarily know objects? Surely that question has a reasonably unequivocal answer in the Jewish tradition. For to say we know God the way we know objects is to turn God into an idol. And it doesn't make any difference if the "object" of our analysis and construction is a physical thing or a pure idea.

But none of this stringency against idolatry is applicable to the way we relate to persons for to objectify or claim controlling knowledge of the other is to deny them their very status as persons. Moreover, when we are convinced we have a genuine relationship it seems foolish to think that we are merely involved with something inside our skulls. (As it were, an I-I relationship.) Please do not ask me "how I know" that the other person is real. I make that request because in our culture answers to "How" questions must be given in I-it form. Too simply put, for us "explanation" means putting things in terms of the scientific description of nature. So in Buber's thought one cannot be true to the personhood of persons and seek to explain a person fully in I-it terms. As long as I remain in the I-it analytic mode I'll never get to know you; I can only get to know you when I stop holding back and am there for you as you are for me. I will only get to know you I-thou.

If Buber is right, we know God the way we know persons. Note, please, Buber is not saying that God is a person. That would be an I-it statement and therefore impermissible in relation to God. All this language about knowing persons is quite metaphorical when speaking about God. Nonetheless it is so real to us we can understand it despite its imprecision. Moreover, it powerfully opens up aspects of God's reality and our relationship to God. We know the God of our I-thou relationship is real in the same way we know persons are real. And as we cannot give an I-it proof that this or that person is truly trustworthy or as real as we are, so we are content with a similar situation with regard to God. But we do, as it were, have a way we can prove whether someone is worthy of our devotion. We try to get together and see if we can become friends. Then we see what happens between us as a result of our relationship. In this odd way we are willing to risk much, sometimes our very lives, on the "reality" of the other person. We do the same with God, seeking God's presence and trying to build up a relationship. At our best, we learn not to cognize God but to love God with all our heart, soul and might. That is the I-thou way of "proving" the other's reality, as strange as it may seem by I-it standards.

Modern religion, esteeming science, created an I-it God. All it could ever yield was myself, that aspect of the self — my rationality, my ethics, my consciousness — from which I created an idea of God. But Buber's God is met, known, related to as the other side of the hyphen, as God is. This God is as real as anyone we truly love. Understood I-thou, God is no longer simply a concept inside my head as the philosophers' I-it rules required them to think. God is an independent other who, like all thous, needs to be met as much on their own (here, God's) terms as our own.

This allows Buber to assert that God — and not just the individual — has an input into our religion. In a fashion that is neither reductive nor obscurantist Buber restores God's revelation to religion. Because Buber has a new way of speaking about the reality of God and religion he can give revelation an extraordinary new interpretation, that what God reveals to us is not verbal. Traditionally, revelation meant that God imparted God's own truth to human beings (in a verbal form they could reasonably comprehend and follow). This classic notion of God "giving" the Torah had been radically inverted by modern thinkers and become some variety of human spiritual or intellectual search and discovery. It was "revelation" only because it opened the secular mind to that which had remained hidden to it because of its secular blinders. With the restoration of a God who is not primarily a human inference/assertion, that real God can now do even more: have independent input into our lives.

Buber's conception of the I-thou relationship, however, now changes the older understanding of revelation drastically. Once God gave words, Torah, and the result is orthodoxy and its pattern of authority. Reinterpreting this in light of the experience of dialogue, Buber says that what God reveals to us is not verbal. As in the most significant human communication, what most importantly passes between us is beyond words. It is we who supply language, the symbolic frame to carry what we have come to know and be. So the Torah and the rest of the Bible arose as a human response to the presence of God. So to speak, these texts are our diary or love letters written by our forebears in the light of what it was like to have encountered God. We call these records Sacred Scripture because we, coming along centuries later, read these texts and recapitulate the experience of our ancestors; the God whom they met, we meet through their words. And if that does not happen as frequently to us as to them, that may well be our fault for being unable to read the ancient words with proper I-thou openness.

To have given us a language to explain how we know that God is real on God's own and not just as a human idea or imaginative projection; to have made it possible for us to understand how God might have a real and significant input into our religion and yet have left significant space for us as God's dialogue partners; to have given us a recognition that this is an ongoing dynamic process which different personalities and different temperaments will express in different kinds of understandings; all this — and much that ought well be said — explains why many of us know that Martin Buber has to be our teacher.

Yet even if we can move this far toward postmodernity, Buber leaves us with so serious a problem that, for all that we learn from him, we are required to go beyond him. We can see evidence of this difficulty in his own thought, one he did not seek to resolve for whatever reason. Buber taught that when we are in the I-thou relationship we are out of time, place and all the common other determinants of which we speak when we describe persons in I-it fashion. I can understand why Buber asserted this. He wanted to say that there is some place inside every human being where one can be touched by the divine and as a result have a basis upon which to judge one's group and one's society. Because this is the case we are rightly able to exercise moral or prophetic judgment upon them. Were this not so, we would be at the mercy of the various determinants which customarily influence our lives and never have a legitimate basis for criticizing the evil that we often see around us. Instead, Buber assures us that in the I-thou we have a pristine moment in which we are suddenly nothing but a pure self meeting with God, as it were, the greatest of all selves.

However, this radical individualism creates the problem of validating communities and community discipline. Buber's own response to this difficulty is that genuine communities arise whenever persons who each individually experience the I-thou also find themselves related with many others at a joint center. That view tends to make communities voluntary and temporary. But Buber also asserts that when such communities are shaped in extraordinary experiences — as happened to the Jewish people at Sinai — they can acquire a national responsibility which is passed on from generation to generation independent of experience. This was not a theoretical matter for Buber as we can see from his special variety of Zionism. (Buber, it should be noted, was an early follower of Theodore Herzl and an important figure in developing the cultural and religious side of Zionism.) Buber argued in several notable speeches to World Zionist Congresses that the Jewish nation had to live up to a charge which had been laid upon it in Biblical times and now still pertained. He specifically applied this in the 1920's to Arab-Jewish relations and then when he came from Hitler's Germany to the land of Israel in the late 1930's he sought to create a movement for a bi-national state in Palestine.

Thus Buber concedes that a command can be given not only to a person but to a community — and given in such a way that it rightly imposes itself on the nation as long as it continues its historical existence. It is an idea which resonates within me and many other loyal Jews, explaining much of what we feel about our relationship to the Jewish people. We Jews today are not a community that starts *de novo* out of our immediate relationships with God. Rather our community hears a compelling instruction coming to us from our history, one which guides us as to how we must live today, and points us toward a messianic future that we sometimes do not have the courage to see or have the foresight to foretell. That corporate vision more than any individual experience goes to make up the heart of Judaism eternal. It is a critical component of our postmodernity. But we cannot derive that essential Jewish sensibility from Buber's notion that when we stand commanded in the I-thou relationship we are outside of community, history and time, properly moved only by what God says to us personally at this moment.

Here Buber fails us. He is, I think, being overly influenced by Kant's construction of the issues of the legitimacy of autonomy and self-legislation. But the reality of our corporate Jewish existence — and of that of any other legitimate religious or social community — has to be more than single individuals momentarily joined together by a centering experience of God. Even to explain his Zionism we require a sense in which we as persons stand within a certain history — one we may seek to reshape and refurbish — and that it is as historic individuals we seek to project our group forward in a way which is consonant with what that community has experienced in the past and the goals that has set for its future. Deeply affected by the Holocaust and its threat to the Jews as a group, renewed in our corporate consciousness by the threats to the State of Israel and by the dissolving entropy intermarriage is bringing into our community, we know that the Jewish people as well as an independent God must be part of our postmodern Judaism.

To elaborate that Jewish philosophy even Martin Buber, in many ways the most appealing of our modern Jewish thinkers, is inadequate, by his very success creating problems he like his modern colleagues could not resolve. A fuller postmodern Judaism will argue that the universal — Buber's individual — does not precede any particularity but is rather an outcome of them.

Postmodern Judaism, One Theologian's View

My discussion of the way postmodernity enables us to preserve Buber's religious gains but now centrally face up to the issue of particularity — a feminist ethical issue as well as one of specific Jewish ethnic concern — must begin with what seems to some of the academic readers of my work, *Renewing the Covenant, a Theology for the Postmodern Jew,* my idiosyncratic use of the term "postmodern." I shall then sketch in something of the results that flow from my application of my interpretation of it.

To begin with, I find the accents of postmodernity particularly congenial because they impose few restraints and tolerate considerable ambiguity. People far more learned than I am in the intricacies of French philosophic and literary thought wish, however, to draw a line at this point. They find it odd indeed that anyone would want to speak of himself as a postmodern and not follow the paths laid down by Derrida or perhaps pursue the fresh developments suggested by Lyotard or others. I find this suggestion strange. How can deconstruction be applied to everyone else's foundationalism but not to its own as it seeks to move from deconstructive criticism to positive statement? Is not a Derridean orthodoxy an oxymoron?

I prefer to read as the critical text of our time the actual history of people questing for reliable meaning. Seeking an ultimate and solid ground of values, a significant minority of people in our civilization have turned from the university to religion to help them understand what they intuitively know to be true, that not everything is relative and that humanhood is intimately bound up with acts we do not do and some others we are bound to try to do. As I see it, many of us find ourselves in the situation of experience seeking understanding. The great French deconstructionists have brilliantly cut the ground out from under the pretensions of others but they have not yet explained convincingly how they can move on to commandingly ground values. Thus in my religio-intellectual quest they can only be of secondary, not primary help to me.

Fortunately, the cultural horizon of postmodernism has been much broader than French critical theory. It embraces a rather broad scale concern with how we might think if we did not take ourselves to be Cartesian selves. Its emphasis on the linguisticality of thought does not create impenetrable barriers for the assertion of religious truth as positivism and many forms of rationalism did. To a Jew, its concern with creative linguistic misreadings awakens memories of rabbinic *midrash* — the classic language of Jewish theology — while its stress on usage rather than pure idea immediately involves us in community and historicity, two notions critical to Jewish faith yet problematic for prior modern Jewish thinkers. It is this amorphous linguistic, communitarian postmodernity that provides me with the least inadequate cultural language I know for speaking of the truth by which I and most other modern Jews live.

Three other features of my variety of postmodern discourse require comment. First, I endorse its polemic against our language's hidden metaphysics or prescriptive logic. I then move beyond its critical preoccupations to positive apologetic formulations via its vague appreciation of the truth of personal experience, of which I take relationship to be the critical instance. I shall say more about this later. Here I only want to make note of the controversy arising from my decision to assert my Jewish conviction that, in contemporary terms, we can have unmediated, compelling, quality-laden religious experience. I devote chapter 19 of *Creating the Covenant* to my reasons for affirming this position against the challenge of many philosophers. Though I necessarily do so in a non-philosophic manner I believe what I do is not only understandable but a variety of thoughtful postmodern discourse. (For the record let me indicate that I do not there discuss this issue in its prior Jewish incarnation, Hermann Cohen's radical neo-Kantian notion of the priority of reason to all experience.) This is but one example of the way my understanding of postmodernity allows me regularly to find a language for my disagreements with modern rationalisms that negate or vacate

God, devalue community and practically reduce the self to the mind. Positively, I can clarify much of the Jewish richness of the connections between God, community and self by means of the metaphor of personal relationship.

Second, as is already evident, my thinking exhibits a certain circularity. My experience as a believer provides me with a measure of certainty and thus too with my most fundamental criterion of judgment. Thus, not surprisingly, as the fuller contours of my faith emerge from my reflection they very much resemble the barely articulate ones with which I began. As a postmodern I see no scandal in this procedure. Once we acknowledge the situatedness of all our thought and deny Cartesian introspection a privileged transcendence of human particularity, we recognize that all serious thinking is significantly circular. That is, no methodology escapes the shaping of time and place, of language and person. The method we choose as appropriate to a given topic cannot claim more than guild or community objectivity — and perhaps only reflects class or person — yet it substantially determines the content that will result from its employment.

Third, the postmodern mood has considerable tolerance for the limitations of system. In fact, my apologetic thought has less coherence than the academic modern mind commonly desires. It is not nearly as tidy as I may have previously intimated here. Though I claim to give Judaism priority in my thought, on occasion, most notably with regard to the notions of revelation and authority, I deviate from my community's classic teaching and allow influences from the culture to reshape my faith. Were I, like most other Jewish thinkers, to insist on the priority of tradition or that of culture, or, indeed, bow to the necessity of settling the issue, my thought would reflect the pre-modern tones of the one or the modern notes of the other. But in the languages for increased self-understanding the culture now puts at my disposal I find I cannot be true to my Jewish relationship with God and myself by forcing myself into a linguistically determined systematic coherence.

I am grateful to postmodern discourse for authorizing those who admit they cannot give reasonably unambiguous voice to the *logos* to speak their truth, sloppy in structure as it may seem to some. This structural untidiness is abetted by my writing with conscious imprecision, a choice designed to warn my reader that my theology does not allow for geometric clarity. Against some postmoderns, however, I do not glory in unsystematic thought. God being one, I seek as much personal and intellectual integration as I can find, so I try to present my ideas in as orderly and reasonable fashion as I can. I have no rule which explains or authorizes this procedure. If I did I would be a rationalist, at least as rationalisms currently present themselves in our culture. Accepting my temporality, I remain open to the possibility that a new construal of thoughtfulness and/or the human condition will allow for more fully integrated Jewish theologies. Until then I look forward to what our community's liturgical use of Zech. 9.14 teaches, that only in the Days of the Messiah will *Adonai's* name be one as *Adonai* is one.

Perhaps all this will be clearer if I speak in less than 320 pages of the substance of *Renewing the Covenant*. It consists of four unequal parts. The first of these provides the experiential foundation for the three analytic, more abstract sections which follow.

Thinking as a postmodern, the religious experience which I turn to is that of my community, the Household of Israel, to be sure, as I individually have experienced and now interpret it. Moderns, of course, thought quite individualistically and thus inevitably had the problem which so plagues us today of authorizing community, a polemical issue of great concern to me. While the university has supplied us with a number of ways of dealing with personal religious experience, it offers no help in speaking directly of what a community has "personally" undergone. I have no presently legitimate hermeneutic by which to validate such a reading; no clear set of criteria by which I arrived at my judgments; and many thoughtful people see things quite differently, though I argue that they and much of our community have misunderstood our situation. I am, however, emboldened in my interpretation of our response to recent events by the uncommonly great breadth of data my view explains, to my mind one much more encompassing than that of alternative explanations. I can only submit my views to the judgment of the academic and believing communities and hope that a significant segment of each will agree with me.

In my view the particular Jewish turn to postmodernity must be envisioned as an aspect of Western civilization's disillusionment with the modern ethos — a consequence of our thorough Jewish modernization and secularization. Intellectually and spiritually, this change of ethos has grown out of our loss of a ground of values. The resulting disenchantment with modernity on this score has resulted in a renewal of Moslem, Christian and Jewish fundamentalisms as well as a proliferation of new religions. Against those who believe that postmodernity means that God is dead — a peculiarly dogmatic assertion for a movement that prides itself on deconstruction — I associate myself with all those who know that our values are not mere word play but are rooted in the universe itself. But against all orthodoxies, I know that some of the spiritual truth of modernity remains valid, specifically, that human dignity involves a significant measure of self-determination and thus now must find a place in a postmodern religiosity which grounds the self in God and community. (This assertion, more than anything else, clarifies why Buber, not Heschel, is the pivotal thinker on our way to postmodernity.) I am confirmed in this view by the fact that, for all their appeal, orthodoxies have not won the hearts of most thoughtful believers in the West, troubled by modernity as they are.

Our particular Jewish version of this development stemmed largely from our response to the Holocaust. Most observers concluded from it that God was dead. I see this, ironically enough, as the high point of the modernistic view of religion, one in which ethics and reason are foundational and God secondary if not dispensable. Even as a descriptive observation this judgment failed; the significant post-Holocaust Jewish movements have not been atheist and secular but religious, even mystical, and that among non-Orthodox as well as Orthodox Jews. Intellectually too, the Jewish death of God movement collapsed as ethics themselves became problematic and the steady evidence of human perversity made a humano-centric faith wildly optimistic. For many Jews, an educated, cultured humankind that can produce or abet a Holocaust is no longer worthy of ultimate confidence.

But now a paradox confronted these once enthusiastic moderns. If the moral chasm between the death camp Nazis and their Jewish victims cannot be relativized but points to a standard of absolute value, if that standard can no longer be found in a secular assertion about universal human rationality, then they needed a new ground of value. They thus came to realize, almost despite themselves, that this conviction of theirs was a matter of faith, that they believed much more than they thought they had. Now a postmodern deconstructive reading of the assertion that God was dead is possible. Following Feuerbach we can say that the opposite of its assertion was true, that the "god" who died in the Holocaust was not the God of Israel's tradition — in Whom few had believed in any case — but the functioning "god" of moderns, humankind, ourselves. And it is this loss of primal self-confidence which so shook the Jewish community and has given it its own version of our civilizations's endemic aimlessness and depression.

A second result of our spiritual upheaval as a result of the Holocaust was our turn from enthusiastic universalism to a pronounced particularism, our version of the communitarianism so characteristic of the postmodern ethos. Many commentators have spoken about this as a result of world Jewry's experience of the Israeli Six Day War of 1967. I do not see how that phenomenon could have taken place had it not been for the discussion of the Holocaust which had been so prominent a feature of the preceding few years. In the threat to the survival of the Jewish community a new issue was posed for the community: was it sufficient for modern Jews to be good people in general with a few Hebraic adornments or was there something in corporate Jewish existence that had a touch of absoluteness about it? Our community is still divided on that question but the rate of intermarriage and its consequences for Jewish continuity continue to force the issue to the center of Jewish consciousness. Clearly, Jewish particularism, in both non-Orthodox and Orthodox manifestation has reasserted itself as a central aspect of postmodern Jewish faith.

Yet it is precisely in both these manifestations that a third insight makes its claims on the bulk of our community: most of us newly believing particularists know that it would be against our most fundamental sense of who we are called to be in our relationship with God as part of the people of Israel if we had to surrender our right of self-determination utterly. That is to say, in our new postmodern religiosity we cannot be Orthodox (as, in effect, Heschel called us to be), nor can we non-Orthodox particularists be unreflective supporters of the State of Israel. Rather we know we need to retain a place for individual autonomy even if our freedom must be rethought in terms of its new context. And it is out of this continuing appreciation of selfhood (reshaped by its postmodern context) that our basis for the desirability of democracy and pluralism, and thus our refurbished sense of universalism arises.

The three affirmations resulting from this experiential foundation set the topics of the theological reflection which follows and takes up the bulk of the book. It should be noted, however, that the idea of the responsible self, so fully adumbrated in modern Jewish thought, is not given independent treatment but accepted as a common item of contemporary exchange. I analyze it only in terms of its new postmodern understanding. That is, I ask what it would mean to speak of the self when it is substantially structured not by pure autonomy but by its grounding in a relationship with God, a relationship it shares in community as part of the Jewish people's historic Covenant with God. The result of all this is a new theory of non-Orthodox Jewish duty, the acts which constitute the primary expression and medium of Jewish holiness.

I then deal, in the first substantive section, with what it might mean that God rightly commands us yet is intimately involved with us. This requires a reworking of the notion of transcendence that is true not only to God's authority but to human freedom and corporate relationship with God. Two other old religious themes require postmodern reconceptualization. First, what can we say about the nature of God and thus about evil now that rationalisms have only a limited hegemony in theology? Second, what dare we assert God actually does now that science has been demythologized into a construction of reality?

Given our postmodern situatedness, these issues, like all others, must be treated holistically. Thus, questions about God necessarily involve me in two other theological motifs, Jewish particularity and, in my non-Orthodoxy, with a self dignified by Covenantal autonomy.

The second substantive section deals with the people of Israel and is founded on briefs for the sociality of selves and the communitarian ground for universalism. All observers agree that Jewish particularism increased as a result of the Holocaust but we differ over whether this imperative has an essentially secular, ethnic root or a theological one, that a certain cosmic quality attaches to Jewish peoplehood before God. Practically, the Holocaust radicalized the question of the significance of Jewish survival and the threats to the State of Israel kept it current. Today it arises in more benign form as Jewish intermarriage increases Jewish assimilation. One hears the echoes of an extreme of modernization in the resigned notion that Jewishness is only another if a laudable cultural form, one which is secondary to being a fine, ethical human being. For a sizable minority among us, including me, good people are not simply Jews without Hebraism but Jewish religious living teaches us that our ethnicity involves a singularly valuable relationship with God.

Intellectually, how can we not be particularists? In a postmodern time how shall we justify beginning with the universal — a theory of religion or of human rationality or experience — and only then seek such particularity as our theory allows? In postmodern humility we must acknowledge that all thought begins particularistically, that giving up our group may mean giving up our universalism. Hence I inquire how the self-legislating, single self and this folk related to God fit together, how their particular relationship with God can be characterized and what this new particularity says about universalism and how it is affected by it.

These two postmodern religious motifs — the turn to God and the particular — are common to Orthodox and non-Orthodox Jewish postmodernity. Their divergent understandings arise, however, from the non-Orthodox insistence on the continuing spiritual validity of a central theme of modern Judaism: that personal dignity necessarily involves a substantial measure of self- determination. (Again, against Heschel.) My religious holism substantially rejects Kant's secular autonomy by incorrigibly linking the autonomous self to God as one of the people, Jewish or human, while rejecting the classic Jewish notions of verbal revelation and God-authorized human law. The issue of feminism as good as settled that question for many of us but there have long been other good reasons for thinking of religion as a more human project than our tradition acknowledged, as chapter 17 of my book indicates.

All this comes to a climax in a theory of Jewish duty, one elaborated by employing though dialectically communalizing the Buberian notion of human relationship as its key metaphor, a notion I defend against its critics. I epitomize these ideas in the classic notion of Covenant now seen relationally rather than in its traditional sense of contract. This makes it possible to understand how a self can be commandingly involved with God and with a people yet remain true to its individuality. It is my hope that this exercise in thinking carefully about our Jewish belief will make it possible for many in our community to live more faithfully as part of the Covenant.

Chapter 11

෪෬

Postmodernity and the Quintessential Modern Jewish Religious Movement

F or nearly two centuries now almost all Jews who could modernize have done so. They knew that modernity was good for them, that the great gains that democracy, equality and opportunity afforded them overrode the Jewish problems connected with modernization. The genius of Reform Judaism, as Michael Meyer has shown in his impressive history of our movement, *Response to Modernity*, lay in adapting to and seeking to transform this determining social development. And since this thrust to be part of modernity still drives much of contemporary Jewish life, it continues to energize Reform Judaism.

But if modernity is losing its allure and we are moving toward a postmodern era then we should be changing certain of our emphases — I propose no more than that but I consider them course corrections critical to our continuing religious vitality. I consider Alex Schindler's leadership of the UAHC so distinguished by his canny perception of the changes in our historic situation that it seemed a fitting tribute to his accomplishments to venture some thoughts about the agenda facing his successor.

Let me immediately qualify my aims. No one can be certain where history and culture are heading so these views are speculative — though they come with considerable evidence behind them and spring from a perspective that uniquely clarifies the many changes we see taking place around us. Then too, I use the term "postmodern" without stressing the "post," though some postmoderns want to create a contemporary equivalent to the ghetto. By contrast, I think it important that we carry forward what we believe are modernity's lasting spiritual insights. Nonetheless, "post" must not be slighted for I am also convinced we cannot import modern spirituality into a changed ethos without reshaping its central affirmations.

The cultural shift called postmodernism did not first arise among Jews out of their unique recent experience. Rather, it was evident all over Western civilization as the twentieth century proceeded and doubts about modernity's beneficence became prominent and widespread. Two particular irritants were political malfeasance and the general deterioration of the quality of life, but disappointment increasingly tinged much of life with dejection. The Enlightenment, the intellectual credo of modernity, had promised that replacing tradition with rational skepticism, hierarchy with democracy, and custom with freedom would bring messianic benefits. The conclusion was inescapable: it certainly hasn't.

On a deeper level, the loss of confidence in Enlightenment values came from the collapse of its intellectual foundations. The assumptions about mind, self and human nature that once powered the bold move into greater freedom now seem questionable. All had a profound influence on modernized Jews, those virtuosi of cultural adaptation. To give three instances: re-reading Abraham Heschel's theoretical works today one hears his plea for an authoritative, God-centered revelation as a premature response to this change of mood. It also helps explain the evanescence of "modern Orthodoxy" into "centrist Orthodoxy" while the most vital growth on the religious right came among those groups who consciously distanced themselves from the modern. And the utterly unanticipated Jewish turn to mysticism now seems a natural reaction against modernity's rigid rationalism.

A Phenomenon Eluding Definition And Lacking A Center

The demystification of modernity is manifest in many fields but it has no accepted ideology though some would like to make the French critic and philosopher Jacques Derrida its central theoretician. For many reasons, I think postmodernism is best described as a moving cultural wave continually redirected by people applying its energy to their activity. Architecture offers the most accessible example. There one sees the sleek, spare buildings of the modern master Mies van der Rohe succeeded by the imaginative, decorative ones of his former disciple Philip Johnson. In musical composition the tight clamps of an earlier formalism now often open into looser, more expressive creations. In academic and cultural circles these developments have been closely identified with literary criticism and the effort to refashion philosophy. Here Derrida's influence dominates.

Let me risk the violence of summing up his highly complex, still evolving thinking in the proposition that cuts to the heart of my concern with his thought: words are all we have. There is no way, as philosophers long dreamed, of starting our reasoning with notions that are simply "given" or "self-evident" and thus uncontestable foundations for all our subsequent knowledge. For if mood becomes thought only as it is verbalized and is then necessarily shaped by the language in which it is expressed, making sweeping claims for one's thoughts becomes grandiose. Thinking and writing should best be understood, Derrida and many others argue, not as unmasking reality, but as elegant word play.

This line of reasoning and other convergent ones have as good as destroyed the supreme confidence moderns had in the human mind — that is, as their science and culture exemplified it. But as they have demythologized the Cartesian notion of "clear and distinct ideas" the postmoderns have also deconstructed ethics and turned moral imperatives into just words about words. No Jewish thinker, no sensitive human being, could fail to be appalled by this potential nihilism, particularly when we have been witness to one ethical outrage after another. With the memory of the Hitler occupation still alive in France, the Derrideans have not been blind to this problem and their writing is often touched by a strong moral passion. But none has yet clarified how a deconstructionist could have a commanding ethics, something with the urgency of Biblical commands. An American philosopher, Edith Wyschogrod, has made a notable effort in this direction by her study of a number of female moral exemplars but the distance between good models and compelling norms remains great.

A Theological, Non-Derridean Approach

My own postmodernism has moved in a quite uncommon direction for against Derrida's confident assertion that it is no longer possible to have any "foundations" for our thought, I know myself to be a Jew first and an adherent of a philosophical system second. What I believe may be obscure, wavering and difficult to put into words but to deny it would be to contradict who I truly am. Despite its hiddenness, my Jewish faith is real, real enough that despite my secularization and skeptical intellect I try to base my life on it.

Postmodernism supplies me with as adequate a cultural language as I can find to interpret and communicate "my" experienced life of Jewish belief. I hastily add about this "my" (in typical postmodern consciousness of the circularity of all thought) that I do not mean by this "my" individual, interior religious experience — which would be the customary way for a modern religious thinker to proceed. Rather, (in typical postmodern particularity) I claim to read ("my"/our) the Jewish people's spiritual experience in recent decades out of my participation and reflection on it. Most of our community is too highly secularized or academicized to scrutinize the religious sub-text of what we have been through. But it is just this which grounds the fuller statement of my views in my book, *Renewing the Covenant, a theology for the postmodern Jew.* I will shortly present its three underlying principles and draw their implications for a postmodern Reform Judaism. But since mine is the first full-scale postmodern theory of Judaism — and a maverick, non-Derridean, theological one at that — let me take a few words to explain why I find the cultural climate created by Derrida's work the least inadequate way today to express my intuition of Jewish truth.

Postmodernism's rejection of foundations ends linear logic's claim to exclusive value and analytic rationality's privileged role as the required style for serious exposition. It thus allows for the kind of "thick" writing in theology that anthropologists have found helpful in describing a foreign culture's many layers. With "objectivity" unattainable — how can any one person's language claim to be adequate to everyone, everywhere's truth? — the religious thinker's particularity (gender, race, class, etc.) now has a proper role in thinking, and that speaks to one certainty of my/ our Jewish religiosity. Lazy, self-indulgent or anti-intellectual writers can, of course, exploit this postmodern linguistic openness to produce works that seem to me less "thought" than effusion. But I trust the

Jewish community to determine in due course which statements of its corporate faith have value.

The Postmodern Difference: My Three Assertions

I can epitomize my understanding of Jewish religious postmodernity as revisions of three modern views: (1) that of people's utter priority to God, (2) that of the individual self's utter priority to community, and, as a result of rethinking these prior two, (3) that of utterly independent personal autonomy.

First, modern religiosity — including the Jewish — is more sure of people than of God. Thus its typical procedure is to identify some certainty about human beings and then move from it toward what people can then reasonably call God. In modern Jewish thought Hermann Cohen's foundation was rationality, Mordecai Kaplan's the experience of growth and development (in a culture), and Buber's the I-thou experience (though his God has some independence). Religion is thus always a personal spiritual search or quest, as secure or as ambivalent as its human base allowed. Making humankind the basis of one's religiosity had the virtue of encouraging people to use their individual and communal power to do the good, a liberation which contributed in countless ways to the betterment of human lives.

This reliance on human knowledge and activism came in conscious rejection of the "premodern" form of religiosity, one dominated by God. Thus in Judaism, God descends on Mt. Sinai, God gives the Torah and, thereby, God transforms an aggregate of slaves into the people of Israel. So in the Bible and prayer book God speaks, commands, listens, answers, observes, judges, rewards, punishes, forgives, helps, saves/redeems, and much else. Founding Jewish lives, individual and communal, on the One sovereign of the universe had the great virtue of bringing stability and security into existence and investing it with incomparable holiness. But by the late middle ages it also tended to make Jews so dependent on God that, by modern standards, they seemed passive and unduly dependent. This perspective made the freedom granted by the Emancipation a means to fuller humanhood and thus highly attractive. However, we can now see that modernity's self-confident activism tended to let human judgment fully replace God as the ground and guide of human value, a gross over-estimation of human goodness and discernment.

For some postmoderns the disillusion with messianic modernism validates a return to classic religiosity with God at its center and this powers the recent rise of fundamentalism in all the religions of Western civilization. But most postmoderns intuit something different: a relationship between God and people that is less God dominated than the traditional religion taught but also less people-dominated than the moderns proclaimed. These believers sense the reality of a God who grounds our values yet makes room for human independence and calls human beings into an active partnership.

With the rationalism that was once Reform Judaism's glory now largely discredited a search for a secure ground of value is underway among us and its code word is "spirituality." But thus far our leadership has been unable to free itself from the inhibitions which a self-confident modernism made standard among us some decades back. That is, placing our trust in humankind we were quite content to put God at the margins of our religious concern. If that did not make Reform Jews agnostics — and a good case can be made for that characterizing all American Jews of some years back — we were effectively agnostic. So, rather briefly, we could confidently welcome the "death of God" because we knew that all the real activity in history was in our hands.

Some among us still hold that position, finding it so intolerable that any "God" should relate to a world like ours that they prefer to place their faith in people. But for some time that confidence in the human has become more problematic than believing in God. Thus it is no longer daring and *avant garde* among us to flaunt one's disbelief or revel in one's challenges to God. That change of ethos is a reproach to the institutional lag which still acts as if the old pervasive agnosticism still reigned. Speaking boldly about God is not without its problems but grounding messianic striving and hope in any realistic view of humankind or social institution is illusory.

The Reform movement must find a way to face up to God's real, central role in our faith — and if that spatial metaphor somewhat overstates our non-Orthodox stance, then let me say more precisely that it is God's real, significant, ongoing role in our covenant partnership with God that needs to be made clear. I do not know how long we can go on trying to be religiously relevant to our most sensitive people tying spirituality to study, observance or liturgical innovation, without ever emphasizing the God who stands behind them. Of course Jewish acts are indispensable. But the spirituality we know we need will not arise without our forthrightly acknowledging the Relating- Other, that Ultimate One who is the ground of the universe and the dynamic source of its values — with God and God's reality understood in any one of the different ways thoughtful Reform Jews affirm. Until that becomes a central, articulated emphasis of the leaders of the Union — and, if it needs saying, of the Conference and the College also — we will have failed the first challenge of the postmodern era.

How Individualistic, How Universal A Self?

Second, moderns thought truth to be fundamentally universal, that is, applying to everyone, everywhere even as gravity applied in the furthest reaches of the universe. So defining something meant relating it to the class in which it fit and explaining something meant showing how it operated in terms of a broad scale natural process. This had the exhilarating effect of indicating how everything could, in theory, be related to everything else and this pervasive sense of nature's unity brought a new breadth of vision into every field of endeavor. This led Kant to insist that only when moral imperatives applied universally — to everyone, everywhere in the same situation — should they be called "ethical," an idea that still powers efforts to include "outsiders" in our communities. Modernizing Jews have had good reason to love this liberating vision and enshrine it in their intense commitment to ethics as the essence of religion.

Again, this reversed the premodern religious view in which God's revelation came to a particular group and not to anyone else. In classic Judaism only the people of Israel received the Torah, Written and Oral, and by its standards the people of Israel understands itself as chosen, dubbing other peoples, "the nations." The people God loves has duties incumbent on it alone and when they are observant they receive God's special favor. This consciousness of God's support made the Jews' indifferent to their host culture's sense of spiritual superiority and armored the Jews for their survival over the centuries.

By contrast to the premodern judgment of others by (God-given) in-group criteria, modern Jews first determine what is true universally and then investigate how Judaism exemplifies it. Thus Cohen, Kaplan and Buber all first determine what is true for everyone — rationality, sociology, or the I-thou experience — and then create a theory of Judaism to conform with it. In the days when the Jewish agenda gave priority to demonstrating Jewish humanhood, this method was invaluable. Its universalistic hermeneutic revealed a dimension of Judaism not previously so evident.

Today a changed Jewish and human situation has made two flaws in the prioritizing of the universal painfully evident. After the Holocaust Jewish survival could no longer be a subordinate Jewish concern. And the notion of diminishing our Jewish particularity so as to gain acceptance in a civilization that could conduct or tolerate a Holocaust seemed ludicrous. Many Jews gradually realized that being and staying a Jew was elementally right and that made the old unbridled universalism wrong.

Moreover, if truth is fundamentally universal, then all particular forms of its expression — including Judaism — are in principle expendable, a view that appears to give sanction to giving up or drifting out of Judaism. In the growing practice of intermarriage these theoretical musings became a disturbing, practical threat — one recent statistical data massively indicate leads to a generational abandonment of Judaism. Jews had to face the issue of whether they were content to be a "terminal" generation, one happy to keep Judaism alive for itself and such of its children as wished to carry it on for a while. For that implied acquiescence, if with reluctance, to the ongoing atrophy of Jewishness and the sapping of its vitality. For those whose Jewishness was too elemental for that, it was clear that the supremacy of the universal was a faulty standard.

Many groups in Western civilization had come to a similar conclusion. People of diverse races and cultures began protesting the moral arrogance of an ideal which said, in effect, that they would be more fully human if they became more like the cultured Western, white man. Another blow against the universality of the universal came from feminists who rebelled against the subordination of their gender to male criteria claiming to be correct for everybody, everywhere. Intellectually, these groups had been preceded by Marxism, psychoanalysis and anthropology, and more recently, by deconstructionism. They denied that anyone, necessarily speaking out of a given class, a given self, a given culture and a given language, could enunciate something true about everyone, everywhere.

If human beings are quite particular and everything we posit arises from our specific situation, then the particular inevitably precedes the universal. Should one affirm the commanding truth of universalism — as most contemporary Jews are led by their folk experience and faith to do — then it arises out of one's personal/communal/historic situation, in our case, by our being Jews who have learned something from emancipation.

This priority of the particular to the universal is thus the second characteristic of my postmodernity.

In many ways it has been easier for the Reform movement to particularize its modern universalism — more precisely, to balance its universalism with a healthy particularity — than to put aside its old agnosticism. History has forced most Jews to recognize the spuriousness of their old claim simply to be people-in-general who happened to be Jews. And those who have persisted in this (often self-hating) dream of transcending their origins generally drift out of our community. Besides Reform Judaism and the other modernized versions of our faith have made clear how much satisfaction there can be in living as a Jew. So, too, the State of Israel (despite our occasional worries about its soul) has by the impressive quality of its human reconstruction added incomparable pride to that lustrous old title "Jew." The overwhelming majority of Reform Jews have rejoiced in the effort to make Reform freedom a means of deciding what of our tradition and creativity to *add* to our lives. Prior generations, avidly seeking acceptance, only saw Reform freedom as authority to deJudaize. They gloried in departicularization and their spiritual offspring still decry as "orthodoxy" any effort to reclaim valuable aspects of our tradition.

We have, however, gone nearly as far as one can go in exploiting the human bases of our Jewish loyalty (the Holocaust, the State of Israel, the joys of Jewish living). Earlier generations of Reform Jews knew that the premodern doctrine that God had chosen us was incompatible with a modern, democratic existence. Not being particularistic wimps, they forthrightly asserted the virtue of our particularity as resulting from the "mission of Israel" to all humankind. Out of a mix of Hermann Cohen's philosophy of Judaism as the religion of reason *par excellence* and their own sense that it was right to be distinctively Jewish, they said we existed as a people because we were uniquely able to teach ethical monotheism to humankind. Our universal task justified our particular existence.

The mission of Israel has long since faded from Reform Jewish thinking though one occasionally hears it or its like in careless rabbinic or lay rhetoric. The notion that Jews have a unique racial capacity — so Kaufmann Kohler — or a unique intellectual insight into an essentially Kantian universalistic idea simply cannot survive acquaintance with other peoples or realism about how modern Jews live. Besides there is something inherently demeaning about having to justify one's existence in terms of what one does for other people. But no new Reform Jewish surrogate for chosenness has arisen to take its place. As long as a growing turn to ethnic roots among all peoples and a post-Holocaust, pro-Israel consciousness intensified our particularity, the Jewish bent for living rather than thinking about Judaism could mask the problem. But as freedom and acceptance have more fully become the condition of Jewish existence, as religion has retreated from our corporate relationship with God to become only each person's private spirituality, Jewish particularity has is in long-term peril.

We Reform Jews are badly divided on what to do about that issue. Large numbers of us affirm the modern notion that a universal humanhood happens in our case to be lived out in the Jewish tradition — a rich and rewarding one. While this view brings some of its adherents to a passionate concern for Jewish particularity, it provides no rationale other than "valuable possibility" for staying Jewish and bearing the sacrifices minority existence entails. Worse, it is a position which makes Jewish existence dispensable or changeable. Allied with this theoretical position are those many people whose families or children have been involved in intermarriages. They do not wish religion to be a barrier between them and those they love. They find the concept of the priority of universal humanhood validating their heart's intuition. And that surely seems a reasonable conclusion from an unreflective Jewish embrace of modernity.

But on what basis can one today confidently assert such a universal truth? It is surely not empirically evident or universally held. Judaism and its daughter faiths can ground it, at least insofar as they have been through the experience of modernization. But they do so because they have their particular faiths in God's unity and God's resulting relationship with all humankind not because they know this from being people-in-general. And all the Biblical faiths consider the historic realization of their universalism a matter for messianic, not historical time.

There is an experiential basis for this affirmation of particularism and it comes from the lives of those who have become conscious on a most primal level that there is something true about existence as a Jew, not just for them personally but for their people. Among other illusion shattering disclosures, the Holocaust made clear that the death of the Jewish people could become a reality; the continuing threats to the existence of the State of Israel confirmed that possibility; and the slow hemorrhaging of Jewish loyalty and dedication through intermarriage have made it a present peril.

As long as the Reform movement does not forthrightly find a way to assert its simultaneous dedication to the equality of all humankind and its unequivocal commitment to the irreplaceable truth of particular Jewish existence it confirms the disparaging charge that it is essentially a "gateway to assimilation." Continuing silence about our commitment to Jewish particularity makes us unwitting allies of those who find the short-term abandonment of Judaism regrettable but rely on universalism to justify tolerate its long-term evolution into ethical living or such. I believe that my restatement of the doctrine of the covenant provides an intellectually solid, humanly sensitive, Jewishly grounded response to that issue. But whether it is my formulation of the universal/particular dialectic or someone else's, only such a forthright affirmation of our particularity will take us beyond the illusions of modernity.

The Third Concern: Retaining But Rethinking Autonomy

With regard to these two matters — greater involvement with God and with Jewish particularity — postmodern Orthodoxy and non-Orthodoxy agree in principle if not in means. They disagree over my third affirmation: the need to keep (but reinterpret) modernity's notion of personal autonomy. Orthodoxy allows individual self-determination only as the Torah, God's revelation, provides for it. Though caricatures of Orthodoxy ignore it, the Torah recognizes substantial areas for personal decision in the observant life. But to stretch these to the point of dissenting from the Law is a sin and, so it is charged in the contemporary polemic, leads to all those human tragedies liberalistic individualism wildly abets. So many Jews, like people of the other great Western faiths, have turned their back on anarchical modernity and its degraded life styles by choosing to be Orthodox.

Despite the appeal of this reasoning the masses of the three widespread faiths have rejected orthodoxies. Many do so out of self-indulgence; they want to do whatever gives them pleasure to the extent that they can. But more reflective people, though they agree with some of the criticism of religious liberalism, have not been convinced that it was fundamentally in error. They have found their personal dignity enhanced by the strong sense of responsibility engendered by its teaching about self-determination. Though they seek guidance from their leaders and traditions they know they are right to then insist on "making up their own minds" about what they have been taught.

In the postmodern context, however, "making up their own minds" cannot mean a return to the self-confident heyday of modernity. Then autonomy assumed that individuals had (or could have) in their minds, their experience, and their learning all the resources they needed to determine what they and society should do. In my postmodern understanding, the self is no monad but an individuality intimately structured by its relationship with God and the particular people within which that self functions. So autonomy now has validity only when it is exercised in intimate involvement with God as part of one's community relationship with God, in our case the people of Israel's historic relationship with God, the *brit*, the covenant.

This theology obviously does not call upon our movement to give up what has been its chief, if occasionally troublesome, glory, its respect for the informed, conscientious individual and its corporate devotion to works of social action. This third principle gives both a solid, postmodern theological foundation. But it also sets autonomy into a new context and that has certain practical implications for our movement.

Once it seemed that "conscience," a purely human, essentially internal faculty, could give us "God's" truth. Of course, this always carried the overtone of Kantian (more precisely, Cohen's neo-Kantian) autonomy, that conscience was utilized in a thoroughly rational manner. That entailed being well informed and testing one's decisions against one's effort to treat others as ends, not as means only, and in terms of their universal applicability. In this process, God stayed very far in the background and the "particular" community considered here was humanity as a whole. Communally, we followed our universal consciences by asking what other liberals were saying and then, generally, joined them by passing resolutions and becoming involved in political coalitions. (Thus Jewish bio-ethics has largely become the preserve of the Orthodox and other traditionalists. Serious inquirers find they may have some distinctly "Jewish" wisdom to bring to bear on such issues whereas Reform Jews will only restate the general liberal positions, perhaps illustrated by some Jewish texts.) Both the older private and communal styles of Reform Jewish ethical decision-making need some reshaping in terms of our emerging postmodern sensibility.

It will be easier to characterize the particularistic component of this shift. On the personal level it requires us to stop making our decisions without essential reference to our most particular communities, our families and the Jewish people. We need to say plainly, "Reform Judaism does not teach that religion is simply a private matter between you and God — or simply between you as part of humankind and God." That individualistic universalism may be an irreplaceable aspect of Jewish religiosity but our faith is violated when those who affirm it do not live it out in community. Thus we need to make plain that Reform Jewish decision-making is not just privately consulting one's conscience. Rather, among other critical guides, Reform Jews facing a significant decision should, to begin with, be vitally concerned with what other Jews (our community, in all its pluralism) are saying on this issue and how our decision will affect our community. But our people is not merely contemporary, it has a vast tradition of seeking to serve God in history. Personally and communally, we therefore need to ground our deliberation in a deep understanding of its prior traditions, specifically, its legal literature, the *halakhah*. Since few of us will be able to do this adequately, education, publication and rabbinic teaching rabbinate are particularly incumbent upon us. Our institutions, however, have a special responsibility to be adequately informed in their decision-making.

There are many social problems which require no profound Jewish study. When the homeless crowd the streets, when people are hungry, one needs no great knowledge of Jewish sources to know what God requires of us as Jews. And while this is more precariously true as one moves into the broad-scale social, i. e., political arena, there surely are issues where the exigencies of time and situation as well as of topic allow for the equation of social action with resolution-passing and program-starting. What is now missing in this largely commendable enterprise is the serious study and careful evaluation of the alternatives in critical areas of continuing social concern. If we have a unique capacity for ethics it is not evident in the publication of much serious Reform Jewish ethical literature in recent decades. Rather one must look to the American Catholic bishops and some of the Protestant denominations for searching efforts to probe the teaching of their traditions, relate it to the specialized knowledge of our time and respond to a complex ethical problem faithful to God's perceived demands. We do not have the resources to fund as many such studies as the confusions of our times warrant. Nonetheless, we need to be steadily at work on some key questions, instructing our people with our occasional results modeling the Reform Jewish conscience sensitized by a thorough study of our tradition as well as contemporary reflection and expertise.

It is far more difficult to state how neo-Kantian autonomy needs to be modified in terms of a living relationship with God. In part that is because attending to God is as much a subtle, inner act as it is actionally and communally expressed/experienced. In part it is because we are unaccustomed to speaking directly about our relationship with God and can become quite uncomfortable when others do. I think that largely comes from our holding on to the modern teaching that human conscience on its own — perhaps vaguely grounded on a "concept of God" — protects us from having to be personally involved with God and God-talk. So we move toward postmodern Jewish autonomy by engaging in the kind of (God)consciousness-raising I am attempting here.

The next thing may well be to change the tone of our public rhetoric from one that radiates self-confidence to one — let me dare it — more piously modest. I do not mean by this to encourage Reform Jewish sanctimoniousness but, as I see it, we generally know a good deal less and are considerably less certain than the current modes of social-political tussling encourage. We generally need God's help a good deal more than we institutionally let on in most matters. And when issues are serious indeed, we should be entering upon them with a certain mix of fear and trembling before God that it is wrong to repress and not acknowledge. In general, we need privately and publicly to be a good deal more prayerful about the stands we know we must take, may God help us. And we need day by day to be building the kind of intimacy with God as part of the people of Israel that will be our chief guide when we come to one of those awesome moments when the little we or our community or anyone else has done or knows helps us divine what God immediately requires of us.

I think that the ideas I have sketched out here are implicit in *Renewing the Covenant* even though I could not have put them so directly there. I am therefore doubly delighted to be celebrating Alex Schindler in this fashion for it has again, as over the years, allowed me to learn from my ongoing if ordinarily more silent dialogue with him and his work.

Chapter 12

℘)Cℛ

Five Letters to Readers of
Renewing the Covenant

1.

Dear ——,

I was flattered to hear that your Faculty study group read and discussed my book. Its gotten a considerable amount of attention, the way these things go, and much of the response has been quite positive. Some readers, to be sure, just don't know quite what to make out of it. They simply read it for the individual points and miss the architectonic quality of the whole that gives the individual points compelling power (as I see it). This bothers me enough that I am thinking of doing a brief statement of the argument of the book to guide readers. The most astonishing response, from someone I normally consider an astute analyst, was a response to the book which completely missed what I had done to the modern concept of the "self." So I was understood to be left with all the modernist/Reform problems I had so carefully worked to avoid. It was as if chs. 11-13 of the book weren't there and the last chapter wasn't tellingly called "The *Jewish* Self." That's an oxymoron to a modern but the whole point of my treatment.

And that brings me to your comment, "as a historian," that what I'm talking about is "only another stage in the modern." Since I've already expressed my own doubts about my "periodization" on pp. 4-5 and elsewhere in the book speak of modernity's continuing influence, e.g., pp. 49-50, I probably agree with what you are saying. But I want to emphasize that this is quite "another stage" indeed. And so your comment that I have "much more in common with H. Cohen and M. Kaplan than you are willing to admit publically" requires me to inquire just how seriously you take the term "another stage." I see it is as quite a shift indeed.

As to the practical aspect of your comment, is there a thinker who has more fully, regularly and carefully indicated, in public, his/her differences with the great masters of our century than I have? My book is full of continuity with them. Normally historians have to go rooting around to find out the intellectual sources of people's ideas. That is because it has been accepted practice simply not to acknowledge them; other people simply don't want to admit how much they've learned from others. On the simple level, I reject your charge.

But on the more significant level, I wonder if you see how radically different my approach is than theirs — no small matter in this day where methodology is the master of content — and how I use the same language they do but, in my revised context, it comes out quite differently.

I differ radically with both thinkers and all such rationalistic moderns on two basic grounds. One, they have such confidence in human rationality that they begin with it, make one of its university styles basic to their thinking, and then utterly reinterpret Judaism, specifically its traditions of God, Torah and Israel, in terms of a university-rationalism. I utterly reject such confidence in the human and in the hegemony of rationalism and thus the notion that the university tells religion what is still true. I therefore, to begin with, ground selfhood not in reason but in a relationship with God, an independent Other, not a creation of the mind in exercise of reason, whether individually located, as in Cohen, or socially, as in Kaplan.

Practically, Cohen's "autonomy" is monadic/Kantian; Kaplan's is situated socially but remains strictly individual, and he doesn't want to think about the possible clash. My "autonomy," is, to begin with, qualified by an "autos" that has no independence of God but exists properly only in relation to that Other. It is relational "autonomy," quite a different thing indeed and one that the moderns would (do) consider retrogressive.

Two, the moderns thought they could think universally, that truth was characterized by universality, and that one therefore first established the universal truth and only then went on to see how it was instantiated in particulars. Indeed, one could judge the value of a particular by its approximation of the universal ideal. So Cohen's rational argument for the Jews. (His sudden Hegelian shift to originators having a historic hold on their insight remains utterly inexplicable by his own standards.)

In the postmodern view, it seems arrogant for these white, middle-class, urban, male, dead Jews to have asserted that they can know how every good mind ought to think or what is the structure of societies everywhere and for all time (and Durkheim's analysis of the "primitives" is simply applied to secular modernity!). It's difficult to believe there is anything left of universalism, rationally, though various guilds still insist on it and pragmatically it certainly helps with many political situations. In sum, for postmoderns the particular precedes the universal. We may have some choice in which particularity that we know we situate ourselves but much of selfhood is simply social. For Jews, that means primary situation in the Jewish people. While it is difficult to explain that in our language, which remains highly modernistic, there is truth in Jewish existence and not merely the health that Kaplan found in accepting the historical accident.

The practical consequences of this shift are radical indeed. For the moderns, there is no ultimate reason to stay a Jew. Cohen still struggles against this implication of his system but what can he do when Kant explains to Moses what he really meant. And Kaplan expressly states in *The Future of the American Jew* that when the American civilization finally has a religious content then there will no longer be any reason for Jews to stay Jewish. Which is about where many people in the American Jewish community are today. But if particularity is fundamental and Jewishness is a true way of being (a folk and not merely an individual way) then there is a command to be and stay Jews. I am convinced that "continuity" will continually be in trouble until some such faith animates a significant minority of the non-Orthodox.

Note what this does to "autonomy," ethics and the lot. Of course the terms are still there and we liberals recognize a certain religious truth in them. But now they are utterly reshaped by having the self operate fundamentally out of its historic/ethnic ground. The "autos" is now as much concerned with what the Jewish tradition said, what Jews now think and how we can get to the messianic days as it is about the insights of reason/conscience. It is radically a *Jewish* self.

Now if that is what you mean by what you say, then I didn't quite pick it up. And if it isn't what you had in mind, then this is what I think. And you may find some of this better clarified in my writing that has followed the book.

2.

Dear ——,

The thing I most wanted to tell you was my reaction to your and your rabbinic friend's comments about my book. Two things stood out, if I recall correctly. One was that since much of it deals with developing a relationship to God, it seemed not to have very much to say to the two of you. The other was that I seemed to be paying very much attention to Orthodoxy, even kowtowing to it, without giving the Reform position its proper legitimacy.

As to the former, I would agree that much that I have to say about God may have had little relevance to you two. After all, you believe in a proper God, so why work so hard at the topic? The answer is that, in case you didn't realize it, the two of you have been and, to a considerable extent, still are greatly atypical of our colleagues, much less our laity. Until relatively recently, covert agnosticism was rampant among them with various kinds of humanistic substitutes for God serving their overt needs. And that kept the laity quite satisfied -- no one had to believe much.

That remains the latent situation with much of our movement today but the change in the past decade, particularly in the past few years, has been quite extraordinary. For all the proper problems with "spirituality," it has gotten people to face up to how much more they believe than they thought. My book was directed to them, to explain their situation, the reasons for the paradigm shift and the directions I think we need to be heading when opening ourselves up to God's reality. I shall say another word about this later.

But with regard to the second point, the fawning on Orthodoxy, I suggest you and your friend may have missed the point in your proper pride in our movement. At mid-century it seemed perfectly clear that Reform or something like it would dominate American Judaism by the century's end if not sooner. In fact, the opposite has happened. The liveliest group in Jewry is the Orthodox. I disagree with them on much of what they care about but that does not change the sociological or theological reality. What interests me is why that is the case.

It will not do to say that if people understood Reform properly or lived it as they should it would be perfectly clear why everyone should be Reform. That is, if they were like you and your friend. But they aren't and a movement that began by facing up to historical change and adapting to it ought at least ask itself why this is the case. And see what we can learn from it.

My answer is that we are undergoing a shift in western civilization from the modern to something vaguely called "postmodern." What is true in Islam and Christianity is also true among us. The right has been able to mount devastating critiques against the realities of liberalism applied to society or religion. Of course, what they say does not apply to those who, like and your friend, are steeped in knowledge and Jewish devotion. But is that how you would characterize the bulk of our colleagues or our laity?

So the fact that Orthodoxy is, from our religious perspective, wrong on the role of selfhood or reason in Judaism has nothing to do with the fact that they have been right in criticizing us for not — in reality — having a serious relationship with God and for not creating any serious kind of life of Torah except for those who thought that the *mitzvot* were fulfilled through social action. Surely you, who have been so strong a critic of our movement, ought to be willing to admit that outsiders might see our flaws equally well, if not better.

So trying to restore a serious relationship with God and a richer life of *mitzvah* are the critical aspects of my book. Which is why I said the bulk of it was devoted to developing a "Postliberal Theology of Jewish Duty." And that, because of my defense and Covenantal recontextualization of "the self," is clearly not Orthodox.

The book has had a decent reception as these things go. That is, some thoughtful people seem to understand it reasonably well and like what it says. But it is interesting how many people whose intellect I admire have found it "hard," which is at least a welcome change from the old days when I was dismissed as a popularizer. The more interesting thing is how many people feel they understand what I said but haven't got much of an idea as I see it. They are trying to put it into their old categories and it won't go as long as it is true to itself. As Kuhn said, the old paradigm had sufficient truth in it that it is difficult to surrender.

And I want them not only give God reality, independence and input but I want them to do this in terms of a living relationship with the Jewish people.

3.

Dear ——,

Let me congratulate you for the fine job you did in your thesis "Borowitz and Beyond." I confess to still being pleased when someone considers my work worthy of serious attention and writes about it. However, your detailed, searching study deserves great praise simply on its academic and intellectual merit. You've read me carefully as well as many others whom you cite to good effect. The arguments are tightly drawn, well presented and set down with clarity. As you can see, I cannot help but read it in my usual professorial advisor's role and reflect my joy at your work.

You invite me to continue the conversation which you initiated with respect and care and I shall try in this letter to do so. That is emotionally easy since it seems we differ on no substantive issue and you generously credit me with elucidating a number of positions you consider critical to our non-Orthodoxy. Essentially, you wish I were more a Gadamerian and drew far more on the current discussion of hermeneutics for the apologetic theology of *Renewing the Covenant*, than as Buberian and "self"-oriented as you see me (not altogether incorrectly) presenting myself. I can be of most help, I think, by explaining myself on matters that relate to your work rather than deal with this or that specific matter that you raised. I hope this will provide another perspective on what unites and divides us.

To begin with, I have no interest in writing philosophy or philosophical theology or shaping my writing in forms which academic philosophers will find appropriate. It is not that I have no interest in or respect for philosophy. But for much of my life philosophy as good as claimed hegemony over religious belief and I increasingly resisted that stance. To be sure, the philosophers were never so brazen as to claim they should tell religionists what to believe. Instead they used numerous euphemisms like "that's not knowledge," or "how can you believe anything if you cannot understand it," or "what evidence is there for believing that," or "that makes no sense to a rational person" (a term of great power though "rational" was always defined in the specific system of rationality propounded by the speaker).   In short, we moderns were expected to do with some philosophy as we did with science, acknowledge that it had the truth and then adapt our religiosity to it.   Something like that was and is the standard liberal religious methodology.

Since a good deal of such philosophy was for a long time secular that meant that any serious sense of God was inevitably ruled out, a notion that despite my questioning and intellectual searching struck me as unwarranted. But as the fragmentation of rationalism became ever more pronounced and just what constituted a proper rationalism became ever more debated, it was clear that philosophic rationalism itself rested on non-rational foundations. Today we have gotten to the point where one recognizes one cannot solve the problem of extra-mental realities so one blithely announces "I am a realist" and then is able to go on with one's arguments. To me that seems more a statement of substantial faith than the mere announcement of a premise for an argument. Except for guild reasons, why are some of my stands in faith not as reasonable a basis for life-shaping as the accepted philosophical faiths? At that point philosophers often want to seize the word "reasonable" and insist that it must mean something like what they do or consider cogent. But I have little difficulty carrying on conversations with thoughtful people in the religious world, a public that in recent years has increased greatly indeed. And this is no mere sharing of certainties but generally involves a good deal of response, probing, counter-argument and counter-formulation. Yes, there are some similarities to philosophic diction in this give and take but though I find it going very deep it would generally not satisfy the rigorous standards of most philosophers. Besides, I am concerned with getting people to live their lives in terms of Jewish belief and philosophy has been notoriously unable to create any significant group of people who actually lived their lives philosophically.

So I purposely write in a non-philosophic cast though I am willing to try to think as hard as I can about what should be the entailments of my religious "experiences," "intuitions," or "insights" — and I purposely try to be imprecise in my language so that I will not give the impression that I am thinking/writing philosophically. The academy has no term for this kind of discourse but if you insist upon giving it a name you might call it some kind of "religionese."

That is one reason why I am not centrally focused on ethics and or care much about elucidating a meta-ethics. To the contrary, it was precisely the mistaken reliance on philosophy, Kant to be specific, that brought Reform Judaism to the sorry state where only ethics constituted Jewish duty and all the rest was "ritual" or "ceremonies." Kantians could command ethics but never find anything remotely as obligating for the non-ethical leading. That led to the classic confession of our time, "If I am an ethical person and try to do the right with all my heart, I don't really have to come to services, rabbi, do I?" I am rather concerned with a broader-scale theory of Jewish duty, with what would be our equivalent of *halakhah* in all its comprehensiveness. My theology is a meta-*"halakhah"* and therefore is not shaped so as to validate ethics, which I hope it will also include, but a far broader sense of what my believing Jew ought to do. To be sure, the one area where I have regularly sought to apply the theology is ethics, in some embracing sense of the term. There are two reasons for that, one apologetic, the other methodological. Apologetically, that is the one thing that semi-believing Jews in our time still care about, that is, insofar as they care about anything, it will be ethics, one of the previous century's intellectual/ spiritual successes. So I talk about what they care about hoping that this tactic will enable me also to get to duty's religious foundations and greater breadth. Methodologically, since I believe there is inevitably more of a personal, that is subjective, element as one moves from people-to-people-duty toward people-to-self or to God, it is somewhat easier at the moment to deal with the people-duty end of the spectrum than to have to increasingly factor in the issue of individuality.

We heard of Gadamer decades back when our German readers, searching for a new philosophic medium for their work, began to make his thought known. I'd guess that even the translation is twenty years old by now and that then caused an explosion of attention here. Having been raised intellectually by neo-Kantians it came as no surprise to me to hear that one thinks out of one's own hermeneutic and, Dilthey being no stranger to our world, that trying to find a way into the hermeneutic world of a "text" was a major intellectual problem. To be sure, Gadamer advanced all this on the basis of the increasing self-critical nature of twentieth century philosophy but, when all was said and done, and an increasing linguistic self-consciousness was sweeping over the intellectual world, of what specific value was Gadamer? So he is still reverently invoked from time to time but is surely not so significant a name or substantive thinker that invoking his name would have apologetic clout in American non-academic circles.

However, you point to one critical, substantive matter where you believe Gadamer's position would significantly improve on my efforts to get semi-Enlightenment types to take their sociality nearly as seriously as they do their self-hood. You epitomize Gadamer's point on p. 30 in these words: "The authority of traditions should be accepted, answers Gadamer, because they demand not obedience, but acknowledgment. This because traditions are reasonable." I do not quite understand the prior sentence since one could "acknowledge" that there are certain Jewish traditions but then ignore them, that is, not grant them any significant "authority" in one's life. So I do not get what you think he means here.

But it is the latter sentence that brings me into radical disagreement with your claim for the usefulness of Gadamer's position. If one tried to tell Jews that the reason they ought to have a more robust regard for the Jewish tradition ("authority" without necessary "obedience") is because it was "reasonable," then I think they would agree only in a relatively trivial way, i. e., "Yes, some traditions are reasonable." But I think they would reject any serious sense of that proposition. Why? Because the reality of most Diaspora Jewish life is founded on our conclusion that Jewish tradition was inherently UNreasonable, and that goes double for Israelis.

Jewish tradition demanded a substantial segregation of Jews from non-Jews and its ultimate authority for this was God's revelation of the Oral Law with its present-day continuation in the system of halakhic authority. The overwhelming majority of Diaspora Jews have never even had to think very deeply about that. They knew in their bones that modernity was smarter and so they abandoned segregated living for equality, gave up Sinaitic revelation for the university and the halakhic system for the urban-intellectual cultural style. And though they may disagree as to how untraditional they want to be and despite their greater traditionalism these days (even a flirtation with Orthodoxy), they know Jewish tradition was centrally wrong and only radically revising it might it make sense today.

Israelis know that also from the reality of Zionism. The most traditionalistic Jews are and always have been anti- or at best non-Zionist. It took quite an effort for a good chunk of the Orthodox community to finally come to terms with the modern nationalistic political movement that brought the State of Israel into existence and there is still always a certain uneasiness about its involvement in secular governments and its co-optation based on the heavy subsidies it gets. I should think Israelis would find Gadamer's thesis as applied to Jewish tradition doubly unbelievable.

This is not to say that some traditions aren't reasonable and worth following — but surely one doesn't need a major German philosopher to tell us that. So, as for myself and the Diaspora world that I was speaking to, it made little sense to invoke hermeneutic philosophy beyond the covert kind of communitarianism I thought I had built up in my own attack on the naked self, its competence and its universalism. All this, while nonetheless maintaining that in the non-Orthodox Covenantal situation, a newly reconfigured, recontextualized kind of selfhood — not in an "Existentialist" sense, philosophical or otherwise — and autonomy — not in a Kantian sense — still have a place simply because Diaspora-niks still largely think in those terms.

4.

Dear ——,

I know of no language-game adequate to describe what I experience/believe. That does not mean it is not true or real or worth staking my life on. I find much of Buber's language the least inadequate way of pointing toward what I have in mind, so I will largely use it.

First, a word as to the infamous issue of the term "autonomy." Perhaps the simplest thing would be to renounce ever using it again which, in prominent public announcement, should be a sufficient penance for my sin. But I do not know of a word which better points to the active, necessary role of the individual in the pious Jewish life, as I understand it. I thought I could use the term, culturally denatured for everyone but philosophic types into something that points to making up your own mind about most things. But in the current trashing of language, I wanted to assert the religious right to point to a somewhat similar activity in the liberal religious life, albeit in relationship to God as a member of a community related to God. That has created communication static with some of my colleagues (as have the words "absolute" and "postmodern"). But what single word shall I use to deal with what is a widespread, absolutely central part of the religious life for us, that there is a legitimate measure of personal judgment involved in our piety? Perhaps I should signal my special usage of the term by always printing in a form that clarifies my reinterpretation of it, e. g. ?auto?nomy?, or "auto"nomy." But I don't think it will help. From now on everyone will always connect me with "autonomy" anyway. But let us get to the substance.

It will help to clarify two levels of the limited freedom of the self(in Israel with God). I shall repeat that formula several times to remind you of my understanding of "self" and if I stop using it after a while, I hope you will remember that this is another of my co-opted, reinterpreted terms.

One level has to do with the immediate relationship with God. The second has to do with its effects, the doing that is entailed by the togetherness. It is easier to talk about the second than the first.

God doesn't reveal content, that is, specific things I(in Israel with God) must do. God, on the first level, gives only presence — but a presence that empowers and sends. Individuals(in Israel with God) respond to the experience of being with God by determining what they must do. In due course the community, Israel, sanctifies some of these by adopting/ adapting these acts. They then acquire significant authority over all those individuals who are in Israel with God. Whether I(in Israel with God) or others created the practice the community has "sanctified" I always retain, alongside my responsibility to listen to the authority of Israel, the right to judge that this or that practice or this or that text, is contrary to what I(in Israel with God) believe God wants us to do as Israel. And I have a right to create new practices that the community has not sanctified and even go contrary to what the community presently deems proper. I(in Israel with God) never do that lightly since my "I" is substantially constituted by God and Israel. My point is, however, that it remains something of an "I" nonetheless. And that is why we have *shitot* in traditional Jewish law, which to some modest extent, recognizes the value of selfhood(in Israel with God). But I believe, with many others, that God wants us(in Israel with God) to exercise a greater self-determination as selves as long as we stand firmly in relationship with God in faithful alliance with the people of Israel.

The harder topic, the one that reduced me to such inarticulateness in our conversation has to do with the self(in Israel with God)'s "freedom" as it stands with God in relationship in the pre-"legislative" situation. There is never any question of this being a relationship between equals. It is true that what transpires can be said to reflect a certain symmetry — sort of like *dibrah Torah bilashon benei adam,* the Torah speaks in human language. One can even speak of it as a "partnership" — but as

I have written somewhere, there is never any question about who is the Senior Partner. That God "comes down" on Sinai is what moderns might call the grace involved in the One God be willing to reveal God to people.

Before going further, let me emphasize a point: as I understand it, language about God always involves God-in-relation-to-people (even as language about people or "the self" always involves God). I do not know any way in which God, as it were, is available to me (or anyone) without a substantial involvement of the human recipient(s) of that experience/understanding. The point of this introduction is that, in a quite postmodern sense, I dare say, the recipient/partner is already part of what is transpiring with God. No me without God; nothing that happens between me and God leaves out me(in Israel with God). Religious experience, revelation, what have you, does not destroy or cancel out the me-ness of me(in Israel with God).

That human aspect of the God-person reality is what can make it suspect; the involvement of people might taint it. Hence there is a second order ?auto?nomy? involved here. I(in Israel with God) must regularly inquire whether this was "God speaking" or, as Buber puts it, "one of his dupes." "God said," "God wants" has been put to demonic uses throughout history and in stunningly evil ways in our time. I(in Israel with God) must guard against that. So, on reflection — which certainly includes extensive concern with what the people of Israel past and present say about this — I may have to say "No" to what seemed for a moment a genuine encounter with God.

The most difficult thing is to try to say a word about (*sic* — was I peeking?) what I might do over- against God, the test of freedom, alas. What I shall now say I recognize as theory, trying to find words and patterns for something for which I have no firm experiential base. I recognize I am extrapolating from what I have been through and for what I have come to think about being with God. When God is there with me(who is one of Israel and its relationship with God), the primary mood is of privilege, awe, openness, occasionally love. So my departing sense of urgency about doing something because of our meeting is rightly described as "commanding." And to the extent that I(in Israel with God) have legitimately given content to the sending, I know I have violated something precious when I fail to live it. Normally, the more closely tied a deed is to what I(in Israel with God) believe God wants of me as one of Israel, its violation is a sin. Some "commanded" deeds I believe reflect more my response to God than God's demand of me; as a teacher of mine once said, "God cares more about how you treated the woman who came to clean your house on Friday than at what instant you lit the Shabbat candles."

Yet, it is conceivable to me(who stand in Israel with God) that even in the first order encounter, God being there with just this Jew and no other (let us say), this particular Jew, not having lost selfhood along the way, might conceivably resist God as God came to this Jew. The easy "out" on this matter is to say that is a matter of faulty "perception." By definition God could not be there in a guise that one had to resist. That makes a certain sense to me and it is something I would like to believe. But I thought that one of the big lessons of the postmodern period was our being wary indeed of using human standards to tell God what God could be. And clearly our forebears from time to time encountered God in forms whose tone and substance are ones I, for all that I am one of Israel and its ongoing historic relationship with God, would, in God's name, have to resist. That is all theory and it is a situation I hope not to have to encounter. I have not in the past been closed to God's reproof or other experiences of God not being what would be easy for me, but thus far I have been able to accept them as genuine. Still, a possibility remains . . . and since you asked and pressed me hard on this matter, to my benefit, I assure you, I have told you what I can.

5.

The Reform Judaism of Renewing the Covenant
An open letter to Elliot Dorff

I'm deeply grateful for your searching review of *Renewing the Covenant*. To be given serious attention is itself a considerable gift but you are also gracious enough to say many nice things about my work over the years and that truly touched me. Many thanks indeed for your great-heartedness. Yet as you surely know, the greatest compliment of all is to have a thoughtful reader probe your ideas with great care and respond to them from the depths of his or her understanding. I was particularly happy that you devoted a significant part of your review to my effort to transform the old Enlightenment-Kantian view of the individuality of the self into something far more congenial to Judaism. As I see it, there is far more overlap in our views than your analysis indicates though I agree that we differ in significant part.

You perceive a great divide between us because you insist that my book must be read "as a distinctly Reform theology . . . Indeed it would be hard not to be, given that Rabbi Borowitz has been the prime Reform ideologue for a generation." As a result, though I climax my "theology of postliberal Jewish duty" with my notion of "the Jewish self" — self-consciously not "the autonomous Jewish self" of my 1984 article — you believe I must not be saying anything much different from what Reform thinkers of prior generations said. All my talk aside, you insist that self overwhelms Jewishness with all the usual deleterious consequences for our Judaism.

Two things about this assertion particularly surprise me. The first stems from your careful emphasis on my six chapters rejecting the isolated selfhood of the Enlightenment and Kant, a notion that dominated the older Reform Judaism (and most of American Jewish non-Orthodox apologetics). Postmodern Jews, I argue need to recontextualize selfhood for Jews as Covenantal, that is, to see the Jewish self as an individuality fundamentally grounded in God and the Jewish people's relationship to God. Moreover, second, even though you know that "This book does not present itself as a distinctly Reform theology" you insist that "it certainly is one." Since you claim that "Reform" necessarily calls for the supremacy of utterly individual autonomy, you can insist that I must also be making the isolated self the arbiter of Jewish duty. You say I write clearly and probingly, so either I cannot mean what I say or else I misunderstand its implications.

I do not know how I can persuade you that "I am not now and never have been a card-carrying Reform ideologue." As to my role in preparing our Centenary Perspective document, I became Chair of the Committee which wrote it only because a previous Commission — of which I was not invited to be a regular member — failed to do so despite several years of meetings. A series of political necessities then brought the CCAR to turn to me. So though you twice credit me with inserting some specific language in it, my colleagues, vigorous exercisers of their autonomy and doughty defenders of their political diversity, never extended such deference to me. They wrote the text in session line by line. Overnight I put my notes (now in the American Jewish Archives) of what they had agreed to say into connected prose. They then went over the whole thing again — as later did the whole membership in a floor debate of the draft. In short, I am not the Reform Robert Gordis, z"l.

Instead, I have always tried to think academically about Jewish belief and its consequences. None of my models — Cohen, Baeck, Kaplan,

Buber, Rosenzweig and Heschel ever did their thinking as part of a movement or in the context of its ideology. They simply tried to think through the truth of Judaism in their day as best they could understand it and I have spent my life attempting to emulate them. Only one of my books for adults and only a few of my articles deal with Reform Judaism. For over three decades I have addressed myself to and written about that overwhelming mass of modernized Jews who, regardless of labels, exercise the right to make up their own minds about what they will believe and do as Jews. Having been misunderstood when I tried calling these people "liberal" Jews, I attempted to nail down my meaning in *Renewing the Covenant* by mostly speaking about "non-Orthodox" Jews. When I mean Reform Jews there or anywhere, I say so.

If you would like some specific if rough examples of my view of Reform Jewish decision-making today, look at my *Reform Jewish Ethics and the Halakhah* (Behrman, 1994). That book, with all its faults, e. g., its fourteen issues were tackled by teams of students who did term papers as my kind of Reform *poskim,* will show you the distance between my functioning theory of duty and the one you have imputed to my theology. Even though the students are far more Kantian than I am, you will not find "autonomy run amok" in any of their papers.

You see three issues dividing us: practicality, Jewishness and philosophy. The first, practicality, has two parts, the heavy burden of being a responsible (Jewish) self and the role of community in our decision-making. I agree few of us can know all we need to know to make a significant decision. When I need help in such cases I do what most people do: consult experts and read the most responsible literature I can find. I see no reason why responsible Jewish selves will not do the same on matters where Judaism is relevant. Thoughtful Jewish writing on contemporary problems today continues to expand, one reason I take it that you and I often seek to make our own views known and do all we can to see to it that rabbis and Jewish educators are increasingly knowledgeable.

You say that the Jewish self will not care as you do about what the Jewish community says on an issue. Maybe "your" Reform Jews are supposed to believe that but not if they took my views seriously. In addition to what you correctly said about my situating the Jewish self inextricably in the Jewish people, consider what I wrote about proper Jewish decision-making as the climax to my argument in *Renewing the Covenant* (pp. 288-295). There I explain in some detail that as a result of its Covenantal situation, the Jewish self should make decisions based on 1, what it believes God wants of it as a member of the Covenanted people; 2, which means it will be concerned with what the Jewish community today is saying on this topic (more of this below); 3, but the experience of Covenant being fundamentally historical, what rabbinic tradition said on the topic must be given reverent attention; 4, as must the messianic, future-oriented thrust of the Covenant. But all those vectors finally come to rest 5, in an individual self whose individuality is not extinguished for all that it is utterly bound up with God and the Jewish people's relationship with God, historically articulated, presently lived and projected to the End Days.

My six chapters and my second vector should make plain that I insist on community concern among Jews and know nothing of the unattached self in Judaism. If that means that I am not a Reform Jew by your standards then so be it. It is equally clear that I am not your kind of Conservative Jew for I do not closely identify "community" with rabbinic law-making as you do.

The issue of law, however, requires me to inquire about your "practicality" in making it so central a tenet of Conservative Judaism. For years Conservative rabbis have lamented the inability of the movement to create a laity that would let their lives be disciplined by Jewish law and recently a good number of rabbis and laypeople who took law seriously abandoned Conservatism for a movement of their own. Realistically, then, how practical is it to ask Conservative Jews to live by Jewish law? Of course, if by "law" you mean little more than "standards," the term with which law is linked in the title of the Rabbinical Assembly Committee dealing with issues of duty, then little divides us. No self-respecting Jewish self could object to hearing about communal standards; that would only help clarify one important factor in determining Jewish duty. We disagree, however, about the possibility and desirability of law fulfilling its common function, being authoritative in our lives. You charge that my sense of "sociality does not . . . require obedience of Jewish law." You are right. But has the Conservative Movement, which has made law central to its ideology, yet found a way to "require obedience of Jewish law?"

Your second objection to my position is that Jewish tradition knows nothing of individual Jews being given "the right to make decisions about what they should believe and practice." I agree that in sanctioning even a Covenantally limited autonomy I, and certainly the Reform Jews who are more radical than I am, have moved away from classic Jewish faith. But by Maimonides' standards of *epikorsut* the Conservative view (like that in Reform) that there is a significant human factor in revelation instantly puts you too in our situation. The issue here is not, as you suggest, a simple realism about what modernity has done to us all but rather how we evaluate what we have learned about the conjunction of human dignity and self-legislation. You are too sensible not to value much that this notion has brought us and you affirm its lasting significance when it does not degenerate into radical individualism, a plague I equally deplore. But I argue that modernity, by teaching us this new sense of self, has made a major, lasting, spiritual contribution to Judaism — or, to be more direct, that this notion is contemporary revelation, a new insight into God's will and thus a present indication of our ongoing Covenantal responsibility. That is, I believe, the theological substrate to the endemic practice of most of contemporary Jewry: listening to their leaders but then exercising what they take to be their sacred right, making up their own minds about what they will and won't do. Community creates duty, as you say, but that is a far cry from anything like authoritative law.

This brings me to your final charge against me, that I have ignored the philosophical attack on the radical individualism of the Enlightenment. That makes sense only if one demands that the rejection of the Enlightenment and Kantian self which I have specifically called "postmodern" and "postliberal" doesn't mean what it says and I have no choice but to be a defender of the kind of individualism you take to be the unchanging essence of Reform Judaism.

I shall allow the defense to rest there. But I must, however, point out that the authority of the self operates in contemporary Jewish law more significantly than you have acknowledged. On the simplest level, why is it that I know that I will find your forthcoming book on Jewish medical ethics highly persuasive, where a similar book by David Novak will be somewhat less so and the writing of J. David Bleich on the same topic will likely touch me only informationally? Surely what divides this trio is not what the legal texts objectively say, for you will all study the same ones. It is also not substantially a matter of consulting the community (though I imagine that your disparate reference groups will have some influence on you). Rather I suggest that we are dealing here with the way in which the self makes itself felt even in legal decision-making. One factor in decision-making, not the only or the most significant matter in the process, is simply who you are as a person and how you act on that individuality. Were you different as person than you are, you would not be the *posek* we know you to be, the author of your *shitah*.

Or let me give a case more internal to the Conservative movement. Consider the situation of Conservative rabbis faced with a split decision of the Committee on Law and Standards. How do they finally reach a decision about a difficult issue? The critical texts can apparently be read in at least two ways and they cannot ask the community to settle the matter for it is just its leaders who are themselves of two minds. I suggest that in significant measure they will follow my five part schema: they will seek to determine what God now wants by filtering their living religiosity through Jewish history, the community's present experience and its ongoing messianic aspiration and, finally, subject the whole to the reality of who they individually are and what they personally believe. You and they may take step three — studying Jewish law and lore — with a somewhat greater sense of obligation than I might but we shall all be following the theology of Jewish duty explicated in *Renewing the Covenant*.

This line of argument can proceed one final step. You assert, in distinguishing yourself from the Orthodox, that there is a significant human element in legal decision-making and your open acknowledgment of it enables you "better [to] discern God's will" than they can. By what authority is that position put forward as a fundamental principle of your Judaism? It cannot be on the basis of Jewish law and tradition for they do not grant human beings that much power. It cannot be claimed that it is self-evident for not only do our Orthodox deny it but so do all fundamentalists and secularists. I suggest that the Conservative sages who founded your movement did so on their own authority as scholars, people of piety and participants in many aspects of modern culture. In brief, they acted on the authority of their autonomy, literally, their right to be self-legislating. And those who have since joined the Conservative Movement have done the same thing in a somewhat lesser fashion. You have more investment in autonomy, Covenantally recontextualized to be sure, than you are willing to admit — or so I see it.

I hope you will take the length at which I have written as a token of my great personal esteem for you and your writings over the years. I have learned much from you in the past and look forward to doing so in the future. I do hope you will have the opportunity before too long to respond to what I have written here and I will look forward to hearing from you about it.

Chapter 13

ೞ಄ಌ

Textual Reasoning and Jewish Philosophy, The Next Phase of Jewish Postmodernity?

A ll of us who rejoice in the eros of intellect have had an extraordinary experience at this conference on Textual Reasoning and Jewish Philosophy. At all other sessions we dipped first into text before an occasional second dip into philosophy. Now for *afikoman,* our festive dessert, we give abstraction prime of place. Let me then say a few words about the philosophic agenda behind this program.

Our meeting has continued the task Rosenzweig undertook in his 1921 essay, *Understanding the Sick and the Healthy,* that is, curing philosophy of its modernist maladies. This seemed critical if Jewish philosophy was to continue to fill the gap which the changed notion of revelation had created in the theory of authority for modernized Jews before and immediately after the turn of the century. In effect, German idealism had explained to them why people who were determined to be modern should stay Jews and it clarified which commandments they still ought to follow. I do not suggest that most Jews then or even their rabbis, those middle-men of Jewish ideas, walked around with the predecessor documents to Cohen's *Religion der Vernunft* as their guide to Jewishness. But they vaguely believed that academic philosophy stood behind the plausibility structure which undergirded the community's efforts to create a life that was both Jewish and modern. Rosenzweig knew that the modernism of his day, Marburg neo-Kantianism and perhaps all of German idealism, was doomed and he sought to move from their sickness to a healthy new form of intellectuality. He differed from us in one critical respect. He believed that the classic philosophic quest retained sufficient vitality that he could create its therapy by philosophic means, though his radical transformations of the old ways are only now being received as philosophically acceptable. However, a century's experience and postmodernism's cogent critique of logocentricity have enfeebled philosophic authority so greatly that most of us believe that a strategy other than Rosenzweig's is called for. And it was this powerful intuition which prompted this experiment in the renewal of cerebration.

Why do we still seek to revivify philosophy? We do so not merely because we find it fun to think and rewarding to attain tenure. Rather we believe philosophy's dedication to abstraction and generalization can give us access to significant levels of truth, or as a theologian might put it, that the mind's stretch for comprehensiveness is another way we approach God's own unity. The social effect of broad-scale rationality confirms its value since it allows us to talk to, to understand and often live peaceably with people of radically different backgrounds than our own. Moreover, we Jews have special reason to care about philosophy's infatuation with the universal. On the theoretical level, the notion of universalism has been the basis for our inclusion in modern societies and remains the bulwark of our security. All this is true and yet postmodernism has convinced us that abstraction and generalization belie the reality that we are all particulars, gendered persons and social beings. It is grandiose to believe that any single mind can have ideas which are true for all people, everywhere, all the time. We all think more particularly than that. Yet knowing this, we also intuit that there is somehow a certain truth to thinking universally. I exemplify our predicament, for only by generalizing about our individuality and speaking abstractly about our particularity, in effect only by refuting myself, can I communicate my meaning to you — a quite common postmodern situation.

Jewish philosophy today suffers from what generalization has done to Jewishness. When Jewish thinkers can transcend the secularity of the general philosophic guild, they identify Jewish belief with having a proper understanding of God and seek to supply that in terms of a philosophically responsible statement. But that accomplishment, for all its value, only brings us to the faith of Noachides, that is, people in general, human beings. Without also positing the election of Israel and the truth of Torah, that is, without the particularity which philosophic generalization eschews, we do not stand in the Covenant of Sinai and have a recognizable Jewish character. A similar reductionism occurs when *mitzvah* is redefined as ethics. Jewish philosophers do that because ethics is the only category of duty philosophy can hope to mandate, a practice, for example, that leads some of our most stimulating thinkers to compress Rosenzweig's notion of revealed law to ethics. Valorizing the ethical commandments may produce exemplary *Benei Noach*, humans, but it will not produce *Benei Yisrael*, Jews. Is there, then, some way of preserving the genius of philosophy, its reaching for the greatest unity, without thereby requiring philosophers of Judaism to denude our tradition of its precious particularity?

This line of thought has led some thinkers among us to suggest that we could link philosophy and particularity by a close reading of Jewish texts. This procedure might well produce the therapy we seek. After all, insofar as we remain Jews, we acknowledge that our classic texts make a claim on us and in some sense, therefore, are commanding. Moreover, though individual voices often sound in them, their collective, anonymous authorship clearly speaks out of the fullness of Jewish folk particularity, as does the exalted regard in which our people has traditionally held them. And we, talking about them today not only carry on their communal discussions but do so ourselves in community. Engagement with our texts, then, commends itself as a therapy for the generalizing ills of Jewish philosophy and may also help us create a new way of thinking about Judaism.

So we have taken a first step in this new Jewish philosophic direction in the two days that we have been together. What have we accomplished? What might we yet do? Let me respond to these questions by presenting six concluding observations. For brevity's sake I shall put these in rather general language but I understand them to be quite personally grounded, not only in who I am but in the special way in which I approach issues of Jewish belief and their exposition.

One, it is clear that textual scholars and philosophers share a common goal. In Dan Boyarin's language, we who are resolutely fixed in western culture and are simultaneously devoted Jews quickly discover that our treasured Jewish texts seem odd to those steeped in a western sensibility. As a result we seek ever more adequately authentic ways to explain their meaning to the general culture and that means finding aspects of current intellectual exchange which will empower us in that task. We seek to state what is common to these two modes of thinking/writing while clarifying what makes them different from each other and gives them their individual character. If earlier generations of Jewish scholars often erred on the side of exaggerating what the two shared, we seek to guard against triumphalism as we work to give the particular its due. In more specifically philosophic guise, we seek to set forth our Jewish view of reality and, most particularly, the human condition — theologically what would be called Jewish faith — with just this same concern for commonalities and divergences.

Two, the textual scholars and philosophers gathered here share a common perception of the cultural resources enabling us to carry on our work of dialogue and translation between our two intellectual worlds. Specifically, the various spiritual currents which come together in the stream called postmodernity. It allows us a certain mental freedom and encourages a greater sense of the layers of meaning in what we take to be the truth than modernity did. For both groups it is not clear that the resources of postmodern ways of reading texts or explicating ideas have yet been exhausted and we are encouraged to proceed along this particular intellectual path. It should be noted, however, that in the presentations here, the textual scholars often exhibit an esthetic which is more sexually oriented than that of the philosophers. The latter seem relatively staid in their creativity where the textualists seem to find greater value in what an older scholarship would have called daring and shock.

Three, we share one great exemplar of our common enterprise, Levi ben Gerson. Despite his notorious scientific sophistication and his rigorous rationality he was clearly influenced by Judaism's received texts. His greatest impact on the later generations of Jews came less through his major philosophic work than from his textual writing, specifically, his commentary to the Torah. Yet the particular distinction of his interpretations of the biblical text lies in the philosophic mentality which infuses them. Thus it appears that in his case philosophy, as it were, largely provides the context for his literary work, the kind of hermeneutic we are quite accustomed to from modern Jewish philosophical readings of our texts. But it would be interesting to know in greater detail how he found text leading or critiquing his philosophy since this might provide us with a model for our particular task.

Four, from this brief exposure it would seem that there are levels to the way in which reasoning about texts becomes immediately applicable to philosophic thinking. When one explicates the reasoning in a given text, or provides a plausible supposition of the reasoning which structures a specific text, that provides Jewish thinkers with a clear, specific bit of intellectual data which will require their attention at some point in their broad-scale constructions. Textualists also often bring together a number of texts and generalize about them, or make similarly comprehensive statements about them based on their expertise with the texts or their hermeneutic theory. Philosophically, such observations may be quite stimulating. Nonetheless, as the gap between what the individual text or texts say and the generalization about them increases, a question arises as to whether the "authority" behind the observation is more to be connected to the reverenced text or to the imagination of the reader. Obviously, postmodern understandings of the intimate interplay between text and reader will not permit us contrast objective with subjective readings here as the moderns were wont to do. Nonetheless, the more texts one wishes to generalize about the greater the distance between the texts and the reasoning. Oft-times this goes a step further, as when one reasons about one or more texts in terms of a broad-scale understanding of history, human nature or reality. In such cases what passes as textual reasoning has largely passed over into the application of a philosophical point of view to the texts in question. Without a full-scale philosophic validation of these covert metaphysics, the reach of textualists for the broadest possible horizon of meaning can only be of limited value to philosophers.

Five, for some time now philosophers have been obsessed with where one begins one's thinking — one's premises or assumptions — and how one then seeks to carry out the analytic/constructive intellectual task — one's method. It seems reasonably clear that the substance of the resulting thought will largely depend upon these two matters but most people do not want to pay much attention to these matters, so critical to philosophers. Thus, scholars of texts largely take it for granted that the particular text they are working with is worth our attention for more than the simple reason that all increases in human knowledge are to be valued. Something similar may be said of the manner in which they carry on their enterprise of revealing what these texts most significantly imply. To be sure, they validate their practice by accepting, perhaps with creative modification, the patterns which their guild has found valuable and commends to all who would have a respected place in their midst. Yet the special passion or hope which pervaded our sessions was almost certain due to our joint assumption that reasoning about texts might transcend its abstract academic value and have significant consequences for living and believing as a Jew. Particularly since something of a normative agenda lurks behind our exploration, philosophers, who glory in validation and what might establish it, will find it difficult to proceed very far until a persuasive case is made for why this text or texts should engage us, what weight it might have in our Jewish lives and by what means a contemporary reader might best elucidate their compelling meanings.

Six, pursuing these several problems to their climax, a daunting clash between the central interests of the two groups of scholars seems to remain. Characteristically, classic Jewish texts resolutely resist generalization. Everything we read is but a partial statement of what we intuit to be a much greater, unitary truth. Yet no statement of that comprehensive truth itself is ever explicitly given us in a text or collection of texts. When, rarely, a given text speaks comprehensively, we find other texts that persist in saying the contrary or flatly contradicting the former. Will not philosophic generalization from the reasoning exposed in one text stand in need of continual expansion by philosophizing from another text's meaning? Or does some synergy assert itself when the texts assert their particularity against the philosopher's desire to think abstractly, opening up to us a new way of thinking as post-ghetto Jews, one which is neither the old philosophy with its suspect passion for universals, or the older styles of exe- and eise-getic reading of texts? Our conference was convened to see what happened when these evocative issues were faced in practice rather than merely in theory and textual scholars and philosophers will agree, I am sure, that our common investigation has gotten off to a stimulating and promising start.

Part Three

What Does Judaism Say About . . . ?

Chapter 14

℘ℛ

Covenant

J ews commonly use the term *berit* in two main ways. In particular, it refers to the rite of circumcision; on a more abstract level, it signifies the central affirmation of Jewish belief: that there is a pact between God and the People of Israel. We cannot properly hope to understand the one without exploring the other and this chapter is devoted to the far-ranging faith, traditional and modern, which ritual circumcision embodies and projects.

The very first time we hear of circumcision in the Torah, (Genesis 17: IN), it is intimately connected with God's promises to Abraham for his descendants and to Abraham's corollary obligations. The first of these to be specified is circumcision: "Thus shall My Covenant be marked in your flesh as an everlasting pact" (Gen. 17:13). It is no wonder then that the rite of surgically removing the foreskin eventually came to be called berit. Yet that identification of ceremony and belief often confuses people about the role of circumcision in Judaism and thus about the nature of our religion. In the overall understanding of traditional Jewish Law, one need not be circumcised to be a Jew, that is to participate fully in the Covenant. Medically exempt males are fully kosher Jews; so are women, a matter on which the Torah is quite explicit in its Deuteronornic version:

You stand this day, all of you, before Adonai your God, your chieftains, your elders and your officials, all the men of Israel, your children, your wives, even the stranger within your camp . . . to enter into the *berit* of *Adonai* your God, [the *berit*] which *Adonai* your God is concluding with you this day . . . (Deut. 29:9ff.)

The term *berit* is also closely associated with other rites, most notably that of keeping *Shabbat*, which is called a "sign" of the Covenant (Exod. 31:16-17). Most frequently, however, the Bible uses the term in speaking of the Ark in which the two tablets of the Covenant were kept, the tablets Moses received on Mount Sinai from God. For that is the larger sense of *berit*, the one which lies between every other usage of covenant in our tradition: our God calls human beings into partnership, initially all humankind, as with Noah and his children, (Gen. 9:8ff.), but later, climactically, all the People of Israel.

Even traditionally, the concept of a pact between God and people is most astonishing. The God who is the only God of the universe and thus transcends it in every way nonetheless is understood to become involved with people. They are known to be frail, perverse or even malevolent. Yet they are created in God's image and, whatever else that might mean, are therefore capable as no other creatures are of being called into alliance with God. More, God has purposes for people and commits these responsibilities into human hands. Were that not surprising enough, God then resolutely refuses to infringe on the human freedom to do or not do what God has commanded. To be sure, God remains free to respond to human sinfulness as to human merit, a matter of no small weight in human accountability, but, despite their inequality in status and power, there were two active partners to the agreement. This was the heart of biblical Jewish faith.

In that unconscious way social groups have of making certain terms central to their ethos, the Hebrews somehow settled on the word *berit* to describe their fundamental religious intuition. As is typical of religious symbols, the original use of the term *berit* occurred in everyday life, in this case in the legal realm. In Hebrew jurisprudence, it signified a contract between two parties, whether the ordinary one of commerce or the more exalted one between one king and another. The critical features of ancient contracts are quite familiar to us: two parties are involved; each party takes on certain responsibilities to the other; these undertakings are entered into with considerable solemnity; and violating them brings serious consequences. To our biblical forebears this model of human relationships seemed the best symbolic expression they could find to represent what they knew to be their tie to God.

Berit was not the only term for relationship that suggested itself to the biblical authors. They occasionally speak of God in a domineering role, as that of an owner to his beast (Isa.1:3) or to his slave ("servant" is too euphemistic a translation of *eved*; Isa. 41:8ff.). This is mitigated in the more frequent use, certainly among the prophets, of the marriage motif, though one needs to keep in mind the male-dominated, Near Eastern marriage which the authors have in mind. It is even more loving and tender when God is described as Father or as Mother concerned with a child. Yet as evocative as were all these other ways of speaking of God's relationship to the People of Israel, none can be said to have become as encompassing as was the legal metaphor of Covenant. (It should be noted, too, that the potential limits of this one relationship, *berit*, were then compensated for by utilizing many other images and, in later Jewish literature, by amplifying them. By extension, the second commandment of the Decalogue warns us that no symbol, no matter how supernal its apparent genius, will ever be great enough to speak to God fully.)

We may conjecture that *berit* was so appealing a term because it conveyed another critical aspect of Jewish faith: that God gave us specific instruction (*torah*) as to how we were to live to carry out our partnership with God. It is, indeed, one of the distinguishing characteristics of Judaism that it claims to possess God's verbal instructions, the story and exhortation as well as the laws and counsel-so to speak, the stipulations of the contract-that are to guide us in fulfilling our awesome role. From this belief derived the Jewish passion for knowledge and the sanctity of study, as well as the activist approach to serving God in community which so runs through biblical teaching.

In sum, Jewish faith has classically centered about the notion of a contract which God, no less, had entered into with the People of Israel, one prefigured in Canaan but properly formalized at Sinai and renewed on numerous occasions thereafter. To live by the Jewish religion meant to abide by the many evolving stipulations of the contract, one of the earliest of which was the circumcision of males.

Put in such bald legal terms, it is difficult for modern Jews to gain a good sense of the living religiosity which characterized our forebears. Most of us, from personal experience as well as by Christian apologetic, tend to find law in general and contracts in particular essentially oppressive. Idealistically, we like to think that if people really understand each other, they don't need written agreements, certainly not in anything so personal as religion ought to be. I shall say something more about that later. Here I only want to say something about understanding the centrality of this legal metaphor in traditional Judaism: it never came close to wiping out the personal side of Jewish religiosity. Think, for example, of how the people's acquiescence is needed for the contract to be made at Sinai, and how again and again the prophets strive to bring the people back, not only to religious obedience, but to spiritual understanding. They are so much real partners to the pact that they can even argue with God about God's conduct as a Covenant partner, though, to be sure, this happens only at exceptional moments. And, if more personal evidence is required, one can simply turn to the Book of Psalms. Better than anything else I know, it conveys a rich sense of the ennobled inner life of the individual Jew in good times and in bad.

Our central Jewish motif arises from a legal basis to do justice to our belief that the service of God is mandated, with a social as well as a personal dimension and activism; it is not centrally personal and thus easily oriented to the inner life and relatively passive about the world. So when Jews left the ghetto and could no longer affirm a law mandated in detail by God, they nonetheless retained the notion of Covenant, affirming its religious vision while giving it new content.

The modem Jewish thinkers who have suggested how Reform Jews might reinterpret the notion of the Covenant agree on one principle: our sense of reality demands that we give greater weight to the human partner in the *berit* than did our tradition. That is to say, we believe that we serve God best by being true to our minds and consciences even where, in significant matters, they clash with our heritage. Reform Judaism itself is a result of such trust in the Jewish People's continuing capacity to meet radically new challenges; Zionism is another such development, though a secular one. Both movements insisted on a human activism that was not acceptable in classic Judaism, particularly as it had evolved in the centuries immediately preceding Jewish modernization.

By taking some liberties, we may say that our modern thinkers have interpreted *berit* less as contract than as what moderns call "a personal relationship." Where the classic notion of *berit* had seen the relationship between God and the People of Israel stipulated in considerable contractual detail-their marriage contract, if you will-modern thinkers stressed what God and Israel meant to one another, thus giving the human partner considerable room to specify the duties that result from this relationship.

This subtle shift of emphasis has many ramifications. Thus, a proper Jewish act would now be judged not simply in terms of what our sages had ruled concerning it-though we might find that still persuasive-but whether the act contributed, as best we can understand it, to our ongoing Jewish relationship with God. Driving to the synagogue for *Shabbat* services is clearly forbidden in the traditional understanding of the Covenant-contract. Yet attending *Shabbat* services, even if that entails driving on *Shabbat*, seems to most modem Jews to be a proper way of enhancing the Covenant-relationship. This shift of standards for Jewish practice remains the major basis of argument among Jews in modern times. While we liberal Jews consider this to be a true understanding of how Jews ought to serve God today, only after many generations of Jewish experience with this new emphasis will our People be able to judge whether we have truly acted "for the sake of Heaven."

Most modern Jews, alas, do not also want to hear about the obligations which arise from this new sense of Covenant. They are delighted that Reform teaches that they are entitled to reject our tradition when it conflicts with modernity and they happily chuck whatever does not come easily or pleasantly. Having been granted Jewish autonomy so that they might be more responsible, they mostly use their freedom to avoid duty. One might call that primal Reform Jewish sin: abusing religious freedom by taking it casually. We will know you care by what, in fact, you do; a relationship that does not have a significant effect on one's life is not much of a relationship. One cannot hope to do little or nothing as a Jew and still claim to have a significant relationship with God as part of the Jewish People.

Modern Jewish thinkers have gone on to specify just where Jews today ought to place major religious emphasis in building their sort of Covenant. Since they stress the human aspects of religion, much of their thought has dealt with the personal relationships which ought to characterize contemporary Jewishness.

The primary level on which this has been worked out has been in an insistence on our Jewish Covenant with all humankind, a relationship which lays upon us the responsibility to be ethical to all human beings. That seems so obvious to most modern Jews that they cannot imagine it was not always a central part of Jewish teaching and practice. To be sure, there always was an implicit mandate for universal ethical obligation in our tradition. But social circumstances made responsibility for humankind as a whole a minor part of active Jewish duty. In biblical times, non-Jews were idolaters, hence involvement with them might mean the loss of the one people dedicated to God. Once Christianity and then Islam had established themselves, they segregated and oppressed Jews, keeping them from full citizenship as long as their countries were intertwined with religion. Only where secular, i.e., non-religious, states emerged could Jews become equals and only then, a matter of less than two centuries ago in Europe, could the issue of Jewish duty to non-Jews become anything other than a highly theoretical topic.

When Jews were permitted to live among non-Jews as equals, they had little difficulty embracing the notion that all humankind was one. The Jewish tradition had said the same thing religiously in its vision of human origins. It told of a single progenitive couple for all people and unequivocally said that all human beings, unconditionally, were created in God's image. One God implied one humankind and the duty to create God's rule on earth meant doing good to and with all other human beings.

The very essence of the Jewish religion, it was now suggested, was ethical responsibility. Jews were now to live out their ancient, ever-new Covenant mainly by how they conducted themselves in the general flow of human life, the matrix in which they primarily lived. The extraordinary Jewish contribution to every contemporary cause for human betterment has its roots in this concept. Indeed, it has affected Jews so powerfully that Jews who have given up the religious notion of the Covenant have regularly sought secular causes in which they could, as they thought, more effectively achieve their ethical ends.

One somewhat technical aspect of this universal ethical stress in the modern understanding of the Covenant deserves special attention. Jewish thinkers have been particularly attracted to ethics in the sense in which the philosopher Immanuel Kant used the term. He insisted that a rational mind necessarily manifests itself in an ethical (as well as in a scientific and an esthetic) mode. Since the hallmark of rationality is its effort to create and operate by rule rather than arbitrarily, rational ethics are characterized not by mood or by quality but by their lawfulness. His disciples thus took the ethical implications of being rational most seriously and they spoke of ethics as moral law. That allowed Jewish thinkers to say our religion is the most rational of religions for we are a religion which emphasizes law and the heart of our law, they asserted, is being ethical. Suddenly, modern reason and Jewish being had come together in a most attractive way. And this understanding of our Covenant with all humankind still has a powerful place in our modern Jewish self-understanding.

What other thinkers found missing in this view-for all its human appeal-was a satisfactory sense of our continuing Covenant with all other Jews; that is, with the Jewish People as an entity of its own. The trouble with making the Covenant with all humankind primary is that it may seem to supersede what had been the basic community of the Covenant, the Jewish People. And there have been and are many splendid Jewish humanitarians who have had energy for every troubled people in the world-except their own. Even logically, this exaggerated universalism is ethically odd; surely loving my neighbors cannot mean that I may not give special, indeed priority attention to my own family. And, almost literally, that is what "the Children of Israel" means. We are, to give that phrase literal effect, Jacob's kids. We are also a community united by a glorious history, a rich heritage, an ongoing way of life (in all its diversity), and a common fate as far as our enemies are concerned. On many human levels, then, our Covenant must not slight our bonds to other Jews.

This motif has even been made the most basic understanding of modern Jewishness by those who point to social groups as the source of the most significant human creativity. Our cultures give us our language, our values, our way of living and approaching life. Through our civilization, structured in institutions, empowered by values, transmitted formally by rite and informally by the family and other human networks, we attain our true humanity. The Jewish People need have no apology for desiring to maintain its distinctive folk culture, considering how richly human it has been-and that includes its incomparable concern with ethical action, now extended to reach out to all humankind. But, like every such folk life, it lives by continual creativity and development. Today, in a democratic age, it will benefit most by a pluralism which will happily embrace its diverse cultural experimentation.

For such thinkers, a Jew is primarily one who actively maintains Covenant with all other Jews, avidly participating in their cultural creativity though free to reappropriate the Jewish heritage in quite individual fashion.

One major manifestation of this sense of folk covenant has been the close sense of identification Jews the world over have with the State of Israel. At its simplest, that is an extension of the notion that Jews have a particular responsibility for other Jews who are in trouble. Surely the State of Israel originally awakened widespread Jewish passion as a haven for refugees and a home in which they might be rehabilitated. But the ties have grown far beyond that so that Jews everywhere somehow look upon the State of Israel as "their" state, in an ethnic rather than a political sense, and personally identify with its accomplishments. Over the decades of its existence, the many human triumphs of the State of Israel have awakened extraordinary Jewish pride-and so, it must be said, have its occasional failures awakened great Jewish concern and soul-searching. We would not care so if we were not so involved.

These impressive human extensions of the Covenant might easily so capture our imagination that we permit it to remain almost entirely a human matter. That is, we become so fully occupied with what we must do that we have little or no concern for our erstwhile dominant Covenant partner, God. Some decades back, in the heyday of Jewish satisfaction with what human beings could accomplish on their own, that seemed like a reasonable strategy. The more people learned, the more they could do to transform all human existence.

History has not dealt kindly with the notion that people, so to speak, could take God's place, that we and our resources are adequate to all the challenges which face us personally and humankind generally. As we have reached greater humility about our powers, we have made more room for God in our lives. In psychodynamic terms, having been through our developmental phases of separation and individuation, we are now ready for reconciliation.

This cultural movement has brought us to realize a fear we have in affirming God's role in the Covenant: won't letting God back in our lives mean we must become Orthodox? Surely that is what many Christian fundamentalists and Jewish "returnees" seem to think. Since modernity causes us such malaise, they argue, its antidote is to return fully to tradition, often with emphasis on its antimodern aspects. Yet that belittles what we have quite properly learned in modern times, that to be a person in the full sense of the term means to have substantial self-determination. Covenant needs to be interpreted in a way that enables us to keep our activist modern sense of human dignity while recognizing that we exercise it in terms of our relationship with God.

The response to this fear has been to recognize the substantial difference between a deep personal relationship and one which is only acquaintanceship. All of us know some people whom we manage to get through to on a deep level and, because of that, with whom we know we have special relationship. Doctors regularly encounter this phenomenon; with some patients you just hit it off, for reasons that aren't at all clear. Then you really become "their doctor" in a way that, for all your friendliness, you aren't with other people. The same sort of qualitative difference distinguishes "just friends" from "good friends"-and, most of all, from those whom we truly love. The binding, life-affecting relationship we call "Love" here becomes our model for the Covenant as a relationship.

This view asks us to envision the Covenant as the Jewish People's long-lasting love affair with God, one that has survived and been strengthened by its many fights and reconciliations, its intimacies and its duties, its inspiration and its unfathomability. As in every deep human relationship, it is sometimes overwhelmingly certain and other times troublingly shaky. And, so too, it needs to be worked at regularly though one can never quite know what will bring it alive just now-and then something quite trivial occurs which makes one realize how real it is and how much it means to us. One key to such relationships is that each partner participates in it in full integrity; neither one is master, neither one is slave, both can make their demands, each partner saying, if necessary, a painful but self-respecting "No." The moments of genuine love, whether in agreement or loving dissent, are our greatest human experiences. They are one contemporary model for understanding what we mean by Covenant.

These three interpretations of the Covenant converge in our contemporary idea of the family. We want it, in some primary sense, to communicate a high sense of human ethics and by its day-to-day give-and-take exemplify what we believe. We also want it to be a living continuation of all that the Jewish People has creatively stood for over the centuries, transmitting as much by its spirit as by its education and ritual the high human sense of what it is to be a Jew and a human being. But, most of all, we want it to touch and reflect the deepest reality that is in us and the mature love that ennobles human individuality and enables us to transcend ourselves.

Liberal Jews believe that the old contract-terms our People has lived by still often give rich expression to our ethical-Jewish-loving relationship with God. So we happily embrace them in historical, communal, personal continuity of the Covenant — and then not infrequently discover that doing them leads us to need deeper understandings of the *berit*, ones we are unlikely ever to have known without our tradition. Sometimes, however, that is not the case and then we feel religiously obligated to move beyond the old and honored patterns. Proudly and loyally, we seek to create our own, new modes of living our contemporary sense of Covenant loyalty. The kiss after Shabbat services is my favorite example.

We continue to work at deepening and strengthening our way of Covenant living. It is not an easy task to bring together a dynamic sense of Jewish responsibility and a modern sensibility which itself is in considerable flux. But when a child is born, we know that by a circumcision or a baby-naming we happily, responsibly want to welcome a child into the Covenant relationship/relationships we embrace — and by doing this we look forward in hope to all that this new person will now do to carry on our Jewish vision until humankind reaches the Messianic Time.

Chapter 15

ଈଠରେ

Zionism [1]

What constitutes Zionism never has been very clear and since the establishment of Medinat Yisrael some Israelis have questioned whether the idea of Zionism makes any sense. Over the decades the only constant has been that Zionists seem never to tire of talking about what Zionism really is, a tradition we now carry on.

I cannot hope, therefore, to tell you what Reform Religious Zionism is but only what I believe it is or ought to be. I mean that statement literally, that what I believe, my religious faith, requires and determines my Zionism. To my surprise, despite ARZA being a religious Zionist movement, my emphasis on the primacy of belief caused my old HUC schoolmate Dick Hirsch to anathematize[2] me as leading a new Reform non-Zionism[3]. For him Zionism means making peoplehood an equal "dimension of Jewishness to belief," and affirming that the Jewish state is "a prerequisite instrumentality for Jewish survival." He thinks our Zionism conforms to the World Zionist Organization Jerusalem Platform which bases it on "the unity of the Jewish people and the centrality of Israel," by which it probably means the State of Israel.

In the public discussion with Dick at the College-Institute it turned out that the misunderstanding between us was somewhat deeper and more unfortunate than I had thought.[4]   The article[5] which provoked Dick's response seemed to me merely a description of what was going on in American Jewry, albeit one to which I believe only a religiously grounded response will be adequate.   Dick had thought I was *advocating* the distancing from the State of Israel based on a classical Reform notion of "belief."   I would have thought that anyone who had read my work would know that was not the case — but we shall see another example of such misreading.   I am glad that the occasion at the College-Institute enabled us to clarify this issue for ourselves and for our listeners.

Since like all thinkers, I utilize terms from the past — our predecessors having taught us much — but then give them my particular slant, let me briefly try to clarify some relevant themes from my theology.   As to my advocacy of "belief," I do not think we take things very seriously unless we believe in them.   So one can be born into a people but not care much about that fact.   Thus, tens of thousands of Israelis have left the country and a good number of them, like all emigrants, have gradually allowed the residue of their former nationality to slip away from them.   So, too, for about twenty years after the '67 War, Diaspora Jews found new riches in their Jewish ethnicity, something that more recently they find less compelling than being a good person.[6]   I do not deny that ethnicity still has some normative power but when it comes to significant issues, peoplehood seems to me a subsidiary, not a primary force.[7]   When, however, we believe God is involved with our people, our folk, our nationality, our *am* or *goy kadosh*, our holy people or nationality, and we know we serve God as a member of that particular group, then our ethnicity takes on a special dignity and power.   That is true because it is not simply we who confer value on this *am* but the one and only God of the universe.

Let us track the relationship of our theology to our Zionism by pursuing an old liberal strategy, separating the essence of the effort from the immediate program which seeks to fulfill it.   Here Mike Meyer's thesis in his Union Biennial paper on Zionism makes good sense.   He suggests that the Zionists rightly criticized the early Reformers for lacking a proper sense of Jewish "collectivity."   As a historical description I think that term too neutral, hardly reflective of the Jewish nationalism early Zionism advocated, but I admit that a more precise term is hard to come by.   [Though our teacher contrasts this to Reform individualism, I suggest, with considerable temerity, that neither his work nor that of Gunther Plaut shows a lot of early emphasis on personal freedom.   The

Reform pioneers' sense of Jewish collectivity followed the models around them and they seemed to think of modern Jews as a church, so they often called it, after the Protestant model, "Reformed."]

In any case, the Zionists insisted that the Jews are not a church. I think they were right though for somewhat the wrong reasons. Still, permit me three quick comments: one, most world religions are not churches, credal associations, as Christianity is; two, they also aren't quasi-philosophical think-groups as it is sometimes suggested Reform Judaism ought to be; and, three, Moslems as well as Sikhs, are, like the Jews, the social hybrids we lamely call religio-ethnic groups. My Reform Jewish Zionism, then, is a direct outgrowth of my religious belief about the people of Israel. And I generally find that the intensity of one's Reform Zionism is directly correlated to the importance one religiously attaches to the people of Israel.

Let me track that phenomenon beginning with our colleagues whose souls are mostly fully identified with humankind. Their attitude to the Jewish collective ranges from benign indifference to that oscillating ambivalence we all manifest toward the far flung family we love but not always very enthusiastically. These colleagues — and those people in our congregations who are leery of being "too Jewish" — are the seed bed of a certain North American Reform Jewish aloofness toward Zionism. Thus, we have colleagues who have not been back to Israel since their year there under College auspices — and an occasional HUC faculty member who, I believe, has never been there. Their hearts are engaged by the homeless, the conflicted, the abused, the addicted, or the like. An emergency in the State of Israel would, of course, immediately bring them to take action on its behalf. But lesser Zionist causes will not deflect them from their heart's dedication to remedying general human injustice and suffering.

Other colleagues with something like this faith balance their love of humankind with their special joy at being a Jew among Jews. Perhaps they feel this most when studying Jewish texts, or swimming in the crazy tempestuousness of Jewish community activity, or, more likely when doing Jewish good deeds or old rites (like mourning and celebration, praying and socializing, discussing what to do or getting together to do it). They simply are enamored of this people which produces such a disproportion of smart, verbal, successful, useful, creative, maddeningly independent, depressingly vulgar and often silently saintly human beings — or is this more me than them?

Regardless, for many of us the people of Israel is more than rewarding; it is important, essential, and not just to us, we believe, but to the world, perhaps even to human history. Suddenly Zionism changes from a religious possibility to a religious necessity. Someone who believes there is something special about the Jewish people — without thereby casting aspersions on any other group — will care passionately about its collective welfare: biological, physical, cultural and spiritual. This understanding of our collectivity produces a close identification with the State of Israel in tranquil as in troubled times. It feeds the sentiment that no Diaspora community is as important to our people's contemporary well-being and morale as is that of the State of Israel. Zionism, most richly understood, is the movement dedicated to assuring the Jewish State's multi-leveled well-being and our widespread Jewish people's continued flourishing. No wonder then that for many colleagues of the generation before mine, Zionism was as good as their entire religion.

A further theological step must now be taken and since some people find this psychologically difficult to do, let me first indicate its common experiential manifestation. Many Jews, including many Israelis, believe that it is not enough for the State of Israel simply to be *k'khol hagoyim*, "a nation like all other nations" (1 Sam. 8:5), that is, to conduct its affairs as do its neighbors, Egypt, Jordan, Syria and Lebanon, or even like the established democracies of the West. As Jews we want it to be better than that and, for some obscure Jewish reasons, we insist that it must be better than that. We certainly do not think any outsiders, those paragons of cynicism under the guise of morality, have the right to employ that supererogatory criterion to make demands on us. And all but a saintly few of us insist that Jewish survival must begin with hard-headed realism. *V'af al pi khen,* nonetheless, at some elemental level of our Jewish being we know that Jewishness requires a Biblical kind of politics, one that works to sanctify power. It takes a full-blown prophet and God's own inspiration to know clearly what needs to be done in any specific political situation and we are not, despite our rhetoric, prophets. But we are, *haftarah* by *haftarah*, their living disciples and we know we must be driven by their Jewish ideals.

There is no good secular reason for having such exalted goals for the State of Israel and, indeed, for our people generally. We will understand this experience better if we cast off another vestige of our secularization and think theologically. We make these special demands upon the Jewish people because of the underground survival in us of an old Jewish religious belief we affirm in our own way: our people is, as a collectivity, intimately involved with God, the one and only God of the universe. And today, as before, the price of ethnic closeness with God is righteousness, personal and national spiritual overachieving. Most of us cannot term that "being chosen by God" or, more rationalistically, the "Mission of Israel" to teach humankind an ethical monotheism we know better than they do. I have made my case for speaking of this as the relationship called Covenant, personalistically rather than contractually understood, but no one's usage has yet captured the contemporary Jewish religious imagination. Still, the experience and the belief remain real if subterranean.

Permit me to reinforce this by pointing to our rabbinic experience. Despite the endless stupidities and frustrations of serving Jews, again and again some Jewish act we do surprises us by touching us with transcendence. Then we are reminded in a primal way that we and our people are involved with what is Ultimate in the universe, or better put, what is Utterly Significant in it. If our secularization does not immediately reduce religious experience to emotion, culture, failure of nerve, or the like, we recognize that this reality we confront in our own knowing/ unknowing way is the one our forebears called *Adonai*. Their usages about this can vex us badly so we prefer to struggle with our own theological language-making. Like our ancestors we know that *Adonai* demands that we become more than we are, even though, for the moment, to use an old anthropopathism, we sense that God, to use that term, is pleased with us collectively.

This mix of demand and blessing is as reminiscent as it is fresh. It results from what our people called "Covenant," its living relationship with God. So even in our own embarrassed, half-believing, half-disbelieving way we know that Jews, individually and collectively, must reflect in their lives this old-new intimacy with God. Because our folk is still called to serve God, it must survive and in our world national sovereignty has become critical to doing so.[8] That makes us Zionists, religious Zionists. And now political sovereignty has, for the first time in two millennia, given us the opportunity to effectuate God's demand for social righteousness in our own, self-determined collective life. No Jew who believes in the people of Israel's collective religious responsibility to God can fail to be stirred and moved by this exceptional religious challenge.

So much for theory. Practically, I regularly find an intellectual correlation between the depth of a Reform Jew's commitment to our people's corporate involvement with God — what we once called "the doctrine of Israel" — and the intensity of their religious Zionism. I will shortly measure the adequacy of my view by the critical Jewish criterion, its programmatic consequences, but I must first briefly speak of two other matters.

First, I suggest that our contemporary theological agenda should no longer center on God or Torah but on the doctrine of Israel. Any discussion of Torah as revelation and applied content depends on who the group is that is supposed to be "hearing" and doing this. That issue lies at the heart of many of our most troubling practical issues: should patrilineality mean that merely matrilineal Jews have no claim on Jewishness?; can intermarriages still be justified now that the statistics show it does not long add to Jewish affiliation?; should non-Jewish spouses and relatives in our congregations find no distinctions made between them and our Jewish members? By contrast, God's reality, once so hotly questioned by some of us, no longer agitates many in our community. The frailty of human nature, the self-destruction of rationalism, the emptiness of the general culture and especially the nihilists we nightly see on television have made us realize we don't believe as little as we once imagined we did. In this waste land, spirituality, not enlightened agnosticism, moves our searching minority. And, fortunately too, our linguistic problems with God-talk are now being eased by feminist Jewish thinkers whose analysis and practice are enriching us with their new coinages about God. So who we are as Jews, collectively, cannot now much longer be ignored.

Second, we cannot turn to the Torah precepts we call Zionism without discussing the critical liberal belief in self-determination. Affirming only God and Israel, we might well have Orthodoxy; granting the self a substantive role in our faith makes us Reform Jews and characterizes, I insist, the *de facto* Judaism of most modernized Jews regardless of their labels.

My use of the term "the self" has caused some people to misunderstand my views, again by putting me back into prior periods of our history. Mike Morgan writing recently in our *Journal* hears in my use of this notion only my 1960s existentialism. He contrasts this and other old options unfavorably with how he and other philosophers currently are trying to think as radically historicized persons — something I thought I had fully addressed in 1991 in my book delineating our postmodern situation.

Ellen Umansky not only knows *Renewing the Covenant*, as Michael does, but cites it in the *Journal of Reform Zionism*[9] only to then indict me for carrying forward the two centuries' old Reform anti-corporate preoccupation with autonomy and personal freedom. Against this, she suggests that the Jewish self exists in covenant not, in my language, "as a single soul in its full individuality" but "as a relational soul in community with others." She urges me to learn from Martin Buber "that no self is fully autonomous" but always exists in relationship. Her reading of *Renewing the Covenant* is so at variance from what other academic critics have found there and so typical of other misunderstandings of my notion of autonomy that I must clarify this issue in order to move on in an orderly fashion to my programmatic suggestions for Reform Zionism.

As to my failing to affirm the particularity of the single self, let me cite what I wrote in 1968 when I was already Buber's most enthusiastic supporter in the Jewish religious community. In the sexist language of those days, I said, "Yet, is the real man of history, in this case, the Jew, simply the I of I-Thou? That is, is his Jewishness, his sharing in a corporate covenant, somehow not essential to his existence but only an accretion?"[10] By 1984 I could articulate a positive resolution of the issue in my paper, "The Autonomous Jewish Self."[11]

In order better to situate my odd spot in the theological landscape it will help to give a quick map of the theological varieties of the territory called "autonomy," the place inhabited by the self. I see the term referring to five separate perspectives. Three of these may be called modern secular views. The classic philosophic view is that of Immanuel Kant who celebrates our essential individual freedom but calls for it to be fulfilled through human rationality and thus morally contained. By Jean Paul Sartre's time human rationality can no longer be philosophically thought of as essentially ethical so he creates an autonomy only out of freedom, thus making the worst sin "bad faith" or insincerity. And that has led on to the vulgar sense of freedom we hear so much of these days, that people simply have a right to their choices since it is their lives they are putting on the line. [How have the mighty fallen!]

These three positions are all human-centered; freedom is exercised in dialogue with oneself. The fourth position radically transforms philosophic self-legislation by converting what once was strictly "auto"[self]nomy into a freedom exercised in relation to an other, ultimately with God. This is clearly a religious view. However, in its fullest early exposition, that of Martin Buber, modern individualism reasserts itself. Buber says that despite group experience of the same "thou/Thou," all decisions are finally determined by what I personally learn from the encounter with the other.

I do not believe I ever spoke of autonomy in the common, essentially humanistic, neo-Kantian, Reform Jewish understanding. When I was a rabbinical student I discovered Buber's religious sense of autonomy and espoused it from then on. But caring about Jewish corporate existence as I did, I soon dissented from Buber's notion of Jewish duty of what God wanted you, a Jew, personally to do. It took me until the late '70s to work out my ethnicized, historicized and, if you will, Zionized conception of the Jewish relationship with God. Because I thought communication with moderns about religion still proceeded easiest when talking about the self and selfhood, I characterized my new, fifth notion of non-Orthodox Jewish "auto"nomy as the peculiar freedom of the "Jewish self."[12] Chapters 12-20 of *Renewing the Covenant* present a detailed development of my particularized, relational theology of Jewishness. I find it difficult to believe that thoughtful readers can escape the way old theological terms are being significantly transformed in these pages.

Let me precis my notion in two sentences. The Jewish self lives in intimate relationship with a real God not merely as a spiritual individual but as a single self ineradicably grounded in the people of Israel's ongoing, historic, messianic, relationship with God. Covenant involves all five of these vectors, God, the Jewish people today, the Jewish tradition, the people living toward "the messiah," and the single selves who are involved in all this.

All this would have been clearer if my text had been cited precisely in the first issue of *The Journal of Reform Zionism*. The omission of a single word there turns out not to be merely a pedantic concern of mine but changes my meaning. The text on p. 49 reads after the ellipsis, "Yet despite the others with whom it is so intimately intertwined — God and the Jewish people, present, past and future — it is as a single soul in its full individuality that the Jewish self exists in covenant." It is this last conditional sentence — "Yet . . . it is as . . ." — which was taken as indicating that I do not hold the prior comments about God and the Jewish people very seriously but espouse the old-line, individualistic Reform Jewish ideology. The capital on "Yet" gives the disjunctive great force. Alas for my meaning, the first word of that sentence really should be "Fifth, yet despite the others. . . ." Perhaps that would have clarified that this insistence on some measure of individuality is only the fifth aspect of Jewish selfhood, the others being, quite seriously, a real God, the Jewish tradition, the contemporary Jewish community and the messianically oriented Jewish future. Selfhood in that binding context, as I was arguing, would then receive a new, quite postmodern understanding.

All this authorial nit-picking is critical to whether my notion of non-Orthodox belief is Zionist or non-Zionist. I summon only the Israeli testimony. Moshe Dann, my recent reviewer in *The Jerusalem Post*, who criticized my non-Orthodoxy, nonetheless felt compelled to call me "an ardent Zionist." And Eliezer Schweid, reviewing *Liberal Judaism* in *Gesher* as long ago as 1986, termed the book a Zionized Reform Judaism. Maybe distance does make the heart grow fonder.

My multi-dimensional notion of Covenant now being clearer, let me specify what it entails with regard to Zionism, our Reform Zionism, and I quickly want to run down thirteen tasks, the first two of which deal with general issues.

One, unlike Dick Hirsch, the State of Israel is not central to my Jewish existence — and I don't know many Diaspora Jews for whom it is. Covenant makes the Land of Israel highly important and contemporary political reality makes the State of Israel close to indispensable.[13] May it long flourish and exert its wholesome influence over world Jewry. Nonetheless, I must add that the people of Israel survived in Covenant faithfulness for two millennia without a state and, may God spare us such a challenge, it could, with God's help, do so again.[14]

Two, critics will say, "That isn't Zionism but the old Reform *shtik* in modern lingo." Our representatives ought to meet such canards aggressively. There have always been more Orthodox anti-Zionists than Reform, the Satmarer alone easily outnumbering the American Council for Judaism at its height. And our so-called "non-Zionism" is religiously identical to that of Agudat Yisrael, because we too make Torah, not the State, the center of our Judaism.

The next half dozen duties refer to the Land of Israel and our people there.

Three, the preferred form of fulfilling the Covenant is social not just personal and this makes *aliyah* a central Jewish demand. I pray that one benefit of ever greater peace will be an increase in the number of Reform Jews settling there. For the rest of us, visits and sojourns must serve as a modest surrogate. We also need to help rabbis who hesitate to take groups of their congregants on tour there to do so. Moreover, the College and Conference need to set up a welcoming, useful sabbatical program for rabbis at our Jerusalem school. Both programs might also get more retired congregants and colleagues to live in the State of Israel.

Four, our congregations and institutions in the State of Israel still struggle against heavy economic odds. They need more money and while all of us have been badly pinched by a budgetary crunch, special causes still draw forth extra funds.

Five, one of the two jewels of our movement in the State of Israel is the Religious Action Center. In a country where religious political action too often means finagling for subsidies we uniquely show how a modern Judaism can have a genuine social concern and a significant social message. The IRAC deserves our enthusiastic financial support.

Six, for Diaspora Jews the heart of our Israeli movement is that glorious complex of buildings the College erected in Jerusalem. It is the result of the vision, courage, tenacity and Jewish determination of one man, Fred Gottschalk, and I suggest we take a moment now to show him how grateful we are for this act of leadership. [Enthusiastic applause then ensued.] But if the general wisdom is correct, that marvelous creation remains a major financial drain on the College. Colleagues, do you have a millionaire or two who are ready to do something that needs to be too big and lasting to be a local project? Perhaps someone who cares deeply about the State of Israel? They will thank you for directing them to a Jerusalem building or project they can underwrite. Do call Fred or John Borden, our development *maven*, and tell them about your possible donor.

Seven, it is time to begin paying more attention to what Israeli Progressive Jews can do for us. They live Judaism in community much more intensively than we do, so they have something critical to teach us. We need better channels for hearing what MARAM is doing and learning. Even an adopt-a-congregation program could encourage the human interchanges which always teach so much.

Eight, we need regularly to meet those special religious personalities whom our Israeli movement will surely be developing in greater numbers as the years go by. Telling us about the experience of being a sensitive Reform Jewish Israeli, they could give us new insight into our own Diaspora religiosity.

My remaining proposals deal with Diaspora Zionist existence.

Nine, the obvious must not be overlooked. We must be vigilant that the political interests of the State of Israel are presented in full virtue and attacks on them are thoroughly refuted. Of course, as religious Zionists we come to this task with our great commitment to ethics of a universal reach. An ethicized politics is not easy but it must apply to the causes projected by the State of Israel as it does to the social welfare of our North American fellow citizens.

Ten, in our narcissistic culture, individualism saps the power of community responsibility generally and of our situatedness in the Jewish people in particular. If our Zionism could intensify a healthy Jewish folk consciousness among us it would help rectify a major moral and Jewish failing of our time.

Eleven, a critical means of accomplishing this is to create a cadre of committed Reform Zionist Hebraists. I deplore my inability easily to present this paper in Hebrew, the result of a poor education and limited stays in the State of Israel. Nonetheless, this is another time and despite our compulsive monolinguality, we should aim, at the least, to create a critical mass of 2500 active lovers of Israeli writing and classic Jewish literature in the original — a number that is merely 1/4 of 1% of our one million American Reform Jews.

Twelve, if Zionism means collectivity, then it needs to influence our praying, that is, it needs to help us break the narcissistic pattern of mentally translating every "we" and "our" in the prayer book into "me" and "my." Jewish prayer is not merely the service of the individual heart but the collective worship of the people of Israel renewing the Covenant.

Thirteen, but the greatest thing a living Reform Zionism could do for us is to lift our messianic imaginations out of the despair fostered by endless examples of the abuse of power. Anyone who has ever tried to run an institution knows how impossible and yet how Jewishly necessary it is to try to sanctify power. So sinful politics and politicians in our midst and on high cannot persuade us that piety requires a retreat to powerlessness. Once, Zionism and human idealism, Zionism and messianism, went hand in hand. We desperately need the revitalization of idealistic Zionism for if we could recreate it, it would invigorate Jewish hope and reempower the Jewish dedication to work and wait for the coming of that glorious messianic time.

Notes

1. Somewhat revised since the CCAR meeting, May 31, 1994, at which it was initially read and critiqued. I have also drawn on a public discussion on this same topic held Sept. 29, 1994 at the HUC-JIR, New York, between Dick Hirsch, Larry Hoffman and myself.
2. Dick was distressed at my use of this term as he wrote me from Jerusalem. I responded that saying that someone taught a theory even remotely related to that of the American Council for Judaism — Dick's view of the new Reform non-Zionism — had as good as been assigned to pariah- hood. That charge was not only made in the *CCAR Journal* but the article which began with that identification was reprinted as the prelude to his Think Tank contribution in the first issue of this journal. Though attacked by name, neither Editor informed me of this treatment or provided me an opportunity to respond in the same issue. See note 3 for the bibliographical details..
3. *CCAR Journal*, Fall, 1991, reprinted in *The Journal of Reform Zionism*, Vol. 1, No. 1, March 1993/Nisan 5753. The third sentence of the article mentions the Council. The damage thus done, the subsequent acknowledgment that very much has changed does not leave the leaders of the alleged new Reform non-Zionism untainted, I alone being named.
4. At the CCAR session I suggested that it was partially "semantic."
5. "On the Passing of the Ethnic Era," *Sh'ma*, 20/397, Sept. 21, 1990. What I said there has since become a commonplace of the Anglo-Jewish press discussion of the situation with regard to Federation budgeting. If more academic substantiation is required, see Jonathan Sarna, "The Secret of Jewish Continuity," *Commentary*, Vol. 98, No. 4, Oct., 1994, particularly his "transformations" nos. 1 and 4, pp. 56-7.
6. A semantic difference between Larry and myself did arise at our public discussion. I often use, even prefer, terms like "ethnic" or "ethnicity" to convey the uncommon social character of the Jews. Larry prefers terms like "people" and "peoplehood." He finds overtones in the ethnicity terms that make the people terms preferable while I considered the people language rather empty. But there was no time then to discuss this further.
7. In his remarks at our discussion Dick cited this sentence as an example of my retreat from classic Zionism. For a fuller statement of my position see *Renewing the Covenant*, ch. 18, "When Community Takes Priority," (Philadelphia: JPS, 1992).
8. I was joined in this view by Larry. Dick's fervent love of the State of Israel did not clarify whether he felt that the principles of Judaism demanded a Jewish state or whether, as we did, that its necessity arose from our political situation. Larry and I did disagree, as I learned at the CCAR

session, on whether "landedness," specifically the Land of Israel, is an immediate consequence of the Covenant relationship, as I think, or, as he believes, a "metaphysical" affirmation of our faith, on a religious par with God, Torah and the people Israel. I assume his article in this journal will reflect this. A synopsis of it, as it were, is found in *Sh'ma*, 25/478, Sept. 30, 1994, 25 Tishri 5755, p. 6.

9. Op. cit., p. 49.

10. *A New Jewish Theology in the Making*, (Philadelphia: Westminster, 1958), p. 144.

11. *Modern Judaism*, Vol. 4, No. 1, Feb. 1984. The paper had been given some time previously in Denver to an early intra-denominational session by the then National Jewish Center for Leadership and Learning, now better known as CLAL.

12. Note how its first academic airing, "The Autonomous Jewish Self," *Modern Judaism*, Vol. 4 No. 1, Feb. 1984, gave too much prominence to a term most people still thought of as secular and individualistic. Hence by the time I came to its full-scale statement as the climax to *Renewing the Covenant* I was using the terminology that is the title of ch. 20, "The Jewish Self."

13. I express here, as against Larry Hoffman's view, the common view of the subordinate religious status of the Land of Israel. (Larry and I agree that statehood is a necessity of contemporary politics, not a Jewish religious requirement.) I believe its subordinate if highly significant status is indicated by: 1) the sense of conditionality with which our tradition overwhelmingly refers to it, 2) the *halakhah* making Torah study a sufficient Jewishness to override the virtue of *aliyah*, and 3) its past and present lack of commanding power equal to God, Torah and Israel (as general folk responsibility).

14. Some people are so accustomed to hearing the ideological notion that the State of Israel is indispensable to contemporary Jewish existence that they are surprised to hear anyone say the opposite. But two thousand plus years of non-state Jewish history in post-Biblical times are a powerful argument of the opposite, particulariy for one who takes Jewish faith and living seriously. Is it too subtle to suggest that something can be of the greatest significance to us but, as we often learn, not "indispensable?

Chapter 16

୨୦୦୯

Apostasy

1) Apostasy from Judaism Today

F ew if any people in our generation with the spiritual and academic status of Michael Wyschogrod have devoted so major a share of their energies and intellect to thinking through the proper relationships between Judaism and Christianity. This interest has been a major motive for his reshaping the contours of his Jewish Orthodoxy, resulting in his notable statement of Jewish theology, *The Body of Faith*. Anything Michael writes is therefore worthy of the most serious scrutiny and that holds doubly true for me since I have had the privilege of decades of friendship with him confirmed in a mutual enterprise, the journal *Sh'ma*. I always expect to be stimulated by his writing and his letter to a Jew — and I shall take the masculine instance to include the feminine case — who has converted to Christianity now confirms that experience. In this case, however, I find myself unusually at odds with what he has written.

It may help to understand my response if I clarify the special nature of my Jewish faith. I am not an Orthodox Jew but part of that great mass of American Jews who may informally be described as "liberal," though non-Orthodox would be more precise. In fact, I am reasonably happily affiliated with the Reform movement, though I stand in its right wing, but there more to the center than at the poles — or so it seems to me. And if that is not confusing enough, I have in my recent book, *Renewing the Covenant*, enunciated a full-scale Jewish theology which claims to be postmodern. Since I find most of my colleagues in the Reform movement (and the Jewish intellectual community as a whole) still speaking in modern terms (though often increasingly troubled by them), it is difficult to say for whom I speak theologically other than myself.

My interpretation of postmodernity bears on this response because it involves somewhat uncommon "liberal" affirmations. These are: that particularity is prior to universality, and thus that the Jewish tradition and community need to be taken most seriously in discussing a Jewish relationship with God. My "liberal" credentials hinge on my then also recontextualizing the exercise of individual autonomy, asserting that it has Jewish validity only when it operates in intimacy with God as part of the Jewish people's covenant relationship with God.

I want to say some things about Michael's discussion of Christianity before turning to what I feel more secure about, how I believe Jews today ought to think about apostasy. I do not know whether my objections to Michael's comments about Christianity are more intellectual that experiential but I shall present them in that order.

First, the data. Seven times, by my rough count, Michael speaks "from the Christian point of view" or discusses problems within "the traditional Christian view" or clarifies what Christian Scriptures really intend to teach or Christian hopes involve (though here he shifts from assertions to questions). I do not understand the basis on which he believes that someone who does not share the circle of Christian faith can reasonably make such statements. It is true that those of us who have studied Christian theology with some care and have spent time talking to Christian thinkers have some idea of the affirmations of the varieties of Christianity we have been involved with. Still, if as Judaism maintains, a considerable measure of belief and practice is required to properly understand what the Torah teaches, it does not seem unreasonable to suggest that other religions feel similarly. (And I have certainly heard echoes of this idea from Christian theologians speaking of the role of the Holy Spirit in properly understanding Scripture and Christian faith.)

Further arguments against this procedure could be adduced in the name of postmodernity's emphasis on the collapse of confidence in realms of universal comprehension and communication, and its emphasis on the communitarian nature of significant discourse. I am not so doctrinaire as to suggest that we really have no basis at all for talking to people of other groups. Nonetheless, surely in matters as intimate and refined as the nature of a group's faith or its immediate entailments, a certain distance of even the well-informed and well-meaning is in order. Consider, for example, how difficult it is even for those of us within a given circle of faith to agree on what we "really" believe or what Scripture "properly" entails.

To all this let me add my experience and that of not a few other Jews. To give the most common example, it is astonishing how what many Christian teachers confidently tell Jews our Bible means differs from what Jewish sages over the centuries have taught us Hebrew Scriptures say. A neutral ground between us could be established if we all agree to speak in academic, that is, secular terms, but that is surely not what we have in mind here. And I have had similar unhappy experiences listening to believers in another religion or even academics speak of the nature of Jewish faith. On occasion I have found such experiences quite distasteful so I may be overly sensitive to adherents of one faith suggesting to people of another faith what they should believe or do. Such reticence seems to me only a proper respect for the boundaries beyond which even an open soul seeking to love others of God's children cannot pass.

Several things about Michael's discussion of Judaism and the Jewish response to apostates also trouble me. Not the least of my difficulties is what I take to be his exaggeratedly positive reading of the Jewish tradition's attitude toward apostates. I think it goes beyond that suggested by this form of communication, a letter to the convert to Christianity seeking his return to Jewish observance. It is, of course, a major Jewish duty to hold the door for return as widely open as possible and one certainly doesn't wish to be offensive when seeking to win the correspondent's assent to a new form of action. Despite that, it seems to me that the tone of our sources and community attitudes is so slanted here toward the positive that the convert might well be surprised later to discover what a more common Jewish response to his apostasy was.

The issue is not whether an apostate from Judaism remains, in the eyes of the Jewish faith, a Jew. Here Michael's emphasis on his never relinquishing his Jewishness is quite right. But the problem begins to make itself felt — and will later bring me to discuss conscience in traditional Judaism — in Michael's passive acceptance of Cardinal Lustiger's self assessment (to his parents), "I am not leaving you . . . I am discovering another way of being a Jew." In the Jewish theological sense, the first assertion is true because we believe he cannot do otherwise. But as far as the Jewish community is concerned, to convert to another religion is to desert the Jewish people, the people of God's covenant. Even secular Jews in our time have understood this, as the refusal of the Israeli Supreme Court to allow Brother Daniel Rufeisen to immigrate to the State of Israel *as a Jew* indicated. And though there are Hebrew Christian congregations in North America, I know of no umbrella Jewish community organization which would even consider placing their application for membership on its agenda. Cardinal Lustiger may believe he has not left us but those of us who in some sense remain caring Jews know he has in significant part done so. And despite our community's tolerance of its deviant members and its occasionally obsequious eagerness to demonstrate tolerance to all religions, races and points of view here a communal limit has been reached.

This issue of apostasy cannot, from the human standpoint, simply be left as opting out. To some extent it involves desertion, even moral turpitude. I do not know to what extent such attitudes remain widespread in the Jewish community. Until a generation ago, it seemed to me — and I am a member of the most other-involved segment of the Jewish community — it seemed to me they were quite strong. The strong feelings on this topic involved many themes: the smallness of the Jewish people and so the special preciousness of every Jew; the persecution of our people which inevitably taints every apostate and assimilator with seeking personal surcease and joining the oppressors; the proud record of Jewish accomplishment now personally thrown aside and made more difficult for others to carry forward; and the like. Not so long ago Christian doctrine was easily disparaged by Jews as neo-idolatry and Christian behavior denigrated by contrast to that of Jews but the experience of living together and the modernization of Christian doctrine has made both charges quiescent. And in the past two generations the Holocaust casts its grim shadow over this issue. To lose another Jew is, in Emil Fackenheim's famous phrase, to give Hitler another posthumous victory, to join the ignoble culture and to associate oneself with a church that for all its high doctrine prepared the way for and then by its general silence abetted the work of the murderers. The feelings on all these matters still run very high among people who care about the Jewish people as much as they care about individual Jewish souls.

This discussion of communal acceptance also has a theological foundation. Judaism denies that apostasy can lead to "another way of being a Jew." There is no such thing. Apostasy is sin, very grave sin indeed, and it is this that Michael faces but quickly glosses over. He does clarify that the convert "from the point of view of rabbinic Judaism" — Michael's Judaism and mine, to be sure — is not "a good Jew." And he adds that conversion is "a very serious matter." If it is to a trinitarian faith then clearly it "is not a good thing to do. In fact, it is so bad that a Christian Jew loses all sorts of privileges . . ." True, as far as it goes, but that is hardly the classic Jewish sense of things. Traditional Judaism has regularly considered the apostate a most grievous sinner. Even Jews converted under duress who lived as Christians for any period of time and then wished to return to Judaism, were asked by our sages for some serious act of penance before they could resume a rightful place in the Jewish community. And here we speak of someone who gave up the Jewish faith willingly. The most that Michael can bring himself to say is that "You have violated some of the commandments of the Torah and you (and I) should repent of these violations." Again, that is true and in some ways it is commendable for the mentor to identify with the sinner in the hope of winning him to proper observance. But surely there is something utterly disproportionate here! I cannot believe that though there is no one so righteous that s/he never sins, that anything Michael has done in violation of Jewish law even remotely approaches the heinousness with which the Jewish tradition invests apostasy.

Others are better qualified than I am to discuss Jewish law's attitude toward trinitarian Christianity and very much has been made of the one recognized authority who ruled that the past barriers between Judaism and Christianity were no longer fully justified under Jewish law. (The reference is to Menachem Meiri, the 13th century Jewish legal authority who lived in Peripignan.) But his voice remains isolated in the ongoing stream of the *halakhah*, classic Jewish law, and that means that, in the specific terminology with which the legal mind operates, trinitarian Christians still customarily fall under the technical category of idol-worshippers. That may seem merely a systemic inheritance since most authorities will, should they ever write in English, skirt the offensiveness of this usage and its practical effects. But the legal categorization is still sufficiently operative for the observant that they will not attend, say, a Catholic mass — at least that has been my experience with most of the Orthodox rabbis, much less halakhic masters, who have been involved in various kinds of interfaith activity. To most Orthodox authorities, then, conversion to trinitarian Christianity violates one of the three inviolable

Jewish commandments — not committing idolatry — the others being not to murder and not to do a sexually proscribed act. Michael does not give us this traditional ideological background which still shapes formal Jewish attitudes toward the apostate who now wishes to become observant.

Despite my great respect for Jewish tradition I do not see how we can usefully think of trinitarian Christianity as "idol worship." While that indicates some non-Orthodox softening of the classic Jewish attitude toward conversion to Christianity it does not domesticate it to the point of being only another sin, say of the kind that Michael and surely I commit. When one compromises monotheism, defects from the primacy of the Jewish people's relationship with God and claims a satisfactory surrogate for the Torah and its way of life, one cannot still claim to be only another of the usual crowd of Jewish sinners.

Some of my left wing Reform rabbinic colleagues appear to disagree, more by attitude and practice than by intellectual defense. Adopting an anthropological point of view, they view all moral faiths as simply clothing the essential truth in different symbols, so, in the last analysis, one ethical faith is as acceptable as another. But most of my liberal colleagues, if I read them correctly, find that does not tell the whole story of the distinctiveness that remains amid the now more evident similarities. They seem to know, without being able easily to articulate it — our culture certainly hindering the expression of normative particularity — that there is a worthwhile difference in Judaism that needs to be maintained. So while they will treat converts from Judaism to another faith with courtesy, I do not find them considering apostates merely another group of the Jewish sinners with whom rabbis spend their lives. More than anything, what has forced Reform rabbis to rethink the question of the theological status of the people of Israel is the growing presence of numbers of non-Jews, often Christians, who participate with their intermarried spouse in the life of the synagogue.

There remains one further matter to discuss, Michael's contention that acting in accord with one's conscience renders conversion to a faith other than Judaism not a sin in God's eyes. When he first enunciated the notion that one must follow conscience even against the Torah (as long as one sought to be faithful to God), it seemed to me more a classic Reform Jewish than a traditional Jewish view. To the best of my knowledge, this view has no support in traditional Jewish legal rulings and Michael remains its only adherent among learned Orthodox Jews. I will be grateful to have my impressions corrected. But if I am right then his absolving the conscientious apostate of the Jewish need to repent for his conversion is an idiosyncratic view, one without the support of any recognized contemporary Jewish legal authority.

As I am not Orthodox, let me speak now of my Reform colleagues' faith in conscience and my own. Earlier in the century, when rationalism still seemed the necessary language of moderns, Reform Jews tended to speak of conscience in essentially Kantian terms, that is, as the exercise of one's rational, moral capacity. There was some acknowledgement, of varying seriousness, of what Hermann Cohen had taught people to call "a concept of God" or "God idea," but many people simply thought of autonomy in the relatively secular fashion of Kantian philosophy. Michael has rightly rejected this and insisted that conscience be exercised in response to one's perception of God's will. But Reform Jewish practice based on the primacy of ethical monotheism rendered Jewishness — the particular aspect of Judaism — inessential, perhaps even insignificant when compared to the grand, compelling quality of universal ethics and that, primarily, it is the reason that Reform Jews have for some time recognized its theological insufficiency.

A theological analysis of this position clarifies the problem. Believing only in the commandments given by conscience exercised in relation to God is the faith of the Children of Noah, that is humankind in the language of rabbinic theology. But Jews are bound to God under the covenant of Sinai to observe the Torah and it, in its historical unfolding, has as much authority over them as does their universal conscience. Reform Jews, such as myself, who take the Jewish people's relationship with God seriously and who therefore must give Jewish tradition considerable sway over their behavior are not satisfied to live, in effect, under the covenant of the Children of Noah.

I am, of course, here speaking out of my postmodern emphasis on the particular as the ground for the universal and therefore call for liberals to exercise their autonomy within the relationships created by their people's covenant with God. To my delight, I find that a considerable number of my colleagues now acknowledge that this or something like it is the faith that makes them not want, as you put it, "a world without Jews." To put it plainly, these liberal Jews know in a Sinaitic way that they are commanded to be Jews. For that reason, even a well-intentioned apostate from Judaism who wishes to resume living the covenant of Sinai, must first repent for having committed a most grievous sin.

I agree with Michael that my negative stand toward apostasy is not likely to stop many Jews who wish to convert to another faith from doing so. But at least they should know plainly what an awesome sin Judaism teaches they are committing. More usefully, I would hope, my attitude might disabuse some people of what in many cases is a self-satisfied move toward syncretism. "Look how democratic we are. I have my faith as does my spouse. We observe rituals from both groups and attend services from time to time at both sanctuaries. Our children are raised in both faiths and when they are old enough, they will make up their own minds as to which faith they wish to choose. This way everyone's conscience is respected and a bold step is taken to eliminate the frictions that often arise between religions." If my negative teaching can penetrate their self-righteousness or their essential indifference to the seriousness of religious commitment, it will at least indicate to them that religious syncretism is not, as far as believing Jews are concerned, the next step in the fulfillment of Judaism's universal concerns.

The convert to whom Michael addresses his letter and Cardinal Lustiger are obviously far more thoughtful and pious than the syncretists I have run into in considerable numbers in recent years. But I worry lest Michael's uncommon theology be used by less responsible people to justify a syncretism my Judaism demands I reject.

2) Are We Too Soft on Apostates?

What should be our attitude to Jews who convert to another religion? Have they abandoned us as the term "apostates" implies or have they properly followed their conscience and should simply be called "converts-out?" Our response depends intellectually on our theology of universalism or, for that matter, of particularism.

Most liberal Jews I know feel that converts-out remain Jews (a term I use with gender inclusiveness). So if they later want to return to Judaism they have an inalienable — though inexplicable — right to do so but with the usual differences over what acts they should do to claim this.

Humanly, our problems begin emerging when converts-out say, as Jean-Marie Cardinal Lustiger wrote (to his parents), in his book, "I am not leaving you . . . I am discovering another way of being a Jew." We may agree with his first assertion but not so easily with the second. With rare unanimity, the organized Jewish community considers conversion to another religion desertion from the Jewish people. Thus the Israeli Supreme Court, rejecting a rigorous interpretation of the classic Zionist notion of Jewishness as nationality, refused to allow Oswald Rufeisen, a

Holocaust survivor but a Christian lay-brother (so, "Brother Daniel"), to immigrate to the State of Israel *as a Jew*. The Court ruled that the Jewish people considers conversion-out defection from the Jewish folk. So too, no umbrella American Jewish community organization would even consider placing on its agenda an application for membership from a Hebrew-Christian congregation.

Certain moral considerations are involved here. Thus, one could not be indifferent if conversion out seemed motivated by personal gain. Albert Einstein is reported to have remained a Jew because he considered leaving a decent people under attack morally despicable. Such a negative attitude was once widespread among us for many reasons: the smallness of the Jewish people made every Jew particularly precious; the reality of anti-semitism taints every assimilator with seeking self-gain and, worse, doing so by joining the oppressors; the proud record of Jewish accomplishment is now personally thrown aside and made more difficult for others to carry forward; and more. These themes are not without continuing validity.

One reason from a prior time no longer commands respect: that Christian doctrine is neo-idolatry (trinitarianism and the veneration of saints) and Christian behavior is neo-pagan (spousal abuse, alcoholism, divorce, crimes of violence, etc.). Having now long lived together with Christians, we are far more impressed with our common humanity. As to doctrine, if we proclaim the legitimacy of liberalizing Judaism, we cannot deny Christians an equal right. At the same time, our post-ghetto experience also includes the Holocaust. Today, converting out is, in Emil Fackenheim's luminous phrase, giving Hitler a posthumous victory. The apostate leaves us for an ignoble culture that tolerated or even abetted the Jew-murder and remains anti-semitic today. Moreover, the apostate to Christianity had taken on a faith which, despite its considerable noble teaching, prepared the way for the murderers and then, by its general silence, condoned their work.

I am sorry if my blunt words have caused the reader psychic distress. But despite familial and personal reasons for repressing these judgments, no significant inter-faith relations can be established without confronting them. Those who care as much about the Jewish people *corporately* as they do about individual Jewish souls are likely to be moved by them.

Theologically too, we must reflect on the unanimous rabbinic stand, until recently, that apostasy was one of the worst possible sins. Thus we may not gloss over the act by saying that though the convert-out has violated some commandments, so have all Jews. At best, this attitude doesn't slam the departure door and avoids erecting another barrier to possible later reentry. Nonetheless, this congeniality obscures the harsh seriousness of conversion-out for most of us are retail sinners but the convert-out has abandoned the Torah wholesale.

One old rabbinic position must, however, be rejected: that trinitarian Christians commit the sin of idolatry. The 13th century Peripignan halakhic authority, Menachem Meiri, did rule that since the gentiles were now largely moral, the laws proscribing Jews associating with idolaters no longer necessarily applied to Jewish-Christian relations. His views are a cornerstone of interfaith activity today but his is an isolated voice in the *halakhah*. No halakhic master will, for example, attend a Catholic mass. So too, in late medieval times Jews who converted to Christianity under duress, as in Spain, and later wished to return to Judaism were not generally required to convert back (they remained Jews) but still had to do some serious act of penance before they could reenter the Jewish community. Except for the Holocaust, we rarely encounter the issue of duress, our converts-out generally validating their act as one done with full responsibility. As to Holocaust survivors who convert-out, while there may be some unforgiving halakhic authorities, most Jews leave all such judgments to God, the inscrutable yet finally merciful One.

My rejection of the notion that trinitarian Christianity is "idol worship" surely indicates a non-Orthodox softening of Jewish law's classically harsh attitude to adopting Christianity but does not turn it into just another sin. When one compromises monotheism, denies the primacy of the Jewish people's relationship with God and claims a satisfactory surrogate for the Torah and its way of life, one isn't simply another face in the usual crowd of Jewish sinners.

Judging from their practice, some Reform rabbis apparently disagree with this view. Adopting an anthropological perspective, they consider all particular moral faiths only different symbolic approaches to a universal truth. The rites of such religions, their holidays, tales and other such group sancta may carry great emotional freight but on the deeper, moral level, one ethical faith is as good as any other another. Since religious symbols, not ethics, have long evoked terrible conflict, conversion from one moral faith to another should not maturely trouble us.

Most of my colleagues, however, believe this view is only part of the truth. Faced with the potential dissolution of the Jewish people they know intuitively that Jewish distinctiveness is religiously, not just institutionally, mandated. Why that is the case cannot easily be articulated, our culture radically favoring universalism. Yet they know that their deep devotion to Jewishness involves more than tribal devotion, that describing Judaism as an impressive ethics adorned with Semitic forms is reductionistic. Practically, the growing number of Christians participating in our synagogues has made them rethink what they believe about the people of Israel. They may treat converts-out with simple human courtesy but rarely consider them merely another of the Jewish sinners with whom rabbis spend their lives.

The critical issue, then, with regard to the Jewish status of conversion-out is the measure of authority we still assign to individual conscience. Reform Judaism once championed conscience as superior to Torah for it justified the modernizers' drive to find Jews a place in the newly opened society. That principle has no standing in Jewish law but was fundamental to the Enlightenment view of humanity, the perspective which undergirded the eventual Emancipation of the Jews.

For more than a century now, sophisticated Reform Jews have discussed "conscience" in Kantian terms, that is, as the proper exercise of universal human rationality, something Kant taught inevitably involved ethical decision making. This philosophy thinks of ethics without relation to God but classic Reform Jews followed the great philosopher Hermann Cohen who taught that rationality involved having a "concept of God" (or "God idea") to structure our worldview. Judaism as "ethical monotheism" made Jewish particularity essentially superfluous, or at least insignificant when compared to the grand, compelling quality of rational, universal ethics. That suited most Reform Jews fine as long as their spiritual agenda focused on becoming accepted in the general society.

Long before Hitler reordered Jewish priorities, conscientious Reform thinkers sensed the problem of over-concentration on universalism and individual conscience. One sees this in their difficulties explaining why Ethical Culture or Unitarianism did not better express their Kantian faith than did Reform Judaism. Their convoluted justifications of particularity seem today a grasping at straws, e. g., Cohen's contention that the Jews had a uniquely rational God-idea; Kohler's notion that Jewish blood produced high Jewish character; and the cultural Zionist, Ahad Haam's teaching that Jews had a special talent for ethics and high culture. Mordecai Kaplan's later view gave up essential Jewish uniqueness and taught only anthropological individuality.

Historical experience then reversed the focus. First Hitler and the Holocaust made plain that there could be a "world without Jews;" then the State of Israel bestowed new dignity and worth on Jewish corporate action; and most recently, social acceptance, that long-sought goal, showed how it might fatally compromise Jewish existence. The decades made increasingly unsatisfactory the survival of "our" (Kantian) ethics while the Jewish people itself atrophied. To use Thomas Kuhn's famous phrase, the cognitive dissonance grew steadily for half a century giving Jewish particularity a place alongside universalism atop the Jewish religious agenda.

In this period, too, Western culture began transforming the Enlightenment's self-confident perspective on rationality and self-legislation. Linguists, philosophers, people of color and feminists found themselves united in attacking universal thinking, an individual's ability to think so rationally that his (*sic*) ideas would be true of anyone, anywhere, any time — something the Marxists, the Freudians and the cultural anthropologists had long charged. The all-competent self famously enthroned by Descartes as the one who rightly first doubted everything and only gave assent after being persuaded by "clear and distinct" ideas began to seem a fantasy. That collapse of the Cartesian self ushered in the postmodern era. In its religious manifestation it best explains the utterly unanticipated Jewish spiritual developments of the past half-century: not the triumph of modern liberalism but rather the death of the death-of-God movement, the collapse of Diaspora Jewish secularity, the loss of messianic fervor in Jewish social action, the vigor of Jewish Orthodoxy, the flourishing of Jewish feminism and the widespread non-Orthodox Jewish concern with meaning and spirituality. These six phenomena all take for granted, albeit unconsciously, the self's limited ability to judge and proclaim all truth, its inevitable particular situatedness and its living relationship with a God not defined in terms of the self.

Theoretically, then, our response to converts-out will depend on how close we stand to the pole of modern or postmodern Reform Judaism. Some of us consider the authority of the Cartesian self unchallengeable. Others, I among them, say particularity precedes universalism. It was the modernization of Jewish faith that made Jews universalists in disproportionate numbers. Converts-out should inquire whether their new particularity will ground their universalism as enthusiastically as Reform Judaism did. With particular faith given priority, we, whose lives are grounded in Judaism, cannot be indifferent to those who have spurned it. I practice the courtesy that keeps the *teshuvah* door ajar to converts-out but I disdain those who have deserted our embattled people, our noble truth and our uncommon record of humane achievement. To me and others like me, they are quite properly termed "apostates."

Our negative attitude will not stop Jews from converting out. They should, however, know plainly what an awesome sin some of us in Reform Judaism believe they are committing. More usefully perhaps, it might disabuse some people of the self-evident righteousness they associate with their move toward religious syncretism. Religious faith is not a leisure-time activity that an unattached self chooses as one might a significant lifetime acquisition. From the postmodern view — and only that? — it is the foundation of the self. So the notion that the children will elect what they wish when they grow up denies the schizoid particularity in which they have begun life. And, for that matter, not having a single, inclusive family religion teaches much the same flawed message. These troubling thoughts will, I hope, make the issue of which comes first, independent selfhood or situated particularity less academic and more practical.

Does this postmodern perspective also affect our attitude to converts-in? It surely mandates sensitivity to the new Jew's loss in joining our people. It also reminds us of the wonder that people have always sought entry into our small, outsider faith. One charming traditional explanation of what brings them suggests that genuine converts are descendants of that "mixed rabble" (Ex. 12:38) that left Egypt with us and who, with their descendants, also stood at Sinai. We are taught to discourage converts-in by reminding them of our particularity, of the special problems being a Jew brings. But many now come to us out of such rootlessness, such spiritual emptiness, such lack of community, that they hear the Eternal voice of Sinai again in our midst. As we rejoice at every wholehearted convert we must also rededicate ourselves to the unending task of assuring that no one in our community shall have experienced life among us as the spiritual waste land this former non-Jew is likely to have left.

Chapter 17

ℰↄℂℜ

Postmodern Jewish Ethics

1) From Cognitive Dissonance to Creative Groping

For more than two decades now thoughtful Reform Jews have been grappling with the need to rethink their approach to ethical decision-making. Since I have described the social and philosophic bases of that development elsewhere it need not be repeated here. Suffice it to say that with political liberalism effectively challenged by ethical conservatism and with liberalism's rational ("Kantian") academic underpinnings eroded, the identification of Jewish social ethics with a presumed universal human moral consciousness no longer evokes conviction. Besides, it seems odd that a religion which prides itself on its ethical emphasis has nothing distinctive to contribute to contemporary ethics other than an uncommonly large cadre of liberal ethical activists. For about two decades now, this change of mood has manifested itself at the New York School of the HUC-JIR by students linking their perennial dedication to ethics with an interest in "text" or "sources." By these charged terms they do not mean study of the Prophets but of classically authoritative Jewish teaching, *halakhah*.

This turn to the rabbis has increasingly plunged us into the current storm of problems clustering around the term "hermeneutics." Texts, we are continually reminded these days, do not read themselves or philologically disclose one true meaning. To read necessarily is to interpret and invest with meaning so academic rationality is not the only sure guide to The Truth but only another possible human hermeneutic. We all "read" according to the presuppositions we bring to the document before us. While some of these can be stated, others remain implicit, perhaps to surface in a contest between rival readings. How, then, are we Reform Jews to read the rabbis? This is not merely an academic issue for us since unlike literary or historical texts — themselves bedeviled by hermeneutic issues — we come to the rabbis seeking to define our religious duty. We grant them a certain authority over our lives (just how much being highly debated among us) so how they may properly help define our moral responsibility, our primary means of serving God, quickly becomes a critical human/religious issue for us.

Though I have called this an issue for "Reform Jews" that is true only on an organizational but not on a personal level. Only Reform Judaism has made informed, conscientious self-determination a formal part of its ideology. In theory, Orthodox Jews follow the rulings of their *rav*, Conservative Jews of their Commission on Law and Standards (or, in split decisions, their local rabbi's ruling), and Reconstructionists the democratic decisions of their community. In fact, most Jews, regardless of label, insist on personal autonomy, listening to their authorities but then making up their own minds. Crypto-Reform Judaism is the effective decision-making mode of most American Jews and this makes the issue under discussion far more than one movement's dilemma.

Once we grant autonomy pride of place in determining our obligations as Jews we cannot be satisfied with our older communal patterns of reaching decisions. The juristic model of the past fails us because the great decisors, the *poskim*, are not expected to persuade the independent inquirer but only to rule for the faithful. For our liberal purposes it is troubling that they do not often go beyond legal reasoning to explain why they read just these texts and not certain others, emphasize some and play down others, arriving, therefore, at just this rather than another conclusion. Jewish tradition — like other legal systems — excuses the judge from significant hermeneutic self-disclosure. This system works as long as one can accept the decisor's special competence but only a minority today will regularly allow their faith in a given sage's scholarship and piety to override "conscience." The same reluctance to share the reasoning behind the "reading" characterizes decisions made by a group rather than an individual.

Modern Jews have until recently avoided this problem by reading Jewish texts — insofar as they cared to do so — with the eyes of urban, liberal culture. The sophisticates did so by applying some version of neo-Kantian universal reason. But neither group granted Jewish texts any independent value in their deliberations. Rather they cited the Bible or the rabbis only to show that Judaism could agree with the enlightened conscience. The many texts which differed with the modern liberal consensus were ignored. The Conservative movement has made a valiant effort to overcome this problem by maintaining fealty to the *halakhah* but reading it with a sense of its historical and thus ever-developing nature. This strategy only postpones facing the hermeneutic issue. No one can tell us just what "the halakhic process" can and cannot allow. (And those who most study and live by it deny the authenticity of such Conservative views as have been put forward.) Moreover, no one can tell us when the claims of historic development must be recognized — as in women's rights — and when they must be rejected — as in the far better historical case for patrilineal Jewish identity.

The need to move toward a new hermeneutic for non-Orthodox Jewish ethics led me to create a course at the HUC-JIR, New York, in which we would respond to the loss of deductive methodological clarity by proceeding inductively. First, students would render a Jewish religious decision on a contemporary ethical issue of some concern to them, doing so according to a schema I worked out (after some initial experience with the course). Having done so, they would then reflect on the experience to see what it had taught them — and us all — about the living nature of Reform Jewish decision-making. I do not mean to suggest by this that ours was an exercise in pure induction, whatever that is. Rather, as will become clear in a moment, we began with certain rough affirmations — contemporary ethical pluralism; the "authority" of halakhic texts; and personal autonomy — and tried to see what would happen as we moved forward guided by them.

After some experience I worked out a six-step schema for proceeding that promised good results. First, students were to find a "fruitful" problem to study. This meant an issue of concern to them, on which the *halakhah* had something to say, preferably with some difference of opinion, and on which there was contemporary general ethical literature, again preferably with differing views. Second, a preliminary survey of the general literature would indicate where the ethical issue was thought to lie, thus clarifying what Jewish study would be specifically relevant.

Third, students were to study the pertinent halakhic material as intensively as possible, paying particular attention to divergent views and disciplining themselves to ask what the sources they intuitively disagreed with might yet have to teach them. Fourth, the general ethical material was to be treated in similar fashion. Fifth, based on their study of the diverse Jewish and general sources, they were to render a decision on the issue. In setting this forth they were to explain as best they could their reasons for arriving at just this decision rather than another. That being done, sixth, they were to step back from the entire process and see what their work had taught them about a desirable method for responsible Reform Jewish decision-making today.

2) *Toward a Postmodern Jewish Ethics*

In hindsight it seems clear that differences in meta-ethics unconsciously make themselves felt in the different ways the student authors [of the studies in this book, *Reform Jewish Ethics and the Halakhah*] utilized the course model for decision-making. The schema itself, it now also seems clear, derived from my growing clarity about a postmodern theology of Jewish duty and I shall be using the term "postmodern" in that specific sense.[1] But other than the session introducing the course there was no time to explain the theological reasons I could now give for our proceeding as I proposed. I could only refer students to my early statement of my views[2] on what one needed to take into account when making a responsible non-Orthodox Jewish decision. Its mature exposition did not take place until the publication of *Renewing the Covenant*[3], by which time all these papers had been written. It will clarify the situation in which liberal Jewish ethical thinkers now find themselves, as I see it, if I explain why I now consider the recommended schema postmodern and what I learned from the actual experience of having students work with it.

Four features of the model strike me, particularly in combination, as departures from various modern patterns of decision-making. First, as against an older liberal view that every rational person's access to the moral law has made possible a direct understanding of one's duty — popularly identified with the work of one's conscience — this schema calls for an elaborate examination of contemporary rational alternatives and historical material (*halakhah*). More specifically, thinkers of a prior generation could easily by-pass most of the study required here. Assuming the identity of Jewish and universal ethics, they only needed to refer to what conscientious (=liberal) general ethicians were advocating and know what Jews, too, ought to be doing. In the series of steps to be employed here, each requiring serious investigation of the available alternative views, a fundamentally different meta-ethical view is at work. The Kantian trust in human rationality and its view of moral law has now been so compromised that a more complex form of moral investigation is required.

Second, and related to the first, Jewish liberal religious ethicians of prior generations assumed that Jewish ethics customarily entailed liberal political stands. It is difficult to trace the source of this assurance. It seems far more likely due to the social situation in which Jews found themselves than to their ethical philosophy. As a minority still seeking full equality in the general society Jews had both pragmatic and idealistic motives for identifying with the struggles of all outsiders for greater justice and opportunity. Rational, universal Jewish ethics then provided the theoretical foundation of this stance. In their eagerness to integrate, liberal Jewish ethicians ignored the possibility that particular Jewish needs might be lost in giving unrelenting priority to our universal obligations. They also so identified conservatism with the rights of privilege and the acceptance of prejudice that they could not conceive of it developing a more humane ethics. But gradually some conscientious Jews were attracted to it, at first because of its cogent criticism of liberalism's failings and then because of its thoughtful response to America and its Jewry's changed historical situation. The method recommended here was open to the possibility that the contemporary conscience might be as well expressed by a conservative as by a liberal political position.

Third, because reason or conscience provided their guidance, liberal Jewish thinkers had little interest in what classic Jewish literature might teach them ethically. The prophets, to whom they looked for inspiration, mainly served to validate their Kantian insight that ethics was to be distinguished from ritual with clear priority given to moral action. When the liberals did cite rabbinic literature, it was largely aggadic and educed to show that Judaism had some sources which agreed with the (normative) modern, rational temper. In contrast, the method called for here requires detailed attention to rabbinic views on a given issue, specifically, *halakhah lemaaseh*, authoritative rulings for action. Moreover, in following the dialectical development of halakhic views, students were asked to pay particular attention to the rabbinic views with which they disagreed. They were to be on guard against simply trying to find opinions which confirmed their contemporary moral intuitions and asked to develop a dialogic openness to what they might learn from our non-modern sages. When they could discipline themselves in this way, two intertwined results were likely to follow. First, the otherness of the *poskim*, the decisors, helped them gain radical insight into their modernist attitudes. Second, instead of resolutely reading the past by the standards of the present, they could amplify their moral probing by equally considering how the present might ethically gain from the wisdom of the past. Because postmodernity finds all universalism rooted in particularity — can any thinker or thought be anything other than particular? — it also takes our participation in the long chain of classic Jewish ethical reasoning as a sign of our Jewish authenticity even if our views ultimately differ with those of the tradition.

Fourth, having opened themselves to all these opinions, students were asked to render a decision, to give their reasons for deciding on just this course of action and, abstracting further from the process, to reflect on what they had learned about decision-making from their experience doing it. Despite all the study and reasoning, the six stages of this process tended to make students radically more self-consciousness about what they were doing in acting as ethical decisors. This emphasis on the personal involvement of the thinker in the thinking is characteristically postmodern. By contrast, moderns prided themselves on their clear, firm, essentially impersonal sense of duty. They considered moral disinterest a major sign of ethical probity and they deemed disciplining the self to the impartial demands of conscience a telling index of high character.

At the heart of this difference in approach is a meta-ethical divergence over human nature. Moderns had unlimited confidence in the enlightened human self, its reason and its moral capacity. Postmoderns have far less certainty about themselves and their abilities, on their own, to discern their responsibilities as they face complex challenges. So where moderns had little interest in what classic Jewish teaching might have to say to them, postmoderns are seriously open to our classic texts, specifically, the *halakhah*. This new found humility may be epitomized in saying that the rational, universal, Kantian self of Jewish modernity has now been displaced by the Jewish self, one which knows itself to be more fully personal than rational and more fundamentally particular than universal, though it remains significantly both rational and universal.

Permit me an aside at this point. I have been surprised by the way in which some otherwise astute readers of *Renewing the Covenant* have only recognized half its constructive argument. In keeping with the greater Jewish interest in spirituality today they have been reasonably receptive to its case for a greater place for God in our lives (chapters 1-10). Restoring a living relationship with a real God would at least bring us beyond the near-secularity of much modern Jewish religious thought. Yet that would only leave us *benei Noah*, children of Noah, with only the duties of Noahides. We do not properly become authentic *benei Yisrael* and take up the fullness of Jewish living until we take our stand in the particular historic relationship of the people of Israel with God, the Covenant. If the task of a contemporary non-Orthodox Jewish theology is to explicate a theory of contemporary Jewish duty, its affirmation of God must be complemented by its equal affirmation of the people of Israel's true relationship with God. Postmodernity provides us with a language with which to affirm Jewish particularity by giving primary emphasis to the way our historicity, our race, our class, our gender, our language and other such specifics, necessarily shape our lives and thought. I draw on this to make a case for the ultimate particularity of the self[4] (chapters 11-13) which leads on then to a rethought doctrine of the people Israel (chapters 14-16) thus establishing the other side of the Covenant. The relationship then in place, a specific understanding of Jewish duty can then be educed from it.

This effort to situate the self primally in its Jewishness — what Louis Newman so nicely calls "Learning to be Led" — apparently troubled some of the authors of these papers. I had the feeling that some of them knew from the moment they decided on the question they would study what its answer had to be, so despite the recommended process, they were really only interested in texts which confirmed their views. Others may have been more open to the argument of the texts that opposed their ethical intuition but this seemed more an academic nicety they could live with since they knew they could always autonomously dismiss them. Perhaps they feared that taking the halakhic texts more seriously might impinge on their dedication to liberal Judaism and render them quasi-Orthodox. However, this fear receives no confirmation from the bulk of the papers for no author wound up agreeing with the dominant halakhic view simply because it was where "the" Jewish tradition stood. So too, none of those who most seriously engaged the *halakhah* evidenced a sacrifice of autonomy to the texts. The writers remained too modern for that.

This persistence of certain modern concerns amid the move to a pattern of decision-making I consider postmodern deserves some comment. It disconcerts some thinkers to be told that there remains a considerable overlap between modern and postmodern modes of ethical deliberation. It centers on the issue of autonomy. Few things if any are as religiously precious to our students as their right to self-determination in thought and action. Their intense concern for this value is confirmed by their deep devotion to compassionate human relations, individual and social. Ethical idealism has long been one of the two major motives bringing students to the rabbinate. (The other is a love of the Jewish people leading to the desire to serve it. How the two relate to one another varies widely.) They devoutly believe that autonomy is confirmed in ethics and this proposition is central to their understanding of non-Orthodox Judaism. I think the same is true of most caring American Jews and to that extent the modernization of Judaism has spoken truly and lastingly to a religious impulse basic to our people's lives.

Let me now qualify what I described above as the patronizing stance modern Jewish ethical thinkers took in relation to the Jewish tradition. Many of the writers and thinkers of prior generations were men (*sic*) of great Jewish learning and broad Jewish sympathies. While they were anxious to parade their broad humanity, much of their thinking was imbued with Jewish sensitivity and sympathy. It really is unfair to them to speak of their universalistic utterances as if there was nothing particularly Jewish in them, subterranean though it might be. Our students demonstrate this same interpenetration of the universal by the particular, perhaps even more intensely than did their liberal forebears. They are, after all, the offspring of some generations of American Jews who have enthusiastically identified the Jewish and the ethically universal. They and our community as a whole regularly show a devotion to justice and a concern for social betterment that cannot be termed distinctively Jewish. Yet the interpenetration of the two continually manifests itself in such odd indicators of continuing ethnicity as the heavy disproportion of Jews working to improve human welfare and voting for liberal social causes despite their contrary class interests. The result is that when American Jews assert their universal ethics without conscious regard for Jewish text or teaching, they are very often far more deeply grounded in their Jewishness than they take themselves to be. So I very often have sensed in these papers as their authors exercised their autonomy to universalize our tradition that there was something quite Jewish even about their reasons for transcending their particularity.

Despite my insistence on a certain Jewish particularity in modern Jewry's universalistic decision-making process, there remains a substantial difference between it and what follows from postmodern commitments. This is more than a matter of balance, the modern utterly subordinating its particularity, the postmodern glorying in it. The more critical issue is that postmodernity substantially transforms individual freedom in keeping with its different sense of the human situation. So to speak, moderns take the "auto[s]," the self, in autonomy quite seriously, individualizing judgment and legislation. In classic Kantian thought individuality quickly becomes socialized since one's autonomy ought to be guided by reason. Since rationality is common to all thinking-beings/moral-agents, a critical sign of proper moral reasoning is whether the duty one imposes upon oneself might be made a law for all humankind. Nonetheless, individual reason is the arbiter of that decision.

Postmodern thought does not have such confidence in the individual or in human rationality. In postmodern Jewish theology selfhood is indivisible from a relationship with that independent Other we call God and with the Jewish people, past, present and future. The "auto[s]" now validly exercises its power of self-legislation (auto-nomy) not as a quasi-monad but in intimate involvement with its relational-others, God and the Jewish people.

It may help to explain autonomy's overlap-with-transformation in directly religious terms. For all the postmodern critique of modernity, some postmoderns, I among them, acknowledge that part of its innovative religious insight remains valid. Modern thinkers tightly linked personal dignity with the right of self-determination in ways previously unknown and unacceptable to our tradition. For a religion based on a revealed text, our "orthodoxy" may have granted substantial individual freedom within the system. Moderns grandly expanded this. While postmoderns agree that they were right to do so, their chastened view of human capacity results in a newly contextualized and thereby delimited view of personal freedom. Thus they affirm "autonomy" as moderns do but mean something significantly new by it.

These theoretical observations indicate something of what the teacher was learning from the students as they experimented with — as it turned out — applying a postmodern view of autonomy to some pressing ethical issues. (Of course, I was also working on *Renewing the Covenant* in this period. That, plus post-publication discussions concerning it refined my theoretical understanding.[5]) It came as little surprise that some students chafed at being asked to exercise their autonomy less independently than their upbringing and religiosity instructed them to do. Modernity remains the dominant Jewish community ideology (certainly its language) even though the signs of its intellectual collapse abound. What came as a pleasant surprise was how congenially most students took to this new (and demanding) schema. They knew that conservative ethicians were often quite cogent and while they might have preferred ignoring them they recognized that evasion was simple irresponsibility. More importantly, for Jewish and human reasons they wanted to know what the *halakhah* said on their topic so they avidly took to this aspect of our work (though it often involved them with texts for which they had received scant preparation). The two concluding, reflective steps — of decision in the face of alternatives and of personally reacting to the process — met with rather a more mixed response. I judged this to be less a resistance to postmodern self-consciousness than a preference for action over speculation as well as exhaustion at completing this paper in one semester. Considering that the students came to this effort with little conscious understanding of or commitment to my view of postmodern meta-ethics and thus the decision-making structure I imposed upon them, I found their general satisfaction with the method — albeit for major, not day-to-day, ethical deliberation — a confirmation of my analysis of our community's move toward postmodernity.[6]

I do not mean to suggest by these comments that these papers, for all their seriousness of intent and depth of research, fully present my ideal of postmodern decision-making. Sometimes their constricted method results from the specific issue being studied for then its particular contours will make one or another aspect of the procedure more or less valuable in dealing with it. However, here students were not asked to deal with three additional aspects of the postmodern decision-making process I deem significant.[7] Two of these derive from standing in Covenant as one of the people of Israel: first, a concern for how our community today is facing up to a given issue, and, second, a consideration of the messianic future to which Jewish action ought to be directed. The third stems from the fact that our Covenant relationship is with God, no less, and so our decisions need to be made with intense regard for what we believe God now wants of us.

To some extent the first of these desiderata, the contemporary attitude, operates in these studies when they invoke the opinion of present day *poskim*, decisors. But that does not often yield what the mass of Jews themselves sense to be their present duty. Taken literally, this criterion self-destructs. The bulk of American Jewry is apathetic, ignorant and non-observant. Shall we really seek their guidance as to what God wants of the Covenant people? And if we limit ourselves to "caring" or "serious-minded" Jews, can we ever say just who they are? Nevertheless, the Covenant is made with the Jewish people and not simply its authorities. In recent generations the Jewish people has not infrequently been spiritually ahead of its leadership, as in their acceptance of responsible contraception, secular education and women's equality. Hence, with all its risks, a postmodern Jewish decisor must seek for what he understands to be the present trend or divisions in the Jewish community on a given issue.

The eye to the messianic future is not often found in these studies but it must have a place in any fully responsive Covenantal decision. At the least, the messianic consideration enters on two levels. The simpler one involves asking whether a given policy has redemptive features about it. So to speak, would instituting it serve to foreshadow the full redemption to which Jews aspire? I termed this the "simpler" level for people readily identify this purposiveness with their determination to be scrupulously moral in responding to an ethical challenge. High morality surely is redemptive. But even an intense dedication to ethics can easily become so time-and-culture-bound that it misses the grand sweep invoked by asking about ultimate redemption. Thus, on the second level one asks whether a given decision is likely to help the Jewish people endure the tests of history in holiness until the Messiah comes. Now Jewish continuity, the subject of so much communal discussion since the Jewish Population Survey of 1990, takes on its proper theological frame. On this level the speculative difficulties increase for no one can tightly connect specific Jewish duties with our people's survival to the end of history. But living messianism is indispensable to Jewish survival in faithfulness. Negatively, one cannot sanction an act which is unlikely to keep Jewry alive in long-term Covenant loyalty. So while we are not gifted with prophecy we must stretch our Jewish imaginations and seek in each decision to connect our deeds with the long passage to the end-time.

To suggest that our relationship with God also must play a direct role in our ethical deliberations often panics liberals. Adamant in their rejection of Orthodoxy, they worry lest religious leaders again be empowered to have God authorize ethical barbarities, the Crusades and Inquisition being quickly linked to Jonestown and the Waco Branch Davidians. They do not care that even in Jewish Orthodoxy God's authority is domesticated, as it were, by the halakhic tradition and community scrutiny. Among the non-Orthodox, of course, "God's authority" is even further conditioned by the emphasis on religion as substantially our human response to God and the resulting centrality of personal autonomy. But only in a thoroughgoing humanism would esteeming individual freedom require that God have no role at all in our decision-making.

Moderns, say those who thought of God as the organizing/integrating idea of their worldview, could easily equate being fully rational in their ethical judgment as attending to God's will. For the less philosophically inclined, this became simply listening to their conscience. For religious postmoderns, the self does not have such omnicompetence and the new humility induced by realism about our limits makes room for a relationship with a real God. "Listening" to that God, trying to discern what one's relationship with God entails, now claims a significant place in decision-making. Thus, traditional Jews not only expect exalted learning from their *posek*, decisor, but exemplary personal piety as well. Liberal Jews vary widely in their sense of God and what it means that they are involved with that God in the Covenant. But their faith always has a sense of our present, ongoing "listening/discerning" to God's "will," our equivalent of revelation, something we claim goes on today as in the past though not as spectacularly. One whose intimacy with God has grown over the years will "know" from time to time, with varying degrees of clarity, what God "demands" or "prohibits." At the very least, their ethical deliberations will be conducted with the seriousness befitting the One whom they seek to serve. I may only have been theologically wishful but I often found the depth of concern manifest in these papers to be the equivalent of the non-Orthodox piety I have in mind.

Even had these papers applied the fullest possible pattern of decision-making they would not likely have remedied an outcome that troubles some people: it may lead people to different results, as some papers indicate. Shouldn't a religion be giving unequivocal answers to questions of good and evil? and is that not a desideratum today in contrast to a liberal secularism that seems able to permit almost everything? I think there are many questions of morality where we could reach near unanimity but for pedagogic reasons we selected issues enveloped in controversy. We hoped that facing a clash of values would throw us back on our own (now richly informed) ethical intuition and bring many of our meta-ethical presumptions to consciousness. In any case, it seems strange for Jews to be asking for a more monolithic (applied) ethics when the *halakhah* regularly features differences of opinion. To be sure, the area of agreement as versus that of disagreement was much greater in our tradition than it is among liberals. Nonetheless, if even our "orthodoxy" tolerates diversity then surely non-Orthodox Judaism will do so to an even a greater extent.

The liberal Jewish proclivity for diversity stems from its recognition of the individual's right to self-determination. Once one's self is allowed a place in the decision-making process, a certain subjective variety acquires authority. Postmodern Jewish theology brings a considerable measure of order to bear on the threatened anarchy by requiring us to exercise our autonomy Covenantally, that is, out of our relationship with God as part of the people of Israel's past, present and messianically future involvement with God. But one thing more remains to be remarked upon: how a change in our actual pattern of contemporary Jewish existence would affect the single Jewish self. Today most caring Jews find themselves quite isolated among the masses of relatively indifferent Jews. Few people share their religious assumptions. So their efforts to determine just what constitutes their Covenant obligations must be pursued in a relatively solitary fashion. My comments here and in much of *Renewing the Covenant* have been addressed to such isolated, devoted Jews. But what if they were able to share in a community of Jews devoted like themselves to the imperatives of existence in Covenant? In that case, I suggest, the corporate patterns of this "mini-people-of-Israel" would have great sway in their lives (as a living extension of the communal criterion discussed above). Were we able to produce such small communities of shared faith/action — and then to link and enlarge them! — the threat of Jewish duty becoming radically subjective would diminish. And though this pattern of decision-making would always oscillate in avoidance of the dangers of anarchy and orthodoxy, its dedication to process over outcome would be less worrisome. Until such local communities of faith become realities, we will continue to suffer Jewishly from the residual effects of a modernization which has over-stressed the virtues of individuality to the point where we are now socially deprived. The postmodern understanding of the Covenant — and of the self which stands within it — restores a more recognizable Jewish balance.

If, indeed, our beliefs prevent our ever escaping the issue of subjectivity in our decision-making,[8] there is one further virtue of the scheme utilized in these papers: it forces us to confront the meta-ethical commitments in terms of which we read our various texts and construct our arguments. Having to make a case against people — whether halakhic or general ethical sages — with whose decisions one disagrees, eventually forces one back to the beliefs by which one hopes to live. Seeing their ethical consequences can strongly reenforce them; it may also suggest they need reconsideration. It takes a strong faith to live with such commitment/openness. I do not see that anything less would be adequate to what our ever renewing tradition requires of us today.

Notes

1. "Postmodern" has turned out to be so useful in many venues of contemporary intellectual discussion that it permits of no reasonably clear definition. I use the term in a theological context worked out in *Renewing the Covenant* (Philadelphia: Jewish Publication Society, 1991). The standard, Derridean understanding of the postmodern denies that such foundational terms like "self" and "God," which I employ, can still be meaningfully be used. But the philosophic/literary postmoderns then divide on whether any sort of reasonably didactic discourse remains possible or only educative forms of word-play. Other postmoderns seek to avoid this difficulty by new/old modes of reading texts or their own lives, I. e., spiritual autobiography. For an early, 1990, statement of some Jewish varieties, see "A Symposium on Jewish Postmodernism," *Soundings, An Interdisciplinary Journal,* Vol. LXXVI, No. 1, Spring, 1993, with contributions by Edith Wyschogrod, Peter Ochs, Jose Faur, Robert Gibbs and Jacob Meskin.
2. "The Autonomous Jewish Self," *Modern Judaism,* 4.1, Feb., 1984.
3. This took place at the end of 1991. Its first nineteen chapters provide the basis for the culminating statement now significantly retitled, "The Jewish Self."
4. See, in particular, pp. 43-48 where, as part of the experiential exposition of American Jewry's postmodern situation, I explicate the socio-historic basis for my later polemic against the adequacy of the self before presenting my argument for the primacy of its particularity.
5. For the ongoing tri-partite split in my theological work — Jewish sources, apologetics, application — see *Renewing the Covenant*, pp. ix-xi. Note that I have been fairly consistent in using the realm of ethical duty as an academic means of exploring what my theological speculations entailed.
6. I refer to the analysis of "Jewish Religious Experience in Our Time" carried out in chapters 1- 3 of *Renewing the Covenant.*
7. See chapter 20 of *Renewing the Covenant*, "The Jewish Self."
8. I believe this is as true of traditional *pesak*, decision-making, as it is of serious non-Orthodox ethical determinations, though there is an obvious difference of degree between the two modes. Thirty years ago, I devoted my column on "Contemporary Theological Literature" in *Judaism* to the topic, "Subjectivity and the Halachic Process" (Spring, 1964). I argued there that an examination of the current literature of each of the movements showed that decisors necessarily could not be fully "objective" about their decisions and that a certain measure of personal insight inevitably made itself felt in their work. This drew a rejoinder in a subsequent issue of *Tradition* (Vol. 7, No. 1, Winter, 1964-5) from Immanuel Jakobovits the

regular writer of its "Survey of Recent Halakhic Literature." He readily conceded that there were certain personal limitations involved in every human intellectual process and pointed out that only Moses knew God's will without distortion. But he then tried to make a case for the objectivity of halakhic *pesak*. I will still happily let readers decide for themselves on the basis of these two statements of the case whether subjectivity is not a significant factor in classic Jewish decision-making.

Were our culture now fully committed to the postmodern identification of text and reader we could simply abandon the pretense that there could be such a thing as an "objective" reading of a text and stop worrying that the reader necessarily is involved in giving meaning to any text. But for the time being, with modern as well as postmodern ways of approaching these issues being current, I shall continue to assume here that the reader is more influenced by the modern than the postmodern understanding of hermeneutics

Chapter 18

ℰℛ

Human Rights

The One God and the Dignity of the Human Person

T he modern idea of human "rights" does not exist in that conceptualization in classic Jewish doctrine for neither the Bible nor rabbinic literature speaks of human dignity this way. It is not difficult to understand why this is the case. The contemporary notion of human rights arose in connection with a strong assertion of property rights; one has such significant entitlement to the property one has legally acquired that government exists in large part to safeguard one's claims in this regard. Jewish tradition over the millennia had great respect for property rights yet it had even greater regard for God's ultimate possession of everything in creation. Theologically, the Jewish equivalent of "rights" derives from the compelling Jewish response to God as the absolute "owner, *baal, koneh,*" in the economic metaphor, or "king, *melekh,*" in the related political usage, or more directly as "creator, *bore, yotzer.*" And it is not difficult to see these notions carried forward in the European euphemisms for God's own, ineffable name, the tetragrammaton, as in the English "Lord."

This affirmation of God's "right" to everything must be associated with the equally strong Hebrew spiritual sensibility that God is one, alone, unique, the Entity incomparably greater than all those non-entities people call "god." Hence, there is almost a hint of blasphemy in the assertion that individuals might have property or even personal rights that could in any way be like God's or, more heretically, allow one to challenge God's absolute status. (Modern writers have made much of the uncommon tales in Biblical and later writings which depict God's worthies directly challenging God. However, they confront God only in terms of the "rights" God has given them as God's Covenant partners, not on the basis of some standard independent of people and God.)

Because this absolutely single God is good and in that goodness creates and relates to human beings, all of them, they have the Jewish equivalent of human rights. I wish to explicate here the theological foundations of this development; for a detailed examination of the parallels in Jewish law to many provisions of the United Nations' Universal Declaration of Human Rights, see the admirable work by Haim Cohn, *Human Rights in Jewish Law* (New York: KTAV Publishing House, 1984).

To begin with, Judaism asserts that an inalienable dignity inheres in every human being and it may perhaps best be understood as a function of two closely related religious themes. The one is the astonishing assertion that God created human beings in God's own "image." Regardless of our exegesis of that richly ambiguous term, there is something about every human being which is identified with the absolute source of value in the universe. An even more daring belief, God's incomparable greatness and goodness being kept in mind, is the central Hebrew religious perception that God had brought humankind into active partnership with God, the relationship symbolized by the ancient Semitic legal term "covenant." As it were, humans are sufficiently Godlike that God can be intimately involved with them, concerned about their behavior and dedicated to their welfare. Their incomparable status among created things stems from this close identification with God and God's purposes.

Responsibility, Justice, Grace and the Dignity of the Human Person

Perhaps no other concept of Jewish faith makes this more evident than does its notion of *teshuvah*, the turning back to God English somewhat lamely terms "repentance." Being a covenant partner of God's involves each human being in precious responsibility; one is not only commanded by God but one is then free to respond thereto in obedience or defiance. Judaism thus understands God as endowing people with the freedom to turn against the very source of their supreme worth and status and thus bestowing on them an extraordinary intrinsic value. But should they exercise this freedom to defy God, to sin, it might conceivably result in their permanent estrangement from God and thus to a loss of all human dignity. To some extent this aura attends the sinner. God being central to traditional Judaism, the wicked, particularly those who self-consciously and defiantly transgress, are loathed — but they never lose their covenant partnership with God, even in just punishment. We see that most clearly in Judaism's proclamation of the ability of even hardened sinners to turn from their evil ways and "live." To Jonah's discomfiture, that is what happens when the vicious Ninevites give up their immorality and throw themselves on God's mercy, which is instantly granted. And rabbinic literature, in law and lore down to the present day, reaffirms this understanding of God's relationship with all humans as individuals and in their collectivities. In sum, Judaism teaches that no one can ever take away from a human being an elemental value which God has bestowed upon everyone and which God never alienates.

This motif is related to the strong emphases on justice and mercy in Jewish doctrine. That all are equal before human courts as they are before the Divine judge, that the rich must receive no special deference and so too the poor are only legal equals, no more but no less, testifies to the inherent worth of each person. But the prophets and sages who shaped Jewish religious life are too sensitive to what God demands and what social realities make of human relationships to think that good statutes and legal procedures alone can produce God's sanctified community. They regularly enjoin us to be merciful as God is merciful to us, giving one another much more than what others might claim by right or we might think to grant them to gain some advantage. Each person symbolizes God and thus ought receive a precious measure of our love and concern.

Positively, this produces an expectation that people will be given the opportunity to develop their humanity through security of person, respect for privacy and reputation, encouragement of education and leisure, the chance to work and be compensated, to acquire property, to marry and found a family, and much else. All this is so fundamental to Judaism that it rarely reaches direct statement in the Bible or the Talmud. Rather, it is simply taken for granted by our sacred texts as the ground of all those many provisions of Jewish law and teaching which specify the details of existence made holy. That these many documents, written over centuries in different social circumstances, have so little need to explain or rationalize their fundamental worldview testifies to its enduring power in Jewish religiosity.

To a considerable extent, however, it is the negative aspects of the human situation that most tellingly indicate whether one has rights. Human relations are substantially ordered by the interplay of power, which means that some people are often able to deny others their self-determination. In such situations of coercion the person with inferior power has little or no defense against the more powerful unless the victim has something like rights to fall back upon and, the realities of power being what they are, some countervailing power that can be called upon to enforce them. The analysis of one such situation, an important one for universal human rights, should clarify what is involved.

The Treatment of Outsiders — A Test Case

Even today in democracies with well-articulated notions of pluralism, aliens often find themselves discriminated against. In ancient times when the individual and the group were not differentiated as sharply as they are today, outsiders would normally expect to be treated with a strong suspicion or outright hatred. Indeed, we often consider it a critical test of one's ethics to see how one treats the outsider, how different are the standards one applies to members of one's own group and to those outside it. On this score the oldest Jewish sources are admirable. The Bible does not begin its account of human history with the origin of the Hebrews. Instead, it speaks first of God's relationship with humanity as a whole and specifically indicates how this comes to include all the 'tongues and nations' into which people have become divided. Two important lines of development proceed from this biblical understanding.

In the Talmud and thence through the rest of the development of Jewish law, the covenant God made with Noah and his children becomes the foundation of the Jewish theology of the Gentile, the non-Jew, and the many laws regarding Jewish-Gentile relations. Structurally, the Gentile relationship with God is the same as that between God and the Jewish people, namely, it is a covenant. God gives seven grounding command-ments to all humankind: the prohibitions of idolatry, blasphemy, murder, theft, sexual immorality and eating a limb severed from a living animal, as well as the positive injunction to establish courts of justice.

Without much imaginative speculation one can infer from these duties the sense of human dignity to which they give social and religious form. Even more to the point, Jewish law substantially equates Jews and Noahides by two presumptions: first, that before the revelation at Mt Sinai Jews were obligated to serve God in exactly the same way as were Gentiles, and second, that after the giving of the Torah, the special revelation to the Jews, there was nothing prohibited to a Gentile that was now permitted to Jews. Of course, the judgment of the biblical authors and the rabbis that the Gentile nations all violated their covenant by their idolatry rendered them utterly wicked and reprobate in Jewish eyes. The critical point is that they were not condemned merely because they were Gentiles, religiously alien, but because of their behavior. Thus, rabbinic tradition came to the authoritative position that pious individuals among the Gentiles, like Jews, had 'a share in the life of the world to come'. Clearly, the beliefs which ground this point of view could in a later age, one of much greater human interaction and equality, make possible a Jewish ground for a universal declaration of human rights.

A similar attitude toward the alien is found as a major motif in the Torah's legislation regarding the stranger who comes to live among Jews settled on their promised land. Empathically the law states that 'you must not oppress the stranger, for you know the heart of the strangers having yourselves been strangers in the land of Egypt' (Ex. 23 - 9). Or again: 'The stranger who resides with you shall be to you as one of the homeborn. You shall love him as yourself, for you were strangers in the land of Egypt. I am the Lord, your God' (Lev. 19-33). God is even described as telling the people of Israel, when reminding them that the land that they have been given remains God's, that 'you are but strangers, sojourning with me' (Lev. 25.23).

This theme requires greater emphasis, for it is not the stranger alone who is powerless in most societies. The Torah often calls upon the Hebrews to be particularly concerned about the widow and the orphan as well as the stranger. These three symbolize all those likely to be taken advantage of by the shrewd and the mighty, and it is just these that are described as God's special concern. Again and again the refrain sounded above, 'I am the Lord', is the only 'reason' given for this decency toward people one could easily outmaneuver. So too, one must not curse the deaf, though the words cannot be heard, or put a stumbling-block before the blind, though they will not know who did them harm, for 'I am the Lord'. God is their advocate and the power behind them, though society considers them insignificant and God will execute judgment on their behalf, in this life and, if not here, then in the life of the world to come. Eschatology as well as this-worldly retribution gives the powerless and thus all people a Vindicator, and one infringes upon the worth God has conferred upon them only with great personal risk.

In much of Jewish history these teachings did not have the universal scope and democratic aura they have today. For centuries Jewish belief and the Jewish people lived under continual threat, for the few Jewish monotheists existed as a most peculiar people in a world of often hostile idolaters. And later, when Christianity and Islam made belief in one God the common faith of the Western world, discrimination and hostility toward Jews made it realistic to maintain a limited Jewish ethical horizon. That their spiritual forebears living in such straitened circumstances had so fundamentally universal an appreciation of humankind seems to Jews today an awesome, numinous accomplishment. Then, when social circumstance changed and persecution gave way to equality, it was not difficult for Jewish thinkers searching their sacred tradition to recover and apply the old Jewish appreciation of human solidarity and inalienable individual human dignity.

Problems of Religious Foundation

Religions of Revelation Versus the Absoluteness of Rights

As often, the problems connected with this religious understanding stem from its very strength. I do not see that these problems arise directly from the specific Jewish character of the faith outlined above. Rather I believe that they come from the difficulties created by modern, that is, Western thought for the discussion of religions based on revelation. One problem derives from the absolute character of the vision of humanity elaborated. Were the one, incomparable God not the source of universal human dignity, then in certain circumstances that dignity might be compromised or qualified. What gives the term 'rights' its high practical significance is precisely its unconditional character. In the face of overbearing power one can assert one's 'rights' and thus, ideally, prevent the would-be oppressors from doing their coercive will. When such rights exist, any effort to justify the imposition of the other's will by seeking to qualify the rights or make them conditional can be quickly identified as immoral and discriminatory. In this context, the absoluteness of rights is commendable.

We are troubled, however, because some religionists claim to know in detail the will of the One, absolute source of value in the universe. Anyone claiming a different or, worse, an opposite position, is then not only absolutely wrong but can be seen as an enemy of God and truth, and possibly in danger of damnation or its equivalent. It is but a step from this to what some rabbinic texts, in another context, term saving a sinner's soul at the cost of taking his life. That is, to be sure, an extreme case, but it is sufficiently exemplified in the history of religion world-wide, even into our own day, that it cannot be ignored. Religions of revelation - and even others which have no such concept - have, by their absolutism, occasionally generated extremism, zealotry and fanaticism. Thus there is a fearsome contradiction in advocating a religious position which can motivate denying others their rights as the foundation of a robust commitment to broad-scale human rights.

Universalism and Particularism

The other major conundrum lies in the paradox that religions of revelation affirm the universal value of all human beings on a quite particularistic ground. That is, everything they have to say about humankind generally comes from their institutional version of what God has said, making the particularity as critical as the universalism. Thus though the Jewish tradition accords Gentiles the fullest human value as a result of the covenant made with Noah, how Gentiles know their status is critical to Jewish law. If they assert their Noahide status as a matter of their own reason, they forfeit their dignity in a Jewish jurisdiction where they must formally accept it as a matter of Jewish revelation or reap the consequences (Maimonides, The Laws of Kings, 8.10-11). This stipulation, which clashes with modern views of tolerance, has a religious logic to it. When revelation is the basis of all truth, to suggest that one might reach ultimate truth by another means is to challenge the premise of all premises. Hence the paradox that to benefit fully from the universal reach of the Jewish tradition, the Gentile must accept it in its particularity at least in part.

This seemed like an egregious case of ethnocentrism in the heady days when philosophers had no difficulty asserting as a matter of simple rationality that their ideas were characteristic of all human rationality. In that context the reference to a special level of human experience — particularly one limited to certain specific persons at some particular time — was adjudged a rather primitive level of thought. Modern secularity claimed to reach beyond such limited horizons of thought to a true universalism and claimed that it was ethically superior to Western religions as a consequence. In that time religion seemed more a hindrance to universal human rights than their needed foundation.

Eurocentrism

Only we no longer live in such self-confident secularity. What once passed for a broad universalism now seems quite particularistic, even Eurocentric, in the language of some critics. Others easily fault it as the guild product of a certain group of university professors, ones largely male, white and either Christian or highly influenced by Christian culture. Today few rationalists can confidently claim to stand above all the particularities of individual existence and speak in some compelling way of what everyone is or ought to be or needs or experiences or deserves — and thus the various rationalisms are no longer able to give a convincing rationale for the existence of universal human rights or the rational necessity to make them an operative reality in our world. Religion, for so long the beneficiary of the ethical chiding of secularists who pointed to its moral nakedness, is now able to return the compliment. How paltry a notion of human reason is the one our intellectuals have come to accept, one so impoverished that it cannot easily contain a substantive, commanding ethics! How shallow a sense of what it is to be human suffuses our culture so that our artists and literati rarely venture beyond criticism to assert something positively and unqualifiedly about universal moral responsibility! In its confident advance beyond its revelatory ground western secularity lost its deep human bearings with ugly consequences now seen everywhere around us.

The Role of One's Own Religion

With contemporary secularity in so sorry a human state, if human rights are to have a sure ground, it must now come from those religions, like Judaism, whose traditions provide ample grounds for affirming them. But that returns us to the problems of the absoluteness and the particularity of such religions. In Judaism as in some other faiths a response to these problems has been widely accepted if rarely articulated. It rests on what may be called with some exaggeration a theological rejection of the logical law of the excluded middle. Either, so the old standards of proper reasoning held, a notion is absolute or it is relative, it is universal or it is particular. These stringent alternatives seem unreasonable to the modern

Jewish religious sensibility. Yes, our faith is sufficiently sure and certain so that we stake our lives and that of our community on it — and will do so until the messianic fulfillment arrives. But though we know our religious truth to be utterly decisive for us we acknowledge our human limits in the religious realm. We do not also assert that we have the whole truth or the only truth about God and humankind. Others we have come to know have what we can recognize as their own truths. Not only must we in due humility give them the freedom to express and refine their truth, often we can learn from them while nonetheless seeing our own faith as decisively correct.

The Actual Contribution of Judaism

Something similar must be said about our particularity. Yes, it is our particular Jewish tradition which gives such power to our affirmation of universal human rights. If our people's God were not the good, concerned, unique Divinity we know our God to be, where would we gain the compelling insight that humankind in all its individual and corporate diversity and moral disability was nonetheless inalienably endowed with ultimate worth? And if we had not made our slavery in Egypt and our exodus thence to freedom a central human truth in our lives, one we have profoundly renewed as we have seen our people granted equality after centuries of degradation and persecution, would we be as dedicated as we are to extending human rights to every creature? Yet this truth we so centrally proclaim as part of our living faith is not exclusive to our people either as religious insight or human experience. Many others, in their own ways, have come to believe what we believe. We are not then surprised when they see in our old Exodus tale their deepest spiritual insight for we know our particular religious vision also to be profoundly and indivisibly universal.

These sentiments are most easily expressed in the various liberal forms of Judaism. These movements, which emphasize the human partnership with God in the evolution of our faith, can see in our recent experience with democracy and pluralism an ethical instruction that we know must be part of our Judaism. Simply put, God has spoken to us in the experience of these two centuries since our emancipation from the ghetto began and we have learned, not the least because of our experience with the Holocaust, the ultimate value of universal human rights.

A large part of our Orthodox community has, in ways befitting its elemental dedication to the Written and Oral Torah as revealed by God to our people, found the notions of democracy and pluralism, so closely linked with that of universal human rights, congenial to their Judaism. For a religion as closely tied to human history as is ours, it is quite natural to take an almost pragmatic approach to the application of God"s ultimate truth to given social circumstances. Perhaps the evident human gains which have come from getting people to live with one another in mutual respect will similarly one day affect the rest of our religious community and those other religious groups who have been reluctant to embrace even an unimperialistic universalism.

Chapter 19

ℰↄℂℛ

Money

(This lecture is dedicated to the memory of Felix Mitchell and in continuing tribute to Eva Rose Mitchell.)

Fifty one years ago, I and other students preparing for the entrance exams to the Hebrew Union College were asked to read a book entitled *Judaism as Creed and Life*. I confess I had not looked at it since but opening it recently in preparation for this lecture, I discovered to my great pleasure that its author, Morris Joseph, was the rabbi of the West London Synagogue. That volume appeared in 1903 but our New York School Library also had a copy of a collection of his sermons, *The Ideal in Judaism*, issued a decade prior. I shall be drawing primarily on these two books in order to characterize the trans-Atlantic spiritual mood of Reform Judaism a century ago.

Those were days of confidence and hope. Almost everywhere one turned one's eyes the world was changing for the better. Only the mean-spirited could deny that progress, though often slow, was the leitmotif of history and Jews, now increasingly overcoming their pariahhood and finding places in general society, rightly often had a special appreciation of history's beneficence. This optimism grounded itself on a rich appreciation of humankind's ability to improve and its will to do so, indeed, even to "perfect" itself. Morris Joseph thought it required no further comment when he said, "Religion is being purged . . . of superstition and error, and slowly and painfully the world is climbing to its moral regeneration." Here and elsewhere Rabbi Joseph was not blind to the continuing ubiquity of sin or the magnitude of suffering in our world but his realism always gave way to an all-conquering confidence in the onward march of human decency. Concluding his sermon on "Pessimism," he characterized faith as ". . . fear(ing) no evil, even in the valley of the shadow. This is religion — optimism if you like. But it is the optimism that makes 'the great world spin for ever down the ringing grooves of change,' that supplies progress with its vital force, that makes life possible as well as worth living. It is the only true, because the only practical, philosophy."

Messianism provided the doctrinal formulation for this attitude and he characterized it this way, "The Jew, then, looks forward to a future of universal religion and righteousness. . . . The world, he holds, is progressive; mankind is slowly but surely marching on to a happier time of faith and goodness. . . . That time is called the time of the Messiah or the Messianic era." Ten years later, shortly before the outbreak of World War I he put it this way, "All the world's greatest men have seen the vision. . . . But the meanest of us share the vision with them. The world is going to be better than it is. We are going to be better."

My desire to extend this theme somewhat arises neither from pedantic nor masochistic reasons but because this messianic faith in humankind has had great staying power. It utterly dominated North American Reform Judaism until the social and historical shocks of the 1960s and, in somewhat muted form, to be sure, humanistic optimism remains the essential faith of otherwise tough-minded colleagues and lay-people. Let me add some words then about human power's expected ability to transform any situation. Said Morris Joseph, "There is no work so humble, no lot so lowly, that faith will not ennoble and sweeten. . . . Though all the world's malignant forces band themselves together against you, they can effect nothing. . . . You are the master of your own fate. You come in very sooth, in power as well as in rectitude, as near to God as is possible for mortal man." Thus, the greatest human beings, he continued, "have proved themselves, by a contempt for their own pain, born of a reverence for the grandeur of their mission. For them all their woes have been dwarfed into utter insignificance by the majesty of their life's task. . . . Suffering has been their badge — the sign of the Messianic nature which lives from age to age."

Such optimism, perhaps no longer as fulsomely expressed or unreservedly asserted, constituted the operative faith with which we progressive Jews faced the second half of the twentieth century. And it has failed us in our ongoing tour through an inferno that includes, among countless lesser hells, Auschwitz and Hiroshima, and has recently made us relatively helpless bystanders to Serbian ethnic cleansing and the Somali disregard for life. We cannot say that this is only how "other people" live for people much like us have schooled us too well in the apparently endless syllabus of the betrayal of trust by local institutions and officials, or even by those closer to home. Humankind is uncannily ingenious at outwitting our safeguards against chicanery and our therapies for rechanneling perversity. We began the century convinced that an educated, cultured, politically activist humankind could remedy the world's ills. Now most of us know we can't even radically transform ourselves. We are, it turns out, as much, if not more, the problem than the solution. And promising us "perfectibility" has doomed many of us to disappointment and a mood of apathy, cynicism and self-indulgence that often keeps us from such righteousness as we might realistically create.

Some such consciousness of this century's frustrated spiritual pilgrimage lies behind the commonly remarked upon limpness of contemporary mainstream theology. Unconsciously, I am convinced, it has also led substantial minorities in the three great western faiths to spirituality. Ironically, the recent Zarathustrian proclamations of the death of God have now given way among Jews — perhaps the most secularized of the western religious communities — to so strong an interest in a more intense personal experience of God that the practice of mysticism has found a secure place in progressive Judaism. Morris Joseph and his rationalistic colleagues would probably have been appalled at such a development.

Elsewhere I have tried to describe this spiritual transition in greater detail. Here I wish to turn our attention to what has not yet often been discussed among us, the economic, indeed the fiscal aspect of the collapse of these great expectations. Surely much of modern Jewry's boundless hope arose from its sense of being borne along on a tide of economic progress. Of course, compared to Rothschild one was a pauper but few had aspirations so grand and rather made their estimate of history's goodness by contrast to the impoverishment that caused their families to immigrate to western countries. For more than a century these East European Jewish emigres radically improved their income by their move, and their living standards and horizon of opportunity as well. The Emancipation was not a fantasy. The barriers anti-semitism still kept in place were less daunting than those of yesteryear and far more amenable to those magical Jewish keys to success: education, drive and a *yiddishe kopp*.

For some decades twentieth century economic development sustained this practical messianism but Victorian rabbis and thinkers rarely discussed this monetary optimism. It would have been an egregious social blunder to do so and many people still become quite uncomfortable when, under spiritual or other idealistic auspices, the topic turns from institutional budgets to individual incomes and assets. One gauges something of the eerie power of this taboo by a comparison to its twin contaminant, speaking openly about sex. That prohibition has broken down much more than has speaking about one's money — though I cannot say that the liberty with which many people today speak of their sexuality is an unmixed Jewish blessing.

If, unlike our teachers, we now turn our attention to the sensitive issue of how our changing means have affected our lives, individually and institutionally, we do so because a new spiritual realism demands we do so. As it were, we have all become Marxists, though in a most modest sense, for there are few any longer who would deny the great role economic status plays in our lives and, more astonishingly, how intertwined our private economic fate is with that of our society. Bluntly put, our countries are a lot poorer than we ever expected them to be and as their economic eminence has declined most of us have become poorer. We cannot now realistically expect the most compassionate of governments to undertake all the social initiatives we would like them to and — may God help us — should they soon emerge vigorously from their present distress, they will still be unlikely to do so. And just when we are in need of ever greater help from our private institutions and thus from the donors who support them, they are in turn similarly short of funds.

We would have a far simpler spiritual response to this situation if our tradition idealized poverty and disdained wealth but it did neither. For nearly four millennia, most Jews lived in economies of scarcity and suffered from economic insecurity. Knowing our God, our people knew being poor brought no religious disgrace. So instead of being defeated by hardship, it developed strategies to sanctify want. At the same time, the centuries of suffering under Jewish penury made clear that we could not sentimentally consider poverty a virtue and asceticism a preferred path to God. Early on Jewish faith took a positive attitude toward wealth even though it simultaneously warned against its demonic potential. If we are to understand how Judaism might guide us in our present debilitating economic distress we need to explore the dynamics of this classic Jewish view of money.

In the Bible God's favor often carries with it the promise of material well-being, a theme which still makes many a high-minded commentator squeamish. Thus the patriarchal families are quite well to do, the Jews leaving Egyptian slavery do not depart impoverished — though the means of their enrichment are troublesome — and, to the consternation of idealistic readers, Job's possessions are doubled after his terrible ordeal. Theologically, this motif instances the unique Hebraic understanding of what we moderns call "religion." For many cultural and political reasons we tend to think of it as essentially a private matter, a state of the individual heart. But the Biblical authors and the rabbis who succeeded them understood our Covenant with God to be as communal as it is individual. It had to be for its horizon is human history entire. Caring Jews therefore live as much in the past and the future as in the present; their lives personally wind about a thread of corporate messianic continuity. If the Jews were to survive in history they needed to be realists, realists for the sake of their ideals. And therefore our religious realism intuited early on that money is a major means to messianic survival.

One day an enterprising Jewish historian will tell us in some detail how Jewish bribes and pay-offs over the centuries helped secure the continuity of our people. And the age-old corollary to that practice has been the insight that over the years Jews have often been acceptable to nations seeking to add or keep a significant wealth-producing minority in their economies. I certainly do not mean to assert that Jewish survival has only been due to our uncommon capacity to increase wealth. I am, however, emphasizing that thesis as a corrective to that common spiritualized Jewish theology of money which stresses to Kantian effect our high-minded interest in good deeds only for their own sake.

The Torah, Written and Oral, has been more immediate and practical than theological. Knowing people, our teachers knew the value of money in smoothing one's way. With a typical mix of hyperbole and insight the Book of Proverbs says, "A poor man is hated even by his neighbor; but a rich man has many friends." (14:20) Deuteronomy may sternly warn the judge not to show partiality toward a rich litigant, or for that matter a poor one, but R. Judah b. Shalom later found it useful to observe, "No one pays much attention when a poor man comes to plead his cause but a rich man gets priority as well as attention." (Ex. R. 21:4) The medieval pietist Bahya ben Asher extends this view, noting that "Wealth lends weight to one's words so that the opinion of the wealthy is heard." (*Kad Hakemach*, s. v. "*osher*") Yehiel ben Yekutiel Anav of Rome adds the social effect. "All come near to the rich person, and they become related to him as lovers and friends in order to benefit from him." (*Sefer Maalot Hamiddot*, s. v. "*maalat haosher*") I like the tart ambivalence of the Yiddish proverb on this topic, "With money in your pocket you are not only wise and handsome but you sing well too."

Our moralists take their customary utilitarian stance toward money as to other desirable but dangerous aspects of existence: it can be valuable only if it is properly used. The late medieval Talmudic commentator, the Maharsha, noted that not only do people want money for honors but because it provides one's family with their needs and gives one independence of the benevolence of others — which, incidentally, says a good deal about what was expected of Jewish males. (Shab. 125b) Maimonides, as so often, goes to the heart of the matter, saying, "In pursuing wealth, the main reason for its acquisition should be to expend it for noble purposes and for the maintenance of the body and the preservation of life so that its owner may obtain a knowledge of God insofar as that is vouchsafed unto human beings." (*Shemoneh Perakim*, ch. 5) Or as R. Elazar ben Azariah's famous apothegm puts it, "If there's no bread, there won't be any Torah." (P. A. 3.21)

It does not take extensive experience in the Jewish or general communities to corroborate that most of these practical dicta of ancient times remain true. Riches still get you very far socially and quickly enhance your ability to do good thereby, incidentally, giving you contacts that enable you to make more money. But all this makes clear that our present dearth of means inhibits our ability to do good and thereby lends a special poignancy to our present situation. Directly put, anyone who sits on a synagogue or other institutional board can almost immediately tell you the worthwhile activities that another thousand or ten thousand pounds a year of income would make possible. Our agencies are not hampered by a lack of responsible programs or of able personnel to carry them out but by a lack of money. This has created a problem utterly unanticipated when we made the transition from a largely volunteer community apparatus to one staffed by a corps of increasingly trained, full-time, professionalized workers. Of course we can make up for their absence by returning to our time-honored, effective emphasis on volunteer effort. But we cannot easily hide from the knowledge and the worthy Jewish pain of knowing how much more good our institutions could do if they were more fully staffed and had the means to amplify their activities.

Then why do we not simply convert our synagogues into temples of entrepreneurship and dedicate them to inspiring Jews to increase their and thus our income? Surely there is good reason to feel that with the passing of immigrant and post-immigrant vigor there has been a lessening of the vaunted Jewish drive to make money. Should we not then initiate programs designed to rededicate us to the economic prowess which has been the substrate to our survival? Cynically one might add that such economic synagogue activities would likely appeal to far more people than the services and adult study which presently occupy us. But, it is just here that the dialectical Jewish negativity to money must begin to assert itself.

Believing Jews know money can be terribly dangerous for it easily becomes addictive. R. Yudan said in the name of R. Aibu, "No one departs from this world with half his desire gratified. If he has a hundred he wants to turn them into two hundred, and if he has two hundred he wants to turn them into four hundred." (Ec. R. 1.13.1) The tenth century philosopher, Saadya Gaon, observed, "I have come to the conclusion that the acquisition of money is good so long as it comes to a person spontaneously and with ease. However, once one passionately engages in the quest for wealth, one realizes that it entails immense efforts of thought and exertion, keeping one awake at night and plagued by hardship by day, so that even when one has acquired what one desires, one is often unable to sleep properly. . . . When a person makes money the object of all his strivings and devotes himself to it with mad ambition and avidity . . . then the love of money becomes for him like a consuming fire, like a wilderness, like death or barrenness that are never sated." (*Book of Beliefs and Opinions*, p. 379)

Even when one resists compulsive acquisition the power that money grants easily leads one to arrogance and the abuse of others. What once one decried in other people one now feels entitled to do for wealth makes us superior to the common moral constraints. This exposes its heretical insidiousness: it seeks to displace God. The Torah knows this root sin well. Some 2500 years ago the authors of Deuteronomy described it this way, "When you have [come into the Land and] eaten your fill, and built fine houses to live in, and your herds and flocks have multiplied, and your silver and gold have increased, and everything you own has prospered, beware lest your heart grow haughty and you forget *Adonai* your God who freed you from the land of Egypt . . . and you say to yourselves, 'My own power and the might of my own hand have won this wealth for me,' remember that it is *Adonai* your God who gives you the power to get wealth, in fulfillment of the Covenant that He made on oath with your fathers and is still the case." (8:12-14; 17-18)

One need not have a lot of money to be tempted by money's empower-· ment and its effects can be devastating even in small groups, the family being a notable example. Whatever the arena, money can give us such sway that we act as if we were God. That makes us idolaters, the worst of Jewish sinners. No wonder Jonathan Eibeschutz, the 18th century talmudist and cabbalist said that of all the temptations one faces, the greatest is posed by money. Perhaps this was what R. Nathan had in mind in his midrash on the priestly benediction. "'May God bless you,' that is," he said, "with possessions. But then, 'May God guard you,' that is, against the Evil Urge which [then] seeks to drive you out of this world." (Num. R. 11.5)

Leery of our ability to resist money's seductiveness many a Jewish teacher has therefore lauded the virtues of poverty. A midrash reports that when Israel asked God, "Who are Your people?" God answered, "The poor," as Isaiah indicated, "For *Adonai* has comforted His people, and has compassion upon His poor." (49.13) "It is human nature," the text continues, "that when someone is wealthy and has poor relations, he does not own up to them. . . . But God is not like that for though 'Both riches and honor come from You' (1Chr. 29:12), yet God particularly protects the poor." (Ex. R. 31:5) Perhaps the most famous of these passages is ascribed to Elijah, who once instructed a sage that the Holy One, examining all the good qualities that He might give to Israel thought the most appropriate one was poverty. Samuel, or perhaps R. Joseph said, that this agrees with the folk saying, "Poverty befits Israel like a red trapping does a white horse." (Chag. 9b)

But for all their worries about the wealthy being closet idolaters the rabbis were too realistic to ask us to spurn wealth in order to show our love of God. These passages commending poverty should be read as a special species of theodicy, one that tries to make the best case for an unavoidable bad situation. Mostly their realism drives the rabbis to decry poverty and yearn to be free of it. R. Pinchas b. Chama said "Poverty in one's home is worse than fifty plagues." (B. B. 116a) The medieval poet and philosopher Solomon ibn Gabirol acidly notes in his book of ethical aphorisms "When a person's wealth diminishes, even his children do not accept his opinion and they contradict his words and commands." (*Choice of Pearls*, p. 119) The 16th century pietist and talmudist, Chayyim ben Betzalel remarked that the rabbis often use the word *dammim* for money whereas its literal meaning is "blood." And he commented, "As blood sustains life, so does money. Thus one who has no money is like someone who is thought of as being dead." (*Sefer Hachayyim*, part 3, ch.5) I do not know whether this is again the preacher's overemphasis on his lesson or another sign that we, even in our reduced circumstances, are still too far from the grinding poverty of yesteryear to appreciate Hayyim ben Betzalel's honesty.

The rabbis' ultimate strategy for avoiding the idolatry of wealth and the despair of indigence is to teach us never to measure our worth by our economic assets. That is, in the worst sense, too human a criterion and one which seeks to put us at the center of all things. But we did not bring this world into being, or establish its order. We may find it remarkably hospitable to us but there are limits to our dominion and rich or poor, sooner or later, we must all defer to them. So though we have some responsibility for what has brought us to our estate, we did not get there entirely on our own. The world is God's and in a way so subtle that even the rabbis knew they could not finally track it, God has had a "hand" in our destiny. If that has meant exceptional blessing, then let us remember the Chronicler's adage, "All is from You and it is your gift that we have given to You." (1Chr. 29:14) And if the blessings have been few or decreasing, then let us not think ourselves the less for that in God's "eyes." We are commanded to be holy, not rich, and we acquire merit in God's "eyes" by doing commandments, not by making record profits, as helpful as that may be.

We believe that — despite all our realism, we really believe that. Once again two views of reality compete for our allegiance and little has changed in this choice for Jews over the millennia. One way is pagan, and it makes the drives and desires of humankind, for good as well as ill, the context of the sacred. The other way is that of Torah, and it makes the sometimes inscrutable, sometimes mysterious, but mostly the evidently ennobling will of *Adonai* the context in which we understand and work out our individual and corporate natures. For all our modern love of compromise and tolerance we cannot love them both with all our heart, with all our soul and with all our might.

Contemporary paganism is not without its truth and we modernized Jews have gladly learned from it. But insofar as we let it rather than Torah determine our criteria of value then we shall look at wealth and poverty with quite different eyes than has Judaism. The rabbis — some few of whom were men of considerable means — knowing what really counted, could be quite simple in characterizing wealth. R. Tarfon was the most quantitative, calling for "a hundred vineyards, a hundred fields and a hundred slaves working in them." R. Yose's practicality led in other directions. He defined wealth as having "a privy near one's table." R. Akiba romantically found riches in having "a wife comely in deeds." And R. Meir called anyone wealthy who "was pleased with his means." (Shab. 25b) The latter counsel reminds us of the more famous comment of a prior generation. Ben Zoma said, "Who is rich? Someone who rejoices in his lot." (P. A. 4.1) We are likely to be a bit disturbed by the passivity implied in Meir's and Ben Zoma's comments but that aside, the insights of two thousand years ago still sound remarkably true; wealth, in a Jewish sense, is more a matter of attitude than of quantity.

Special duties, personal and communal, follow from the Jewish sense of money. As the Book of Proverbs puts it, "Honor *Adonai* with your wealth, with the best of all your income." (3:9) R. Tanchuma Berabbi epitomized the fundamental rabbinic understanding of this verse as follows: "You are only my steward. If I have given you anything and you possess anything of Mine, honor Me with a portion of it." Another master made that specific, "God gave you gold and silver; do deeds of charity with them." (Pes. Rab. 25:2) The law here follows Mar Zutra's categorical dictum: "even a poor man who lives on charity must himself give charity to another poor man." (Git. 7b)

I take it this audience does not need another sermon on the importance of *tzedakah* or a rehearsal of Maimonides' perennially fresh eight degrees of charity. Nonetheless, it would be irresponsible in this context not to remind you of the eighth. "The highest degree, than which there is none higher, is [attained by] one who upholds the hand of a Jew reduced to poverty by handing him a gift or a loan [interest free, of course], or entering into a partnership with him, or finding work for him, in order to strengthen his hand, so that he will have no need to beg from other people." But let me remind you of some of the rest of his classic summary of our Jewish duty to help others. "You are commanded to give the poor man according to his lack. If he has no clothing, he should clothed. If the has no house furnishings, they should be bought for him. If he has no wife, he should be helped to marry. If it is a woman, she should be given in marriage [that is, supplied with a dowry and given an appropriate wedding]. . . . if a giver cannot afford [what is needed] he should give as much as he can afford. How much is that? Ideally, up to 20% of his possessions; more customarily up to 10% of his possessions . . . but never less than a third of a *shekel* a year. . . . If someone poor you don't know asks for food, don't investigate whether he's an impostor but feed him. If he needs and asks for clothing, investigate first. . . . If a poor man refuses to accept alms, one should get around him by making him accept them as a present or a loan. But a wealthy man who starves himself because he is too miserly to buy food and drink, pay no attention to him."

Judaism being as much a community as an individual religion, the communal aspects of the law also deserve some attention. Here is a bit more of Maimonides' statement: "He who refuses to give alms, or gives less than is proper for him, must be compelled by the court to comply, and must be flogged for disobedience until he gives as much as the court estimates he should give [even by seizing his property]. . . . In every city where Jews live, it is their duty to appoint from among them well-known and trustworthy persons to act as alms-collectors, to go around each Friday to collect from the people. . . . This is what is called the *kuppah*. . . . And I have never heard of a Jewish community that doesn't have one." (M. T., *Matnot Aniyim, passim*)

This sense of corporate obligation resulted in the medieval Jewish community's sponsorship of a range of activities that went far beyond seeing to the welfare of the poor. These were likely to include care for the sick — including the provision of physicians, pharmacies and hospitals — for orphans, for travelers, for the redemption of captives, for free loans to the needy, for dowering brides and for burying the dead. Medieval Jewish communities being relatively small and mostly of quite modest means by our standards, there was rarely professional staff to attend to these matters. Not infrequently these volunteers organized themselves into a group devoted to a specific cause, the most common one being the *chevrah kadishah* whose members attended to the dead. Our contemporary, highly developed form of volunteer Jewish philanthropy may be traced back to these origins.

Jewish communities often felt there should be restraints on the rich as well as help for the needy and they not infrequently supplemented moral exhortation by sumptuary laws designed to curb ostentatious display.

Thus in 1418 the North Italian communities, seeking to get Jews to stop spending more on banquets than they could afford, limited wedding guests to 20 men, 10 married women and 5 girls plus relatives going no further than second cousins. The community of Furth in 1728 prohibited having more than four musicians, including the jester, and terminated their services at midnight. It also proscribed serving coffee and tea at such feasts or giving late guests any courses previously dished out. The Constantinople community in 1725 limited wealthy members to a dowry of 1000 piasters — those in the middle class being restricted to 700 — and banned wedding gifts that exceeded one fifth the value of the dowry. Gaudy clothing apparently was a constant problem. So in 1629 the Poznan community ruled that no artisan accept an order for a garment of silk or damask under penalty of a fine. The Cassel community must have had some wealthy families indeed, for its ordinance of 1719 forbade men and women servants from wearing any diamonds, or caps or slippers embroidered with gold or silver. Human nature being remarkably constant and money rendering one remarkably influential, most historians believe all such legislation was largely ineffectual. The problem of guiding the wealthy to use their means wisely remains a perennial one.

We can confirm the essential timelessness of these teachings by listening to what Morris Joseph made of this heritage a century ago. Speaking of the problems which rising affluence brought into many lives, he wrote, "I have said before from this place, and I repeat it now, that the pursuit of wealth is not only defensible but even commendable. It is at once a necessary condition of the world's progress and a valuable builder of character. It is the parent of enterprise and discovery. It often calls out in the individual such sterling virtues as industry, sincerity and self-restraint. It may be, in short, a moral discipline. But, on the other hand, if these benefits are not to be neutralized, it must be engaged in for the sake of something better than the material prizes at which it aims." In another sermon he spelled out the contrast between common materialism and Jewish idealism. "For now they are so living as though bread and all it stands for — the sustaining of the lower, the false self — were the one desirable thing; whereas then they would live only to nourish and develop their higher, their true selves. Now they are dominated by a base hunger — a hunger for riches, for luxury, for sensual joys — a hunger which they will often sacrifice their integrity to appease, and which nothing can still save the hand of death; where as then there would be . . . an unquenchable desire to measure human duty in all its height and breadth and depth, and to make life a faithful reflection of that larger knowledge; then they would live."

Yet with characteristic rabbinic realism, Morris Joseph did not ignore the large number of people whom a growing economy had bypassed or exploited and he did not want his community to forget them either. "I should like to see a band of workers associated with this congregation, who will pledge themselves to accept guidance as to the way in which they may turn benevolent, yet vague and barren aspirations, into practical and fruitful service. Little or no money is needed . . . what is needed is much helpfulness, much energy, much sympathy, much love. . . . If the bread-winner of a family is without employment, swift feet would hasten to seek for it; if there is a sick person to be comforted, a neglected mind to be instructed, a solitary soul to be blessed with companionship, gentle hands would be outstretched to proffer the needed boon; if there is a downcast spirit to be upraised with a cheering word, there would be lips ready to speak it."

The tone of these messages is more rosy, less tough-minded than the intervening century has taught us to be. Here, for example is Rabbi Joseph's view of economic competition. "I may rightly contend with my fellow man for the prizes of life; but I must not overreach him. . . . But rivalry does not imply a conflict of interests, as ethics understands them. In truth, there is no such conflict. To do my best for my neighbor is, after all, to do the best for myself. Philanthropy and self-love are identical. . . . If ever there is a seeming collision between our neighbor's well-being and our own, if ever we hesitate between serving him and serving ourselves, it is only because we form a wrong conception of well-being, and mistake selfishness for self-service." I do not think the preacher thought he was being merely idealistic in uttering these views and we too would agree, I think, that in some final sense our welfare and that of our neighbor are identical. But in a shrunken, stagnant or declining western economy, we cannot easily take so benign a view of human rivalry. Our times are simply more Darwinian, or, to be fair to the objective realities of life at the turn of the century, our consciousness of what money means in our lives or might mean to us and others has radically changed. That makes us newly susceptible to the old temptations of making money our god or estimating our worth in its terms.

But the gritty realism this century has rubbed into our psyches does more than threaten our integrity. It has also awakened us to a new possibility of faithfulness. I can describe that best by another reference to medieval Judaism, this time taken from *kabbalah*, our mystical tradition. Isaac Luria, the extraordinarily influential teacher of mid-16th century Safed, sought to explain the suffering of his post-Expulsion generation by a daring, intriguing, mystic image. Turning logic to his uses, he asked how it was possible for God to create the universe. For if God is everywhere, there would be no place for the universe to be. So to make creation possible, Luria said, God first carried out an act of *tzimtzum*, that is, God contracted, concentrating Divinity, as it were, to make space for creation. And in the hollow God had vacated, creation came to be in its odd magnificent, flawed fashion.

When this century began and increasingly for many people through its turbulent decades, human self-confidence and aspiration expanded, pushing what remained of God to the periphery of human concern. We were the Messiah and by our intelligence would redeem ourselves. Today we are fortunate if, after all that we have done and seen, we can retain significant confidence in human beings at all. I suggest that what we are going through is a postmodern *tzimtzum* of our own, a contraction of the omnipresent, omnipotent human. And in our new found humility we have increasingly made space for God once again to be God. We are not called upon to do everything, as if there were no God. We are only asked to do what, in a Jewish sense, we can. And that, in a progressive Jewish sense, means not relying on God to do what it remains possible for us to do for ourselves and each other. Having done that we resolutely trust that God will complete the work we have begun and never can finish.

Is this the theology of the losers, the plaintive rationalization of those ground down in the economic scrum of recent years? Not if we listen to the message of the Jewish ages on true value and human duty. For very little has changed in all this time. Human nature remains as conflicted as ever whether to serve the glittering calf or our sometimes inscrutable, sometimes embracing but always demanding God. Realism has humbled us but Covenant continually reempowers us and history remains the trying domain in which we continue to live out our messianic faith.

Chapter 20

⁊)Ƹ

Finding a Jewish View of a Just Economy

The human and Jewish foundations, social and intellectual, which once seemed to make the liberal religious case for Jewish social activism compelling have eroded. As I see it, the ethos of modernity is giving way to a religious variety of Jewish postmodernity, a cultural shift whose ground and implications I have explicated in my book, *Renewing the Covenant, a Theology for the Postmodern Jew*. This paper moves on from that work, drawing on its judgment that this new understanding must include much of the religious insight of modern Judaism, which means in this instance, its dedication to social activism and the high estimate of human agency on which it was based.

This presentation therefore proceeds somewhat chronologically. For Jews the modern ethos came with Emancipation and, overwhelmingly, their modernization included a secularization in which human self-confidence knew few limits. By contrast to this Enlightenment optimism, we may speak of the pre-modern as that piety in which God was the most significant actor, though some considerable scope was given to people for self-determination. Because of their revelational context and living sense of God's activism I speak of the classic sources of Judaism — the

Bible, Talmud and subsequent halakhic literature — as pre-modern. My constructive theological contribution to this is postmodern, based as it is on our relationship with a God on whom we are more dependent than were the largely humanistic moderns yet thereby called to greater human initiative than were the pre-moderns.

These admittedly exaggerated distinctions immediately situate the theme of our discussion in our modern experience. Without Rousseau, Kant and the American Founding Fathers, without Hegel, Marx and their successors, we would not be asking about a "just economy" and what our Judaism might direct us to do to create greater righteousness in our economic order. Despite the numbing challenge of joining the perplexities of justice to the complexities of macro-economics, we assume that Judaism mandates our involvement with America's social problems and our using our creative capacity to remedy them as best we can. This impatience with injustice, this insistence on make compassion effective now is what makes the modern temperament at its moral best so admirable.

By contrast our tradition does not explicitly think about a just economic order and it envisions human responsibility largely as a response to God's commands rather than as a matter of human inventiveness. Nonetheless, certain fundamental Jewish commitments unite modern and pre-modern Jews and these constitute the theological meta-ethic on which our common concern with this issue arises. Jewish duty arises from our relationship with the one God of the Universe. Our God's holiness includes God's goodness and identification with justice. In some monotheisms, the Ultimate Unity is beyond all distinctions, including justice and injustice; not in Judaism. God's concern for justice infuses much of what God commands us to do and no contemplative state or ritual act can supersede God's demand for righteousness. This leads to particular attention to those easily disadvantaged in the reality of social relations: the widow, the stranger, the orphan and the poor. Every human being possesses an unalienable dignity God requires us to respect, allowing early on for the rights (as we term them) of proprietors and workers alike. The list could be made longer but one matter demands special emphasis: in Judaism individuals are necessarily social beings. Each person is indivisibly part of a family, a neighborhood, a town, a nation, humankind and has duties to them all. The group, too, has duties to God and regularly stands in judgment before the Heavenly throne to determine how well it has fulfilled its responsibility to its members. Libertarianism and totalitarianism alike are unthinkable in a classic Jewish context.

Certain other characteristics of our traditional pursuit of justice tend to differentiate our classic period from more recent times and these need greater attention. The first of these is its microeconomic focus. In the Bible and more elaborately in rabbinic literature, our teachers focused on the specifics of exchange. The call for just weights and measures is prototypical but their concern extends to the myriad details of contracts, acquisition, sales methods, restraint of trade, working conditions and the like. For two millennia our sages gave their major intellectual energies to such matters. While they did not often speak explicitly of the relation between a specific ruling and the abstract principle of justice, their ultimate concern in these legal pursuits is clear. They had no doubt Whom they served in what seems to moderns their pedantic arguments over text and counter-text, or about the alternate foundations of a law, or of which precedents were properly analogous or not. Their subtle structuring of economic relations was and is Torah and so their efforts to apply it to a new situation, no matter how trivial, was in some mysterious but real way God's own revelation.

Knowing they were serving God invested the work of our rabbis, at its best, with a special urgency. To be sure, they occasionally indicate their sensitivity to various social and institutional realities and respond to them. But in defining the Torah that could only come to life in the context of their economic reality what was finally at stake for them and those who attended to their teaching was their relationship with God. For a rav to rule improperly or even stupidly is more than personal embarrassment and collegial disgrace; it is a *hillul hashem*, a profanation. And for ordinary Jews to transgress the *halakhah* is more than shameful; it is a sin, a sin against God and not merely a matter for regret and self-reproach. Sin renders one liable to God's punishment in this world and, worse, in the life of the world to come. I am, of course, describing the theological ideal, not how the masses of Jews actually lived. But the ideal and its effect on Jewish life are so unlike our secularized temper that we easily underestimate how alive prior generations were to God's reality and retribution and their effect on Jewish lives.

This confidence in the nature and activity of God also gave classic Judaism its unique "optimism." I am not referring here to a 19th century notion of inevitable progress in human affairs but rather its opposite. It is not confidence in the benignness of human nature or trust in human reason or in some impersonal natural drive that gave our prophets and sages hope. Being sensitive to sin, they saw too much of it to be naive —

and that may well be a motif in their legal constructions. Their confidence in the coming of the Messiah had no empirical foundation; if anything we would call it highly counterintuitive.

Traditional Jews know rather that the Messiah must come because God rules and God's dominion on earth will not forever be delayed. Why that great, awesome, desired day does not dawn is one of the central mysteries of our classic faith, one that pious Jews have lived with — sometimes most impatiently — because of their certainty of God's character and supremacy. Having that faith meant that no historical setback to justice, no collapse of another dearly built, decent social order could reduce our people to despair or sap their dedication to the holy deed and the sanctified social order. Survival is too lame a term for this Jewish endurance in hopefulness and commitment.

Does the counter-evidence refute the conclusions I have drawn from this breathless dash through our intellectual history, that traditional Judaism had a microeconomic focus grounded on its theocentricity? I begin with the case of the most important macroeconomic institution in Judaism, the Jubilee year. It is unquestionably a most extraordinary plan, one which still makes a strong impression on us despite its antiquity. But what we know about it hardly demonstrates a macroeconomic concern in traditional Judaism. As far as we can tell it was never practiced. Perhaps it could not be since it involved having a fallow seventh Sabbatical year prior to the Jubilee year in which again the land was not worked. More important, the law applied only in the Land of Israel. No Jewish community elsewhere ever sought to put it, or something like it, into effect. And until modern times with its emphasis on human activism, the model of the Jubilee year never inspired a Jewish thinker to create even a theoretical macroeconomic plan applicable to his [*sic*] social situation.

The concept of the Sabbatical year, though we do have a history of its observance, is similarly exceptional in traditional Judaism. Once again, the macroeconomic remittance of loans was not so central to Judaism that it applied outside the Land of Israel or stimulated later Jewish communities to emulate its practice in some fashion relevant to their situation. To the contrary, when it was in effect in early rabbinic times it caused such economic hardship that Hillel instituted the famous *prosbul* which, by transferring a debt to the Jewish court, prevented it from being canceled by the Sabbatical year. Apparently the traditional Jewish commitment to this macroeconomic invention was insufficient to keep it fully in effect even where it was applicable.

Some thinkers have cited the case of the *prosbul* as evidence that, for all the rabbinic God-talk, human initiative not God's stated revelation now effectively determined the content of Torah. Other examples of providing an alternate to the explicit commands of the Torah can readily be cited, the nullification of the *lex talionis* by a *reductio ad absurdum* being perhaps the most dramatic example. A considerable rabbinic creativity can also be adduced, such as the introduction of the *ketubah*, the groom's promissory note to the bride, which effected a major legal change in the economic relations between spouses. And surely one of the highlights of rabbinic economic initiative is Simeon B. Gamliel the Elder's action to reinterpret the law on sacrifices to break the extortionate pricing of the bird dealers. One need not be a modern, eager to prove that human agency had a great role in classic Judaism to be impressed with the scope of the rabbis' authority. When one knows something about religions other than our own one can hardly be prepared for a God-centered, text-oriented legal system giving human initiative such leeway.

Nonetheless, the evidence for rabbinic independence, though impressive, does not imply that rabbinic Judaism had displaced God's dominating presence with an essentially autonomous rabbinate. Though one could add to the examples I have given and cite some similar activity in later centuries, radical rabbinic initiative is exceptional rather than characteristic in Jewish law. Overwhelmingly, our sages have simply worked with the economic system in which they found themselves rather seeking to revise it. Perhaps an example will help. The *halakhah* rather consistently accepts for Jews the stipulations customarily made in a locale between employers and laborers or those commonly in effect among people doing business with one another. Moreover, they have little difficulty doing the same with gentile economic law. Some scholars suggest that the underlying basis for Samuel's famous dictum, *dina demalkhuta dina*, "the law of the (gentile) land is (Torah) law (for Jews)," was economic, to allow Jews to participate in the national legal system by which commercial relations were governed. Theologically, the significant point is that, without significant alteration, the rabbis regularly accepted as proper for pious Jews doing business with gentiles, the gentile patterns of acceptable exchange.

Through the middle ages, the Noahide command that gentiles establish courts, *dinim*, that is, a legal system, was understood as approving their normal sense of legitimate economic activity. Some authorities rooted this command in God's revelation, thus perhaps setting a Jewish criterion over common practice. Yet they and others also derived the Noahide command of *dinim* from simple human reason or as a necessity for the peaceful functioning of society. In any case, the Jewish attitude toward gentile economic law was essentially accommodating and shows little Jewish drive to reshape the economies in which they found themselves.

This somewhat passive, meliorative, microeconomically focused, theocentric approach of classic Judaism to economic relations underwent profound transformation with the rise of modernity — but that is true only for that vast proportion of Jews who modernized when given the opportunity. Some Jews never accepted the modern ethos and others never were truly emancipated. In due course in Europe and the United States particularly, most Jews accepted modernism's emphasis on human creativity as self-evidently true and desirable. Yet, like most other moderns, they did not become revolutionaries. Only significant minorities, the various Jewish communists and Marxist socialists agreed with the Nietzschean proclamation that God was dead so human beings should now, in full responsibility, radically refashion their economic destiny. Most Jews remained meliorists and regularly supported in great statistical disproportion their country's liberal parties. They did so, one may speculate, because they considered it their Jewish responsibility to reshape their social orders and wanted the kind of government that would provide leadership in this regard. Much of this history can easily be seen as the result of modernization's identification with secularization.

Two aspects of this development seem to call for theological analysis. The first of these is the way in which ethics provided a heavy ideological overlay for these movements. They often used the language of social betterment, asserting that they would accomplish by revolution or the ballot what pietists could never achieve by prayer and ritual. Moreover they would do so with a universal reach which transcended the narrow purview of religion. They and all enlightened humankind would be "the Messiah" — the exaltation of human initiative went this far. But why did they needed to be so moralistic (it being assumed, with some reason, that there was a considerable measure of sincerity in what they said)? There is nothing intrinsically moral about secularization or relying on human effort or seeing economics as central to human relationships or turning to politics as the means of effecting significant social change.

A second such anomaly may be seen in the continuing affinity of a disproportionate number of Jews for liberal political causes. The phenomenon can be observed in a number of countries and has lasted over a considerable period of time. To some extent this can be explained as political self-interest, the conservatives generally supporting the established social interests and thus traditional prejudices. Yet as Jews have risen in the socio-economic scale and been widely accepted in their societies, acquiring class interests that would normally lead them to conservativism, they have largely remained liberals. The locution "Jewish vote," so despised by Jewish apologists, as applied to modernized Jews, still refers to that statistically unexpected number of Jews who continue to want government action to improve the effective reach of the economy and the social welfare generally.

These phenomena are closely connected and, theologically, they are a logical consequence of secularization's transformation of the traditional Jewish attitude toward the just economy. Modernized Jews did not utterly abandon the basic principles listed at the beginning of this paper. God and holiness no longer played an effective role in these Jewish lives but the goodness connected with them was still seen as fundamental to the structure of the universe. Thus, the essential human duty remained increasing goodness and was still understood in a social, not merely interpersonal mode. God's revelation of duty was replaced by the ethics common to all rational people. This view, primarily in its neo-Kantian formulation or in versions derived from it, became the major plausibility structure for modern Jews. In this system, universal inclusiveness characterized rational injunctions so humanity as a whole became the ideal field of social concern. As a result, the microeconomic horizon of pre-modern Jews expanded to embrace the host nation and thence the world. So, too, bringing the messiah now rationally became the central task of humankind entire, one whose pursuit was the essence of humanhood. For enthusiastic modernized Jews, this was best pursued through education and politics rather than via *talmud Torah* and the observance of mitzvot.

The Emancipation — a personal or familial experience for modernized Jewry — gave this doctrine powerful reinforcement. After roughly 1300 years of increasing segregation, degradation and persecution, Jews were — theoretically and by fits and starts — given social equality. As Jewish equality increasingly overcame ingrained prejudice and became reality, Jews had living confirmation that goodness was basic to the universe and humankind could indeed respond to it. They also saw efforts to extend benefits to other pariah groups as a reenactment of their own liberation and a reinforcement of the ethical activity which had given them opportunity and security. Theory and experience alike motivated a continual flow of Jews into activities for human betterment and it is difficult to think of one in which they have been welcome that they have not been over-represented.

One further aspect of this transformation deserves emphasis. The Emancipation came about because of human action, that is, political change. Moreover, this radical shift in the status of the Jews resulted from decisive government leadership rather than a growing grassroots sentiment or as a direct outgrowth of market or other social forces. The effect of this moral leadership (regardless of what cynical motives accompanied it) by government has registered on the psyches of most Jews. They have benefited incredibly from national initiatives in social reconstruction and therefore remain committed to its worthwhileness.

I do not consider it a great exaggeration — though surely its basis is more homiletic than empirical — to suggest that the experience of Emancipation has been something of a recapitulation of our Exodus experience and similarly has religiously transformed us. Because we were slaves in our segregated Egypt, the ghetto and shtetl, we know the heart of every stranger seeking effective equality in our society. And because with a strong hand and outstretched arm enlightened nations redeemed us from our pariahood, we accepted the secularized covenant of ethical concern for humankind. Something like that has served as modern Jewry's version of the classic Jewish covenant and while it was and remains primarily a political vision it could not help take on strong economic overtones as politics and economics grew ever more closely intertwined.

Alas, we expected too much of ourselves, that collectively we would be the Messiah. What a shock it has been to discover just how flawed we and our best plans are. The failure of communism, the economic inefficiency of the socialisms and the various problems connected with democratic welfare states have bankrupted the left — and the present stagnant condition of the economies that underwent a Thatcherite reaction to the welfarists has indicted the right. We have lost our confidence in our ability to manage our affairs as redemptively as modernity taught us we could. So privatism and cynicism often rule where once conscience did and our new realism about the complexity and unresolveableness of our problems has paralyzed the morally healthy. In the face of these realities hope has become an uncommon achievement and we tend to limit our investment of energy to the near at hand and personal projects.

In this bleak social ethical environment many prefer the pre-modern ethos with its moral certainties and assurances to a modernity which knows the glory of freedom but not how to set its limits. Fundamentalisms have found new life all across western civilization teaching that revelation is more reliable than human reason and ingenuity. What then becomes of the role of human agency in our religious life and the possibilities of innovative social planning led by governmental initiative to help us carry out our ethical responsibilities? Does the collapse of messianic modernism require us realistically to reduce our reliance upon human creativity and inventiveness to the scope that our pre-modern tradition prescribes or permits? What "Judaism" has to say about a just economy would then become essentially "What did the *halakhah* previously advocate or permit and what do recognized *poskim*, decisors, rule it can validate today?"

I am not suggesting that classic Jewish law lacks the means of moving in new directions to confront the issues that face us. I am asserting that the history and ethos of those communities which most study and live by Jewish law — the ones in the best Jewish position to determine what is halakhically valid — makes any bold halakhic action in our time most unlikely. Those halakhists who do call for significant new action in the face of this traditionalistic refusal to act are themselves already committed to a positive, modernistic view of human agency. The only issue for them, then, being how much initiative to allow.

Let me now state what I take to be the view that roughly represents a large majority of the caring Jewish community (if their behavior can be taken as a criterion of their belief). Not unproblematically, to be sure, we do not understand why, in the face of compelling human need, contemporary Jews must limit themselves to what our law once commended or might now widely authoritatively advocate. The spiritual benefits of human creativity free to move outside the *halakhah* seem plain to those of us who love democracy and its pluralism, social arrangements created by essentially secularized modern types. Besides, it seems to us that on a number of critical issues Jewish law is wrongly restrictive.

Consider a single problem, one generally approached only from an ethical point of view but of equal interest as an economic problem. I refer to equal opportunity and equal payment for women in our society. Without substantial, sustained human initiative and government leadership women in our society will remain unable to make a full contribution to society for reasons having nothing to do with interest or ability. With

Jewish women the most highly educated group of women in human history our community, while emotionally unable to give up speedily its long-standing patterns of male dominance, increasingly recognizes that it must make place and pay for a change in our society's treatment of women. In the ongoing struggle for women's rights Jewish law and its protagonists seem less part of the possible solution than of the continuing problem. And it is for this reason that most of the Jewish community finds conscience a better guide to what God wants of our community than is tradition.

Two major factors often radically differentiate us from those Jewish communities for whom our law was elaborated. They lived in economies of scarcity and in societies that segregated and often oppressed them. Classic Jewish law spoke to their specific situation. It is most unlike ours, for we live in an economy of abundance if not affluence under conditions of tolerance and equality. And our different situation often suggests possibilities that would have seemed strange or undesirable to our tradition.

The issue before us is not whether we should seek to learn from our past and its experience in sanctifying existence under the most diverse circumstances. Where there are models in the past that still commend themselves or guidance that can direct us, we can, like prior generations, be its grateful recipients. But in issues like job creation for the unemployed, welfare for the needy, medical treatment available to everyone, and the regulation of interest and credit for the benefit of the society as a whole, having understood what our tradition says, shall we not then respond in creative respect to what we experience God demanding of us as Jews in our specific context? Jewish responsibility, then, must involve the free exercise of human imagination built upon reason and experience as well as the urging, idealism and example of Jewish tradition. The specific plans and programs that might remedy our problems lie far beyond the capacity of experts in Jewish law or theology. Such matters test the competence and ingenuity of the area experts and the politicians whose lives have been devoted to studying and responding to them. Educating them as best we can to what Judaism has taught about human responsibility we can respect the God-given capacity of each generation, particularly as it faces new problems, to sense what God asks of Jews today and to respond to it in faithfulness. In that respect I remain a child of modern Judaism.

If I differentiate myself from my teachers it is because I do not share their optimism about what human beings, essentially unaided, can accomplish. The work of righteousness remains our simple Jewish duty regardless of its long-range effect; of course, we pray that it may, indeed, make us all reflect more truly God's rule in our lives. But dearly bought realism has made my aspirations more meliorative than messianic. After all that we have seen of what the best and the brightest of us can do, after the chastening that has come with our finest institutions creating evil along with good, I do not expect that humankind is the Messiah or even that our spiritualized politics will bring the Messianic Age. If I have more faith in human initiative than Jewish tradition validated I also have more faith in God and God's role in redeeming history than modern Judaism did. It is this sense of living partnership, of being summoned to action and endurance by the One behind every particular, of a personal humanhood defined by my people's ongoing, historic relationship with God that constitutes my postmodernity. God gives me, us, no rest from responsibility and no release from my complicity with the social sins that we might do something to rectify. God lifts me above my moods of cynicism, of fatalism, of selfishness and despair. God gives me hope that I, we, you, might find a better way to be human together for I know that God's goodness has its own power and that one day it will be fully manifest on earth. And that gives me the courage, to try once again, this time with your help, to face the daunting details.

Chapter 21

ℰ⳽ℭℛ

Psychoanalysis

About two weeks ago there appeared in the *New York Times* an unusual obituary. It dealt with a certain Pierre Verger who died at 93 and was described as a photographer and a Brazilian voodoo priest. It was, I guess, the latter item that attracted me to him and made me read the obituary as a whole. It discussed the way in which as an adult he had become involved with a Yoruban religious group known as candomblet. This is what he said about that religion, "What I like about candomblet is that it is the only major religion not based on good or evil, right or wrong." The reason that I want to begin my remarks here is that it is quite precisely central to the Western religious faiths, the only ones I shall deal with, that their adherents do good and avoid doing evil. Unfortunately, I cannot speak about Islam because its relationship to psychoanalysis is essentially unknown to me. So when I speak about "religion", I am speaking only about Christianity and Judaism, as I have come to know them, and certainly not about a broader conception of religion which would include candomblet.

The fundamental Judeo-Christian insight is of the human closeness to God. As Rabbi Akiba put it, "Beloved are people because they were created in the image of God. Even more beloved were they that it was made known to them that they were created in God's image." In the Biblical view there is an expectation of human beings that, being created with this likeness to God, they will do the good. It therefore comes as a surprise to the authors of the Bible and their successor leaders of the Biblical faiths that people do such great evil as they do. In a way, it is the problem of human sin that centrally engages both Judaism and Christianity. Please try to keep this schematic in mind as our discussion proceeds, namely, that people who have a unique capacity to do the good do a disturbing amount of evil.

In each of these religions there is a balance between what people do to help themselves overcome the will-to-do evil and the fact of their exercising it, and what it is that God does in this regard, acts variously described by terms such as "redemption" or "salvation." Yet despite what God may be expected to do, there are also, in varying configurations, things which people should also be doing to help themselves with this basic problem of evil-doing. Though there is a great variety of situations in which this fundamental notion of the cleansing power of Divine-human intimacy is to be played out, this partnership is fundamental to the religious teaching of both faiths. What I should like to address my remarks to is the way in which psychoanalysis becomes a powerful ally of religion in fighting sinfulness and increasing our potential for doing the good and does so by enhancing the human side of bringing about a measure of salvation.

While I have no formal cases to set before you to illustrate this thesis I wish to recount an incident to you which I hope will serve in their stead. I can readily identify the person involved since I do not need to keep confidentiality in this instance. It was me. It had been a very dreary week and the ghastly winter refused to let up its depressing grip on us. I was feeling somewhat down. I had in certain ways been having an emotional tiff with certain students over what I knew was not a terribly essential matter yet I was not disposed to give in. While I was teaching class in this mood a student was making a presentation so I was, as is my wont in such circumstances, standing at the side of the room. Withdrawn as I was, I felt a sudden, unaccustomed, tremendous surge of primitive rage in me. It was almost uncontrollable.

That was a moment when the critical issue of impulse control came into play. What should I then do about this impulse to wound, to hurt, to destroy? May I point out the power situation at that moment. I am a tenured professor. I am, moreover, the senior, tenured professor at my institution. What could anybody do to me if I gave in to that impulse to let fly at this student or at any bunch of students? As this sense swept over me I somehow also immediately recognized it, in the language of my community, as an inducement to sin. For the rabbis, this kind of anger is a fundamental sin because it is a kind of idolatry. That is to say, some other god than God, as it were, takes over the guidance of what it is that you do or are supposed to do.

What happened then was most interesting, probably the reason I am recounting this anecdote to you. As soon as I had this insight into what was going on, all of a sudden I also had the recognition that acting destructively was not what I wanted to do. I recognized the impetus to sin for what it was, a flood of some childhood rage bursting up out of my unconscious. Almost instantaneously I became very calm, quiet, even relaxed. And then I spent much of the next several days thinking about and trying to understand what had been going on in me.

Obviously, I wouldn't likely be telling you this story if I had acted on that impulse and in fact had smashed the student presenter to smithereens as my old professors were accustomed to do to me and my colleagues. But in this case the insight itself was remarkably transformative. For some days I was very much quieter inside myself, indeed very much more myself than I had been for some time. Had that rage persisted, or had it somehow increased — though at the time it swept over me that hardly seemed possible, it was so intense — I would obviously have needed some professional help to deal with it. But in this case, the exegesis of the incident became part of my inner life and with the skills that I had learned in analysis, I was able to transform myself in what I recognized at the time was remarkable immediacy.

Now let me describe this experience in terms of the Talmud's metapsychology. My inner evil urge, one that every human being has, had strongly tempted me to sin. My inner good urge, here obviously strengthened by the result of my learning, of my religious practice, of my being part of my religious community, and my introjected sense of my analyst and the psychoanalytic process, had all worked together to enable me to meet this moment without doing something I would later rue. And, if you will allow me, they had all worked together to allow me, however fleetingly, to have a taste of the life of the world to come.

I present that to you as a case of religion and psychoanalysis as allies. I think that alliance worked so effectively in this case because my functioning analyst, myself and my introjected analyst, had a common value system. But what if Pierre Verger had been my analyst? What if his value system, one that included neither right nor wrong, neither good nor evil, had been operative in me? Allow me, please, to pursue this line of thought by presenting you with two real analysts, ones of a somewhat prior time, and one make-believe analyst, and let me discuss what would have happened if they had been the analyst introjected in me.

I begin with Franz Fanon who, about twenty or twenty five years ago was a highly significant figure among those trying to utilize the wisdom of psychiatry and the practice of psychoanalysis, to deal with the problem of black rage. Fanon's position was that black anger was so deep, so intense, that it would never be properly dealt with unless those of African descent were able to act on it. After all, aggression is as much part of the human being as is love. Here, you see, my value system said "No, you should not act on this impulse you feel. Love is hierarchically more significant than is aggression and to the extent that you are able in a given situation, love ought to indicate the controlling direction in which you ought to act." My religion had taught me that. It had given me this hierarchy of values. I do not see that I would have gotten that relative ranking of values simply by gaining insight into the dynamics of human emotion. So in a general sense, my belief system, what I am equating with religion, is fundamentally to be understood in terms of where do the values come from?

Let me give you a second example, also of that period. Perhaps you recall the name R. D. Laing. Laing had the interesting notion that schizophrenics should not be considered deviants. Considering the kind of world in which we live, it might be as reasonable to meet what reality throws at one with some sort of schizoid or even schizophrenic response as trying to integrate all aspects of the personality, an inevitably futile quest. Now why should integration of the self be so significant a goal of ours? One might just as well see it in its hopelessness as simply loading another burden upon us when we already are feeling we are trying to carry too much emotional freight. But our religions, Judaism and Christianity, suggest that the fundamental reality we detect behind the diversity in the universe is one. That oneness, being ultimate reality — or as the Biblical language has it, our being created in its image — is a goal we ought to reach for. Or, to say the same thing from the human side, being created in the image of ultimate reality, we ought to try as best we can to increase the integration of self. If Laing had been my analyst, perhaps I could have allowed myself my aggressive days and then occasionally had my loving days. Why not? But in my moment of decision, the faith that accompanied my psychoanalytic insight made me realize that I needed to try to knit myself together in terms of my higher goal.

Let me now turn to my imaginary analyst. One of my favorite thoughtful movies of the last ten years is the Woody Allen film *Crimes and Misdemeanors*, not, you will notice, crime and punishment. Today all we have are misdemeanors. Of the two protagonists of the ways we have in which to meet the problems of the universe, particularly the problem of sin, one is the psychoanalyst Louis Levy. Levy is the only real figure in the film who never appears in person. He only appears as film clips or sound over quotations. I am sure that will prompt considerable speculation but I want to move on to the substance of what he says. Levy's remarks about reality as he, the representative of psychoanalysis sees it, indicate the kind of values he might bring to bear upon a given situation such as mine. If you recall, he said that the world is, in itself, value-free and we because of some mix of our growth, our love and our understanding come with certain value systems which we impose upon the world. As long as we do that positively we contribute to the world what people normally consider constructive acts. When he, Prof Levy, gets to the point that he no longer has the inner resources to impose himself upon the unfeeling world, the film informs us that he "went out the window." In other words, one keeps up this quixotic notion that one is somehow going to build or create something of value as long as one has the inner power to do it. But the world itself is ultimately indifferent to all that, so when the positive resources run out one might just as well commit suicide. If that had been my value system standing in my classroom then why should I have cared one way or another as to how I responded to my impulse?

Let us intensify the issue. In a universe indifferent to our common values, why should anyone care to be a faithful analysand? Or, for that matter, why should one be a faithful analyst to meet day after day, week after week, with troublesome, wearisome people who grind one down with their emotional problems and difficulties and who somehow manage to find the most ingenious ways of not making progress despite our exquisite treatment? Why do we do that? Is it not an utterly frustrating way to spend one's life? Not if one believes that value is inherent in the universe and, indeed, inherent in every individual so that working with individuals, helping them, is a sacred task.

But we can suggest one further analytic strategy to meet this issue of values. One might say that one doesn't want to bring one's personal values to the analytic situation for I am only involved in the analysis of the human personality. Society will give us a value structure and if this analysand wishes to get along in our society then let him or her recognize what are likely to be the consequences of following a set of values uncommon among us. Yes, that is a possible analytic stance and to return to my case, society would not be surprised to hear that a senior, tenured professor sniped at students and did them the benefit of cutting their inflated egos down to a more sensible size. Not to mention the right of senior, tenured professors to exercise their own oversized egos.

But what then would there be ever that would prompt us to correct the evils inherent in a society? Where would the values come from by which one would judge whether the society itself was corrupt or praiseworthy? Or, indeed, in a society as pluralistic as ours, where would the values come from by which one would judge that this aspect of our society was positive and a competing trend among us was negative? In our time reason has shown itself to be almost entirely inconclusive when it comes to matters of value and unable to bring us, as it once did, a commanding sense of duty, that I am suggesting that what our Judaism and Christianity at their best and most mature teaching can bring to us is a recognition of a standard and power in the universe greater than that of society or anything people individually or collectively have yet conceived. Trying to get a sense of that, trying to understand it better, trying to make it part of our lives, trying to find ways to let it give us guidance and allow its power to help us fulfill ourselves, makes it possible for us to carry on what most of us who have been raised in this Judeo-Christian civilization know to be the work that we need to do. Whether in the person of the Hebrew prophets or rabbis, whether in the person of the Christ, there is a transformative power which is not just our own but which we can join in order to make this universe the kind of place it ought to be.

Now I know that there is very much more to be said about the possible problems and indeed about the possible hopes for the alliance between religion and psychoanalysis, but I wanted to present one specific example where I think this new cooperation is a reality and where I think it functions most usefully. There is much more to be said: what happens when the analysand has taken his or her analysis as far as it can go? Now that we can meet our problems as more mature human beings, how are they to be faced? What then does it mean truly to be a whole person? What is it to have proper accomplishment in a lifetime? What hope is there for humankind writ large? How shall we face death? These are the questions which religion also turns to. But I have said enough I think to open up this conversation. Moreover the very fact that the Long Island Center for Modern Psychoanalytic Studies wanted to participate in such a discussion it is itself a sign of the movement forward in this area. And I hope it will give us all a taste of redemption.

Chapter 22

ℰↄ℧

Religious Pluralism

Introduction

Four separate meanings of pluralism impinge on the liberal Jewish educator and demand attention. One, there are many religions in the world which have truth in them. Two, there are several differing interpretations of Judaism, the religion we hold to be most true for ourselves. Three, in our own interpretation of Judaism, Reform, there are numerous views about what properly constitutes our belief and practice. And four, among religious, Jewish and Reform Jewish educators, there are significant differences of opinion with regard to the content and the method of Jewish religious education. We can best discuss these problems, we feel, by first indicating our position with regard to the last issue, educational pluralism. Indeed, by doing so we hope to be able to set an example of the approach we would take to the substantive religious issues.

We do not believe it is possible to speak to the educational (or religious) differences by offering a single theory which will satisfy everyone and resolve the problems inherent in this realm of thought. We believe that to be true because of the inherent logical difficulties with our approach to pluralism and because of the variety of human factors involved in education. As to the first, we believe that religious, in our case liberal

Jewish, education is not so open as to include anything one wishes to introduce into it, yet not so closed as not to take account of the staggering variety of factors that impinge on liberal Jewish education. Hence, we wish to marry a content we cannot specify rigorously to a freedom whose limits we cannot easily define. We affirm both these impulses to be basic to our faith and educational practice, though there is considerable clash between them.

These inharmonious premises render our approach essentially dialectical and dynamic rather than defined and linear. Were our faith less fluid, we should still be daunted by the numerous ways our colleagues suggest most effectively transmitting it to our people in this society at this time. And as any veteran of educational activity knows, there is no way of achieving a meaningful consensus on many long-disputed educational issues, even were we to agree on the basic purpose of education in general. Here we tend to side with those who take a generally liberal approach to education, finding this view most consistent with our belief, and yet we remain cognizant of the elements of a more conservative educational ideology that often demand our attention.

We propose to speak to the issue of pluralism in religious education from our particular point of view, recognizing that there are other points of view, seeking to be fair to them particularly when we differ with them, specifying our commitments so that readers know where we stand, all the while seeking to be open to truth others have that we may have slighted or not seen. It is this openness which, while making our educational practice seem fluid, also allows for the "living" quality of Reform, liberal Judaism.

This response to educational pluralism exemplifies our approach to pluralism generally. That is, we seek truth wherever we can find it, including that seen by those with whom we disagree. Yet, we affirm our own truth which, for all its difficulties, we seek to make plain to others, thereby respecting their dignity - part of our faith - as well as refining our own belief. The one factor we would add, were space not a consideration, is the responsibility to communicate the views of others fairly and fully as part of teaching one's own, a liberal commitment which leads us to advocate a place for comparative religion, comparative Judaism, and the varieties of liberal Jewish thought as an integral part of a satisfactory liberal Jewish education.

The Problem: the Particular
Jewish Context of our Views

At a meeting of the Religious Education Association in 1930. J. H. Randall asked. "Can a man entertain all ideas as provisional hypotheses . . . and at the same time cherish in feeling and action the conviction of the prophet and saint of old? . . . can he pour out his soul in worship of a force or an ideal he knows may be superseded tomorrow?" Does the idea that in today's pluralistic world many truths exist create in the minds and hearts of human beings this dilemma when it comes to religion and, therefore, religious education. If so, how do we educate to the beauty of the particular truth without denying the others and yet not become dogmatic? This is the essence of the general problem of pluralism. We know that many of the religions will not be superseded tomorrow, that our challenge is to live with them today.

These general problems of pluralism are by now well known and need relatively little further explication. That is not true of the special factors which we, as Jews, bring to this discussion. For historic reasons, modern pluralism is not a relatively recent challenge to our community. Ever since Jews have been permitted into non-Jewish society as equals it has been the premise of our social lives and a major concern in Jewish living. The matter is so important to understanding the Jewish community that it is worthy of some elaboration.

Before the eighteenth century Jews were not allowed to be citizens in many of the lands in which they lived. In some they were confined to certain areas of the city or land, called ghettos. In others they were forced to wear marks that set them apart. Often this led to theological aversion and persecution. Only when nations became pluralistic (which stemmed from eighteenth-century social and political thought) were Jews able to become citizens. Jewish modernity is therefore based on pluralism in society. Jews found that their security and opportunity for social and economic advancement was tied up with the social-political pluralism of a society.

As Jews accepted modernity in increasing numbers since the early nineteenth century, they faced several challenges from within the community and from without. From within, Jews could not always agree on how to modernize and face the new society. A radical change in the authority/discipline of the community created questions of authenticity in the variant patterns of living Jewishly; a split with regard to the authority of Jewish law as Jews entered the world of modern scholarship added to the complexity with which Jews approached modernity. Thus various movements within the Jewish tradition developed which led to a pluralism within the community itself. As mid-twentieth-century democracy with American values such as its philosophy of individualism has spread, the differences in the Jewish community have also grown, and sometimes the differences are dramatically different from each other. For the liberal Jewish community, this has led to a considerable acceptance of these differences within the Reform movement itself. The pluralism within the community manifests itself as a respect for the value of diversity. Liberal Jewish life and thought has extended this openness both within and without the community.

Having become then so thoroughly involved in the general and pluralistic life of America and of Western civilization itself, there have been three pivotal experiences which have led to a greater interest today in the particular. These experiences - the Holocaust, the birth of the state of Israel, and the decline of preeminent faith in Western culture - have led Jewish educators to a new stage. The new stage is how to now stress and incorporate the particular into the plural.

From the previous paragraphs one can understand why Jewish educators generally approach the problem of pluralism from a somewhat different perspective than that of many of their colleagues in the field of religious education. They are often largely concerned with how now to be open to the truths of others; that is, how to see the universal dimensions of religious truth. Most modernized Jews (not all of the community to be sure) appear to have integrated that notion into their lives, that is, at least as far as the legitimacy of Jews to living as equals among others are concerned. Thus they have integrated the idea that all people possess dignity and other religions have some truth and are entitled to some or considerable respect. In this way they have been substantially universalized. Out of our success with universalization has come its dialectic counter-problem: how in the face of our sense of widespread ultimate truth to affirm our own particular version of it, indeed the one that we take to be the most true for us? The problem, "Why, then, be Jewish?" strikes us with particular force because of our sociology and history. How to affirm our unique vision of the world, how to "choose" to live by that vision and pass it on to future generations in the pluralistic culture becomes the challenge.

Being a minority among a majority in most countries of the world is not easy. There are very strong pressures to assimilate, to be like everyone else. Reform Judaism gives the freedom to individuals to choose their level of observance. Choosing to observe customs and traditions or to hold to values which may go counter to the culture in which one lives or which may make one seem to be "peculiar" or "strange," is often difficult. Added to these problems is the continuing presence of antisemitism, even in American society. It is hard to forget that the Holocaust, the attempt to eliminate Jews from the world, occurred in an educated country where supposedly there was equality for all people. This fact makes us especially conscious of our particularity. Even the pressures placed on the state of Israel add to the demand that we recognize our identity as Jews and as citizens of other nations.

Thus for us, the particular version of the question of pluralism which we address is not: how cope with the universality of truth? but, that being taken for granted, how do you educate for that fundamental affirmation while recognizing that a higher priority in our times needs to be given to our particular faith/group? That is the special sense in which we need to talk about pluralism.

The particular situation of Jewish educators facing this challenge of pluralism can easily be generalized. It then becomes the more broad scale philosophic problem: Must pluralism imply relativism as was suggested by J. H. Randall that one person's truth is as good as another person's? And is there any way of asserting one's own truth without thereby denying or denigrating the truth that might be found elsewhere. Or, in sum, does particularism necessitate intolerance? For most liberal Jewish educators, we believe, the values are clear. With wounds still aching, we know there is a cosmic, qualitative difference between Nazis and their victims; thus, for all our openness, we are far from relativistic. However, seeing the human indignities perpetrated by religious intolerance in our own community and elsewhere, we know we are committed pluralists. With our eyes to our own truth and our own survival we approach our particular version of educating for Jewish life in pluralism.

Content: Comparative Religion, Judaism and Reform Judaism

In many religious schools and day schools across the country Comparative Religion is a course of study. Often in the teen years, Jewish children will learn about the major world religions by hearing guest speakers (often ministers and priests), by attending religious services in churches, and by comparing the tenets of the other faith to the Jewish ideas that they have studied up to that point. There are several texts that educators may choose to reinforce or introduce the knowledge, and there are many additional materials available.

In most Liberal or Reform religious schools and day schools, Comparative Judaism is a common course of study In these courses, Reform, Orthodox, Conservative, and Reconstructionist philosophy, lifestyle, traditions, and prayer are discussed and explored. Students may again have speakers, Rabbis or educators from the other movements, and may visit other synagogues and temples in the community. Often exchanges between classes in one religious school and another are arranged. Implicit in this curriculum is the acknowledgment that Jews act and believe differently within their own religious tradition.

Both of these courses help teach an appreciation of others while stressing the value of what is present in the Reform Jewish expression. The books, materials, and courses are all done with such titles as *Our Religion and Our Neighbors*, *Four Paths to One God*. Often there are active discussions about the need for such courses, even among Reform Jews, but in most schools they continue to be an important part of the curriculum.

With regard to pluralism in our own movement, Reform Judaism, we can approach our task with a certain philosophical advantage. A decade ago our Rabbis group issued a statement about the nature of Reform Judaism which deals centrally with the problem of diversity of interpretation among us. The document states: "Reform Judaism does more than tolerate diversity: it engenders it." Understanding that our age will continue to present challenges that will be responded to very differently by different individuals, the document says:

> How we shall live with diversity without stifling dissent and without paralyzing our ability to take positive action will test our character and our principles. We stand open to any position thoughtfully and conscientiously advocated in the spirit of Reform Jewish belief. While we may differ in our interpretation and application of the ideas enunciated here, we accept such differences as precious and see them as Judaism's best hope for confronting whatever the future holds for us. Yet in all our diversity we perceive a certain unity, and we shall not allow our differences in some particulars to obscure what binds us together.

Living with this challenge often proves frustrating and always proves to be exciting. Educating within this framework calls forth the best that is within us.

The Learner, the Teacher, the School

Obviously, the balance between differences of opinion and our sense of what we hold in common will vary with the age and, to some extent, with the social circumstances of the learners. These days even very young children grow up with a sense of the variety of people, languages, and life-styles. If they do not learn it in their neighborhoods they will quickly get it from television. Sesame Street, for example, makes this one of its major themes. And families very quickly have to indicate that different families do things in different ways, sometimes even when people are cousins. The religious school can build on these bases to extend that sense to religion and religious understandings. Perhaps the easiest way of introducing this to the young child is allowing students to give their own interpretations of various stories and symbols. As they become accustomed to their opinions being sought and respected, even as some other ideas are old and honored, they will be learning the mix of individual and group faith which is the heart of our liberal Jewish pluralism. As children grow and become more socially oriented, the content of their comparative understanding can expand, visits being a particularly vivid way of carrying out such instruction (as was mentioned earlier in our description of the comparative religion and comparative Judaism courses).

In the teenage years, self-assertion grows, calling for increasing room for pluralism of opinion, all the while preserving the group cohesion in which it is being fostered. It thus becomes more difficult to maintain the delicate balance between accepting views yet indicating that some are more central to our tradition than others. Fortunately, with each year students also become more "philosophical," able to think abstractly, and concerned about the greater questions of life. Here, too, we encounter the idealism that wishes to reach across all bounds and to embrace a human beings in friendship. At a time when an unhealthy narcissism threatens to engulf us, it is important to our faith to foster such social concern. But with it we must deal with the realities of seeking to expand and intensify human concerns. Most families have difficulty living in love; how much more so do the problems multiply as groups expand and intensify their differences. At this point we have reached the adult problem of pluralism, one we face all our lives.

Special attention needs to be paid to one individual who is often overlooked in this process; that is, the teacher. Surely as the learners are entitled to their points of view, so is the teacher. At some point in the discussion the teacher, too, needs to be permitted a say. And should that be somewhat different from the point of view espoused by the religious movement, or the local clergy, or the school leadership, it needs to be balanced against what the institution wishes to impart. The obvious difficulty this creates is that, by virtue of position, the teacher's views seem to come with special authority, thus effectively contradicting the prior commitment to plural understandings. To some extent, that needs to be the case. If the teacher has no special knowledge or insight to bring to the class then that teacher should not have been employed to instruct those in need of greater knowledge. The dilemmas of group and individual here again reassert themselves, and there is no rule which can assure teachers that they are respecting students even as they are respecting themselves and their traditions as they seek to teach in this open yet guided way.

As the guide of all these complex processes we call education, the teacher provides instruction in a proper sense of pluralism simply by classroom management. On a deeper level, as the teacher indicates by the "management" how to keep diversity and unity in healthy tension, the learners are subliminally taught how to manage their own lives and how to participate in and guide their society. To be sure, if this is not made explicit at some point, if it does not reenforce fundamental values learned at home, if it does not find echoes in the broader social structure, if it is opposed by the thousand and one other compelling forces which strongly shape our character, then it will not come to fruition. But for schools committed to pluralism as a fundamental value, the teacher's role as exemplar is as critical as any specific curricular content.

Teachers, in turn, will take their cues from the way in which their school demonstrates administratively its own commitment to pluralism yet tradition. Does it, in fact, allow a variety of personality types and points of view to be manifested in its faculty? How does it deal with certain sensitive issues about which there is a difference of opinion in the congregation and the movement, e.g., the celebration of Christmas by Jewish families? How does it seek to provide guidance to its teachers for dealing with such issues, and what is its own sense of the limits within which the expression of individual views is tolerated or unwelcome? Does the administration encourage self-evaluation among students and faculty as well as the responsibility to the group and its evaluation of issues and problems? The social context of the school, then, its "culture," is also critically important to such instruction.

One issue of the "culture" of the school can be illustrated by the difference found in the "religious" vs. "ethnic" nature of Judaism. In this setting of critical thought and celebration of diversity, Reform Jewish education may in some situations no longer be religious education. This problem is more often a problem of the split between a religious perception of Judaism and an ethnic view, rather than one which has grown from the pluralism of the society. For many Reform congregations, Jewish education can be historical and cultural with little or no religious content. How can one define a religious educational experience in a spirit of diversity? We choose to define it by suggesting that it contain consideration of the following: 1) that ideas and experiences concerning God be presented and explored in an open fashion; 2) that a reverential attitude be expressed and hopefully developed toward the values and symbols of the religion which has nourished the people without the denigration of other ideas and symbols; and 3) that a seeking for transcendence, for a sense of the past, present, and future, and the extension beyond one's self toward God be offered as one of the aims of the content. In this way it is understood that the teacher will have to be involved in both cognitive (facts, texts, concepts, etc.) and affective (feelings and values) processes of education and model to the students that religious expression in all of its diversity involves the mind, body, spirit, and feelings of a whole human being.

Reference has already been made to the crucial role of the teacher in communicating this approach to pluralism. We believe the teacher as model is the single most important factor in communicating the dynamic approach to life we have been discussing. For a central role in the teacher's ongoing instructional activity — in every aspect of it — is to mediate between the individual learner's needs and those of the group; that is, of the other learners individually and collectively. Hence, respect for others, particularly for the individuality of others, must always be balanced against respect for self as well as for the group's need to move ahead.

Conclusions (if that is Possible)

At a recent Bar Mitzvah the family chose to write its own service. Some of the work was original, and some was pulled from the prayer book. One of the prayers they included demonstrated the comfort of the American Jew with being Jewish in a pluralistic society: *0 God, the Guide and inspiration of all humanity, you have spoken in a thousand tongues for all to hear. In every land and age, we, your children have heard your voice and imagined you in our separate ways. . . . We give thanks for the sages and teachers of all peoples and faiths, who have brought many to a deeper understanding of You and Your will. Gratefully, we recall that among them were the lawgivers and prophets, the psalmists and sages of Israel.*

The inclusion of these thoughts illustrates part of our argument. The problem of pluralism that the Reform Jewish educator faces is how to structure the educational process to answer the question of "why" be Jewish and "how to make Jewish choices in this modern world."

Judaism is not only a religion; it is also a way of life. Hence Jewish people can become involved in the "how to" of that life without concern for the "why." Good Jewish religious education asks both the "why" and "for what purpose" questions that help one to find meaning in human existence while teaching the varieties of how to live Jewishly,

For the Reform Jew, making informed and serious Jewish choices in this world is in a sense participating in the ongoing process of Revelation. Every generation has added religious insight and knowledge in the process of interpreting the ancient sacred texts for today. Reform Jewish religious education participates in the art of hermeneutics so that modern Jews may interpret and translate the texts for themselves. Helping people become newly sensitive to God through liturgy, ritual, and scholarship, or through music, art, and social action is a way of participating in the ongoing process of revelation and in insuring the future of this tradition. Living in a pluralistic society has meant that many more avenues and images are open to awaken the sensitivity, and there are many more possibilities for hermeneutic response.

What this means is an affirmation of both freedom and tradition, a recognition by choice that autonomy has its limits. In Eugene Borowitz, Professor of Jewish Religious Thought at the Hebrew Union College-Jewish Institute of Religion has suggested that for Reform Jews the proper criterion in every choice is, "As one who shares the Jewish people's relationship with God, what constitutes my proper response to God?"

The Jewish religious tradition and Jews have existed throughout the centuries because of the truths that human beings have found in their texts, values, and traditions. Every religion is a way of trying to understand the world and the meaning of life; each religion has attempted to explain the mystery of the world, human nature, and of God. Judaism, with its passionate relationship to One God, and its ability to awaken the adherent to the miraculous in life, to the responsibility we all have for each other, and to the best that is within us has created a religious tradition filled with beauty, variety, and depth — both intellectually and emotionally. As Reform Jewish educators and teachers model the struggle to live Jewish life to its fullest in this pluralistic society, we confront the future, with faith and optimism, understanding that the dilemmas that confront us offer challenges in which to grow stronger.

Chapter 23

ℰටℭ

Healing

1) *"Please, God, Heal Her, Please."*

Two experiences, thirty years apart, frame these ruminations.
In 1963, I and some others addressed groups at the CCAR meeting
seeking to persuade the Reform rabbis to replace their establishment
rationalism with existentially oriented thought. My presentation was on
"Faith and Method in Modern Jewish Theology." Its plea to acknowledge
the primacy of faith in our Judaism was greeted with an incredulity
typified by the question of a colleague somewhat older than me.
Restraining his sarcasm, he said that he doubted that I now wanted us to
begin reciting the *refaenu* instead of relying on the science of medicine.
I wonder if today, a spry 84 year old, he has changed his attitude. Back
then he nimbly expressed the wall of separation dividing the clinic and
the synagogue, an attitude still stoutly supported by many Jews today.

In recent months my practice of many years standing, praying the
refaenu and other prayers for the healing of specific people I know, has
been especially fervent. My overriding concern has been someone whose
affliction has not lessened despite extensive consultation. All else having
failed, a highly risky operation of uncertain promise was undertaken.
That made me pray with even greater intensity. The operation failed and

the prognosis is now uncertain. Though saddened to some primal depth, I have not relented and continue to ask God to heal this hurting soul.

Thirty years ago my practice would have caused most modernized Jews to shudder or shrug. Today, many in our community will, I trust, reach out to me in empathy.

Consider: six years ago, when Rachel Cowan first broached the idea of a project on Judaism and healing, it wasn't clear if any Jews cared, or were doing anything, or could learn something useful if they met to share what knowledge and experience they had accumulated. This assembly, co-sponsored by two great American Jewish institutions, has had to turn worthy applicants away for lack of space and it is only the first of about a half dozen such meetings whose mailings have reached me.

What brought about this radical change of ethos? Why has a skeptical community become one in which a sizable minority eagerly seeks to learn about and practice Judaism's counsel for the work of healing? Let me spin out a theological hypothesis which explains this development to me and which you can test against your own experience and the rich data of the sessions soon to begin.

Thirty years ago my colleague felt certain he could refute faith's role in a modern Judaism by reminding us of the absurdity of asking God to heal the sick. Whence did his dogmatic liberalism arise? Not out of his Jewish knowledge for he knew the halakhic texts requiring us to recite the *refaenu* daily (e. g., Meg. 17b, A. Z. 8a). Biblical prayers for healing are difficult to ignore, the most famous probably being Moses's astonishingly concise, four word plea that Miriam be cured of leprosy, *"El, na, refa, na, lah."* (Nu. 12.13) R. Eliezer is reported as reminding his disciples of it as their proper model for brevity in Jewish prayer. (Ber. 34a) In his petition, Moses dispenses with the customary sequence of praise, request and thanks, while also eschewing any artistic embellishment. He knows God heals so he asks God to do so. Yet not exactly, for he doesn't "ask" at all but, employing that odd usage of Jewish prayer of which Heinemann reminded us, he addresses God with an imperative, "Heal, please." (*Hatefilah Bitekufat Hatanaim Vehaamoraim*, Jerusalem: Magnes Press, 1966)

By linear Greek standards the Jewish attitude toward medicine defies logic. When a teacher upholds Judaism's strong sense of God's providence, he says the Master of the Universe is the source of illness. In that mood too, God is the only legitimate physician. Ex. 15:26, "I, *Adonai*, am your healer," is its classic text and Asa, King of Israel, who sought the help of human physicians rather than God, is its whipping-boy. (2Chr. 16:12) Yet that attitude coexisted with the notorious old Jewish esteem of physicians and love of medicine. The rabbis of the Talmud, often pictured as powerful healers, frequently rest their bio-ethical *halakhah* on the determinations of medical experts and themselves pass on treatments for a variety of afflictions.

These paradoxical views may explain the slenderness of the rabbis' proof that the Torah — God — commands physicians to heal the sick, namely, the duplication of the verb "to heal" in the list of damages that one who injured another must pay. (Ex. 21:19, B. K. 25a) The classic Jewish theology of medicine is dialectical. God sends illness — often as punishment for sin — yet God also commands doctors, and by extension all of us, to cure those ailments. This is the most dramatic example I know of rabbinic Jewish theology's view that there is not just one but two effective sources of energy in this universe, God and people. God, being God, may act independently; people, having only derivative, "imaged," status, may not. They act with God but the way the human and Divine energies intertwine in our world is beyond our sorting out.

We call this bi-partite notion of agency "covenant" and the resulting non-linear quality of rabbinic theology arises from this Covenantal dialectic, as I have termed it. As various unnamed Talmudic sages said, God rules but *olam keminhago noheg*, "The universe goes its accustomed way." (A. Z. 54b) Accepting the partnership of the human and the Divine may well be the theological root of the historical anomaly Shatzmiller points out, that medieval Jewry had no religious difficulty accepting new medical procedures based on changing scientific knowledge. (*Jews, Medicine and Medieval Society*, Berkeley: U. of Calif., 1995, ch. 1 *passim*.)

What agitated my colleague was not the Jewishness of prayers for healing but their clash with modernity. They implied that God acted in the natural order as an effective cause, a notion that violated science and thus the modernization of Judaism which had accommodated to it. In that worldview, natural events occurred only for mechanical or electro-chemical reasons. These might eventually be given mathematical form, thus proving that such processes, like their mathematical delineations, had inherent necessity, obviating the need for God or other supernatural forces. In short, modern causation was immanent so God was irrelevant except as invoked by the still pious to explain nature's origin, order and values or the occasional experience of a numinous presence.

This modern God could no longer be asked to heal, a task now in the hands of the medical team. At best, God lay behind the orderliness assumed by treatment and research, the values which moved people to seek and apply them, and the presence which might give patients and caretakers a psychosomatic boost. That vision frames the prayer for the sick provided in the Reform *Rabbi's Manual* of 1961: "In this hour of her great need, our hearts go out to our sister _____. Bestow on her Thy help and healing. Guide her physicians, Thy servants. Give them understanding hearts, skilled and tender hands. Sustain her dear ones with faith in Thy goodness and love. May she find constant strength and comfort in Thee, O God, now and evermore." (p. 55) Believing more than that I want a richer text but I could begin my praying here.

This limitation of God's effective role to the psyche of the ill or their care givers was the accepted ideology of modernized Jews some generations back and most people still fall back on it when speaking of this topic. Here is some of a prayer for the sick in the home prayer book published by the Reform rabbis last year: "In sickness I turn to You, O God, for comfort and help. Strengthen within me the wondrous power of healing that You have implanted in Your children. Guide my doctors and nurses that they may speed my recovery. Let my dear ones find comfort and courage in the knowledge that You are with us at all times, in sickness as in health. May my sickness not weaken my faith in You, nor diminish my love for others. From my illness may I gain a fuller sympathy for all who suffer. I praise You, O God, the Source of healing." (*On the Doorposts of Your House*, 153) These words touch me more deeply not just because they were written for private prayer while the text in the *Rabbis' Manual* was for use at a congregational service. The new book also sounds a fresh and important note: respect for the power of healing that resides in each person, a topic I shall return to later. Now, I only want to note the 1994 prayer's continuity with that of 1961. God still does not heal, as Jews once thought God did, but God is, at best, the God of healing, the backdrop for the processes by which people naturally induce the restoration of health.

Mordecai Kaplan's naturalism lent a certain clarity to this perspective. Writing to a hypothetical sufferer from infantile paralysis he says: "When the doctor relieves your pain, when he helps you to get back more strength and better control over your muscles, it is with the intelligence that God gives him. When you use braces and other devices that help you get around and do some of the things you want to do their manufacture is due to the intelligence and the concern for your welfare, that God puts into the minds of those who make these devices. Do not feel that God does not care for you. He is helping you now in many ways, and He will continue to help you. Maybe some day you will be restored by His help to perfect health. But if that does not happen, it is not because God does not love you. If He does not grant you all that you pray for, He will find other ways of enabling you to enjoy life. Be thankful to God for all the love and care that people show toward you, since all of that is part of God's love, and do not hesitate to ask God for further help. If the people around you are intelligent and loving, that help will come to you." (*Questions Jews Ask, Reconstructionist Answers*, New York: Reconstructionist Press, 1956, 119-120.)

In these and other such passages, Kaplan speaks for all those Jews for whom science still explains reality. But it is just this erosion of the old certainty paradigm which has deeply shaken us in the past decade or so. Everywhere we turn these days — economics, nutrition, politics, therapy — what once was authoritative is now, at best, a plausible construction of reality. In medicine, we no longer regard doctors, even the greatest experts, as gods. We know them and their helpers to be fallible and the most humane of them share with their patients the limits of what they know and might be able to do. The infant in me wants my physician to tell me exactly what I have and how long it will take me to get over it, if I can; but the adult in me responds better to a caring discussion of the likelihoods of my condition.

These days, too, we do not smugly scorn alternative forms of treatment as quackery. MD's now commit the onetime heresy of going to a chiropractor, some obstetricians have collegial relations with midwives, and acupuncture and herbal medicine, with no scientific basis the west can fathom, often have effects exceeding mere psychosomatic expectations.

I am not saying that medicine has been discredited and that I now refuse an occasional sonogram or have substituted *tai chi* for my daily dose of beta, calcium and angiotensin inhibitors. Medical science still remains our best way of fulfilling the commandment to "guard our souls" and stay healthy. (Dt. 4:15, Ber. 32b) What is at stake, rather, is whether medicine, and science generally, still adamantly insist on a monopoly of insight into nature. But increasingly, medical personnel and institutions welcome religion as bringing to their work an independent, significant understanding of people and the universe. Not infrequently too, it is we Jewish leaders, who are the recalcitrant ones, stubbornly holding on to a prior generation's achievement of allowing hard-nosed science to restrict what Judaism could still teach and do. I guess we are afraid of returning to the magic and superstition which once characterized much of the pre-modern Jewish healing style. However, we need not trash every aspect of modernity as we make our transition from a modern to a postmodern Judaism. That paradigm shift, from the modern to the postmodern, is the theological realignment which is the tectonic source of the rising interest in Judaism's role in healing.

Exactly what postmodern Judaism commends in this area is, typically enough, disputed, a delightfully consistent indication that postmodernity has diverse potential. Once, piety's place in therapy could only be justified by humanistic motives, the ethical and the psychological. The new view I discern adds to these, at the least, an appreciation of the mysterious, non-empirical ways in which the mind, better, the soul, affects the body. Many now believe that what transpires in our depths, and not only in our unconscious mind, influences our organs and limbs for good and ill. With the old empirical censor silenced, we can stop filtering out those fleeting intuitions we have of our inner healing power and, redirecting our spiritual energies, we can newly employ our primal curative capacities. And some people, for reasons utterly beyond us, can do this so well that they can reach out and cure others. All grandiosity aside, we do not yet know our own power.

But as long as we speak only of what humans do — even using the word "God" but meaning only human activity — we will not appreciate the depth of the new religious involvement in healing. Jewish postmodernity, confounding the Nietzschean pronouncements of modern secularity, centers on God, the One we sense to be utterly independent of us yet simultaneously intimately involved with us. A reverse *tzimtzum* is underway. Modernity expanded human agency so fully that there was little space left in our universe for a God-not-ourselves. Now, with science demythologized and culture unable to command worthy values, messianic humanism seems utterly unrealistic. Chastened by the human record in this past half century, people accept the self-contraction contrition mandates. The *tzimtzum* resulting from humankind's new humility has left space in our world for God — and we, conscious of our limitations and the reality of our new/old God, are groping for better ways to let God's presence and God's power into our lives more fully.

Consider the prevalence of services for healing and healers or the efforts to provide prayer and meditative material for the ill. Or think of the increasingly popular Clinical Pastoral Education programs for clergy, ones which seek to blend the insights of psychotherapy with the uncanny reach of religious practice and belief. In these and other activities, God's being there with us bestows on us a certain increase in our power that is a consecration of self and a model for what we are sent to do with others. Twice, Deut. Rabbah (6:13) refers to this bi-partite exercise of power, interpreting Moses's opening plea on behalf of his sister, "*El na*," "Please, God," as saying, "If You will heal her, that is good; but if not, I will heal her." And Radak, interpreting Jer. 17:14, the source of the *refaenu* prayer, says that the pain and injury from which he asked relief were really his own sense of shame and accursedness. It is no diminution of what we can do to reach for what God might also do that laboratories cannot depict. Hesitantly shedding the old constricted rationalism, gropingly moving as our new experience of bi-partite Covenant guides us, we have begun turning to God for what God might independently do for the ill. And sometimes we find that God heals in ways we must call God's own.

Not always. I am still praying fervently that God cure that dear soul whose recent operation failed. Of course I want God to infuse with new power and unfaltering endurance those superbly informed and deeply feeling souls who stand that watch. I also ask my Intimate Other, the One who has so often granted me the little healing of presence, to accept my anger and my frustration, and raise me from my bitterness and gloom that I may see my duty and do it. For years the balm of knowing God was with me has kept me faithful in my liturgical vigil for the sick I regularly pray for. But for some time now, I have sought more. I want God to heal them. "*Refa, na.*" God being God and I being me, a believing Jew, I can no longer ask for anything less than God's independent action to stop this suffering and to restore today's list to health. "*El na, refa na*," "Please, God, heal, please." I may not be as blunt or as peremptory with God as Moses was, but, niceties aside, that is the burden of my postmodern praying. And no matter how many times my prayer has not been granted, no matter how many years now my Alzheimer's patient has sunk deeper into physicality, I resolutely come back and pray it again. Not for me that curious modern trait, that when the prayers for healing "fail," we bitterly attack God, but when they succeed, as mine often have, all the praise and gratitude goes to the care givers and some, perhaps, to the patient.

No, I do not know how God can be an efficient cause in the natural order — but I do know that in our culture "how" questions can only be satisfactorily answered in the empirical terms of science, a mode of description which bars God. Yes, I am unhappy that I cannot integrate the scientific view of causation with my conviction that God can independently heal — but I know that these days all we have to work with are the fragments of various broken systems. When I was young, I was taught to glory in amplifying certainty; today, the maturity I esteem enables one to live humanely despite the enveloping uncertainties. My kind of postmodern Jew treads warily between pooh-poohing science and kowtowing to it, and seeks with every capacity of mind and soul to approach ever closer to the ideal Unity without denying the realism that befits an era awash in disillusion.

I know no easy rule for negotiating the narrow ridge of postmodern Jewish existence but I can suggest a helpful exercise. Shall we bring back amulets? That is, shall we enlist the aid of various angels or heavenly powers or of a particularly efficacious name of God to cure the sick? The rabbis believed that amulets healed and allowed wearing efficacious ones as an exception to the strict Shabbat *halakhah* about adornments. Shall we now move on from prayer and rite and meditation to amulets, and begin seeking expert writers? Some time ago I would have dismissed this notion with a snort if not a tirade invoking Maimonides. Today, with a nod to the Rashba and Nahmanides, I cannot be so dogmatic — yet despite my hard-gained openness, I am not ready for amulets. Such scientific explanation as still influences my faith militates against my doing so.

But my postmodern faith does not always hint at a closet rationalism. The second request of the *refaenu* prayer, *hoshienu venivashea*, "Save us, and we shall be saved" links healing to salvation. Every cure is a small redemption, surely an underground reason why Jews in disproportionate numbers spend their lives doing therapy. They want to help usher in the Messiah.

What we but taste now, the rabbis foresaw fulfilled in the promised future. Resh Lakish is repeatedly cited as teaching that there is no Gehenna in the World-to-come but the sun, released from its sheath, fiercely punishes the wicked. However, as Mal. 3:19 teaches, "Unto you who fear my Name, the sun of righteousness will arise with healing on its wings." (A. Z. 3b-4a) In Ex. Rabbah (14:21), an anonymous exegesis of Isaiah's eschatological promise specifies as part of the first of God's ten innovations then that "When anyone is sick, God will order the sun to heal them." Do you not, as I do, long for that world without sickness, pain and suffering? I have no difficulty envisioning God's goodness joined to God's power to recreate the world so that we all can sit under our vines and fig trees in good health. Until that day we must live in the hope of this messianic healing and recollect it as we work at the everyday redemptions of *refuat hanefesh, refuat haguf.*

2) *Crisis and Confidence, an Introduction to Psalm 90*

Our lives tend to shift between two moods. I do not mean dramatic swings between great elation or deep dejection but rather the simple shifts that are part of the quiet rhythm of the everyday. They raise us from the stability of routine to a warm feeling of confidence or lower us into doubting that anything really matters or is worth our effort.

Our Psalm speaks to me of this alternation of temper. We begin it confidently enough. After all, it is a Psalm, part of our sacred literature, something Jews have recited for millennia and perhaps familiar from the early part of the Shabat morning service. It announces itself — quite uniquely — as "A prayer of Moses, the man of God." If Moses could say this then surely we will benefit from his words. And, like all good prayers, it reminds us "before Whom we stand," as the common synagogue ark wall motto has it. We turn to God, this time addressed as the Ever-was and Enduring One who has been a lasting source of help to us. (vv. 1-2) God's deathlessness initially seems only a basic expression of trust but it will soon return, rather ominously, exactly what a mood swing does to us. For beginning in verse 3 a more troubling tone appears. God wants us to stop taking ourselves and our accomplishments so seriously. Looking back now on the accomplishments we worked so hard for over the years, what happened to them? What were they really worth? Can we even remember all the things that we were once so intense about — or took such care to evade? And if we still esteem them, what really do they amount to in God's "eyes" for whom, "a thousand years . . . are as yesterday . . . or a watch in the night," "a flood," "a sleep," or the overnight grass? (vv. 4-6) Useless, all useless; empty, all empty. A sigh rises from the soul.

The mood intensifies, moving on now to what we see as the cause of our dis-ease: God's anger, fiercely executing God's justice. (vv. 7-9) For we can not stand before God claiming to be wholly righteous and thus worthy of God's good gifts: life, health and all that properly goes with them. In simple truth, we haven't done all God wanted us to do — and though we can't think of anything so terrible that we did, we are reminded that God knows even our "secret sins." (v. 9) So, in a bitter charge, the Psalm says all our life, brief as it is, has been permeated by God's wrath. Surely there are people whose lives have been an unending succession of tragedies.

Despair threatens to overwhelm us — but even as we feel that, another thought arises in us: this is a prayer of Moses. "The man of God" may fearlessly acknowledge the aching sense of human transitoriness but he does not lose hope. And, so we trust, neither will we praying a "Prayer of Moses."

A subtle hint of confidence now asserts itself, that the human life-span is seventy years, occasionally eighty — no small matter when the average child born in biblical times was lucky to make it to thirty five. (v. 10) The numbers are comforting and remind us of what often happens. But the numbers will not magically banish all our momentary feelings of loss and deprivation. There is too much about their caustic realism that is true. Life can easily grind us down and before we know what has happened it has flown away. When this distemper seizes us, we see God as very fierce and unrelenting indeed. (vv. 10 end and 11)

Is it too modern to say that all this harshness ascribed to God may, underneath, say more about us than God? We are angry, mad that another trouble has come upon us. But now the several references to our sins are highly suggestive. Perhaps, we are particularly sensitive because we fear that our inattention or misdeeds may make us partly (largely?) responsible for putting us in harm's way. Acknowledging these very deep, disturbing feelings — which confess our possible complicity in what has happened — doesn't turn life into a yellow-brick road to dance down. But it helps us distinguish our passions from our sober sense of God's nature.

In any case, this emotional discharge has had one effect for the poem's tone now changes. To begin with, we admit that maybe we might learn something from all of this. As we say, "If I ever get over this I'll be a different person." (v. 12) Then, too, we find ourselves hopeful enough to ask God quickly to turn our tears to joy and keep us untroubled in the future (v. 14) or at least to compensate us for all our suffering (v.15). More, we'd like all that love and kindness we have known from God to be manifest, not just to us but to our children as well. (v. 16) And, since we must not forget how ephemeral we really are, we ask God to invest our striving with some of God's own enduring power. Yes, all things considered, we are again quietly confident about life and its promise —

as long as we have God's help. Once more we say, "God, establish the work of our hands." (v. 17)

Will our prayer be answered? That is for God to determine. But in one sense, it already has been, for we end this prayer different from when we started it.

Chapter 24

ℰ)ℭ

Aging

I n the course of Jewish history, little can be described as monolithic, especially in regard to the characterization of Jewish thinking. What is presented in this chapter is fairly representative of the general discernible trends in aging throughout Jewish history when viewed through the lens of a particular period or context (Glicksman, 1990; Rosen, 1990). Thus, it is our intention to divide this chapter into two sections along accepted historical standards: (1) the biblical, which merges into the rabbinic and separately, (2) the modern. While the Bible forms a foundation for insight and understanding, there is much more textual material available from the rabbinic period. However, the rabbis introduce very little actual new material regarding "theology," and thus such a merge of material is necessary. The history of Jewish experience is an indispensable ingredient in presenting a theological approach to aging. Entering into a sacred dialogue, each generation adds its own layer of experience to the core of the primary Jewish experience. This historical experience enters into the memory of each Jew through one's ongoing interaction with history (and the sacred literature that records this history).

The Biblical and Rabbinic Periods

Through the simple accumulation of years, the historical memories of older Jewish adults are deeper and more broad-based and their covenantal bond with the Deity potentially more secure. But the intersection of aging and Judaism does not begin with old age. It really begins with birth, with the growth and development of each human being, fashioned in the image of God. The biblical author saw this quite clearly. Reading the text through a twentieth-century perspective, Rachel Dulin has pointed out:

> The ancient Israelite writers viewed aging as the last part of an ongoing developmental process. Each phase of life was marked by physical and psychological changes as maturity set in and old age approached. . . . Aging is an inescapable part of the human experience. Congruent with the multiplication of our cells and the growth and maturity of our bodies, genetically programmed biological clocks are counting our finite years. Slowly, but inexorably, deterioration) and weakness become the dominant symptoms of life. Biblical man *[sic]* observed that old age was that stage in which decline was most visible. (1986, 50, 51)

Hence, the *locus classicus* of the biblical view of aging found in Leviticus is: "You shall rise before the aged and show deference to the old. You shall fear your God. I am Adonai" (Lev. 19:32). Recognizing the need to raise the weakened elderly for God's protection, the law requires one to rise when an old person approaches and not speak before the elder had spoken. For example, in the Talmud (Kiddushin 33a), we read that Rabbi Yohanan rose up in the presence of an aged ignoramus out of respect for the suffering endured in the course of a long life. Indeed, the text implies a direct and necessary relationship between respect for the elderly and reverence for God. Ecclesiasticus, the apocryphal Wisdom of Ben Sira (25:4-6), makes this line even stronger. Ben Sira wrote: "How beautiful is the wisdom of old people and thoughtful advice of individuals who are honored. Much experience is the crown of old people. Their enhancement is reverence for Adonai." Later, in the Talmud (Berachot 8b), this respect is even demonstrated for the one who has lost his learning (e.g., wisdom): "Respect even the old person who has lost his learning for there were placed in the ark of the Covenant not only the two perfect tablets of the Law but also the fragments of the tablets that Moses shattered when he saw the people dancing before the Golden Calf."

Yet, in the treatment of the biblical material many find a tendency to overstate the "golden age syndrome" and underplay what is better classified as biblical realism. The hope for a good old age is ever present in the text, but it may be more of a reaction to the reality of young deaths and difficult living than theological speculation. As Shlomo Balter has pointed out,

> One should not be lulled by these passages into believing that Judaism viewed aging with either equanimity or anticipation. It must not be forgotten that these passages and attitudes emerged within the context of the world in which the average life expectancy was limited and the rate of infant mortality very high. Understandably, in such a society those who survived and grew old were granted a special staus. (1978, 9)

Long life was seen by many as a reward for righteous living. This was probably more wishes and hopes, a sense of God's special gifts, than the reality of most lives. As Benjamin Blech has shown, old age thus became both a blessing and a curse. While being alive is itself considered good, there was never a guarantee that the maladies of old age would be prevented, even among those "blessed" by old age (1977, 65-78). The twelfth chapter of Ecclesiastes spells it out graphically, if metaphorically:

> So appreciate your vigor in the days of your youth, before those days of sorrow come and those years arrive of which you will say, "I have no pleasure in them; before sun and light and moon and stairs grow dark, and the clouds come back again after the rain:
>
> > When the guards of the house become shaky,
> > And the men of valor are bent,
> > And the maids that grind, grown few, are idle,
> > And the ladies that peer through the windows grow dim,
> > And the doors to the street are shut —
> > With the noise of the hand mill growing fainter,
> > And the sound of the bird growing feebler,
> > And all the strains of music dying down;
> > When one is afraid of heights
> > And there is terror on the road.
> > For the almond tree may blossom,
> > The grasshopper be burdened,
> > And the caper bush may bud again;
> > But humans set out for their eternal abode,

With mourners all around the street.
Before the silver cord snaps
And the golden bowl crashes,
The jar is shattered at the spring,
And the jug is smashed at the cistern.
And the dust returns to the ground
As it was,
And the lifebreath returns to God
Who bestowed it.
Utter futility — said Koheleth —
All is futile!

(Eccles. 12:1-8, adapted frorn Ginsberg, 1982, 399-400)

In the Midrash Rabbah to this chapter, the author identifies each metaphor as a specific reference to a part of the body which deteriorates and ceases to function properly in old age. While one may read the chronological years of many of the long-lived biblical personalities as metaphors as well, it is patently clear that the author intends the reader to understand that ancestors were given long lives as rewards for their righteousness. Rachel Dulin further indicates:

Four conditions were illustrated by the Biblical text to describe blessed old age: lack of infirmity, presence of children, economic success, and being accorded respect. The Biblical heroes who achieved blessed old age were endowed with at least one of these attributes in addition to long life. Although each hero was blessed in a different way and to a different degree, each becarne a symbol of God's blessing. (1988, 79-80)

Therefore, if persons are blessed with old age, then they are the veritable embodiment of holiness. Having lived so long, elderly Jewish persons then intensify their level of covenant through living righteously and through the performance of mitzvot.
Rachel Dulin notes:

Regardless of what biblical people knew about the debilitating nature of the aging process, they still wished to live long. With the yearning to hold on to life, the reality of growing old was altered and the concept of old age at times was given an extended meaning. It was transferred, theologically, to a higher plane in which old age lost its physical dimension, its debilitating nature and became a symbol of reward. By ignoring the traces of the imprint of time, by overlooking decrepitude and suffering, biblical people projected their wish to live long into old age with dignity as a reward given by God to the righteous. . . . And once old age with dignity was conceptualized as one of God's rewards for humans, appropriate projection, not living into old age, was realized as part of God's retribution for wrongdoing. (1986, 77-78).

Aging associated with dying and death is, however, not a joy. For the biblical authors, all one had to anticipate was Sheol, the great pit under the earth to which the shades of the dead were gathered. While a theology of aging without a serious concern with death is denial, the rabbis eventually transcended this challenge when they introduced the notion of eternal soul and resurrection. It is well to keep in mind the dialectic of the biblical view. As the psalmist wrote,

> Do not cast me off in old age; when my strength fails, do not forsake me. I come with praise of your mighty acts, 0 Adonai. I celebrate your beneficence, yours alone. You have let me experience it, God, from my youth. Until now, I have proclaimed your wondrous deeds, and even in hoary old age, do not forsake me, God, until I proclaim your strength to the next generation. (Psalms 71:9, 16-18)

This psalm indicates the classical Jewish realism and separates the other streams of thought as ideals and hope. While the value of the latter should not be underestimated, much of their glorification of Jewish attitudes may never have happened. Even the phrase *al tashliheni* — "do not forsake me" — is repeated in the liturgy and has become part of folk Judaism, an indication that everyone was not engaged in a communal effort to treat the elderly with respect.

In general, the Jewish notion of reverence for parents reinforced the laws commanding deference for the aged. This attitude helped to establish the basis for what would eventually become a social system of caring for the elderly. While the rabbinic views of aging — including those that believe that the age at death is determined by individual acts of goodness and evil — are fraught with theological challenges, reverence for those who live to old age then becomes representative of all later Judaism. With the rabbis, this theme of reverence for old-age wisdom becomes institutionalized. As the rabbinic way of being a Jew becomes more accepted, a major social form in which age counts is introduced.

The question of how long one lives is a major theological issue. The rabbis discussed it on numerous occaslons. In Megillah 27b-28a, for example, a group of teachers in the academy are asked, "Why have you merited long life?" While no real conclusions are drawn, it is implicit that the premise of the statement is, as Richard Sarason points out, that "lifespan is a function of proper conduct, and that a life lived in study and observance of God's revealed Torah will *ipso facto* be lengthened" (Chernick, 1989, 101-6, Bayme, 1989, 107-8; Ben Sorek, 1989, 109-110; Sarason, 1989, 111-112).

Sociologist Allen Glicksman sees respect for the elderly as tied to the more dominant issue of authority in the Jewlsh community, a salient theme that literally shapes the development of' the Jewish community throughout its history. But Since the Talmud saw learning as the *sine qua non* for community authority, somewhat of a compromise seems to have been reached. The assumption was made that if one lived a long time, that person learned a great deal about Jewish tradition and was consequently deemed wise (Glicksinan, 1990, 5). The ideal state, of course, was a combination of wisdom and old age. A Yiddish proverb says it best: "Old age to the unlearned is winter. To the learned, it is harvest time."

Beyond the general notion of inspiring reverence, Jewish tradition views the aged as a group imbued with a special purpose: to pass on traditional wisdom and sound advice to the young. The rabbis viewed the past as a guide to the present. "Remember the days of old," the Bible taught them. "Consider the years of ages past. Ask your parents, they will inform you. Your elders, they will tell you" (Deut. 32:7). Given the choice between listening to the old or heeding the impetuous voices of the young, the rabbis almost invariably went with experience and listened to the elders. A famous rabbinic text (Tosefta Avodah Zarah 1:19) referring to the rebuilding of the Temple in Jerusalem in Hadrian's time explains why: "If young people advise you to build a Temple, and old people say destroy it, listen to the latter. The building of the young is destruction while the tearing down by the old is construction." While this sounds like a formula for community conflict, the traditional Jewish ideal was actually far more harmonious. The goal remains a world where young and old might work together for common ends, earlier envisioned by the prophet Joel (2:28): "And it shall come to pass afterward that I will pour out My spirit on all flesh. Your sons and daughters shall prophesy; your elders shall dream dreams and your young see visions."

Human beings are created in the image of God. This does not refer to a physical representation. Rather, it goes beyond the corporeal by definition. Like God, the human species is creative, albeit on a significantly more limited basis. As a matter of fact, in every case where the imitation of God is apparent, the limitations are also made clear. God is eternal. Human beings are mortal. However, they approximate or imitate immortality and the ability to create through the act of procreation. Thus, the relationship between young and old is necessarily tied to our relationship with God. And all Jewish attitudes toward the elderly are refractions of the guidance of the Jewish tradition in regard to the idealized relationship between adult children and their parents. By comparison, little is really said by the rabbis about the elderly *per se*, unless it is placed in the context of the relationship between parents and children. In the mouth of Malachi (4:5) God speaks: "Behold, I will send you Elijah the prophet before the great and terrible day of Adonai. He will turn the hearts of parents to their children and the hearts of children to their parents, lest I come and smite the land with a curse. " Jewish tradition argues that such lack of regard for the elderly is an outright rejection of God as the Source of life and law in the universe.

Such an analysis is particularly poignant if Robert Katz's notion that old age may be the "sabbath" of human life is accepted (Katz, 1975; Olitzky, 1988). If one assumes that among the many functions and purposes of the Jewish Sabbath is to force the individual from "creating" and be reminded of her or his mortality (in contradistinction to the eternal creative ability of God), then this notion has profound theological consequences. It is the day that moves the individual to a higher plane where mind and soul can take precedence over body and flesh. Old age thus becomes the period in which our active energies are transformed into spiritual energies that sustain the soul more than the body. This is to say that the focus of this creativity, as in the focus of Shabbat, is on a higher plane of existence. Old age — because of the wisdom of experience and the consequent growth of knowledge — leads the individual to this higher plane.

Jewish tradition, which speaks of the aged in lofty terms, also evidences a common sense approach to old age (Reuben, 1976). The frank realism that was expressed in both biblical and rabbinic literature can be summarized by this text from Genesis Rabbah 69: "There is old age without the glory of long life and there is long life without the ornament of age. Perfect is that old age which has both." Like the authors of the Bible, the rabbis were not blind to the frailties of the human condition. In their book of wisdom for everyday living, Pirke Avot (4:20), they ask, "What is one like who learns in old age?" The answer: "To ink written on erased paper." They also wrote in the same mishnah: "What is one like who learns from the old?" This time the answer was, "To one who eats ripe grapes and drinks old wine." These attitudes can be considered synthesized by Rabbi Meir who suggested later in the same text: "Do not look at the flask. Rather look at what is in it. There may be a new flask full of old wine and an old flask that has not even new wine in it."

They understood the need to offer incredibly profound sage advice, based on a lifetime of living, but they also knew what it was like to face the physical limitations of the body. Old age, according to this view, is dark and dull, without music or the sounds of the world. They proclaimed in the Babylonian Talmud (Shabbat 152a) that the intelligence of the aged is dissipated. The speech of the old is faltering. The ears of the elderly are unreliable. To an older person even a little hill seems like the greatest of mountains. They even urged the individual (in Midrash Tanchuma Miketz 10) to pray that "in his older years his eyes may see, his mouth eat, and his legs work, because in old age, all powers fail."

From reading texts like the following from Avodah Zarah (17b), we know that the inspired instructions of the rabbis were not always kept by the people. In this passage, Elazar ben Prata is asked why he had not been to the house of study lately. His reply, "I am too old and was afraid that I would be trampled down under the feet of the crowd." A similar sentiment is expressed in Bava Kamma (92b): "Now that we are old, we are treated like infants." This last stage of life is described by so many as pathetic and without hope. Consider this selection from Midrash Tanchuma:

> Apelike, his disposition changes. Childlike, he asks for everything, eating, drinking and playing like a child. There he sits, even with his children and the members of his house mocking him, disregarding and loathing him. When he utters a word, he hears, "let him alone. He is old and childish." Yet, when the angel of death arrives, he starts to weep and his cry pierces the world from one end to the other.

The perspectives of the rabbis on old age, both positive and negative, were not just filtered through the protracted lenses of the academies or through the leisure of theological speculation. Instead, they learned from the people, sharing their joy as well as their pain. One text from the Jerusalem Talmud (Beitzah 1) says it so poignantly: "Stones which we sat on in our youth make war against us in our old age." In this respect, things have not changed greatly. While medical advances have brought life expectancy in closer proximity to lifespan potential for the human species, the fear of finitude and dependency among human beings that permeated the rabbinic mind resonates within contemporary attitudes as well, and reflects the human condition.

Perhaps the balance of rabbinic views should be read as a juxtaposition of a Jewish ideal to a human reality. Persons often find themselves in the situation described immediately above. This is the reason why Jews are commanded and exhorted to treat the elderly with respect. In one way or another, as much as persons must face the unavoidable reality of death, none among them truly wants to die.

The Modern Period

In turning to contemporary Jewish life, a paradox immediately suggests itself. As a thoroughly modernized, secularized community, Jews rarely approach practical issues of living by directly reflecting on what their people's religious teachings might have to say about them. On the practical level they tend to operate out of their own sense of what they consider right. Being generally more affluent than their grandparents were and living longer than prior generations did, possibilities open up for them that were unknown in the past. The many positive aspects of this development are offset by the obstacles our culture particularly creates for the elderly. These problems include: segregation and separation from family, no clear place in the social scheme and the threat that respect for privacy will become abandonment, among others. All of these problems plague the Jewish community as much as they do non-Jewish society.

Yet, one also sees a certain skewing of the statistics and a general ethos which can be distinguished from what is operative in the general society. The latter emerges most clearly in the way in which organized Jewish communities in the United States have moved to create special residences and services for the elderly. If that indicates the continuing power of the classic Jewish ethos, one can then see its further effect on the many Jews who consider respect for and care of their parents a major indicator of their humanity — and, by extension, of the community's treatment of the aged.

It is the theologian's or philosopher's task to try to give some cognitive insight into the religious bases of this ongoing commitment, often to strengthen or redirect it. And it is a sign of the relative newness of this issue that there has been almost no direct treatment of the theme. In a sanguine mood that might be attributed to the adequacy of Jewish tradition on this topic, it did not really require any academic reconsideration even in the changed modern circumstances. To some extent, this is the position of many traditionalists, stressing the primacy of Jewish action over abstract reflection. Perhaps the problems of aging have intensified, or human and Jewish resources now seem less self evident than they once did. This sense makes it desirable to provide a more abstract reflection on the Jewish religious attitude toward aging. Perhaps, too, one can gain new insight into the present duty by such an exercise. This chapter will now proceed by an exploration of four contemporary models of Jewish thinking and seek to draw out their implications for aging (Borowitz, 1983).

The oldest still effective pattern of thinking about Judaism is ethical rationalism, exemplified most fully in the neo-Kantianisin of Hermann Cohen (Borowitz, 1983, 29-52). In a typical Kantian shift of emphasis from traditional religion's concern with what God had instructed people to do, to what the modern mind could itself teach us about proper human duty and aspiration, Cohen continued the classic Jewish concern with deeds. But he gave this activism a special interpretation that his left its mark upon much Jewish self-understanding: Rational people ought to be self-legislating and need to make their universal ethical regard the center of their existence. Both themes invested personal agency with an intensity they had not had in prior generations. This becomes particularly evident when one keeps in mind Cohen's liberal shift from (rabbinic Judaism's) this-and-otherworldly faith to one that needed to be lived in this world alone.

The resulting emphasis on ethical action as the telltale sign of true Jewlshness has dominated much of popular thought about Judaism. Equally, it has had its effect on specifically Jewish action. The astonishingly disproportionate involverrient of Jews in the various causes for human betterment in recent generations is tribute to the widespread appeal of this reinterpretation of Judaism. As a result, much of the Jewvish concern with the aged must be seen in the context of this fundamental yardstick of Jewish faithfulness. In an academic sense, this can be taken a step further. The Kantian emphasis pm the universal horizon of rational ethics means that one must extend dignity to every moral agent — a notion that still has revolutionary implications for the further humanization of our society and planet. But that means that one cannot simply "cast off "the elderly regardless of how unproductive, infirm, or troublesome they appear to be. As moral agents they must be treated to the extent we possibly can as "ends in themselves" and not as "means to an end."

The dark side of this doctrine is connected with its easy conflation to the capitalistic notion of individuals shaping their own destiny, of "making a life for themselves," as social-cultural entrepreneurs, or economically, by providing for themselves, preferably well. The ethical activism of the Cohenian self was quickly assimilated to the American practical bent while, of course, also modifying it. But it is this emphasis on the self's usefulness, on what one does or can do, and, at its worst, on what goods are yielded, that creates a special problem for becoming old in America. Too often, humanity is identified with a need to be in control rather than simply with the ability to initiate. Action is no longer enough; effectiveness has become critical. Fully being a person means not being dependent upon anyone else, always being able to do for oneself.

This concept surely has its own promise. It encourages persons, at whatever age, to try new things, to see what they might yet become, to undertake such long-deferred dreams as they might now reasonably seek to make reality. Doing often brings great joy and satisfaction. But what happens when one tires, and would simply like to be, not having to prove by actions that one still retains one's humanity?

Productive action is a futile standard even for the young. How many can fully take advantage of all their abilities or of the opportunities that present themselves to them? But it is a devastating challenge for most of the elderly who cannot hope to do what they once did physically, emotionally, or economically. And it is the threat of losing such areas of control that one has established for oneself that depresses persons as the years lengthen. As long as one cannot simply be, as long as one feels one must continually do and by the doing demonstrate one's humanity, old age devalues rather than dignifies.

The Jewish ethical rationalists should not be blamed for this degradation of their teaching. There is nothing in what they said to demean whatever capacity a person has to be a moral agent. It is not difficult to argue that years and experience can bring moral insight. But in the way that this theory has been coopted by the productive genius of our society, it has been an unwitting accomplice to the transformation of youth and vigor to be the honored age of our society.

A second model of contemporary Jewish philosophy has emphasized the social over the individual. As elaborated in the naturalism of Mordecai

Kaplan, Judaism is the evolving religious civilization of the Jewish people (Borowltz, 1983, 98-120). Critical of the exaggerated individualism of the Kantians and impressed with the way in which individuals are shaped by their culture, Kaplan argued for reconstructing a full ethnic existence for Jews in order to remedy the ills brought into Jewish life by patterning modern Judaism in terms of the Protestantism that dominated the democratic countries. Instead of individual faith and ethics being the ground of a Jewishness worked out through religious institutions, Kaplan called for a Jewish life in which the social whole rather than just the synagogue shaped the character of Jews. Hence the land of Israel, the Hebrew language, the Jewish calendar, folk traditions and lore, Jewish art, music, and dance, and a full range of communal institutions to support these variegated aspects of Jewish civilization (as Kaplan called it) would now give Jewishness its vitality. It is easy enough to see how these cultural components would transmit Jewish values, particularly with the survival of the folk itself as a major criterion of Jewish duty. However, following Emile Durkheim, Kaplan argued that religion and personal spirituality would result from a vigorous ethnic existence rather than being its cause.

Kaplan said nothing special about the elderly in his philosophy of Judaism, but several of its themes suggest a special approach to the topic. Honoring the people and its traditions, imbued with a strong sense of how individual existence is the result of folk creativity, he would probably argue that the years one lives form a prominent part of Jewish existence and thus express an appreciation of the aged, the bearers of the tradition. As a result of the explicit humanism of this approach, its insistence on the humane values Jews have inherited from their premodern forebears, Kaplan would make the historical teachings about honoring the hoary head a living part of contemporary Judaism. Finally, with the group and its creativity central to the continuity of Judaism and vitality of individuals in contradistinction to the notion of individual initiative, it would be easier for people to see themselves as dignified, even if increasingly passive, in the ongoing life of the folk. And, if it needs adding, the community's own responsibility to all the constituencies within it would, in this reading of the centrality of the folk, lead to a vigorous, respectful concern with the aged.

The very strengths of this position have, however, also led to its limited effectiveness as providing a new conceptualization of aging. When the ethnic group becomes the generator of one's norms — with the

exception of the moral law that Kaplan asserts is inherent in the universe
— one has little basis on which to chide the folk for the ethos they have
come to accept. That is particularly true in this case, as Kaplan
enthusiastically spoke of living in two civilizations. Of course, he
anticipated that one would take what he pointed to as the humane best of
both cultures: American and Jewish. But with regard to the elderly, the
Jewish community, as it has increasingly acculturated, has often come to
be as youth-dominated and as action-oriented as has much of America
with much the same result. The Jewish tradition once honored the aged
because God instructed us to do so. It believed that the wisdom of the
past or of accumulated years was better than that of the present or of the
young. A philosophy committed to change as people react to new
situations, for all that it seeks to remain loyal to its ethnic roots, is far
more likely to honor the recent and the new and have no independent
basis for dignifying the elderly.

In a striking address to the White House Conference on Aging in
1961, Abraham Joshua Heschel produced the only sustained Jewish
theological treatment of the topic of aging (Heschel, 1981). Typically, it
was not a systematic analysis. Instead, it was academic in frame and
abstract in approach. Heschel assumed that a systematic statement would
concede too much power to human reason in its contemporary technical,
impersonal mode, as if detachment from a concern as human as aging
were the proper way in which to confront it. Rather, here as elsewhere,
Heschel's concern was to transmit or even evoke a new vision, one that
would alone make it possible for us to change our society's pervasive,
pernicious attitude toward the elderly. He did this in two ways that were
closely related. The first was polemical: an insistent, persistent critique
of the style our culture teaches about relating to the aged or to thinking of
oneself as old. The second was visionary: giving us tantalizing glimpses
of what we might yet do and be. Both lines of his thought were carried
out in his uncommon gift for the striking phrase, the telling aphorism,
the stunning reversal of the anticipated. Quite consciously, he reached
for the heart as well as the mind, knowing that if he did not affect the
whole person then no amount of intellectual brilliance would accomplish
his purpose (Borowitz, 1983, 165-83).

Not only did Heschel express broadscale generalities with incredible
insight, but he also exposed a steady stream of specific follies for judgment.
In large part, his extraordinary perceptiveness must be attributed to the
different standard that he confidently brought to bear on secular American

life. On the simpler level it had to do with the fatal preference for space over time. Americans want time to serve them as a means to conquer one or another manifestation of space. They seek to use time efficiently or, when that cannot be done, to kill it pleasantly. So years have to do with productivity. When the elderly cannot any longer compete with the more vigorous time-users, they are considered a burden and consider themselves "useless." Society then recommends that the elderly play or otherwise amuse themselves since, by this standard, there is nothing serious for them to do.

The root of this insidious vision of existence is the exaltation of the thing, another way of saying idolatry. The clear and present measure behind Heschel's view of living is the God of the Bible, the One whom no thing can represent although to whom anything might awaken one. Knowing God is real, more real than any human theory of reality could explicate, and concerned with each person, in a dignity conferring relationship that nothing, not even sin, can obliterate, Heschel knew time was given as an incomparable endowment of humanity. In some sense persons are things and certainly can be said to occupy space. However, in neither aspect can they be said to be most truly what their relationship to God discloses them to be.

Consider, for example, persons' pressing concern with their needs, or their need to be needed by others. It builds their lives on themselves or their society as the source of their worth and significance. It is a bloated humanism which takes their justifiable recognition that they are not isolates but social animals and turns it into a compulsive way of life. And then come the years when persons feel that no one needs them anymore and one difficulty or another makes it impossible for them to fulfill what for so long they took to be their rightful needs. Their problem is not, therefore, essentially one of better techniques or arrangements but of a functioning spirituality. In Heschel's memorable closing words, "it takes three things to attain a sense of significant being: God, a Soul and a Moment. And the three are always here. Just to be is a blessing. just to live is holy" (1968, 75).

Heschel called for conversion, for giving up the false gods that gave persons false standards. Instead, he urged persons to confront the living God who calls them to sanctify time, whatever time is given them.

Something of this recognition that human value is not self-bestowed or earned in social usefulness is carried over into the fourth model of a Jewish theological reflection on aging, the postmodern covenant theology of Eugene B. Borowitz (1991). Only in his view, God, the real and independent One, mysteriously but lovingly gives people a substantial measure of self-determination, making them capable of being full, if subordinate, covenant partners. Relationship rather than hierarchy becomes the instructive model here, allowing God's uniquely normative quality to yoke itself to the free, self-making power of humans while thus keeping it, ideally, from self-worship and its inevitable dehumanization.

Once relatedness becomes the heart of spirituality and the finest mode of a person's service of God, the elderly attain enhanced dignity and continuing power. For with the self forever unable to satisfy itself or its needs except in relation to others, the covenant between the generations takes on its commanding power. Persons would never have come to be or been the selves they now are without the forebears who had the faith to bring them into being and nurture their selfhood. How much of what they take to be their very individuality they owe to their relationships with those older than them. And how much more of themselves have they gained as they risked relationships with those younger than themselves. Rather than lives being measured in terms of an eternal present or compared to some idealized, vigorous youthfulness, it is faithfulness over the years — the model of God's involvement with humans — that provides such glory as a human being can accomplish. And even when debility makes it difficult or even impossible for persons actively to carry on their relationships, they remain those whose partnerships over time exercise their proper demands on others.

Increasingly, individualism carried to extremes shows its destructiveness. Borowitz would give the individual more room in contemporary religiosity than would Heschel, for Borowitz recognizes the spiritual benefits involved in reasonably autonomous living. But he insists on persons exercising their autonomy in relationship to God as part of a humanity covenanted to God. It is a far more social and theological vision of existence than many in the Jewish community are ready for. But in the stubborn insistence of so many Jews to affirm their ethnic roots and freshly open themselves to to their people's historic relationship with God, a new theological possibility of refreshing and enhancing the old Jewish esteem for the aged makes itself presently manifest.

While there are those in the modern Jewish world, primarily right-wing or Orthodox, who would still hold that there is a necessary relationship between righteous living and old age as a blessing by God, most Jews would argue that righteous living is important but not the primary cause for old age. Nature and nurture play indispensable roles, and the human species is limited in both life span and life expectancy (Kushner, 1981, 1980). The major reason for the abrupt change in the theology of aging from rabbinic to modern times is the loss of faith in the system of a tight reward and punishment. Jews observe that things do not happen as they were taught in the rabbinic period; they are not rewarded in years for their good deeds. Thus, rather than searching for all understanding regarding the years of their lives, they work to increase the life of their years through their relationship with God, the Source of all life.

Chapter 25

ℰ〜℧

Life After Death

To Be a Jew

For me, being a Jew is fundamentally a religious matter, one that derives from the ongoing validity of the people of Israel's historic relationship with God, the Covenant. The classic Jewish books, the Bible and the Talmud, testify to this assertion, for they center about God and the service due God. Until a hundred or so years ago, it did not seriously occur to many people that one could be a good Jew without believing in God. If anything, belief in God was so much a part of Jewish life that one did not need to talk much about it. Though often unspoken, everything else in Jewish life depended on it. Thus, the weight of Jewish history, tradition, and practice connects believing in God with being a good Jew and opposing theories must bear the burden of demonstrating their Jewish authenticity.

I also find that the passage of time has lessened the once nearly universal opposition by liberal Jews to the notion that a good Jew believes in God. Since the 1940s ended, we no longer consider atheism great sophistication. Even the agnosticism that allowed us to dispense with God because we trusted culture wholeheartedly increasingly shows its obsolescence. A spiritual shift has begun among serious Jews in our community, and a growing number can now speak of God in personal ways that would have made us uncomfortable some years back. With our new appreciation of the extraordinary openness with which Judaism has allowed people to talk of God, "my" good Jew believes in God but not necessarily in my view of God. We have numerous differing interpretations of what God might mean to a contemporary Jew, and in my several books I have tried to help liberal Jews understand the various modern notions of God, from rationalism through existentialism and on to religious experience and beyond to mysticism. (*Liberal Judaism*).

The Covenant

For me, the ideal Jew cannot be someone who believes in God but has no concern for the Jewish people — as some among us once contended — nor someone who loves Jews and Jewish culture but denies or ignores God — as did the Yiddishists and classic Zionists of yesteryear and the Israeli nationalists of today. Only in the relationship between God and the Jewish people, the Covenant, does authentic Judaism appear. My good Jew, then, believes in and lives in the Covenant (*Liberal Judaism*).

Liberal Jews consider Torah historical but not time-bound. We associate it particularly with Mount Sinai, but we understand it also as a continuing creative stream of Jewish spiritual search and self-expression through the ages. We know it can find authentic forms in modern times as it did in yesteryear. Often the tales and practices from ancient times and distant places not only express our Covenant sentiments but instruct us in their proper depth. Sometimes continuity falls short of our needs or even impairs living out our faith. Then out of our immediate sense of Jewish duty to God as part of the Jewish people we creatively add to the repertoire of Jewish teaching and living.

As to beliefs, then, I see a good Jew having a living relationship with God as part of the people of Israel and therefore living a life of Torah. Three major areas of Jewish responsibility arise from this situation.

First, the Covenant obligates Jews to sanctify their lives and their relationships with others. Of all such duties, none has a higher place than that of being ethical. We may even say that this command rests more heavily upon Jews than upon humankind for the Jewish people claim to represent God in history. The primacy of ethics in Jewish duty flows naturally from the faith that all humanity has but one God and that God "cares" about nothing more than that people treat one another with righteousness.

Other duties flow from grounding one's life as a Jew upon God's reality: daily prayer, study, and religious observance. The week moves toward Sabbath observance; the year is punctuated with Jewish holy days; each life has its beginning, end, and other major moments marked by special rites. All these events have more than purely personal significance. They have a communal dimension, for life under the Covenant involves the Jewish people as well as God. The Jewish family provides the critical link between the individual and the folk at large, so Jewish duty largely centers on participating in a rich Jewish family life. A good Jew participates in synagogue activity, for there the community regularly renews the Covenant through liturgy, deepens it in study, and refreshes it by association. That institution, in turn, leads Jews on to serve the Jewish community locally, nationally, and worldwide — and through it, all humankind.

Ours being a time of special Jewish peril and attainment, the good Jew will be especially concerned about the survival of the Jewish people everywhere, most particularly in the State of Israel. The Holocaust mandates an overriding Jewish concern for other Jews. We cannot depend on others always to be of help to our tiny people. So wherever a Jew cries out for help — Argentina, Iraq, and most dramatically recently, in the Soviet Union — other Jews need to be listening and active in their response. Or, more positively put, a good Jew ought to support every activity that upbuilds and enriches Jewish life anywhere (*Liberal Judaism*).

God

Though I try to teach Jews about the many ways of thinking about God in contemporary Judaism, I have my own position among them. People have relationships that are deeply significant for their lives without fully or nearly understanding those with whom they have such relationships. I find the personal the best model we have for talking about God. As against rationalist models, concepts of God (clear intellectual envisagements of God) are of subsidiary interest in traditional Judaism — if not positively discouraged. Making concepts of God primary tends to make thinking about God a substitute for relating to God and implies the human mind is capable of apprehending God. In a relationship, thought is not abandoned, but it must not dominate. It serves as a critic of faith and as explicator of its consequent responsibilities. This is the safeguard against superstition and cultism. At the same time there is openness to many forms of envisaging God. That is, any concept of God that makes relationships possible (or is appropriate to living in Covenant) is acceptable here. This seems closer to the traditional model of agadic thinking than liberal theologies have been in prior generations as a result of their emphasis on an idea of God as the essence of Judaism. And it provides for continuing intellectual growth in our understanding of God, a characteristic of all of Jewish history, particularly in our time.

The perception of a transcendent demand upon us to preserve the people of Israel, the affirmation of a transcendent ground of value in the face of contemporary nihilism, have led many Jews to a restoration of the relationship with the other partner in the Covenant, God. The absence of God and the hurt we have felt are not intellectually explained. Yet it is possible, despite them, to continue the relationship. For the intellectually determined, the most satisfactory way of dealing with this issue is to say God's power is limited. For those to whom this raises more problems than it solves, there is acceptance without understanding. Both positions are compatible with relating to God in Covenant. I find myself constantly tempted to the former though mostly affirming the latter, a dialectic I find appropriate to affirming the Covenant (*Choices in Modern Jewish Thought*).

Who and What Am I?

For all that I am intricately related to my body, I know myself to be a person and not merely a chemical structure. I do not say I have a "soul," a term heavy with Greek philosophic and medieval metaphysical overtones, for in today's culture I would not know how to substantiate the existence of such an entity. Still, there is something about me that enables me to share in God's reality. I know a bit about God. At my best, I consciously serve God, and my acts help complete God's work of creation. I occasionally have a glimpse of what God wants of me and of all humanity. Sometimes I am capable of rising above the frailties within and social ugliness without to dedicate my life to a purpose far transcending my small existence. This exalted human capacity deserves as much attention as does the chemistry of our life stuff — or more, for it is what makes us characteristically human. And it is the experiential base of our sense that we are like God and thus may be privileged to share in God's eternal life.

Naturalism, the modern intellectual current dominating America at midcentury, hoped to find what is truly real by reducing everything to its smallest physical constituent. The other view, mine, and I think that of Jewish tradition, sees reality most clearly in the most complex thing we know, a person. The one perspective breaks everything down to impersonal energy. The other says we see ultimate reality more clearly as we build upward from human nature to what transcends and fulfills it. If God is the most real "thing" in the universe, then we may hope that, as we make our lives ever more closely correspond to it, we may personally share God's eternity despite our death. And knowing ourselves to be most fully human through our individuality, we trust that the God who is one will preserve our oneness and grant us personal survival after death (*Liberal Judaism*).

We Do Not Understand Death

Don't try to imagine what it is like being dead. (I'm not yet talking about life after death.) In the first place, whatever you come up with has to be awful. Death being the opposite of life, as far as we can tell, all you can imagine is different kinds of nothingness. The point is, however, you won't "be" dead. Think about it: When you're dead that means "you" are dead and you won't "be" or "feel" anything, not even bad. The words "being dead" make no sense together. If you have "being," you're not "dead." Either there is some sort of life after death, and "being dead" means what you're doing in that existence, or else you're dead, in which case "You" won't know it. So you can stop trying to figure out what it is like to be nothing.

This discussion already illustrates the problem with this topic: How do you talk about something you've had no experience with? As difficult as it is to discuss God we can say that through our minds or in our lives we've had some personal sense that God is real. How can we think about death? All we know is life. The closest thing to death in life is sleep — only we are very much alive when asleep though not very conscious of it. How can we figure from life to its opposite? Death is a real mystery, one none of us can avoid, and that makes it frightening (*Understanding Judaism*).

Death Is a Mystery

Death is a great mystery. We do not know life without a physical base. We have no experience of what existence the other side of death could be like. Against that ignorance we balance our recognition that life itself is mysterious, that death is part of life and the creation God ordained. Death, like life, comes from the God who we know daily showers goodness on us. We trust God's goodness even in death. We cannot believe that, having shared so intimately in God's reality in life, we do not continue to share it beyond the grave. Our creaturely existence, which enables us to rise to the level of participating in the ultimate reality in the universe, God's, now may aspire to extend and fulfill that greatness we came partially to experience in life. Having reached such heights precisely in our personhood, our individuality, we likewise trust that our survival will be personal and individual (*Reform Judaism Today*).

Life After Death — A Personal Statement

As a liberal I am dedicated to humankind's significant role in achieving God's purposes. With that sense of faith, I am unlikely to give up my activism and patiently wait for the life of the world to come. True, because I do not consider people the only agents of fundamental change, I will not bring a messianic enthusiasm to every immediate social struggle. But should my projects fail, I will not be as dispirited as many onetime liberals have now become. Believing there is only one life, they have grown discouraged, even bitter, because they were not able to bring the messianic age in their time. Often they now despair of human progress altogether. Why should they spend their only existence suffering continual defeats, why sacrifice their precious few years to the painful task of resisting evil?

Believers who do not expect vindication in this life alone are saved from the spiritual rot that easily sets in when humanity proves obdurate to change or malevolent in interest. They trust God to reward them in another existence for what they have suffered for God's sake in this one. They may even be strong enough to see their defeats on God's behalf as joining them to God's reality. Their lives will be fulfilled no matter what happens in this world, for they have a life with God yet to come. And, trusting God, they know history will one day be redeemed by the One who will not ultimately be defeated.

I do not know much more than that, how I shall survive, what sort of judgment awaits me, or what I shall do in eternity. I am, however, inclined to think that my hope is better spoken of as resurrection rather than immortality, for I do not know my self as a soul without a body but only as a psychosomatic self. Perhaps even that is more than I can honestly say, though in the use of this term I may lean upon Jewish tradition with which I share so much else. Ultimately I trust in what I have experienced of God's generosity, so surprising and overwhelming so often in my life. In such moments I sing wholeheartedly the last stanza of the hymn *Adon Olam*: "In God's hand I place my soul both when I sleep and when I wake, and with my soul, my body. God is with me. I shall not fear" (*Liberal Judaism*).

Part Four

My Teacher, My Friend,
My Dialogue Partners

Chapter 26

ℬↃℭℜ

Abraham J. Heschel

1) Thinking about Our Teacher

Richard Rubenstein and I entered the Hebrew Union College in the same class, that of September 1942. I do not think memory fails me when I report that he was the first person of that large entering class, twenty two, who made a specific impression on me. The occasion was our spending together, in mutual consolation, a part of the evening before our morning's Hebrew language entering examination. It was the beginning of a relationship that has lasted over these fifty years even though we have gone very different ways in theology, ethical politics and careers. Perhaps we should have taken it as an omen that our dormitory rooms that first year were directly across the hall from one another. This festschrift, a happy celebration of his busy, useful life, once again brings us together and in continuing appreciation of his keen intellect and religious seriousness I should like to say some words about the theology of our common teacher and master, Abraham J. Heschel.

Let me begin by pointing to the extraordinary communal role assumed by Dr. Heschel (as we young students called him). More than any other American Jew, he exemplified where the Jewish left and right should have stood as the second half of the twentieth century progressed. Consider the split which grossly disfigured Jewish social ethics in the late 1960s. To the left were Jews so motivated by universal concerns that they fought the Vietnam War with unparalleled energy and creativity. To the right were Jews so filled with love of their people that they devised increasingly effective ways of making the plight of Soviet Jewry an immediate concern of our community and the world. But, as painful as it still is to say, these groups generally had nothing to do with one another. Not only did they keep a certain distance between them, they often disparaged the Jewish ethics of the others and, sometimes, their Jewishness as well. In that critical time, the one person of stature who stood firmly in both camps, indeed, who provided leadership to them both was Abraham Heschel. He knew that Judaism laid a prophetic demand upon us to correct the errors of our nation's leaders even as it required us not to forget our own family as we sought to mend the world. Visibly, dramatically, he defined the vital center of American Jewish life, if not as it was, then as it ought to be and as he, apparently alone among our leadership then, was determined to have it become. More, many then sought the fame an emerging television journalism had begun to confer on public figures and thereby benefited our people by their involvement with the media. His preeminence, by contrast, arose from our knowledge that he was the servant of his primal Jewish faith and his sophisticated Jewish reflection. Because of him, we knew that the bush would never be consumed.

For all the glory of his thought made deed, I do not see that we can identify his philosophy with American Judaism's ideological center. That surely was not his intellectual situation at the Jewish Theological Seminary in the last decade or so of his life. In my contacts with him during this period, brief as they were, he did not feel that he was at the center of things either in this institution or the Conservative movement. His call for personal religious faith as the heart of disciplined Jewish living aroused little response and brought him few genuine disciples. The academic elite preferred text and more text while the pragmatists happily skirted the problem of piety as increasing American ethnicity made it possible for them to work at enhancing *Yiddishkayt*. Many loved him as moral hero or as the poet of Eastern Jewish spirituality or contemporary Jewish sentiment. But that, realism suggests, is about all — which tells us a good deal about the superficiality of our community then and now.

This anomalous combination of adulation and distancing demands greater analysis. Since he was a philosopher first and foremost, we must look to his thought to seek the causes of this odd phenomenon. Clearly, he correctly delineated the central problem of our community then and now: a Judaism whose discipline is defined only by universal ethics cannot be satisfactory to anyone who understands the difference between being a *ben noah*, a responsible human being, and a *ben brit*, a responsible Jew. At the same time, it is contradictory to fulfill meticulously the statutes of reciting the *sh'ma* but not then make loving God in overflowing measure the Jew's primary task.

He was prescient. The caring American Jewish center wants a disciplined Judaism that is founded on what can be a living religious experience for us in this time and place. Once it is clear that the center wants tradition and change, the issue shifts to how they are to be accommodated one to the other. That brings us to the central issue of clarifying Jewish obligation: when may old Jewish disciplines be replaced by new ones? Or, better, when may they be substantially adapted from what they were to meet our Jewish situation as best we conscientiously understand it? If we are to ask whether Abraham Heschel's thought, as against his life, defines the vital Jewish center for us, then we must inquire how he dealt with this issue.

I inquire about this matter with some recognized handicaps. I never discussed this issue with Dr. Heschel and I do not know any of his still unpublished materials except those which from time to time are brought to my attention. Thus, in what follows, I am limited to the rich but limited treasure of his publicly available documents. To begin with, I do not recall him writing about any analogous case from which we may now extrapolate his teaching on this matter. That is, I have not come across his mediating a specific instance of a clash between ethics and *halakhah* and his explaining how, in general, such matters should be dealt with. I suppose that is because he did not see himself in the role of a *posek*, a decisor, even an occasional one. And he apparently did not think it important to specify how his thought might be applied to troublesome situations. Instead, he dedicated himself to the meta-halakhic level, believing that only if the religious foundations were once again secure could we build sanctified Jewish lives and holy communities.

His meta-halakhic position may most concisely be given by contrasting it with thinkers he knew and whose positions he found wanting, Mordecai Kaplan, the naturalist, for one, and Martin Buber and Franz Rosenzweig, the existentialists, for another. Heschel rejected Kalpan's self-proclaimed "Copernican turn" to social humanism. Heschel, rather, placed God, a transcendent, commanding Other, at the heart of his philosophy. Thus, it was more than theological polemics that caused Heschel to limit his discussion of the Jewish people to some few pages at the very end of *God in Search of Man*. When one believed in a real God — part one of the book — one could accept real revelation — part two of the book — and thus could make Jewish discipline arise from God's compelling word, not hope it might arise out of loyalty to the folkways of our intriguing people.

But once revelation is restored to modern Judaism, the question of its nature, that is, of its content, becomes critical for the *halakhah* or the quasi-*halakhah* that is its consequence. Classically put: does God reveal a Written Torah which is verbally authorized, and does God somehow also reveal the Oral Torah in all its dynamic unfolding? Or, to set the question in existential dimension, does God "reveal" — if the same verb may yet be used — something else which becomes the human base for the two Torahs which are one? Obviously, tradition and change will mean different things depending upon one's response.

Buber and Rosenzweig posited a revelation of God that was contentless and whose legal expression was then substantially human. Because Rosenzweig believed revelation was as personal as love, he could never explain what validated his other bed-rock intuition: that Jews are yet obligated to follow the *halakhah* — except, as once he tersely and mysteriously put it, when they are not "able" to do so. To take the paradigmatic case of our time, when, then, the senior members of the Talmud faculty of the Jewish Theological Seminary ruled that in their judgment the *halakhah* bars women rabbis, I do not see how Rosenzweig could have voted against them. The most he could have said was that this was a law he was "not yet" able to carry out.

Heschel decisively rejected the Buber-Rosenzweig stand on revelation. The prophet's personality may be the medium through which the message is refracted. In that sense, Biblical texts are often quite personal. But Heschel insists that the prophet, with Moses as their chief, is not creative in revelation. He does not supply its content or fill it out in any way. He is merely but supremely empathic, empathic with what God truly feels. Thus, his message, given to us in the Bible, is accurate. Heschel clearly believes, against all the liberals, that God gives us a contentful, Written Torah. The text as we now have it may have occasionally been disturbed in transmission but it remains fundamentally God's message to us, not human beings' spiritual perceptions of God. And in a telling sentence, Heschel gives equal status to the Oral Law. He said, "The prophets' inspirations and the sages' interpretations are equally important" (*God in Search of Man*, p. 274).

I take the word "equally" in that sentence with full seriousness. For him, the Oral Torah is as fully revelation, in its own dynamic fashion, to be sure, as is the Written Torah. That not only coheres with all else that he wrote but that position alone can explain his famous lecture to the Central Conference of American Rabbis on form and regularity in prayer. The issue between him and the Reform rabbis was not discipline in religion. They accepted the notion of Jewish discipline but they then specified that it was the discipline of ethics. Note, please that they regularly called it moral law and spoke of it in terms of Jewish duty. When Dr. Heschel called them to Jewish discipline his argument with them had to be that the sages are authoritative for us and not merely the prophets as the Reform rabbis read them. Only if God authorized the sages' interpretations equally with the prophets' inspirations is it clear why Jews have an obligation to recite the *maariv*, evening, service, to mention the striking personal example in the lecture.

Having read and studied his books, it is clear to me that Abraham Heschel hoped by his writing and teaching to make classic Jewish belief accessible and acceptable to modern Jews.

I do see evidence in his writings of two themes which mitigate the apparent orthodoxy of his theory of revelation. The one is his passion for the ethical, a theme brilliantly adumbrated in his life as in his writings. The other is his insistence that there has been far more interpretation in our tradition than there has been revelation. But I do not think we can take that to mean that we can, except in the unusual case, interpret away what God has given us in the Oral Torah of ages past. Such a liberalistic stand would belie the theocentricity of his religiosity and his argument that the interpretations that constitute Oral Torah are not merely historic precedent but fully equal to God's revelation.

Heschel's writings, juxtaposed to his life, create a quandary for those of us who consider him our teacher and turn to his books for guidance in dealing with the difficult issues of our time. What would he have said about the issue which recently agitated the Jewish Theological Seminary and Conservative Jewry in general: should a movement dedicated to *halakhah*, in a dynamic reading, to be sure, ordain women as rabbis? How would he have voted? From the record of his life, it is inconceivable that he would not have been in favor of so ethical an innovation. But from the record of his thought, it is not clear how he could have done so since he considered the interpretations of the sages equal to God's revelation.

In sum, then, his life remains a vibrant reminder of what a modern Jew can and ought to be. But as we now read his theology, it is, at least, problematic. For the vital center of American Jewry, it seems clear, supports the full equality of women in Jewish religious life and thus the ordination of women, a historic, spiritual reality the Jewish Theological Seminary courageously recognized. If so, only a theology which unequivocally makes possible such a reshaping of our tradition can be said to speak for us, a challenge which American Jewish thinkers since him should now seek to meet.

2) *Abraham Heschel and Prophetic Action*

Abraham Heschel's significant role in the protest movements against our sinful racial laws and practices, and against the evil of our waging war in Vietnam are well enough known that twenty five years after his death we gather in these numbers to remember and celebrate his life. Not as widely known but still unforgotten is his role in helping awaken the American Jewish community to the spiritual genocide practiced against the Jews of the Soviet Union. If, today, Abraham Heschel is one of American Jewry's mythic heroes and heroines, it is because of what he stood for and what he then did about it in the troubled social circumstances of his maturity. I only add to this record that he was my teacher at the Hebrew Union College during the second half of his near six years at the Hebrew Union College in Cincinnati. Though we had only sporadic contact after than, we maintained a warm relationship that allowed us to resume communication instantly whenever our paths later crossed.

I am grateful to Fordham University for its kind invitation to participate in this fifth annual dialogue carrying forward the message of Nostra Aetate and to do so by sharing a platform with Fr. Dan Berrigan, himself a mythic figure of imposing stature, though one happily still with us. Fr. Berrigan has had his own strong influence upon me as upon so many others even though we have never met before this evening. But no one alive to the ethical issues of securing and maintaining a moral world in our time could fail to be challenged by the prophetic initiatives which he and his brother and their courageous colleagues have undertaken over the years. In his presence as in hearing about him over the years, I am again made anxious about how well I have lived up to what I have taught and why I have often acted with timidity when moral boldness probably was required. Thus by his life he too has been my teacher and that of many others, a goodness that I am happy to have the privilege of acknowledging to him before this community.

Thinking about these two great figures suggested to me, perhaps because of the mood of self-examination they evoked in me, that I might best contribute to our discussion by ruminating on two concurrent themes. Mostly I should like to speculate on what, for all their comradely ethical passion, made Abraham Heschel take a somewhat different approach than Fr. Berrigan did to acting on the imperatives of the prophets. Doing this will also allow me to make some generalizations about the path of Jewish ethics as a whole.

My principal theme came to me when, as I thought back over those now rapidly receding exciting times, I could not recall an occasion when Dr. Heschel went to jail for one of the great causes to which he dedicated himself. When I checked that impression with his biographer, Samuel Dresner, I was told that my memory had not failed me in this matter. Sam also reminded me that shortly before he died, Dr. Heschel had been among those who waited outside the Danbury federal prison to greet Fr. Philip Berrigan on his release from his most recent sentence. I am ill-equipped to analyze why most members of his order and of his church, indeed most Christian ethicists generally, did not emulate Fr. Berrigan's interpretation of Christian duty in those years. However, I can say something about how my teacher's theology and the thrust of Jewish ethics generally led him to his more law-abiding approach.

What is at stake in this divided sense of duty is our response to the example and teaching of the prophets, those extraordinary teachers of our obligations to other people as a critical aspect of our responsibility to God. In the preferred interpretation of Jewish and Christian thinkers, it is the prophets who most clearly enunciate the ethical thrust of Biblical faith, particularly as it relates to our societies. Their standards are so exalted and compelling that living up to them has long been a major trial for believers; thus, the devastating critique they directed to their own generation has turned out to be a timeless rebuke and inspiration to those who attend to God speaking through their words. Difficult enough as these prophetic messages are for us, we are far more perplexed by the example they set of how to overcome the stubborn resistance of their community. Many of them were moral provocateurs, conscious violators of community convention, wild-men unable to stop acting out their impulse to proclaim God's truth and get people to live by it. A false prophet like Zedekiah goes around with iron horns on his head (1Kings 22.11); a relative insider like Isaiah summons Judah's leaders to hear that he is calling his newly born son *Maher-Shalal-Hash-Baz*, which is more a political statement than a name (Isaiah 8.1-3); Jeremiah variously does symbolic acts with loin cloths (ch. 13), potter's ware (ch. 19), a real estate purchase (ch. 32) and the wearing of a yoke around his neck (ch. 27); Hosea marries a whore (Hosea 1.2-3); and Ezekiel, who may be the consummate virtuoso of bizarre symbolism not only lies down for over a year to simulate the coming siege of Jerusalem but manages to get God to agree that during that demonstration he should not have to cook his bread over dry human feces but can do so with cow dung (Ezekiel 4.1-15). If God's command fills one's soul today in some way as it did the prophets and if the sins of one's society are as egregious as those of ancient Israel, should we too not be moved to strong action? Moreover, since we can do so much more damage to one another than they could, and since we, unlike them have grown up with the Bible and communal traditions of living its precepts, should we not know better than they did what constitutes sin? And should we too not then be moved to do acts of prophetic outrageousness so that God's demands will no longer be ignored? Something like that, I surmise, moved Fr. Berrigan and his colleagues to their acts of defiant but non-violent moral witness.

If I recall correctly, though a number of Jews joined the campaigns involving acts of civil disobedience, some going to jail for it, Jews were not attracted in notable numbers to religiously motivated acts of high ethical symbolism. In part that is because the Jerry Rubins and Abbie Hoffmans of that time were essentially secular in their orientation, believing that, at best, activist ethics was all that remained lasting in Jewish teaching. But Abraham Heschel identified just that modernist confidence in the self, its secure reliance on its own reason and conscience, as the root idolatry of our time. His works brim with his imaginative, learned, insightful efforts to make God the central reality of our lives. And his oft-commented upon inimitable literary style, one so uniquely inspiring that it still speaks evocatively to fresh readers today, is exquisitely suited to his goal of raising us out of our dogmatic secularity and opening us up to the reality of God and God's revelation.

Why, then, was so God-centered a teacher as Abraham Heschel not moved to perform acts of prophetic provocation? I think the answer we may presume to give to that question must grow from his unique understanding of the prophets and that, in turn, must be set within the greater context of traditional Judaism's attitude toward civic responsibility.

If Dr. Heschel's primary concern was to restore consciousness of the independent reality of God to modern Judaism, its immediate corollary was the restoration of the reality of revelation. In all the theories of modern Judaism that preceded Dr. Heschel's, human initiative had been substituted for God's action. Thus Hermann Cohen, Leo Baeck and Mordecai Kaplan, in their various fashions, substituted human discovery for God's input to humans. They stretched human reason as far as suggesting that some people are genuinely inspired, a humanistic notion that only substitutes surprise at the exceptional for the more mundane notions of human growth or evolution. Even Martin Buber, and similarly Franz Rosenzweig, who spoke of relationship with a real God, one not ourselves, though allowing for independent Divine input, made human beings so important a factor in the process that, from Dr. Heschel's point of view, both God's stature and the authority of what had been communicated were compromised. Already in his doctoral dissertation at the University of Berlin, later reworked as the 1936 book *Die Prophetie*, he had striven to explain the reality of prophecy in western intellectual terms. Specifically, he utilized phenomenological categories, to indicate the believability, perhaps even the truth, of the prophetic insistence that they spoke God's words for God and not out of their own genius. God had, in fact, revealed the Divine will to human kind. Revelation was as real as it had all along claimed to be and Dr. Heschel was the champion of its credibility.

Contrast this Heschelian neo-traditionalism with what prior modern Jewish theologians had made of revelation. For them, following the leadership of Cohen, the prophets were the heroes of eternal Judaism because they had the first clear insight into the mandatory nature of ethics and its universal reach. As Leo Baeck put it, the essence of Judaism is its universal ethics, one any rational human being might come to know but which was first given lasting historic power and social sweep by the Jewish people and its devotion to this humanizing idea. Prophetic Judaism, as many ideologues began to term it, was the Judaism of ethical dedication. From this notion stemmed the unparalleled participation of modern Jews in every movement for human betterment in which they were permitted to take a role. Even as they secularized, Jews disproportionately retained this commitment to ethics.

For modernized Jews, then, the prophets were still of interest as superb teachers of ethics, mostly because they went beyond face-to-face righteousness and spoke of what would constitute a society acceptable to God. In a day when democracy had made social policy a matter of every citizen's concern and when the vagaries of history kept raising new challenges and opportunities for humanizing our collective existence, prophetic Judaism was a vision of telling relevance. Of course, it could easily degenerate into mere exhortations to civility or an acceptable means for furthering the self interest of Jews in securing their status by hiding behind a concern with all minority rights. Nonetheless, no matter how great the evasions or mix of motives, ethics became the passion of the modernized Jewish community in a manner that still manifests itself today.

For Dr. Heschel that limited reading of the prophets reinforced the sin of modernity in replacing God with human reason and reducing the full scope of the Torah's commandments to doing good to one another. His two great systematic statements of the 1950's, *Man is Not Alone* and *God in Search of Man*, have almost no extended discussion of ethics, an unheard of reading of Jewish duty in those days. I said "almost" because there is a passage in *Man is Not Alone* which deals with the topic and it is entitled, "The Inadequacy of Ethics." There Dr. Heschel inveighs against the adequacy of the reigning Jewish understanding of ethical responsibility which spoke of it in the rationalistic neo-Kantian terms of Hermann Cohen. He finds this philosophic construal of ethics false to the realities of human existence and oblivious to the human proclivity to sin. I do not think that his reticence at discussing Jewish ethics in these works should be seen as anything more than his polemic against what he considers the current minimalization of what God requires of us. And it is to that broader vision of Jewish duty that he devotes himself and his message. Within it, he has no hesitation in speaking positively of the need to do what is ethical, even if all his mentions of it are tangential to his larger purpose.

It is only in his 1962 volume, *The Prophets*, that he allows himself a full scale statement of God's requirement of us to do good to others. It does not come in his treatment of the seven individual prophets he first devotes himself to. Only after establishing his understanding of the broad reach of their message, and particularly of the validity of their claims that this is in fact, God's message, does he move on to present a substantial thematic discussion of justice, both the justice of God and its implications for human action. Here, finally, does the full Heschelian devotion to what others call "ethics" manifest itself. "Amos and the prophets who followed him not only stressed the primacy of morality over sacrifice, but even proclaimed that the worth of worship, far from being absolute, is contingent upon moral living, and that when immorality prevails, worship is detestable." (p. 195) "The greater masterpiece still undone, still in the process of being created, is history. For accomplishing His grand design, God needs the help of man. Man is and has the instrument of God, which he may or may not use in consonance with the grand design. Life is clay, and righteousness the mold in which God wants history to be shaped . . . God needs mercy, righteousness; His needs cannot be satisfied in the temples, in space, but only in history, in time . . . Justice is not an ancient custom, a human convention, a value, but a transcendent demand, freighted with divine concern. It is not only a relationship between man and man, it is an *act* involving God, a divine need . . . It is not one of His ways, but in all His way*s.*" (p. 198) The temptation to go on citing him is great indeed and, summoning more strength than I can often muster, I resist it.

Of course Dr. Heschel was deeply, passionately devoted to what most other Jews, less theistically oriented and with much narrower horizons of Jewish duty, called "ethics." For both of them that involved feeling as much as it did mind, the mercy and compassion which the rabbis taught were primary characteristics of the Jew. And it involved a sense of commandment, in the Kantian language a categorical imperative, though Dr. Heschel insisted on acknowledging its transcendent source to be the word and will of God. Where they differed, and it was no small matter, was the issue of context. His predecessor modern thinkers believed that the ethical impulse set the bounds within which all Jewish duty was to be evaluated and in which our understanding of God was to be shaped. Dr. Heschel insisted that God's revelation to the prophets alone should determine what constitutes Jewish duty.

But now, having taken you this winding intellectual way, I can, I believe, state my explanation of his civilly obedient dedication to acts of righteousness. The Biblical prophets did their acts of spiritual provocation because God had told them to do so; they often complied reluctantly and grudgingly, doing what they sometimes considered thankless, impractical, and even personally repulsive acts, because they knew that was what God wanted them to do. Dr. Heschel believed that people in our time, Jew or non-Jew, might equally have so intense a relationship with God that they could hear the Divine behest to do something similar today. But because it did not happen to him, because God never called him to be a prophet, only, *nebbich,* a Jewish teacher, he did not do such acts himself.

And in that understanding, let me now much more briefly add, he was reflecting the vast bulk of Jewish teaching and experience in this area. Recall, please, that after the first century C. E., Jews increasingly lived as minorities in Diaspora communities. Though not always persecuted there, they were a people apart, social inferiors and thus, often, severely discriminated against. (The record is much darker in many places as the centuries became millennia.) Jewish law had to take this new embattled social posture into consideration and in early Talmudic times it did so through its doctrine of *dina demalkhuta dina*, the rule that, for Jews, the civil law of the state carries the authority of Torah law. One major qualification of this rule is relevant here, that it must be a just state and the criterion for this is whether in legal matters it treats Jews as it does all other citizens. Naturally, over the centuries and the diverse polities and economic orders in which Jews found themselves living, there were special interpretations of this principle. But it has remained relatively stable down to the present day. Jewish law demands respect for a reasonably just society and Jewish prudence, reinforced by a long history of exclusion and discrimination powerfully reinforces that attitude. As a result, over the fifteen hundred or so years that Jews have lived by *dina demalkhuta dina* we have only the rarest evidence that they have thought God commanded them to confront their governments and by their unconventional acts to pass judgment upon them.

Only in the last two centuries has the spread of democracy given the broad mass of people a say in who rules them and how they are to do so. It thus authorized, even encouraged, new forms of critique and action. As societies grudgingly opened themselves up to Jews and other outsiders, the possibility of Jewish action against the government became a significant reality. Characteristically, Jews in free societies have largely supported the political forces seeking to secure everyone's rights and expand their effective freedom — but most Jews have shied away from the radical groups who sought to do this by revolution. In the minority that leaned strongly to the left there were far more Jewish socialists than communists, though the latter certainly got more public attention. The American labor movement, in contrast to its European forebears, rejected becoming a political party and concentrated instead on working for the improvement of wages and working conditions, an ethos for which authorities deem its leader, Samuel Gompers largely responsible and who, others have suggested, had deep roots in the tradition of Jewish social prudence.

I am suggesting that Abraham Heschel's passionate ethical activism grew out of the twin strands of the revealed law reinforced by the lingering pains of Jewish experience. For Dr. Heschel, Moses is, as the Torah says, the greatest of the Jewish prophets and Jewish law is the heart of God's revelation. The *halakhah* commands with God's authority behind it even though its dialectical development is carried out through human initiative. When one reads his rhapsodic treatment of the holy deed as the place where God and humans meet, one needs to include *dina demalkhuta dina*. Surely that principle has special force for American Jews who live in a Diaspora equality unique in Jewish history and unparalleled anywhere in the world today. And, if I may now express my own sentiments, when one has seen German democracy authorize the murder of most of one's family and countless others, it is blasphemous, to suggest that, as was suggested in those days, that this country should now be called *Amerika,* and not honored as the one nation courageous enough to keep expanding its freedom to one pariah group after another. Dr. Heschel found ways to respond to what he knew was God's unceasing imperative to do something about injustice and he had a powerful effect then and now on American Jews as well as on many other citizens, believers and unbelievers alike. He was not called to be a prophet but few in our time have set a better example of what it means to be a caring Jew and a spiritual heir of the prophets.

3) *The Heschel Our Community Venerates*

Franz Rosenzweig once made a famous quip about the Jewish community's intellectual interests. He called attention to the fact that at the German university it was customary to have what was called "the academic quarter-hour." The students were required to wait in their seats for fifteen minutes for the professor to arrive. Only if the professor had not arrived by the end of that period were they free to leave. Rosenzweig commented that the Jewish community had something of a similar custom, an "academic quarter-century." It preferred to wait about twenty five years before it began to take any professor's ideas seriously. It therefore occurred to me that perhaps now, finally, we are ready to give proper attention to the thought of Abraham Joshua Heschel.

There are, however, two separate groups who have felt his impact and remain influenced by him. The first group is those of us who knew him personally and now fondly remember him. His immediate impact upon us was very much greater than the still quite extraordinary impact he has had on those who have come to know him as a figure of legend, of picture and, of course, of the extraordinary body of texts he left behind.

I am fortunate to be a member of that first group for he was my teacher at the Hebrew Union College in Cincinnati from 1942-5. I knew him in those days as the beardless European intellectual one sees getting older in the series of portraits of him that *Tikkun* magazine included in its recent symposium on his thought. The three years I spent as his student, not atypically, forged a bond between us that allowed us at all our later occasional meetings to pick up our relationship instantly and carry it forward. For that group, I only want to add my voice to what others who knew him longer and better have written. He was a great thinker, scholar, writer and doer. But above all he was a singularly memorable human being.

I do not mean by that to suggest that he was a saint. He had his faults and could be quite disturbing to his admirers. But like many others I cherish mostly the occasional walks we took and the talks we then had. Please consider it a measure of our regard for him that all of us now seek to pass on to a later generation the impact of his person on us, a task made all the more urgent to us since with the years it is not our tales or the tapes but the texts and, to some extent, the photos of him, that are the medium of his influence.

Therefore, the bulk of my remarks has to do with his impact on those who know him only through these media. I suggest that he continues to influence the bulk of our community in three ways: First, as stylist; second as phenomenologist of Jewish practice; and third as the prime exemplar of Jewish ethics in its universal outreach.

It is as the supreme stylist of Jewish spirituality that he still reaches most people. In part this is because of his phenomenal skill with language. Those who are competent to make such judgments say that he could write with equal facility in all of the many languages he commanded. And he applied this skill to a topic that was most unusual: spiritual reality and its truthfulness.

His first notable American publication, *The Earth is the Lords* appeared in 1950 and his most enduringly popular work, *The Sabbath*, appeared in its original and then its supplemented edition in the two successor years. That was a time when science reigned and positivism made it possible to spurn the synagogue. Yet Heschel, in those very days, wrote movingly, intelligently, appealingly of belief and practice.

He wrote with such cogency, that his style still has unique power. So I decided to do an experiment and choose a page at random from his *magnum opus, God in Search of Man.* I came up with these two paragraphs from his chapter on "The Sense of Mystery." Here is Heschel at random:

> We live on the fringe of reality and hardly know how to reach the core. What is our wisdom? What we take account of cannot be accounted for. We explore the ways of being but do not know what, why or wherefore being is. Neither the world nor our thinking or our anxiety about the world are accounted for. Sensations, ideas are forced upon us, coming we know not whence. Every sensation is anchored in mystery; every new thought is a signal we do not quite identify. We may succeed in solving many riddles; yet the mind itself remains a sphinx. The secret is at the core of the apparent; the known is but the obvious aspect of the unknown. No fact in the world is detached from universal context. Nothing here is final. The mystery is not only beyond and away from us. We are involved in it. It is our destiny and "the fate of the world depends upon the mystery."
>
> There are two kinds of ignorance. The one is "dull, unfeeling, barren," the result of indolence; the other is keen, penetrating, resplendent; the one leads to conceit and complacency, the other leads to humility. From the one we seek to escape, in the other the mind finds repose.

Here is Heschel, using evocation as the antidote to a failing rationalism. And it never failed him until his heart did.

Closely linked to this is the second aspect of his influence: as no one else among the thinkers in our community, he opened up for us the inner life of Jewish observance. Mostly, in those days, and sometimes, alas, today, we knew Jewish practice as the realm of rules and details, of the continual struggle of our leaders to keep a modernizing generation faithful to the demands of Jewish duty. Everything seemed external; at its best it merely reinforced our ethics. Heschel suddenly exposed us to the possibility that Jewish doing was a form of spiritual expression and development. Suddenly he made of our duties a service of the heart.

The extended essay on *The Sabbath* remains, nearly fifty years after it was written, the classic entre into his teaching. No less notable in their continuing relevancy are his two great papers on what it means to pray as a Jew. In the one he chides the Reform rabbis for their unconcern about *keva*, regularity, and in the other, he reproves the Conservative rabbis for inattention to *kavannah*, intention.

Here is another random example of his writing in *God in Search of Man*, this time from the chapter on "The Meaning of Observance:"

> What is a noble deed? A hungry soul on the rise. To some the act is fresh and precious, though its meaning is partly here, partly beyond the stars. To others it is like disposing of a burden, leaving a wake of regret and frustration. The test of *kavannah* is in the joy it calls forth, in the happiness it incurs. "Rejoice the soul of Thy servant, for unto Thee O Lord do I lift up my soul" (Ps. 86:4). He who knows how to lift up his soul above the pettiness of momentary meaning will indeed receive the blessing of joy.

> What we accomplish is infinitely humble, moving but an inch toward a distant goal. But what we attempt is noble: to lend a sacred aura to common deeds. What is a mitsvah? A deed in the form of a prayer. Jewish observance is a liturgy of deeds.

> It is a sacrilege to grieve when the task calls, and God is grateful in advance for the service we shall render unto Him. The fruition of a sacred deed is in the joy the soul reveals. The Psalmist (100:2) proclaims: "Serve Him with joy." His service and joy are one and the same.

> To meet a mitsvah is to discover His presence as it is meant for me, and in His presence is "fullness of joy." What is piety? "A song every day, a song every day."

Thus, against Spinoza and even Mendelssohn in his own way, Heschel is arguing that Judaism is not a legalism. It is a spiritual discipline for soul-making. And it has taken our community, as Rosenzweig guessed, twenty five years to catch up to this message.

Yet closely linked with this revitalization of Jewish spiritual life is his exemplification of Judaism as having a universal ethical outreach. The picture of him marching with Martin Luther King is as close as we come to having an American Jewish icon. We love that picture and identify with it. And we love the late pictures of him with the hair flying and beard extended. We may not have much use for the notion of Prophetic Judaism but in the elderly Heschel we have the prophetic figure we love.

In this stance, as Jewish civil rights notable, Heschel epitomizes the American Jewish community's image of itself as having in unique disproportion fulfilled our ideals at a critical moment in American history. For, in many ways, this remains the continuing touchstone of our judgment of true spirituality: does it know the problems of people and our planet generally? and does it seek to do something about them? In Heschel's day we did not yet call this *tikun olam*. He would more likely have understood this phrase in its Lurianic, kabbalistic sense. But in recent years it has come to be our shorthand for universalistic ethics and issues of civil rights remain its critical concern.

In our mind's eye we see Heschel as the scholar-pietist in action and one who is instantly identifiable as a Jew. He is us as we would, in another time, still like to see ourselves and our Jewishness. No other European or American Jewish thinker has had such an ongoing impact on the American Jewish community as has Abraham Joshua Heschel.

Yet there is a curious omission in this list of extraordinary accomplishments. Heschel was a serious, systematic thinker in his own fashion, yet, despite all the adulation, there are few Heschelian thinkers in the Jewish community today, disciples who follow the central line of his thought.

I had one day taken a class from the Hebrew Union College to visit with him at the Seminary. When class was over and we walked down Broadway he commented to me that he found it difficult to understand why people did not see his systematic development of his central thesis.

Let me now, briefly and most inadequately, try to describe this. The purpose of his evocative style and indeed of his phenomenological exposition of Jewish practice was to move people not only to a personal relationship with God but to the Bible as infinitely more God's communication than that of its human authors. And he insisted that the writings of the rabbis and the sages be given a similarly incomparable status. His is a near-Orthodox interpretation of revelation and though he found it desirable to qualify this position, he consistently rejected the more human centered theologies of Rosenzweig and Buber. Rather, he sought to make it unambiguous that the creative investment of the prophets was minimal in terms of what they received from the Divine. And it is that which our generation, for all its increasing love of God and Torah, has not been willing to accept. We will not follow Heschel in what was dearest to him, his teaching about the Torah and its uniquely sacred quality.

In two other significant respects, our community does not celebrate his ideals. The first of these is that he was, of course, as much involved in protesting the Vietnam War as he was in the civil rights movement, and perhaps more so. Here he emerges as the fearless critic of the United States government, though one who respected its laws enough that he did not transgress them and go to jail as others did.

The second is that he was passionately concerned about the fate of Soviet Jewry and identified himself publicly with a cause that was directly and particularly Jewish. In those days, if you were a Jewish activist, you were either against the Vietnam War or you were interested in fighting for Soviet Jewry. He was the one person in whom Judaism expressed itself both in the universal cause and in the particular one.

Neither of these stances is broadly popular in the Jewish community today. Even the thoughtful people in our community, the ones who are concerned about what the Torah can teach us about our relationships with humankind, are not sanguine about taking stances against the U. S, government and its failures. And many other Jews still have a certain hesitation about identifying themselves with causes which are too closely identified with the particular as against universal Jewish concerns.

In sum, the mythic Heschel our community now cherishes is, not surprisingly, the *rebbe* of centrist contemporary Jewish spirituality. He is the lover of God, the appreciator of Jewish acts and therefore the soul animated by universal ethical human concerns. We have made of him the *rebbe* we want these days and that is, as I see it, about all we want from Abraham Joshua Heschel.

Would our master himself be disturbed at this development? I think not. He knew very well the substantial gap between the *tzaddik* and his followers. Only a few can hope to stand close to where the *rebbe* reaches with his own spirituality. The followers, the *chasidim*, will have to make of him whatever they can and they will surely be benefited by that. Most important of all, they not only esteem their *rebbe*, they love him. And anybody who remembers Abraham Joshua Heschel well can testify, he would have loved that.

Chapter 27

℘◌ℭ

Arnold Jacob Wolf at Seventy

A rnold Jacob Wolf has been the finest English stylist in the American rabbinate for decades. Were he a writer of fiction — he once took a flyer at play-writing — or of impressionistic vignettes, as some other rabbis are, that would already be high praise. But Arnold's flashing style has been at the service of ideas, the abstractions we employ to give faith self-consciousness and politics its justifying substrate. In the diverse fields which have engaged him, as you will see, he has written with unique clarity, penetration, belief and sophistication. Disdaining the common academic turgidity and religious sentimentality, Arnold has abjured cant and evasion. His writing, as the midrash says of revelation, "smashes against the ear." Even in the stillness of reading him, one can hardly miss his uncommon quality as rabbi and person.

Yet the style, for all its virtues, is not the man nor its content the whole of his person or his rabbinate (though I doubt that the two are separate in him). His riches of person have decisively shaped his way of being a rabbi and, being a Jew to his utter depth, his Jewishness, focused in the rabbinate, has shaped his eventful life. His writings, then, exemplify the strange reality that revelation obscures, for in disclosing the unknown it points to how little one yet knows. Or is that only my paradox as I try to apply my perspective as his fifty-two year intimate to my friend's exemplary career?

Arnold came to rabbinical school as the scion of an extended German-American family proud of its long record of Jewish service and centered around the scholar-rabbi Felix Levy. He not only knew the Reform rabbinate from inside but identified serious Jewishness with an elitism of mind, heart and person. That quickly isolated him from the many then (and since) who were satisfied with lesser standards. His holism — the word was not yet current — also alienated him from those student mini-elites whose devoted Jewishness was simply social justice, or inter-faith relations, or Zionism. Undismayed, relishing the give and take of argument, congenitally provocative, Arnold prefigured in those student years his ongoing relations with his colleagues — and to some extent to the community as a whole.

Not the least of Arnold's early otherness came from his depth of faith. Almost every student thought something needed to be done to give Reform services new life (certain modern Jewish problems being unending) if only to make it "more Jewish." Nonetheless, most resigned themselves to the conventions, preferring passivity to the pains and perils of change. In truth, they were representative of that great mass of mid-century Jews whose mild agnosticism easily bracketed issues of faith and prayer so as to concentrate on the commanding calls of ethics and Jewish duty. Arnold, however, cared about making God manifest in life so he, with some few others, experimented as best they could with prayer and rite (all this long before "spirituality" became a generation's rallying cry). In the popular mind, this self-conscious faith changed him from mere peculiarity to threat, for he might flush out the agnostics' dirty little secret ambivalence toward religion.

Arnold balanced this elitism by an utterly uncommon respect for students and congregants. They, too, had something important to contribute to our ever-developing Reform Jewish practice. So he scorned teachers who just lectured or rabbis who acted as if they had all the worthwhile wisdom. Using the University of Chicago method of teaching by discussing, he confronted high school kids with Jewish sources or human situations and had them think things through among themselves, albeit with a leader's guidance. This led on to students creating their own services and, immediately following ordination (1948), helping develop the NFTY Camp Leadership Institutes model for member-directed youth groups. Later, the extraordinary creativity of Congregation Solel

— its member-written prayer book, the earliest synagogue Holocaust weekend commemoration, its rousing theo-political discussions — resulted from this continuing faith in what the people, with some guidance, could bring to Judaism. His was no self-serving elitism but the empowerment (another unknown term) of anyone willing to reach for high Jewish standards.

Looking back over these nearly five decades of Jewish service, it seems clear to me that early on Arnold was determined to give new meaning to that increasingly empty motto, "Prophetic Judaism." When Jews cared mainly about validating their participation as Jews in the general society, Prophetic Judaism largely meant stressing Judaism's universally human teaching, that is, explicating its ethic in a neo-Kantian mode. No wonder why many Jews found Ethical Culture — if they were humanists — or Unitarianism — if they sought the comfort or cover of the least unbearable church — preferable to Reform Judaism. Within the movement itself, as Arnold saw it, were their fellow reductionists, those who condensed Prophetic Judaism to social betterment or the imitation of upper-class Protestant church style. He considered their narrowness of focus a travesty of prophets who spoke only because God said they must and whose message was God's own. They addressed the Jews, almost always about their communal obligations and failures, seeking to make them better Jews, not just fine people-in-general. Intuitively, perhaps half-consciously, Arnold saw what was needed and set about living and articulating it. More important, he began challenging congregants, students, colleagues and the community with his radical message: they were not being true to their own avowed standard. Only a radical politics grounded on a rich Jewish piety and practice deserved being called "Prophetic Judaism" or, in fact, "Judaism."

Despite the constructive side to this critical stance, it carried a high social price. The prophet is necessarily an outsider, sometime more, as Amos and Jeremiah were, sometimes less, as is true of Isaiah and Haggai. The estrangement may vary but the prophet cannot become an insider and continue speaking from the Divine perspective, whether in condemnation or comfort.

Arnold, of course, never claimed to be a prophet, only — but what an "only!" — a rabbi. He has lived as an institutionalized Jew and not as one who disdains ordinary folk responsibilities while criticizing the community from its margins. He has given synagogues and a Hillel Foundation budget-and-program-conscious leadership, participated in rabbinic organizations and done his member's duty there and elsewhere. It sounds like an eccentric manner of renewing Prophetic Judaism until one remembers Martin Buber's teaching: the rabbis of the Talmud are the true successors of the prophets. We see that most clearly when they use their genius for routinization and democratization to sanctify the everyday. To be sure, as with all human enterprises, structure tends to become an end in itself, in the rabbis' case by sanctifying a bureaucratization which can suffocate the soul. Then the Jewish spirit must renew itself as it so amazingly always has. Arnold, it is now evident, has sought in our ever turbulent times to model Buber's rabbi, the one in whom the prophetic impulse lives within the community.

Perhaps no event in his near-half century of service epitomizes better the dialectics of the prophetic rabbinate than does his Presidency of Bereira in the mid-1970's. (Or was he only the national "Chair," as befit those heady, anti-hierarchical, anti-sexist days?) It was a time of widespread intolerance of some Jews by other Jews. The established organizations were solidly against any criticism of the State of Israel within the community and any such position directed toward the general public moved much of American Jewry to fury. Nonetheless, against the common wisdom that the Israelis had no choice but to refuse taking any first steps toward peace, a group of idealists — academics, rabbis, caring laypeople — said there was indeed a choice, a *bereira*. They publicly called for the establishment of a Palestinian State as the only long-range political solution to the Arab-Israeli conflict and the only Jewishly just alternative to incessant conflict.

Politics having a rare power to fire the soul, the community and a large proportion of individual Jews burned with indignation against Bereira and its supporters. B'nai Brith was pressured to fire Arnold from his post as Hillel Director at Yale and many a rabbinic colleague shunned him for years. All this and much more because of what by then might have been considered a most gentle kind of political action: founding an organization and issuing a statement. Some years later when Arnold was interviewed by the Pulpit Committee of KAM Isaiah Israel he told me of the following exchange: "Rabbi Wolf, you have a reputation for being controversial though you haven't said anything so far that is. Can you say something controversial?" Arnold then replied, "I believe in the establishment of a Palestinian State." To this his questioner responded, "Well, that's controversial" but left it at that. That is how recently the taint of a principled Jewish political stand clung to him — though we should immediately note, he got the job. Still, even in the early 1980's when most major American Jewish organizations were themselves publicly endorsing responsible Diaspora criticism of the State of Israel, people in the Jewish community still condemned him for his violation of what they had once considered an unalterable Jewish duty.

Arnold had not sought to head Bereira though he had long espoused a position similar to the one it took. He certainly did not seek its special pains, for Bereira fell apart after about one year, as much from internal dissension as from the implacable community campaign against it. Arnold bore the contumely with simple dignity but with an absolute refusal to renege on what he knew was his ethical, that is, his Jewish duty. And if he felt Jewish responsibility required him to dissent from an uncommonly united community but not to withdraw from the give and take of Jewish life, surely he was not the first worthy Jew to do so.

Anyone who has known Arnold for any length of time soon learns that what may seem provocative and self-serving behavior in others is Arnold's natural way of trying to respond — and get others to respond — to what he hears as a Sinaitic categorical imperative. He plays with kids and teases teen-agers in that same intense devotion; he once wrote funny skits and plays, and was no mean performer of them. His kind of prophetic rabbi knows one can only make demands when they are structured by love; and any love without demands demeans the lover as the beloved. It is a hard if mature Torah.

Two other paradigmatic acts remind us of his kind of contemplative devotion to the God of Israel. The first of these points to his theological pioneering. In 1965 Arnold put together *Rediscovering Judaism*, a collection of essays by the diverse adherents of a nascent theological movement later called Covenant Theology and its first major statement. Some of these ideas had already surfaced in articles by Reform and Conservative thinkers as well as at meetings of the Central Conference of American Rabbis. Arnold's book broke new ground not only in giving some dimension to the new thinking but in transcending all denominational divisions to show the pluralistic commonality of Judaism as it struggled for a new self-understanding. Most of its authors had been at one or another of the several small meetings of like-minded theological seekers at the UAHC Oconomowoc Camp Institute, a group Arnold helped inaugurate. (A few years later a larger group, this time under modern Orthodox auspices, met for several years in Canada, laying the groundwork for the present Hartman Institute in Israel.) *Rediscovering Judaism*, prefigured much of the theological development of subsequent decades. Subsequently, Arnold made his contributions through inimitably insightful and judgmental reviews and articles, no small achievement indeed since unlike the academics who came to dominate the field, he has had to focus on Jewish concerns other than the mind.

He made another contribution through a daring experiment in Jewish observance (for it, of course, is the twin of Jewish thought). In the 1970's Arnold decided to act on his mounting concern about the erosion of disciplined Jewish living, specifically about the fate of Jewish law, *halakhah*. He felt compelled to accept, that is, to live by its strictures, at least as defined by Conservative Judaism. He therefore joined the Conservative rabbis' association (while maintaining his membership in the CCAR). He enjoyed the Conservatives' Jewish style and pattern of observance but, his prophetic side quickly drove him to their margins. Wanting more change than they were ready for, he found himself among their halakhic left, and, those being the Bereira days, he was one of the small number of their radical political left. Among the CCAR colleagues, a number of whom were more sympathetic to his politics, the challenge of his life-style — that the Reform movement proclaim that Jewish observance involved far more than ethics — relegated him to the tiny Reform far right. He had too rich a Jewishness for either group but neither could easily ignore his presence as message.

Like all contemporary Jewish theologians, he still struggles with the fundamental non-Orthodox conundrum, how "objective" Jewish law can channel the free human spirit without violating it. Rosenzweig resolved the issue by simply positing the primacy of the law in this, the ultimate dialectic of the modern and the Jewish. Arnold sometimes sounds like he has his own version of that stand but that puzzle remains for him, as for most others, work in progress. One can do much worse than to stand with so noble a thinker as Rosenzweig pondering this mystery of Jewish faith.

When we were students fifty plus years ago, we dearly wanted to edit the student publication called (when we arrived) *The HUC Monthly* (and soon reduced to *The HUC Quarterly*). Three times we ran for that office and three times we lost. If memory may be trusted, the last time (or was it the last two times?) we lost by one vote. It hurt and, in some secret way, still does. No doubt our prophetic eagerness was so overlayed with elitism and ego as to bring about our colleagues' rejection of our leadership. But something else must be considered. Despite the mellowing effect of years and psychotherapy, the colleagues rightly do not trust Arnold (or me) to say the accepted thing and observe the conventions of safe rabbinic leadership. They worry lest he say one of those things that tear the cover from our religious compromises and force us to confront the duty we know we should do but evade. Yet for that very reason, many a colleague and congregant love and revere him as our generation's incomparable instance of the prophet become rabbi.

All this says much too little about Rabbi Arnold the person. No appreciation of style, of acumen, of stance can take the place of that extraordinary creation, the living Arnold Jacob Wolf. He has inimitably fulfilled this era's new commandment: to create oneself. Gloriously alive and involved, profligately scattering sparks of true being, he is that utter rarity, person and Jew as one and no less real in either aspect for being so much the other. No pages can properly describe that. But let it at least be noted that only in the enigma of human becoming can one meet Arnold's true greatness.

Chapter 28

ℰ⃝ℂℛ

John Hick: Advocate of Adjective-less Religion

L et me begin by expressing my thanks to Auburn Theological Seminary for the invitation to participate in this program. I do so with a double sense of special privilege. James Chapel reminds me of the very happy year and a half I spent as a graduate student at Union Theological Seminary, an experience which remains a living part of my life. And, of course, I am honored to share this platform with Professor John Hick from whose esteemed writings on the philosophy and nature of religion I have learned so much over the years.

The Talmud prescribes that when a Jew meets a sage of the Gentiles he is to pronounce a blessing: *Barukh atah Adonai, Elohenu melekh haolam, asher natan mechokhmato livasar vadam*, We bless you, Adonai our God, ruler of the universe, who has shared His wisdom with flesh and blood. Amen.

My remarks this morning proceed from a fundamental agreement with Prof Hick and that is on the ethical/political goals which can often be attained by a humanistic approach to religion. The religious pluralism which results from such an approach is so fruitful that I should like in every way I can to encourage those who work for it. But I feel so strongly about this because I am a Jew and the virtue of pluralism has been taught me by my tradition as refined by the experience of modernity, both its great suffering and the unique happiness we have had at being accepted as an equal partner in society. This statement already leads me into disagreement with Prof Hick for he has criticized such reasoning about pluralism as inclusivist. He sees it as perhaps a covert claim of absolute knowledge and he seeks to supplant this limited commitment to the truth of other religions with his theory of religion as such.

I am troubled by two closely related matter in this proposal. First, his system, as I see it, does exactly what he has chided others for doing. It prides itself on its comprehensiveness and does so by showing how all religions fit neatly into its purview. I shall argue that his view is itself another inclusivism, one which denies to any single religion the right to make the kind of judgments that issue from his theory of religion as such. Once again we have a disparity of discourse. He is too astute a student of religion, too humane a person, too appreciative of what he can see as the truths that historic religions contain, to do other than applaud our insight and celebrate our acting upon it. Nonetheless anything that a representative of an individual historic religion wishes to say about other religions is relativized and it is his system which is the normative one. But, second, reading and listening to his lecture I found myself confronted with an appeal to change my faith, to expand its vision from its historic-experiential base to the more cosmic one from which he speaks and to which he is devoted. I shall then question the bases on which he makes this appeal.

Normally when I find myself in a situation in which the discourse seems to me weighted to one side — that one of the partners speaks from a truth which relativizes the other person, me — I seek a quiet way to disengage from the conversation and leave. However, I have learned too much from Prof. Hick to allow so black-and-white a model of dialogue to dominate this encounter. Let me then at least explain the different basis upon which I can participate in this discussion. Prof Hick speaks as a philosopher in the universal tones so common to the Hellenic tradition as enriched by the experience of a continually shrinking world and the emergence of a global human community. I speak from a Jewish stance, one rather unusual in our community for I claim to be a Jewish theologian, a class with very few members indeed. Moreover, a good chunk of our community would happily agree with Prof Hick in his fundamental assertion that all religions are equal. But I am part of that other sector of the Jewish community which rejects that simple universalism but which believes that there is a truth given in Judaism which is foundational and enduring. This truth, for all the difficulty I and others have in trying to put it into the words of contemporary American English, is the truth through which I see and understand the world. And for all my appreciation of the truth to be found in other religions — something my tradition knows about — I do not believe that I ought to shift my paradigm for construing reality from the particular truth associated with Sinai to the universal truth taught by Prof Hick and other distinguished scholars of religion.

I shall now attempt a translation of my normal theological language which will allow me to speak to the philosophical issues here. The two themes I wish to address are: first, what I see as the privileged intellectual position implicit in Dr. Hick's presentation and, with some greater brevity, my questions about the normative authority he brings to our discussion.

My reflection suggests that there is a certain premise basic to Dr. Hick's stance that he has a perspective which goes far beyond that of the specific faiths and which they, on the basis of their own commitments, would do well to share. Negatively put, it is that nothing can accurately be said of the Ultimately Real — and with that neither traditional nor liberal Judaism would have any quarrel. He then, however, further suggests that he has what I shall call the least inadequate conception of the Ultimately Real. In the written text supplied to me in advance of this session, Prof. Hick acknowledged that this claim of least inadequate statement was something of a contradiction to his negative principle. (That is, if no one can give a fully adequate statement about the Real, how can you logically assert that what you say about it is the least inadequate of all other statements concerning it?) But he there further considered this a "logic triviality, with no consequence" and therefore passed on to other matters.

Even philosophically, however, this move is heavy with consequences. Specifically, it allows the person holding this position to speak with a certainty — limited, to be sure — that it denies to statements made on the basis of their revelation/experience by believers in the historic faiths. Prof. Hick is wise enough to add that his logic generates only "purely formal statements" about the religious order. Yet as he continues to speak to us we discover that he is not engaged in a purely formal logical exercise but that his thesis has made a quantum leap from its original algebraic orbit and now seeks to influence the real world. He is suggesting that we believers broaden our perspectives so as to make them fully comprehensive.

What philosophic procedure allows Prof. Hick to assert this claim to a uniquely significant perspective? I suggest it is something like the common Kantian procedure in which the rational mind rises to a transcendental intellectual level, one where one can gain cognitive insights unattainable to those whose attempts at rational understanding remain radically involved with the phenomenal level, the one on which the historic faiths find themselves. While Prof. Hick possesses a vast knowledge of the phenomenal reality of the world's religions, it is precisely his prescinding from this data, in a quite Kantian fashion, which allows him to reach his "transcendental" understanding with its superior rational wisdom.

Modern Judaism has had a long love affair with Immanuel Kant and therefore also a long tradition of philosophers who have urged universalization upon us for philosophic reasons, i. e., because Kantian reason was our best means of determining truth as the modern mind understood it. But it has seemed to many a modern Jewish thinker that if there are going to be such serious consequences from this Kantian position that we first require a sturdy defense of Kant. Ever since the period before World War 1, Kantian rationality as a self-confident understanding of the way in which any rational mind ought to proceed if it is to lay claims to sophisticated rationality has been under increasingly telling philosophical challenge. Surely, in the face of deconstructionist critics and the current emphasis on the particularity of all thinkers, the very least we require is a rational defense of a methodology for inter-faith discussion which may begin as a formal procedure but then soon turns out to have radical practical effects.

I suggest an alternative reading of our discussion. There is a philosophical movement called critical realism, one composed of those philosophers who ground their reasoning on the assertion that the human mind can gain rationally reliable knowledge about the real world. Among them there is a small group who include in this area of potentially true knowledge the realm of religion, more specifically, that aspect of it called religious experience. This group of thinkers has now given us several thoughtful volumes in which they present us with a new mythic structure about the reality which lies behind everything in a comprehensive, all-embracing way,. Some have called their vision of things a "world theology." But two things need to be noted about their proposal.

Philosophically, their argument rests on a non-rational stance, for their fellow rationalists, the philosophers, largely disagree that critical realism is rationalistically valid, and, in addition, even their fellow critical realists largely deny that reason can grant any significant substance to religious experience. Thus their view is essentially grounded in what a religionist would call faith. The sociology of this philosophized religion yields a picture of a leadership which is largely white, middle-class, academic, most often professors of religion, and a constituency of many in our Western civilization who would just like to be good people and, put off by the insidious institutionalization of the classic faiths, would like their religiosity to concentrate on just helping people to be good and survive trauma. Such a faith, however, should recognize itself as just another one of the historic faiths and, like many of them, one that inclusively claimed, on the basis of its faith, that it could understand the other faiths better than they understand themselves. But my tongue has been in my cheek long enough, and I turn, more briefly, to my second concern.

I question the grounds of Prof Hick's normativity, a stance I detect because it seemed to me that he was trying by his presentation to get me to want to modify my faith substantially. I wish to respond to this in three different ways, by looking at his evidence for unity, and then his definition of religion's purpose, and finally, the practical result of this change of view he espouses.

Prof Hick suggested that several items might be taken as indications of the transcendental unity of all religions, the Golden Rule and the lives of saints being the most notable, though the ideals of King Ashoka also were adduced. Permit me a word about Hillel's formulation of the Golden Rule in Judaism. I know of no teacher in the whole history of Judaism who has ever made it a significant practical statement about our religion. The context of the story is the rabbinic tradition in which learning is considered a primary religious activity and knowledge a major means of developing an effective relationship with God. This gives the tale in which the rule is found its particular charm. Judaism would not have developed the devotion to intellect which still characterizes most Jews, despite their intense secularization, if Hillel's dictum had ever been taken with reasonable literalness and given a major place in Jewish teaching. Of course, it has had a place in Jewish teaching as another of those marvelous evocative teachings we call *aggadah*, lore, which seek to uplift the spirit and motivate us ethically. Thus, I suggest that we cannot know whether what on the surface looks like similar meanings of statements in the world religions would remain so similar when we take them in their specific context. And I do not know of any serious study of this or any other alleged theme demonstrating the unity of the world's religions which has ever been subjected to such scrutiny — but this may only testify to my lack of knowledge.

Something similar may be said about the argument from the saints. I must ask that we first eliminate the modern ones from our discussion since they are all cases of people who, as a result of their experience of a shrinking world, have begun to integrate a sense of greater unity into their faith. When we turn to the premodern ones, however, there is little doubt in my mind that while they might speak grandly of the unity of reality they did so as inclusivists. They spoke out of their specific tradition and saw in it an exalting vision of the unity of all things. I know of no study of the saints which indicates that in any significant way they believed they had risen beyond their spiritual traditions and their teachings to a new understanding of religion that, in one way or another, would on this point, supersede their faith. It will not do to read into their narrower purviews the transcendental vision of religion as beyond all its specific embodiments though necessarily practiced by most people in such forms. Again, if there is a contextual study of the historic saints that proves Prof Hick's point, I do not know of it.

As reported to us, I find King Ashoka's words highly appealing to my Jewish soul. But my modern mind instantly reminds me of all the contemporary reasons to live by the Biblical injunction not to put one's faith in princes. One need not be even a distant Marxist but only someone who has been sandbagged by 20th century history to know that when rulers talk religion they really mean politics and that means power.

I turn now to the second of Prof Hick's evidences for the unity of all religions, their common purpose, which he identifies as a rough salvific parity among them. Perhaps this is perfectly plain to those professors of religion who understand their expertise to be not just what, to use the Christian term, "religions" are, but in that which designates them a class worthy of having a special university discipline devoted to them. However, as I follow the debates in the Journal of the American Academy of Religion that is a matter of considerable debate not only in the guild but on campuses more broadly. Surely, on the surface it is difficult to see that Moses, Buddha, Jesus and Mohammed were really talking about the same thing, even in central effect — and if we dare add Confucius, a disputed question indeed — the matter becomes even more complicated.

But let me conclude with a different query. Prof Hick suggests that all religions are salvific but he specifically denies that he wants to go out and start a new world religion with his view. I ask, "Why not?" Practical issues aside, should statements which claim to give us a more comprehensive sense of religion than those we have had heretofore not do what all religion is supposed to do, be salvific? Is Prof Hick's statement about religion salvific? If so, then why does he suggest his view is merely explanatory and not one which should be taken into action? But if, as more likely seems to be the case, his view is not salvific, then by his own standards is it really a significant statement about religion?

I began by indicating my political/ethical agreement with Prof Hick about the need for religious pluralism in our world. For me, religious liberalism is a far more satisfactory way, religiously and intellectually, to go about achieving this. We religious liberals include a certain humility in the spirituality which structures our lives. It acknowledges that such revelation as we know does not substantially overcome the limitations of human nature and relieve us of the necessity to be partners with God in working out the realities of Divine service in all its forms. But that means that we must allow for others both within and without our circles of faith to conceivably have access to a truth we do not know. Pluralism is central to such a religiosity and not an afterthought. But so is particularism, for we also know that just this tradition, with all its limitations and unanswered questions, is the finest truth we know. So our lives are grounded by it and by the specific community which carries it through history and itself is a major factor in working out its present version of its ongoing truth.

In my case this means that I share the Torah's teaching that God has a covenant with all humankind, a tradition which our teachers through the ages have continually reaffirmed. I therefore do not find it difficult to see and to find real religious truth in many places and thus many true religions in the word. But I know this, I believe this, because I am a Jew. Were I convinced that this were but a relative truth, a nice Semitic story and fine Jewish teaching, but not something which in its specific contours has trans-cultural and trans-personal truth, would I be willing to give my life to it? I doubt it. But, as it is, I take this teaching as God given if humanly shaped and I therefore know myself required to live up to it. May God grant that I am regularly able to do so.

Chapter 29

ଐଔ

Frans Jozef van Beeck, Advocate for Roman Catholicism

1) Foreword: **Loving the Torah More than God**

This book fascinates, inspires and challenges all at once. It can be read as an entrancing excavation of the fruitful misreadings which go to make up a tradition, whether Jewish, Christian or Judeo-Christian. It is also a theological rumination which is learned and incisive, yet deeply moving; we do not often see an erudite thinker responding in openness to a searching critic of his religion by seeking to untangle the authentic from the misguided in his received doctrine. Moreover, centuries of unhappy exchanges between protagonists of Christianity and Judaism have, even in the advent of civility, rarely produced a document such as this in which admirable self-respect is equally respect for others. And it breaks new ground in inter-faith discussion by suggesting, in a most irenic, gentle but compelling fashion that it is time to move to the most difficult question, what Jews might consider learning from Christianity.

All this arises by way of a story and a commentary on a commentary of a translation of a translation of the original! The immediate focus of the author's theological reflection is Emanuel Levinas's radio lecture based on the French version of the Yiddish rendering of Zvi Kolitz's

English tale, "Yossel Rakover's Appeal to God." Thus, this intellectual feast begins with a fiction about fact, a story about a believing Jew's last statement as he awaits death from the Nazis finally ending the rebellion in the Warsaw Ghetto. The moment was rendered with such verisimilitude that the fiction came to be accepted as a historic document when submitted as such to a Yiddish journal by an Argentinian Jew, its apparent translator. And, it should be added, that it was widely accepted as such long after Kolitz called attention to its origins.

This data is important because the title of this work, *Loving the Torah More than God*, derives not merely from Levinas's own original title but from a theme in the Yiddish translation, one that is not found in Kolitz's English story. We can, I think, learn a good deal about modern Judaism, better, about the efforts to modernize Judaism, if we attend to what each of these authors has sought to convey.

Kolitz's Yossel is a Gerer Hasid, a member of one of the most observant and pietistic of contemporary Jewish groups. His words rehearse traditional Jewish beliefs about God's justice, or apparent lack of it, about human suffering and dignity, and about the character and destiny of the Jewish people. Yet Yossel is also surprisingly modern for a Hasid. He writes in a thoroughly westernized fashion, with almost self-conscious attention to good style and apt language. Coming from a community which normally approaches these topics by *midrash* or tale, he is remarkably abstract and reflective about his beliefs. Most significantly, however, he is a political activist, a rebel who takes up arms against his people's oppressors. Should an occasional Hasid argue with God, we would not be surprised; Levi Yitzchak of Berditchev set the model for such post-Job-ian daring. But it is quite another thing to suggest that a devout pietist would forsake the quietism of his movement to take up arms, even against the Nazis. Thus today in the State of Israel, most dedicated Hasidim do not, as a matter of principle, serve in the armed forces.

Our intellectual journey therefore begins with Kolitz's inspiring creation, a figure in whom he integrates the profundities of classic Jewish piety and modernity's passion for dignity as self-assertion, particularly against evil. Surely a major reason this fiction was later so widely accepted as fact is that Kolitz reflected here what many Jews would like Judaism to be, richly traditional yet fully modern.

The anonymous Yiddish translator gave Yossel a radically different point of view. After line 255 of the original he interpolated these two striking sentences: "I love Him, but I love His Torah more, and even if I had deceived myself in His regard, I would nonetheless observe His Torah. God means religion, but His Torah means a way of life, and the more we die for such a way of life, the more immortal it becomes." Read quickly, these words simply slip into Yossel's diction. He is, after all, an observant Jew. But on reflection something very much more is at stake, indeed something that utterly transforms Kolitz's already recreated Gerer Hasid.

The anonymous translator is almost certainly a Yiddishist and the provenance he chose for his "translation" was the great Yiddishist literary journal functioning after the Holocaust, *Die Goldene Kait*, The Golden Thread. In the spirit of Yiddishist secularity he has by his interpolation made the erstwhile pietist Yossel the spokesman of his ideology. All this goes back to the late 19th century when several modernizing Jewish movements took it for granted that sophisticated moderns could no longer believe in religion; it was the Jewish version of what a later generation would call the "death of God." Unlike the Zionists who secularized into nationalism and, in due course into Hebraism, the Yiddishists believed, following the European model, that nationality could exist through language and high culture alone. Since the common Jewish language of the mass of European Jews was Yiddish and not Hebrew, they sought to make it the language of modern Jewish expression and continuity. By "Torah" they meant a Yiddishist cultural "way of life," one whose immortality is found in achievement in this world, not in any supernatural promise. A Hasid could not easily love the Torah more than God, being commanded by it, as he knew by his several daily recitations, "to love the Lord, your God, with all your heart, with all your soul, and with all your might." But a secular Yiddishist would gladly give up the old piety, which many Yiddish writers had attacked, for a life of high humanistic Yiddish culture. Isaac Bashevis Singer remains the great exemplar of this fading possibility — and though he still writes in Yiddish, almost all Jews today read him in English.

This interpolation was, in fact, intensified in the French translation so that it now read "but I love his Torah *even* more." (Was this because it was to be published in a French Zionist journal? or French rationalism asserting itself?) Delightfully, it was precisely this intensified interpolation that caught Levinas's' eye and became the pivot of his lecture. Only he comes to these words not as a cultural secularist but as a deeply religious philosopher. For Levinas these sentences reflected his modernistic reinterpretation of "Torah," one derived from his predecessors in modern Jewish rationalism though given his unique phenomenological grounding. Essentially, he understands "Torah" and the Jewish "way of life" that it enjoins as ethics. Like Hermann Cohen, the great neo-Kantian who first fully gave this theme academic exposition, God is the foundation of our moral striving, the critical effort in which we find the fulfillment of our humanhood. He can, then, speak of loving Torah "even more" than loving God because, in the line of neo-Kantian rationalism now become phenomenology, the ethical is more certain than the theological and religious truth logically builds from its base.

Levinas also takes up and continues in his own telling fashion the neo-Kantian Jewish polemic against Christianity. Its teaching is insufficiently ethical, a failing that arises from the nature of its belief which is blind to the centrality of the good deed. After the Holocaust and what Jews perceive to be the gross display of all the old inadequacies of Christianity in their non-response to it, the old attack comes with a telling bite. And let me add, that though most Jews today do not share, even in some popularized fashion, the neo-Kantian or phenomenological framework that gives rise to this committed Jewish ethicism, they largely agree with its basic thrust. Judaism, they will say, is essentially ethical action and that makes it superior to Christianity which centers on gaining and exemplifying a saving faith. So Levinas had little difficulty in picking up the Yiddishist call to make high culture primary and reading into it his own message, that the (Jewish) ethical act is more significant than (Christian) faith in God.

And now to this steady procession of misreadings Jewish tradition calls the "chain of tradition," I have taken the liberty of adding my own. In exempting the author of this work from that list I mean to compliment him for the high academic and human standard of his own reading of these documents. Exercising exemplary discipline he is as careful as one can be to try to read what he sees before him, indeed carefully comparing versions and texts so that redaction criticism will help him clarify just what it is that he is commenting about. In the long ugly history of interfaith exchange we have not often seen such a meticulous effort to understand "the other," his heart as well as his mind. Of course, it is one of the author's primary points that for a believing Christian, Jews ought not be simple religious "others" but part of the family of one's faith, though not in its immediate core.

This careful reading has led the author back to his own belief to see if there is substance to Levinas' charges, whose ethical standard of judgment he accepts as applicable to Christianity. His measured, sensitive evaluation of where he finds some of its historic developments have not been true to its sublime truth and his careful, deeply felt exposition of what he understands that truth to be as it applies here, made me not only a deeply respectful but also admiring reader. None of us finds it easy in the face of cogent criticism to obey the moral imperative to transcend defensiveness and learn what we can. It is a particularly precious ideal for the leaders and teachers of all religious traditions since they properly stake their lives and eternal destiny on the truths they proclaim.

I shall look forward to seeing how other Catholic writers and Christians generally respond to the author's interpretation of Christianity. But I do not wish to conclude these remarks without calling attention to what I find to be the climax of this extraordinary work. In his last pages, having opened his heart to Judaism's wounded cries to Christianity, having searched his soul to ascertain where the Jewish indictment might have merit, having then restated what he takes to be authentic Christianity, he most gently wonders if Jews might not be able now to do something somewhat similar, to see what they can make of Christian truth. His suggestion grows from the logic of his argument for if, as his Christian faith affirms, Jesus is a fulfillment of classic Jewish faith (though not thereby an invalidation of it), might there not be something Jews could learn about their own belief from Christianity? These soft sentences say a lot about the relationship between believing Jews and Christians that the author now hopes is possible. Beyond treating each other with dignity and acknowledging all we have in common, beyond being able civilly to discuss our past hurts and present differences, the author is ready to move on to the level of mutual challenge. He accepts that of Judaism and responds to it with nobility — and then in all self-respect and in equal respect for the maturity of Jewish thinkers, quietly inquires if they might be ready to do the same.

I welcome his loving queries though this is not the place to respond to them. They reminded me of an address I gave in Chicago, the city of Loyola University, to the 1966 convention of the Religious Education Association. Though that body had for years been one of the few places where Catholics, Protestants and Jews met together to discuss and work on matters of mutual interest, this assembly had a special air of excitement about it. The Protestant community was heady with talk of ecumenicism. The Catholics were present in unprecedented numbers and good will under the impact of Vatican II. And we perennial outsiders, the Jews, were astounded at the prospects for a new openness and mutuality among the faiths of the American religious community. I was invited to speak as part of a three-faith plenary session on the general theme of the ecumenical spirit. What I said was that we should not truly exemplify it until we had gone beyond good-will and deeper understanding to the point where we could argue our differences with love, in what I then called I-thou polemics. It has been a long wait to see if that hope could be fulfilled on either side. In this book, it has.

2) *The Holocaust and Meaning: Two Letters*

(When the eminent Catholic theologian Frans Jozef van Beeck sent me an advance copy of his sermon on the Holocaust entitled "Two Kind Jewish Men" — later published in Cross Currents, *Summer 1992 — I wrote him a letter which prompted a response from him and a further letter from me. While not originally intended for publication these letters later appeared in* Cross Currents, *Fall 1992.)*

March 25, 1992

Dear Joep,

I was most touched by your naming me as one of the persons to whom you dedicate your sermon — and with such gracious words! I am more than ever in your debt. That aside, I found reading the sermon an important emotional, even spiritual experience — exactly what I would want a sermon of mine to do. Yet its concluding sections left me uneasy, so I shall try to explain to you — perhaps to myself -why that is the case.

I begin with an experience. Some years ago Stanley Hauerwas sent me a sermon he had preached at the Rockefeller Chapel at the University of Chicago. He did so at the urging of Jewish friends. His point, most sensitively and compassionately made, was that as Christians increasingly come to understand and acknowledge in act as well as word, the Christian complicity in Western civilization's antisemitism, perhaps the time had come for Jews to begin forgiving Christians for their role in making the Holocaust possible. He had sent it as a submission to *Sh'ma, a journal of Jewish responsibility.* Since I consider the teeny journal an American (not Israeli) Jewish community forum for discussion, I have not invited Christians or others to publish in its pages. But the quality of Hauerwas's statement was so high, the issue so real, the "rule" so artificial, that I quickly accepted and published it.

Nothing in the twenty-two-year experience of publishing the journal has produced a greater response — not even articles attacking the state of Israel or even denying that it had a necessary right to continue in existence. Nothing has even come close to that deluge — by our standard — of mail. All of it utterly rejecting the possibility of this generation's assuming the right to grant forgiveness to anyone for the Holocaust — and the variations on that theme went in many directions, hardly any of them in the direction of mitigating that negative stand.

Perhaps things are gomewhat different now a decade or so later, but if we are talking about seriously caring Jews I think the most that I would expect from them in seeking some commonality with Christians through the Holocaust is silence. They may not be as assertive in their negation as they were then, but I do not expect them to be able to do very much more than be quietly pained and sad. Perhaps I am wrong.

In one respect, however, I think you will find some among us who will agree with you that radical overstatement about the Holocaust, using it to browbeat others or to claim Jewish special righteousness is a desecration of the victims and a simple sin in its own right. I think many of us would see this as a matter of our flawed human nature, the sinful psychic mechanism whereby we turn the sacred into the profane. We see this in all religions and all worthy causes, so it seems not to teach us anything special about the Holocaust or our relationship to it. Such people seem to be too small and insignificant a target for so noble a sermon as yours.

But what shall we do about such admirable human beings as Elie Wiesel and Emil Fackenheim who assert the qualitative uniqueness of the evil of the Holocaust? They hardly fit the portrait of the people you describe, yet it is they and other quiet, saintly persons like them who are the respected protagonists of this view among us. I do not know whether they have ever said that those with special standing in a religious community should have a higher standard of virtue applied to them than ordinary people — though all of us are sinners — but it has been a classic Jewish teaching for centuries. Some of that rests upon every Jew simply by being in the Covenant — their actions affect God's own "status" among people generally, their sins cast a blemish on God. Rabbis and scholars, even significant lay leaders, carry even more responsibility. It seems simple reasoning to most Jews that those invested with greater religious dignity should behave better than the rest of us. Ordinary virtue should not, by Jewish standards, entitle one to extraordinary stature.

I now see that it can come across as extraordinarily offensive for someone to assert to a Christian that another sin could be more historically, even cosmically significant, then the unjust, cruel death meted out to Jesus. It sounds remarkably like arrant blasphemy. But I surmise that the premise of this judgment is that the awful acts were done to the Son, to God, and thus were more directly sinful than any other act could be. For those who do not share a trinitarian faith, the evil has "only" human dimension. And, to risk an effort at comparative evil, one man, as versus millions; one day, as versus years; an act done by pagans, as versus one done by a Western civilization (the abettors as well as the perpetrators) fully and self-consciously informed by religion and culture. But I may have said too much already.

What I think will be most troubling to your Jewish readers-hearers will be the implication of your statement that "The Shoa is simply too appalling and painful an event for anyone to have a right to claim to be right about it." Perhaps I misunderstand your first reference to having "a right to claim to be. . . ." If all you mean is that none of us can claim we have some special basis for ensuring how to judge this "event" and to do so correctly, I think that point almost goes without saying — except perhaps to the psychically troubled I mentioned above. What it sounds like you are also saying and here your emphasis on maturity equaling compassion and mercy but not justice conveys this impression — is that we do not have a right to make a judgment about the Holocaust and consider ourselves right about it. It sounds as if interhuman solidarity should overcome the utter sinfulness that confronts us here. Note, please, that I am not denying the humanity or the God-relatedness of the sinner. How could I even call him a sinner if he did not still remain God's child and thus even in this wretchedness have some claim upon me? But as you put it, the qualitative, cosmic gap between the death-camp operators and their Jewish and other victim has been somewhat closed. And I do not believe most caring Jews can accept that. Indeed, I believe the recognition of this reality overcame the modem Jewish preference for universal tolerance — its relativism — and has led to our current minority spiritualism.

But I am now off on my revisionist view of the Holocaust and our relation to it. Permit me to ask you to take a look at p. 42 of my recent book [*Renewing the Covenant: a Theology for the Postmodern Jew*] which

I am putting in the mail to you. (Indeed the whole chapter may be of interest to you in relation to your sermon.) As I see it, it is the Holocaust which restored to many modern Jews a recognition of the limits of relativism and thus of the way back to absoluteness and, finally, God. If I am right, this is the opposite of the direction you ask us to take. And this, I make bold to my, is our way of reasserting today our classic Jewish understanding of what is ultimate in the universe.

I look forward to worshiping with you in Princeton.

Gene

June 23, 1992

Dear Joep,

I am sorry indeed that an unusually hectic schedule has prevented my responding sooner to your heartfelt, heart-seeking letter. Once again I am uplifted by your friendship and instructed by your faith.

There is much in what you say that I agree with. Were that not the case I guess we could not move on together to the subtle but significant difference between us over the balancing of our values, mercy/compassion and "responsibility" (as you put it); "justice" (as I did).

Perhaps I can best clarify the issue as I see it and avoid the traps of "distant rage" or "high theory" by bringing our discussion closer to home and as near as our television sets by discussing the case of Rodney King and applying your position to his case. Perhaps no one should assume to have the one right understanding of what the police officers did to him. But aside from the jury, some of their neighbors, and a silent number of other Americans, the matter of rectitude seems fairly clear. Worse, the incident testifies not only to a sin that some men committed one night but to one which infects our white society generally.

To be sure, that does not justify a response of "rage" or "violence" and that sinfulness likewise needs to be judged and opposed. But the explosive response to the innocent verdict seems to me far different from the "explosive" responses of the police to Rodney King's actions. For all its criminality, the riot forced us to look at what our society has not done for the inner city and its residents. And the kind of hesitant, paltry response that has been made to this problem indicates how unwilling we are as a people to try to overcome, as best we can, this evil. Yes, 'the poor will always be with you" and ultimate justice is beyond us — but is this all the redemptive action we owe our suffering human kin?

I assume I have thus far said nothing you do not already know and agree with. Yet in the balance of your message you seem mostly worried about our turning Rodney King and his fellows into a "cause" and mostly you commend our trying to turn this into a "human fact" which then can be "suffered in neighborliness." To be sure, you ask the offending community itself first to practice conversion (though you imply that the victim's "kindness enables" it). I do recall a considerable number of white people who went into the destroyed areas and volunteered to help clean it up and there were other such acts which spoke of clean hearts. But I do not see that there has been much conversion in Orange County or the United States. Thus it seems to me prematurely eschatological to suggest to Rodney King and other victims of American racism that we find our spiritual strength and our present human path primarily in "an embrace that calls for universal reconciliation and kindness, not discrimination," leaving it utterly to God to distinguish between the sheep and the goats.

You will, I know, be able to see where my argument leads as applied to the Jewish response to the Holocaust. Suffice it to say that while I, unlike Wiesel and Fackenheim, have rejected the notion of the qualitative uniqueness of that horror, I also find myself overwhelmed by what a "civilized" government did in murdering 6,000,000 Rodney Kings and countless others, not to mention the many utterly traumatized even in "survival." And while I know some Christians to whom I would entrust my grandchildren (if the decision were mine) should such a thing ever overwhelm us here, I see no general conversion on the part of Western civilization and considerable ambivalence on the matter among its religions. Until the Messiah arrives fully manifest among us I must not speak of the virtue of suffering without doing all I can to alleviate it, nor of compassion and mercy without an equal emphasis on the imperative of pursuing justice.

May God's dominion speedily become real among us.

Gene

Chapter 30

ഇഏ

Masao Abe, Advocate for Zen Buddhism

1) Buddhism and Judaism, Some Further Considerations

Prof. Abe has so usefully clarified the broad distinctions between his Buddhism and my Judaism that I can limit my continuation of our discussion to some refinement of the similarities and differences between our religious intuitions. I shall do so around three foci of interest to which I shall append a fourth matter.

I begin by commenting on some things that believing Jews should find stimulating in Prof. Abe's view of dynamic Sunyata. His steady concern to see life and reality, particularly socio-historic occurrences, from the ultimate perspective can prod us to inquire whether many of the everyday matters we invest with great religious seriousness properly merit such attention. Writing as I am immediately after the High Holy Days with their great emphasis on God's transcendence, the religious call to see things *sub specie aeternitatis* sounds quite familiar yet fresh.

To some extent this also applies to his discussion of the great death, that of the ego. Particularly after the modern aggrandizement of the human partner in the relationship with God, religion has sometimes tended to become little more than self-assertion, occasionally even self-serving.

When the self threatens to become an idol or significantly to assert equality with God, then it needs to be broken of its pretensions. A number of things in Jewish practice — like the custom of some of the pious to wear their shrouds to services for the Day of Atonement — make this an ongoing experience for us.

Moreover, his emphasis on dependent co-origination and collective karma might well expand the horizon of the Jewish sense of one humanity and of its universal responsibility to God. Believing as we do in a common human nature for Jews and gentiles, the problems of the "urge-to-do-evil" and our consequent sinning remain the same for all who stand this side of Eden. We are all necessarily involved in a common web of weal — which modern Jews have mostly emphasized — and woe.

What most fundamentally divides Buddhists and Jews is their understandings/experiences of the relationship between ethics and religion, between the historical and the transcendent. A semantic observation may offer some additional insight into Judaism's stand on this matter. The notions of "ethics" and "religion" are foreign to Judaism and have no reasonably close terminological equivalents in classic, i.e., biblical-rabbinic, literature. There are, of course, deeds Jews should do in the service of God but these do not properly divide in claim or significance into what one must do in relation to people as distinct from duties directly to God. Rather, the supposed two levels substantially interrelate so that Jewish misbehavior toward Jew or non-Jew not only can constitute a sin in itself but the additional one of *hillul Hashem*, the profanation of God's name among people. Thus, the thought that duties toward people and toward God are on qualitatively different levels is foreign to Jewish thought until late Jewish mysticism and is one reason scholars have seen this period as influenced by a reemergence of Gnosticism.

Speaking of his Buddhism, Prof. Abe clearly indicates how, though there is a clear distinction between the qualitative significance of the realm of insight from that of ethics, the two may not be separated and thus true Buddhist understanding will always result in significant ethical devotion. As in the Christianity which emphasizes faith over works (though not wanting to separate grace from law) this treatment of ethics does not seem to me and other Jewish thinkers to give it sufficient weight. It is difficult to explain why we feel this way because it is a matter of religious "tone" and its effect on duty. That which is not finally critical may, of course, still have direct though derivative urgency behind it and thus surely be important. But its consequences are nonetheless substantially limited as compared to the effects of placing an ultimate imperative quality behind it as, for example, Buddhism does with the value of overcoming *avidya*. So to speak, the best Buddhists devote themselves mainly to attaining insight (while also practicing ethics), while the best Jews devote themselves mainly to doing acts that God has willed; and their respective literatures would seem to display precisely this difference in emphasis. From the Jewish religious perspective God far more wants our doing than our understanding. (See below further on this matter.)

Then too, the sharp distinction Prof. Abe draws between the historic and the transcendent realms has only a highly limited resonance in rabbinic Judaism. We just do not know very much about God as God knows God's own self and we do not generally find that a disabling agnosticism. Classically, what Jews know about God is what God has revealed to us about God and that, whether in the Written or Oral Torah, is almost entirely about what God "wants" us to do, not what God is or what God's transcendence means or consists of. And what God wants us to do concerns this world and its utterly contingent history; the one God of the universe is that involved in human affairs. And there is almost no sense in Judaism that this concern with history in any way impinges on what we intuit to be God's simultaneous utter dominion over all being.

Prof. Abe's delightful Buddhist *midrash* on "no man can see My face and live" is that one must first die to one's selfhood and then one *will* see "God." Jews generally understand the text to mean quite simply — so it seems to us — that, for all that there is revelation (certainly to Moses!), there is an ultimate, qualitative gap between God as God is and God as people may know about God.

This brings me to the new insight I gained from Prof. Abe's response, one that gives me deeper insight into the difference between the Buddhist and Jewish intuitions of ultimate reality and which underlies our division over the relationship of ethics to religion. Permit me to take two steps to try to clarify this. On the first level, it would appear that Buddhist religiosity is far more philosophical than is Jewish spirituality. Again and again Prof. Abe confronts Profs. Moltmann, Cobb and Ogden (in the section prior to the response to me) and like-minded Jewish thinkers with what he sees as the unhappy *logical* consequences of our religious position. Thus he wants to know "how we should understand" — that is, in some logical, coherent fashion — the relationship between the historical/ethical and the universal religious dimension of human existence. His problem is precisely rational for, as he understands the realms, they are "essentially or qualitatively different from one another." The climax of this argument is that ethics as such must be overcome "because when carried out as far as possible, ethical life falls into a dilemma and finally collapses." It inevitably results in a "dilemma" — illustrated by Paul's famous lament on sin — and this logically requires, in a Buddhist sense,: the 'death' of ethics"; he later calls this "conflict" a "hopeless dilemma," an outcome so unhappy that it creates the imperative, "Only through . . ." What concerns me here, I reiterate, is not the substance of the discussion — though I shall say a word about that later — but the form in which it is cast: reason requiring us to understand ultimate reality in its terms. And one can see this again in his argument against treating Buddha and nirvana as transcendence or in any way as substantialized or reified. Since this permits distinctions in them, it "must be overcome," as must even the nonsubstantiality and emptiness of Buddha and nirvana, logic having this much sway in his Buddhism. On this level, it would appear that Buddhism allows human reason a very much greater role than traditional Judaism allows it in determining the nature and direction of our religiosity.

But on a still deeper level this conclusion must be wrong. As Prof. Abe made clear in his original statement, Buddhism has had a long history of distrust of human reason. Rather it has taught that "only by completely overcoming rational and conceptual thinking can one awaken to suchness, as-is-ness, or the 'original' nature of everything in the universe. . . ." We must, then, not confuse the western philosophic language which Prof. Abe has kindly adopted to try to clarify his faith for us with its essential teaching. It is not logic or reason which leads Prof. Abe to his understanding of fundamental truth but the non-discriminating sense of *tathata*, of suchness or is-ness, which he has acquired. I would like to know more about where reason is allowed to function and where it reaches its limits but I sense here a pattern in which reason operates essentially in the service of religious insight, a pattern I utilize in my own way.

In some sense I quite agree with Prof. Abe's position as I understand it. If I may say so, my rock-bottom Jewish faith comes not from any reasoning or even from the accounts of the history of the universe and the Jewish people's place in it but out of a simple, non-discriminating insight into *tathata*, so to speak, the simple way things are. Only our understanding of "the way things are" differs radically from each other. But I, like he, reject the adequacy of human reason when it comes to rendering suchness accessible and that is why I, apparently unlike him, am not swayed by the need to live without dilemmas or paradox.

I must conclude my response by returning to the issue of what I considered Prof. Abe's unfortunate construal of Nietzsche's comment about the three stages of human sacrifice. Prof. Abe, in response, points out that neither he nor Nietzsche ever used the word "premoral" to characterize the first stage, the one that Prof. Abe identified with the time of the Old Testament. That is correct. But this is what Nietzsche did say and Prof. Abe quoted: "Then, during the moral epoch of mankind. . . ." I should think it would be quite plain that the term "Then" separates a time which was not something from a time that was something, in this case, moral, hence my invocation of the term "premoral." Regardless of my word, the implications for the first epoch of calling only the second epoch moral should be quite clear and therefore shunned.

In my original letter I avoided the substantive issue of the identification of the Old Testament (*sic*) sense of sacrifice with that of the first epoch. A word on this topic is now in order. In fact, Isaac was not sacrificed — surely one great point of the story — and except for Jephthah — whom Jewish tradition excoriated — Hebrew Scripture knows only the fullest condemnation of human sacrifice to God. Is it too much to suggest that a good thousand years before the New Testatment a moral epoch of mankind had begun?

May I now call attention to another unfortunate usage of Prof. Abe's, one which while slighting the faith of others whose religious insight differs from his, happens also to embrace believing Jews. It occurs in his discussion of the inevitable self-contradictions of ethics, specifically in relation to Paul's dilemma about the sin he would not do yet does, resulting in a wretchedness from which he seeks deliverance. Prof. Abe then comments: "This is not peculiar to St. Paul but inevitable to all seriously reflective persons, including Buddhists." As a statement about the depth and passion of Prof. Abe's own faith\understanding, I can appreciate what is being communicated by this statement. But what of those many humanists who find that, despite all their failures, their pursuit of ethics and the improvement of society has not made them wretched and conflicted but happily fulfilled as realistic human beings? Are they and the many religionists who believe that God cares more about the *effort* to sanctify life than about its triumphs not "seriously reflective persons?"

And what of believing Jews who since at least the time of Ezekiel and the writing of the book of Jonah have known that "God desires not the death of the sinner but that he turn from his evil way and live."

When Saul of Tarsus took on himself all the responsibility for overcoming his sins he was properly overwhelmed by it and, finding refuge in Jesus the Christ, became Paul. Had he remembered the Jewish teaching about *teshuvah*, the turning, he would, as Jews understand it, have had no need for a special act of God to save him and humankind. For the Jewish sense of *tathata* is that God is not only commander and judge but forgiver — "for He remembers our frame, He considers that we are but dust and ashes. Therefore he has removed our sins from us. . . ." That is, as Jews have long understood and lived it, "simply" God's nature. It does not make the sin any less painful but also enables us to face with some confidence the many ambiguities with which we appear to have to live. Despite centuries of contact with many other faiths and worldviews our community has not found one truer than this.

2) *Masao Abe's Challenge to Modern Jewish Theology*

I have never met Masao Abe and I have long realized that has been a considerable loss for me. For over many years now he has been a spiritual companion of mine, one whose ideas have given me insight by their direct relevance to my faith or indirectly, by the shock created by our disagreement on certain fundamentals.

We "met" almost two decades ago when I read his article, "Non-Being and *Mu*: The Metaphysical Nature of Negativity in the East and the West" (*Religious Studies*, Vol. 11, No.2, June 1975, pp. 181-192). What struck me as extraordinarily significant in his argument was that it challenged the very basis of the Western philosophical tradition. Why, even when one was inclined to dismiss much of the development of philosophy as a betrayal of its origins, as was the case with Heidegger, did one still insist on asking, "Why is there anything at all?" Why not, instead, respond fully to the ephemerality of all things — philosophic systems included — and begin one's most serious thinking with the question which has grounded much of the philosophical/religious tradition of the East, "Why is there nothing at all?" To explain why this article made such an impression on me I need to make a somewhat lengthy digression to explain the particular context in which I, as one of a handful of Jews concerned with "theology," received it.

Abe's challenge being issued long before the days when multiculturalism gained a certain normative power it was still possible for much of the liberal and philosophic establishments to dismiss his argument as "simply not being how one did philosophy." To me, it seemed quite odd — "damning" is closer to the truth but not as euphemistic — that this should be the response of people who proudly called themselves "rationalists." It obviously is not a rationalistic defense of equating philosophy with rationalism to argue that "This is how it is done in the West," or, "This is what our guild considers acceptable subject matter and procedures and if you want to participate in our discussions you will have to abide by the rules of our language game."

If I put this somewhat crudely today it is not because the multi-culturalists and postmoderns have suddenly empowered me. Rather I remember quite clearly the similar emotional response I had back then to what seemed to me the unwarranted assumption of authority over all thought, most certainly including religious thinking, that philosophical rationalists claimed for their standards of serious thought. They insisted that any structure of ideas which claimed the earnest attention of reflective people must meet their criteria of cogency. (The early years of *Religious Studies*, though they celebrate the willingness of some philosophers finally being willing to argue religious ideas as serious thought, amply illustrate this cultural situation.) While this self-assertion was most flagrantly displayed in English speaking philosophical circles it was similarly found among the remnants of continental idealism (whose neo-Kantianism still dominated common Jewish discussion) and other more robust intellectual currents. These academic tendencies were socially reenforced by the dominant Western ethos which, impressed by the triumphs of science, took it for granted that a naturalistic worldview should provide the context for what remained of religion. Many religionists it should be noted, had conceded this power to specify the criteria of responsible thought to the rationalists. By and large only the "fundamentalists" resisted the hegemony of the philosophers. But if the choice were between modern and quite traditional religious thought, few academics indeed were then ready to buck what seemed like the inevitable onward movement of the *zeitgeist*.

The problem of intellectual context had particular relevance to me. I wanted to create a viable — consider the implications of that term — Jewish theology for the changed situation in which the Jewish people found itself in the second half of the twentieth century. Reason had played a critical role in validating and directing the nineteenth century Jewish Emancipation, the movement from the European ghetto or *shtetl* into those societies which granted them social equality. In some adaptation of German idealism, though regularly more Kantian than Hegelian, rabbis and writers explained the meaning of the radical social transformation taking place. Through the Kantian primacy of ethics and the Hegelian sense of historic progress, they justified their government's acts of liberation, their own subsequent dedication to good citizenship and their right to abandon many of the ritual practices of their tradition. Insofar as they remained religious, their faith was typically liberal: human centered, science-trusting, God-aspiring, more universal than particular, and with God's revelation reduced to human spiritual discovery. In the works of the great Jewish system builders of early in this century, Hermann Cohen, Leo Baeck and Mordecai Kaplan, this intellectual development received neo-Kantian, Schleiermacherian-Otto-ish, and American naturalistic expression. By mid-century, as my Jewish intellectual search matured, the American Jewish ethos was resolutely rationalistic and thus effectively agnostic, ethically and politically activist, and where it was not obsessed with social integration, ethnically Jewish.

Even before the community became conscious of the Holocaust, there were minority signs that these older approaches to modern Jewish life were unsatisfactory. At both the Reform and the Conservative seminaries a new sensibility was making itself felt in experiments in practice and, most unexpectedly, by the interest of some few students in working out a contemporary Jewish "theology." As it were, "philosophy" seemed dogmatically rationalistsic with devastating results for Judaism. In short, philosophy, trusting to the primacy of the mind, required atheism, or at least agnosticism, though it could sometimes muster a patronizing tolerance of various nominalistic reinterpretations of the term "God." For those of us who had sufficient doubts about human omnicompetence to allow for a more substantive understanding of God, "philosophy" thus seemed an inadequate way to understand reality. This attitude also opened up the possibility that the Jewish tradition should no longer be read only to determine where it was in agreement with "the best of modern thought." Rather it should now be studied to see what it might independently say to us, even though we were not "fundamentalists" and committed to always accept its ideas or follow its dictates.

To some extent our renewal of involvement with God could also be detected among liberal Christians. But among the Jews it was intertwined with a strong particularistic thrust. The rationalistic ethos not only negated God but also made dedication to the robust survival of the Jewish people quixotic. The rationalistic philosophies were united in their common assertion that truth is to be found on the universal level and only in a derivative fashion in any particular embodiment of it. To be sure, the universal truth could not exist in history simply on its own and, as it were, "required" some particular interpretation in order to play a role in history. That was as much validity as could be granted to a particular religion, culture or institution. But by making all such embodiments essentially inferior in truth and instrumental in value, this validation also justified their abandonment with the appearance of a more effective means to the final end. For a minority such as the Jews, seduced by the lure of the majority culture and burdened with the disabilities of being a Jew in a secularized Christian culture, the instrumental argument for Jewishness seemed only a palliative on the way to assimilation. Even Mordecai Kaplan, who sought to give a rationalistic defense of Jewish particularity, could only do so by making a sociological case for the power and value of ethnicity. But description had no normative effect so the argument held only as long as Jews retained strong ethnic ties, ones, he acknowledged, which might one day equally be replaced by those of Americanism.

In hindsight it seems clear to me that a radical shift in social agenda had begun to make itself felt among some Jews. Prior generations of emancipated Jews had been passionately devoted to discovering how Jews might best find a place in the general society. For them — and for many Jews today — the underlying drive of their Jewishness is the quest to be more fully universalistic. But the new search took integration into the modern world for granted. That changed the operative question for us and we wanted to know just what it meant for us moderns to be concerned, caring Jews. We did not propose to give up the strong universalistic commitments that modern Judaism had by life and thought made convincingly a part of our faith, but we knew these now needed to be balanced by a particularism of equal cogency.

How we knew then that this intuition of the commanding power of a non-fundamentalist Jewish particularity still had sufficient truth to demand our dedication was not clear then nor is it now. In part it stemmed from our sense of the hubris of reason and the limitations of science. In part it arose as a reaction to the anti-semitism which was so significant a part of Jewish life even in the period before the Holocaust. But if my experience may be taken as reasonably typical, it mostly came from living with reasonable self-acceptance as a modern American Jew and finding in it something ultimately true and compelling, and presently without proper intellectual expression. Hence was born the seemingly idiosyncratic interest of some few to give culturally acceptable articulation to this fuller view of the truth of Judaism.

For some years, existentialism promised to provide an intellectual structure for such a new Jewish theology. Its initial appeal was polemical for it undercut the rationalistic claim to be self- validating by its argument that existence preceded essence. By focusing on the "I" who was doing the thinking (skeptical or constructive), it made clear that every form of rationality necessarily began from a non-rationalistic ground. If so, more attention should be given to the pre-rational than to the rational and any claim that sophisticated reason must be the exclusive arbiter of what was worthy thought and action could be seen as contradicted by its own ground. If, however, the self rather than the mind could be taken as the basis for one's thought — reason as the handmaid of existence — a much broader understanding of the human spirit could reach expression and thus room be made for spirituality. Here the existentialists divided between two groups. Some, like Heidegger and Sartre, had "systems" which ruled out the possibility that existentialist thinking might include place for God. Others, like Kierkegaard and Buber (in their quite different ways), gave the lived quality of existence more weight than how one thought about it. And for both these religious existentialists, the particular, not the universal, was the place of truth.

In the early 1970s the balance of Jewish intellectual leadership had begun to shift from the rationalists to the "existentialists." Masao Abe's article thus came as stunning confirmation of the anti-rationalism that seemed so critical to the insurgent thinkers. It not only asserted a new basis for denying the normative primacy of rationalism but it radically undercut what remained of that notion in the atheistic existentialisms, such as those of Heidegger and Sartre. Yet its polemic was not bought at the cost of obscurantism or the denigration of reason (as in some of the New Age religions of more recent years). Rather, Abe made his case by a carefully argued, thoughtfully stated examination of the nature of reality, one readily accessible to the Western reader but which led in an utterly unexpected direction. The combination was so uncommon and yet so compelling — and in many ways has remained so — that I knew then that I should always benefit by reading his work and, in my own movement from insight to articulation, following it.

Why did I not then become his follower and explicate Judaism in terms of his Zen understanding of ultimate reality? I put the question this baldly because, in fact, serious inter-faith encounter means opening oneself up to the possibility of conversion. But though I took Abe's thought most seriously, I found myself in respectful but unqualified disagreement with him on the ultimacy of Dynamic Nothingness. I was convinced that such a vision would inevitably undercut what I knew to be the ultimate qualitative difference between good and evil — what by that time already had impressed itself upon consciousness as the incomparable model of the distinction between them, that between the Nazi death camp operators and their Jewish victims.

Our relationship would have remained at this level of my appreciative readership had it not been for the graciousness of John B. Cobb. He had become involved in another of Abe's many efforts to engage in Buddhist-Christian dialogue, one in which a serene irenicism combined with a call to find the more comprehensive religious truth, thus making direct engagement with him a uniquely profound experience. John, assisted by Christopher Ives, was heading up a literary exchange (published by Orbis in 1990 as *The Emptying God*) in which a major essay by Abe would be responded to by a number of oft-published figures. As usual, Abe's lengthy paper was distinguished by a careful, respectful reading of Western literature. But it was a sign of his exceptional openness to other views that his sweeping analysis included a challenge to Jewish theologians. This he based on his reading of some of our leading thinkers seeking to come to terms with the Holocaust. John invited me to respond to this section of Abe's paper and thus, honored by the suggestion, I became involved in an active, intense and enlightening exchange with Abe.

His question to Jewish thinkers may be epitomized this way: Zen Buddhism more comprehensively responds to the critical issue of contemporary Jewish theology than does any present Jewish thought. If the Holocaust reveals God's absence and otherwise overwhelms every effort based on prior thought to come to terms with it, why do not Jewish thinkers carry their experience of absence to its logical conclusion, that the ultimate reality is Dynamic Nothingness? In fact, Richard L. Rubenstein, whose work had sparked the discussion in the Jewish community, had himself used somewhat similar language in seeking to describe his own post-Auschwitz spirituality.

In prior generations, those few Jewish thinkers who had touched on Buddhism, would have dismissed any suggestion that it might be of religious relevance to them by accusing it of other-worldliness and of lacking an activist, redemptive ethics. In those days these charges were common among self-confident religious liberals. It was another sign of Abe's genuineness in dialogue that he not only knew of these criticisms of his tradition but sought to learn from them. Of course, he did so in terms of his grounding insight into reality but the result seemed to me an extraordinarily creative interpretation of Zen. Thus he included in the exposition of his position a section on how the emptying work of Dynamic Nothingness, which effects everything, must therefore also eventually include "itself." The logical effect of a negativity of negativity is a positive, and thus Abe's Zen mandates a far stronger ethics than Westerners had been accustomed to hearing about from Buddhists.

Abe's challenge forced me to think through at least two major aspects of my religious heritage and to ask just how I now felt about them. The first of these was the Jewish understanding of God as, so to speak, Nothing. Offhand that seems utterly incompatible with the central Jewish affirmation that God is One. Yet even a little reflection indicates that if God is absolutely unique then nothing can be said in human language that is adequate to God's reality. But to be able to say nothing is to acknowledge that God is, in human language, finally Nothing. While some such notions flitted in and out of Biblical and rabbinic Judaism and medieval Jewish philosophy, thirteenth century Jewish mysticism, *kabbalah*, gave them more substance. Its theosophy understood God as both the ten *sefirot*, the energy centers of the Divine self manifestation (about which a bewildering plethora of things might be said) and the *En Sof*, the No Bounds, and thus "something" about which nothing might be said. And, mysticism asserted that these two understandings of God were, in fact, inextricably One. Through the work of the eighteenth century Hasidic teacher, Dov Baer of Meseritch, an intensification of the "Nothingness" of the *En Sof* (and thus of the largely illusory nature of created things) became a major theme in subsequent Hasidic thought. In various transformations it remains a continuing part of Jewish mysticism. Abe could, as I suggested in my response, probably find his most congenial Jewish dialogue partners among such contemporary Jewish mystics and the more hard-headed people who followed in Rubenstein's path.

I was now led to ponder why most of traditional Judaism from the middle ages on found this reinterpretation of Judaism unacceptable, perhaps even suspect. More important, even in today's more spiritually tolerant climate, traditionalists and non-traditionalists have over-whelmingly rejected this response to the Holocaust. I had little doubt that their reason for doing so lay more in the consequences of the theory than in their not having had a mystic experience to confirm it. The hegemony of Nothingness does explains the irremediable awfulness of what transpired. But it does so at a stunning cost: it wipes out the distinction between the murderers and the victims. Within the Nothing there can be no distinctions and as it is the only reality, so even the distinction between good and evil finally is not real. When one truly knows the One via mystic experience in Judaism or enlightenment in Zen, one learns that evil and good have no true reality but are only appearances. For most post-Holocaust Jews that is far more than they can assert — or bear.

On the theoretical level, the issue now became, what ultimacy did I, did Judaism, did most other Jews, attach to goodness (less inadequately, the good/holy). Was there a "dimension" in which God transcended the good or was it "part" of God's nature? For me, as for most Jews, there is no such "place" in God or a God-beyond-God. Indeed, that is what makes the Holocaust so heinous, that it violates God's very nature and thus is "diabolic." Without the ultimate standard, whence the outrage at the Holocaust?

This should not be taken to imply that Abe was insensitive to the utter tragedy that had occurred. His discussion shows his sharing in its suffering and, as a result of his positive attitude toward activist ethics his determination that nothing like it should happen again. But ultimately, what "makes sense" of the Holocaust to him is insight into the reality behind it and all other phenomena, namely, that the only ultimate reality is Dynamic Nothingness.

For me this philosophy made ethics very important but not essential. To the Jewish spirit, as I understand it, a certain ultimacy attaches to a holy deed. For those who share it, no act of insight or understanding ever takes the place of doing, as valuable as the inner life may be on a secondary level. And to teach people that deed-doing is a derivative rather than a primary value is inevitably to lessen the motivation which prompts people to act. Crudely put, most Jews, whether leftish secularists or right-wing-pietists, believe there is more genuine holiness in political action to prevent another Holocaust than in any metaphysics.

Abe's response to me in *The Emptying God* — and in part that to some of the Christian participants who had somewhat similar attitudes toward the ethical — clarified the points at issue between us and restated his views with great cogency. This rich, rewarding exchange might have rested there had two things not then happened. It was now suggested that the participants in the original discussion, perhaps joined by some others, might find it valuable to carry the discussion another step forward. The resulting symposium has now been printed in the annual, *Buddhist-Christian Dialogue 1993* (University of Hawaii Press).

While this was in process, I was emboldened by Abe's graciousness in our first exchange to ask him for a personal favor. As publisher and editor of a Jewish journal of ethics, *Sh'ma*, it was my custom to thank contributors to our annual fund campaign by sending them a copy of something I had written. I suggested to Abe that he allow me to publish our two exchanges in a booklet. I also asked permission to include with them an independent piece of mine on inter-faith exchanges between theologians. This resulted not only from what had transpired in our dialogue but by comparison with another that had gone on at the same time with the well-known Episcopalian theologian, Paul van Buren. (This study was published as "When Theologians Engage in Inter-faith Dialogue" in my collection of papers, *Exploring Jewish Ethics*, Wayne State University Press, 1990.) Abe could not have been more cordial about this project, extending himself particularly so as to make the manuscript of his latest rejoinder to me available in time for its private publication by *Sh'ma*. This was, of course, in addition to his generosity in allowing me to utilize his prior statements and suggesting which parts of his lengthy original paper in *The Emptying God* he thought provided a proper precis of his position. The result was a booklet of 68 pages entitled *A Buddhist-Jewish Dialogue*. (I still have a limited number of copies which I will gladly send to those requesting one from me at 19 Reid Ave. Port Washington, NY, 11050.) I mention it to indicate not only that a self-contained record of this rare instance of direct Buddhist-Jewish dialogue exists but to call further attention to Abe's commitment to inter-faith discussion and the genial way in which he carried it through.

In this final exchange we realized that, for the moment, we had come as far as we could. How does one move beyond laying bare the bedrock understanding on which all the rest of one's worldview is built? For Abe, that was the realization that beneath all the apparent realities there is truly only Dynamic Nothingness. For me, it meant the recognition of the Holy One who is beyond creation yet intimately involved with it and the humans in it. As it were, for Abe, the truth comes as that illumination that "this," simply, is the way it is. And, in a different context, that is what I know. Only we differ rather significantly on what the "this" is.

One might then ask what value was there in speaking when, as might have been anticipated, we ended up in radical disagreement. At least four answers might be given. I came to understand that Zen has creative possibilities that I would otherwise not have imagined it to possess. Abe's searching challenge, one given added power by his evident spirituality, brought me to understand my own faith in greater depth. The human and spiritual concerns in his activist Buddhism and my post-liberal Judaism turned out to have a much greater overlap than I had anticipated. And the exposure to so fine a spirit is a precious human experience indeed. So I am happy to be able to add my words of appreciation to those of the many others who have been the direct beneficiaries of his sojourn in the West.

I must, however, add to this account some words about the one matter on which we not only disagreed but about which our exchanges seemed only to produce a certain measure of surprise that the other was unable to see what was so plain to each of us. As not infrequently happens, it relates to a matter not central to the discussion but only one peripheral to it, in this case a citation from Nietzsche's *Beyond Good and Evil*. The great iconoclast as educed by Abe divides history into what I characterized as pre-moral, moral and post moral periods. He identified the first stage of history with "primitive religions." Abe then applied this by identifying that period with the time of the Old Testament, reserving the second, the "moral" stage for the time of the New Testament and the following Christian era. I bridled at this, seeing it as testimony to the ingrained anti-semitism of much of Western culture, and, believing Abe had inadvertently absorbed this with his immersion in our way of thinking, was appalled that the academic colleagues who had obliged him by a pre-publication reading of his paper had not called this to his attention. Abe, in turn was most regretful that any such imputation could be brought against his citation or against his readers since it was the furthest possible thing from his mind to cast aspersions on any religion. To clarify this, Abe then gave his interpretation of the passage, seeing it as concerned with different aspects of sacrifice and not historic sequences of morality (neither Nietzsche nor Abe ever using the term "pre-moral). This reading, he believes, was also what his colleagues found in his text.

In my response I acknowledged that I had introduced the term "pre-moral" into the discussion, justifying myself by the correct citation, "Then, during the moral epoch of mankind [the time of the New Testament and the succeeding Christian era]. . . ." To me this plainly indicated that a time [of the Old Testament] not yet moral had been succeeded by one that was, hence I remained offended. Abe responded with a more detailed exegesis of his intentions at this point in his argument and in the light of this he felt that his previous explanation of his understanding of the contentious citation should now be clear. And were there any remaining question he wholeheartedly agreed with my view that a moral era of civilization had begun at least a thousand years before the time of the New Testament.

Have I been unduly sensitive about a possible remnant of anti-semitism which has unwittingly found a peripheral place in this noble thinker's paper and have I over-reacted to a possible implication of Nietzsche's phrasing? Or is the deprecation of Jews and Judaism so endemic in our culture that despite our own good will we unconsciously transmit the germs of anti-semitism to anyone who comes to participate in our intellectual life? I must leave those questions to my readers who have all the relevant documents available for their own study and evaluation. This is, I am certain, a somewhat "incorrect" matter to raise as part of a celebration of an uncommon spirit's greatly valued contribution to our continuing religious growth. I suggest it would not properly honor Abe if I felt I had to repress a matter of considerable ethical urgency to me and to deny my readers here this important if prickly point about inter-faith dialogue with Jews.

About the Author

Eugene B. Borowitz, the dean of American Jewish philosophers, is the Sigmund L. Falk Distinguished Professor of Education and Jewish Religious Thought at Hebrew Union College-Jewish Institute of Religion in New York. He has taught there since 1962. In 1996 the National Foundation for Jewish Culture bestowed upon him its medal for lifetime Jewish Cultural Achievement in the realm of scholarship, the first time it has been awarded for work in the field of Jewish thought.

Other Books by Eugene B. Borowitz

A Layman's Introduction to Religious Existentialism. Philadelphia: Westminster, 1965.

A New Jewish Theology in the Making. Philadelphia: Westminster, 1968.

Choosing a Sex Ethic. New York: Schocken, 1969.

How Can A Jew Speak of Faith Today?. Philadelphia: Westminster, 1968.

The Mask Jews Wear. New York: Simon and Schuster, 1973.

Reform Judaism Today. New York: Behrman House, 1978.

Understanding Judaism. New York: Union of American Hebrew Congregations, 1979.

Contemporary Christologies, a Jewish Response. Ramsey: Paulist, 1980.

Choices in Modern Jewish Thought. New York: Behrman House, 1983, second expanded edition, 1995.

Liberal Judaism. Union of American Hebrew Congregations, 1984.

Explaining Reform Judaism. (With Naomi Patz) New York: Behrman House, 1985.

Exploring Jewish Ethics. Detroit: Wayne State University Press, 1990.

Renewing the Covenant. Philadelphia: Jewish Publication Society, 1991.

The Jewish Moral Virtues. (With Francis Schwartz) Philadelphia: Jewish Publication Society, 1999.

DATE DUE

Demco, Inc. 38-293